Indian Tribes of Oklahoma

THE CIVILIZATION OF THE AMERICAN INDIAN SERIES

Indian Tribes of Oklahoma

A Guide

Blue Clark

UNIVERSITY OF OKLAHOMA PRESS : NORMAN

ALSO BY BLUE CLARK

Lone Wolf v. Hitchcock: Treaty Rights and Indian Law at the End of the Nineteenth Century (Lincoln, Nebr., 1994)

This book is published with the generous assistance of the Wallace C. Thompson Fund, University of Oklahoma Foundation.

Library of Congress Cataloging-in-Publication Data
Clark, Blue, 1946–
  Indian tribes of Oklahoma : a guide / Blue Clark.
    p. cm. — (Civilization of the American Indian series ; v. 261)
  Includes bibliographical references and index.
  ISBN 978-0-8061-4060-5 (hardcover : alk. paper)
  1. Indians of North America—Oklahoma. I. Title.
E78.O45C575 2009
976.6'01—dc22

                                        2009002192

Indian Tribes of Oklahoma: A Guide is Volume 261 in The Civilization of the American Indian Series.

The paper in this book meets the guidelines for permanence and durability of the Committee on Production Guidelines for Book Longevity of the Council on Library Resources, Inc. ∞

1 2 3 4 5 6 7 8 9 10

Mvto vcululke.

In the Mvskoke (Creek) language, this means
"thanks to our elders." Thanks to all those who have
gone before and who have made today possible.

Contents

Illustrations

Preface

This work is intended to serve as a guide for all readers who are interested in American Indians within the current state of Oklahoma. Since prehistoric times Indian peoples have resided in the area that would become Oklahoma. American Indians are an intimate part of the state's makeup and of its history. They often played key roles in major events shaping the region's past.

What should we call the Native peoples? Early contacts with people from other continents, such as the Vikings in A.D. 900 or Africans or Asians at unknown dates, did not provide any long-used labels for indigenous peoples. When Christopher Columbus first made landfall in 1492 in the south Atlantic islands, he mistakenly assumed that he was off southern Asia and near India. He referred to the Native peoples as *indios*, which became anglicized to "Indians." Later a European mapmaker borrowed the first name of another explorer, using "America" as the name for the Western Hemisphere. The label "American Indian" stuck as a convenient name for the Native peoples. It is not accurate, however. Neither is the other often-used phrase, "Native American." Indians usually refer to themselves by their tribal name (Quapaw, for example) or their Indian community ("I live in Hanna," a Creek community), then clan (say, Eagle), followed by family connection and genealogy (descendant of a former chief, for example).

The emphasis in this guide is on economic activity among tribes and within tribes as well as on cultures and ceremonies. Since prehistoric times indigenous peoples have engaged in barter, manufacturing of items, and trade. Federal government policies have also encouraged economic development trends, especially since the 1980s. Contemporary gaming revenue has provided investment capital for some tribes and has helped a few tribes stand out.

Of course, traditional ceremonies are distinguishing features for tribes. Their cultures make them unique. In spite of efforts to suppress and change Indian cultural practices, they have persisted. Descendants of Indian nations now in Oklahoma represent much of the entire indigenous experience in North America, because their ancestors came from throughout the present United States. Some of their predecessors were among the first to encounter Europeans along the coastal rivers of the continent. Other ancestors dominated their regions as Mississippian royalty, who looked down upon their followers and their kingly domain from atop a major truncated earth mound. Some carry on ancient sacred ceremonies, bringing them into the present. Others whose antecedents converted to the Roman Catholic faith in the Great Lakes region and befriended and shielded French Jesuits there have perpetuated their devotion to the Catholic faith to this day. Still others are ardent Protestants. Tribal stories embody centuries-old ties to unique cultures. They also encompass essentially American stories that tell of survival and persistence under the severest of circumstances. Their history is truly the story of America.

Much has been written about the American Indian since naturalist, traveler, and journal-writer Thomas Nuttall lamented in 1819 that "both they and their history are buried in impenetrable oblivion! Their existence . . . blotted out from the page of the living!"

In addition to the works in the Suggested Reading list below, other sources can found online. The Oklahoma Encyclopedia from the Oklahoma History Center (http://digital.library.okstate.edu/encyclopedia) and the Handbook of Texas Online (www.tsha.utexas.edu/handbook/online) from the Texas State Historical Association and the University of Texas General Libraries also offer information. In addition, many tribes have their own websites (such as www.cherokee.org). Individual Indian tribal museums (such as www.cherokeeheritage.org) give their own insights into their cultural histories. American Indians are the best source of information on their own tribal experience.

The Native American Cultural and Educational Authority will soon have a complex in Oklahoma City dealing with contemporary Native American culture and arts and can guide people to sights and sounds in Indian Country (at www.aiccm.org). The Red Earth Indian Museum (at www.redearth.org) in Oklahoma City offers exhibits and a CD-ROM on Oklahoma tribes. The History Center in Oklahoma City (at www.oklahomahistorycenter.org) provides venues for a better understanding of the roles of Native peoples. Other museums within the state, such as the Sam Noble Oklahoma Museum of Natural History on the campus of the University of Oklahoma (at www.snomnh.ou.edu) and the Gilcrease Museum in Tulsa (at www.gilcrease.org), provide dioramas, objects, and paintings of Native lives. David C. Hunt's guide and the National Museum of the American Indian website (www.AmericanIndian.si.edu) offer information on some tribal museums. The Oklahoma Indian Affairs Commission provides basic tribal information and addresses online (at www.oiac.state.ok.us). The State Department of Tourism (at www.travelok.com) can direct those who are interested to large public Indian gatherings such as annual tribal powwows, rodeos, and festivals.

In the interest of serving all readers, references within the body of this work are to authors' names or to legislation, not to specific titles with lengthy citations. For example, John Lawson paused during his 1701 tour of the Carolina territory and provided an eyewitness observation of southeastern Indian ritual practices. He described the all-night dancing as "nothing but a sort of stamping Motion" of the dancers' feet. In such instances, only the author's name is cited in the text. The reader who desires to know more can consult the Suggested Reading list.

Useful listings of sources are also found in the *Handbook of North American Indians*, the Columbia Guide to American Indians series, and historian Arrell Gibson's wide-ranging bibliographical survey, for those who want more detail on a vast literature. Sometimes specific historic sites are mentioned to encourage readers to visit them and to recall the valor of ancestral endeavors.

For each tribal entry, a brief list of suggested readings is appended for those who wish to explore that entity further. The tribal website is mentioned for those tribes that offer one. The small maps at the beginning of each entry depict the locations of tribal headquarters. The terms "nation" and "tribe" are used here interchangeably, as are "American Indians" and "Native Americans."

Archeology plays a role here. Terms such as "period," "era," "phase," and "focus" are used by archeologists to indicate a time in the dim past. I urge the reader not to get lost in the details. Rough periods of prehistory are as follows. "Paleo-Indian" or "Paleoamerican" marks the earliest humans. The Archaic follows, from 9000 B.C. to 1500 B.C. The Woodland period is next, beginning about 3,500 years ago at 1500 B.C.: Early Woodland to A.D. 100; Middle Woodland from 100 B.C. to A.D. 500; and Late Woodland for the thousand years before the arrival of Europeans. The Mississippian in the eastern forested region lasted from A.D. 700 until after the European presence, with the last period being called "postcontact." Dating is approximate, of course, and may change with each new rock that archeologists turn over for scientific examination, altering our understanding of the past.

SUGGESTED READING

Baird, W. David, and Danny Goble. *The Story of Oklahoma.* Norman: University of Oklahoma Press, 1994.

The Columbia Guide to American Indians. Vols.: *Northeast, Plains,* and *Southeast.* New York: Columbia University Press, 2001–2003.

Debo, Angie. *A History of the Indians of the United States.* Norman: University of Oklahoma Press, 1970.

Do All Indians Live in Tipis?: Questions and Answers from the Smithsonian's National Museum of the American Indian. New York: HarperCollins, 2008.

Gibson, Arrell M. "Indian and Pioneer Legacy: A Guide to Oklahoma Literature." *Chronicles of Oklahoma* 56 (Spring 1978): 3–33.

———. *Oklahoma: A History of Five Centuries.* Norman: University of Oklahoma Press, 1984.

Gilbert, Claudette Marie, and Robert L. Brooks. *From Mounds to Mammoths: A Field Guide to Oklahoma Prehistory.* 2nd ed. Norman: University of Oklahoma Press, 2.

Handbook of North American Indians. William C. Sturtevant, general editor. Vol. 12: *Plateau.* Vol. 13: *Plains.* Vol. 14: *Southeast.* Vol. 15: *Northeast.* Washington, D.C.: Smithsonian Institution, 1978–2004.

Hoig, Stan. *A Travel Guide to the Plains Indian Wars.* Albuquerque: University of New Mexico, 2007.

Hunt, David C. *Guide to Oklahoma Museums.* Norman: University of Oklahoma Press, 1981.

Indians of Oklahoma: Past and Present. St. Clair Shores, Mich.: Somerset, 1999.

Lawson, John. *A New Voyage to Carolina* (first published 1709). Edited by Hugh Talmage Lefler. Chapel Hill: University of North Carolina Press, 1967.

Nuttall, Thomas. *A Journal of Travels into the Arkansas Territory during the Year 1819*. Edited by Savoie Lottinville. Norman: University of Oklahoma Press, 1980.

Utter, Jack, *American Indians: Answers to Today's Questions*. Rev. 2nd ed. Norman: University of Oklahoma Press, 2001.

Indian Tribes of Oklahoma

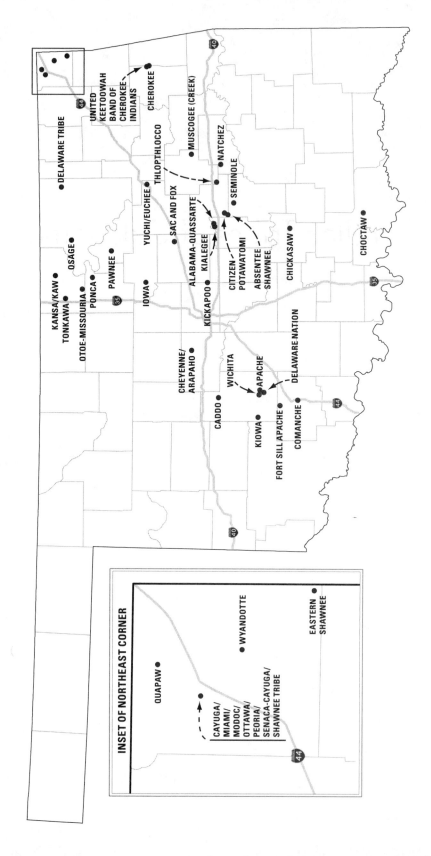

Indian Nations of Oklahoma

Introduction

Native peoples have resided in what is now the state of Oklahoma since primordial times. Recent scientific examination of remains demonstrates the antiquity of Native occupation of the region that is now Oklahoma. While the dating is controversial, a dig called Burnham in the far northern reaches of the state near the town of Freedom may show evidence of the earliest provable human presence in the hemisphere, 30,000 years ago and perhaps even earlier. Whatever the determination of the dating within Oklahoma, occupation of the region over a long period is beyond dispute.

Prehistoric peoples sometimes lived in caves or rock shelters along canyons through the far western portions of the current state. Archeologists call this period with Ice Age glacial sheets the Pleistocene. The Native peoples used what scientists call Clovis and later (finer) Folsom stone points fastened to lances or spears to hunt game. The points are named for the location of their first discoveries in the American Southwest. Domebo near the town of Stecker, south of Anadarko in Caddo County, is a Clovis site dating to about 10,500 years ago where flint blades were mixed with the bones of now-extinct mammoths. Archeologists found human-made spear points firmly embedded in the bones of animals that are no longer in existence, which proved that early humans, called Paleo-Indians or Paleoamericans, lived in the region. They hunted huge mammoths, mastodons, and giant early bison, among other animals. Seasonal residents used thrusting spears and a Siberian-style throwing stick called an atlatl to hunt game. Spear points have been discovered elsewhere in the rib bones of now-extinct prehistoric animals in excavations, offering proof of their presence to about 8000 B.C. Excavation in the 1990s revealed a Folsom point among bones from about 10,500 years ago in northwestern Oklahoma at the Cooper site, located along a tributary of the North Canadian River near modern Fort Supply. At this largest Folsom-era bison kill site archeologist Lee Bement also found what is viewed as the oldest artwork on the North American continent. He unearthed a bison skull with a zigzag red line painted on it, perhaps representing a thunderbolt. An early shaman could have used the skull in a religious ceremony to "call" bison to the kill site.

During the following period, called the Holocene, the glacial sheets gradually withdrew northward. Pleistocene spruce and pine forests receded. This long span with its gradual warming left behind what is essentially today's landscape with its recognizable deciduous forests, flora, and fauna. Trees disappeared as the climate dried through the continent's midsection, and grass remained to form the prairie. Giant mammals like the mammoth and musk ox retreated northward until they became extinct. The earliest human residents lived in small kin-related groups that moved seasonally after game and resources. They foraged for plant foods because they did not yet have agriculture and used baskets woven from native plant fibers to hold and store their foodstuffs. This period after roughly 11,000 years ago is called the Archaic. They made points for their lances from local gravels but also could have imported colorful flint from a large quarry at Alibates, north of the modern city of Amarillo in the Texas Panhandle. Their Clovis and Folsom predecessors also traded for the flint and used it. Later the people made use of clay deposits to produce pottery vessels. They also pecked images, called petroglyphs, on cave and rock walls (at the Kenton site in the Oklahoma Panhandle, for example).

About 4000 B.C. during the Middle Archaic a nomadic group called the Calf Creek people used broad stone points to pursue modern bison throughout present-day Oklahoma and the Texas Panhandle and into central Arkansas. They experienced a tough time. A 250-year dry spell throughout the Plains replaced the remaining trees with grasses, except along watercourses. This was just before the erection of Stonehenge in Britain and during the period when Ice Age people walked the Alps in Europe. In Louisiana at about the same time Archaic people first constructed circular earthworks at Watson Brake and other locations. Three millennia later at a site called Poverty Point in northeastern Louisiana the Tamaroas erected a substantial community center with huge earthen structures that faced a tributary or bayou of the nearby Mississippi River. Those residents utilized their own long-distance trade system after about 1500 B.C. Many such centers were ultimately sprinkled throughout the Southeast. The people did not practice agriculture but intensively gathered plant foods and tended squash and bottle gourds, as well as fishing and hunting for game. Elsewhere across the continent during the Middle to Late Archaic era, predecessors of Native languages (like Proto-Algonquian, Proto-Caddo, and Proto-Iroquoian) are believed to have appeared.

Eventually the Archaic period of earliest occupation turned into what is called the Woodland period by about 3,500 years ago. Woodland peoples at first combined more intensive gathering of plant sources with horticulture for vegetal foods; then their womenfolk slowly developed true agriculture, which ultimately focused on the trilogy of corn, beans, and squash. In the nearby mountains of Arkansas that bear their name, Native people perhaps 4,000 years ago cultivated the first Ozark wild gourd, as Bruce Smith has shown. The plant developed into the varieties of domesticated squash that we know today. Native peoples started tending squash between 2,000 and 3,000 years ago and maize about 1,200 years ago. Beans entered their diet sometime around 700 years ago. They also hunted a wide variety of game animals. Indians who relied heavily upon agriculture are believed to have been matrilineal (that is, members belonged to their mother's clan or extended family). Indians who depended mostly on Plains bison hunting and were more nomadic tended to be patrilineal (following their father's clan). Woodland people also used clays, which they formed and fired to make pottery and decorated with distinctive designs. In addition, they constructed funerary mounds over deceased leaders. These features are characteristic of the Woodland period. Exchange networks over long distances that brought far-away goods for use in leaders' rituals and burials also marked the Woodland cultures. (Noteworthy Woodland earthen centers in Ohio and the Mid-South are called Adena and Hopewell.)

Some of the Woodland people on the fringe of the prairie who spoke a language that would later be called Caddoan resided in the forest lands of today's eastern Oklahoma. They traded rabbit-fur yarn, salt, bow-making wood, velvety deerskins, and prepared bison hides to their neighbors. After A.D. 700 they gradually adopted mound-building, heaping basketloads of earth into low tumuli. Through ensuing years they constructed a temple-mound culture similar in outward appearance to the culture of their Mississippian neighbors. Priests tended perpetual fires in temples atop mounds where chiefs lived. They oversaw burials of elite leaders deep inside some mounds. Their societies are believed to have been hierarchical chiefdoms. Just before the advent of the Mississippian period, they adopted the bow and arrow (ca. A.D. 600–700), making hunting more efficient. That culture peaked during the Mississippian (ca. A.D. 700–1650). It long preceded the arrival of the Europeans on the continent but also began to decline in importance prior to their appearance.

Spiro Mounds in the far eastern part of Oklahoma, the jewel in the crown of the Mississippian period, marked a climax of Mississippian culture. Its extensive burials contained a treasure trove of exotic grave goods that revealed much about the people's way of life. The park now covers about fifty acres and is one of the most important archeological sites east of the Rocky Mountains. After A.D. 1200 priests presided over impressive funeral rituals during which they interred their revered leaders with elaborate grave goods imported from as far away as the Great Lakes area.

Craig Mound at Spiro Mounds Park, Oklahoma *Photograph by Jay Miller*

A wide-reaching trade network provided the exotic goods. It is likely that important priestly ambassadors carried Mississippian beliefs, rituals, and artistic design motifs far afield.

Archeologists believe that Spiro priests and residents in the surrounding region were predecessors of later Wichita, Pawnee, Caddo, Kichai, or Tunican tribal peoples. Spiro ritualists lived under a hierarchical chief with rigidly divided and ranked social classes, who resided inside fortified ceremonial centers. Corn was the staple food, although the people consumed a wide range of flora and fauna. With corn, residents engaged in genuine agriculture. Earthen mounds had solar, lunar, and cardinal direction alignments, which are believed to have been crucial to an agricultural society and its ceremonies. Farmers needed to know when winter ended and spring commenced for planting. Celestial markers provided guidance to the initiated. Spiro's location along the Arkansas River, a natural strategic east-west avenue of trade and communication, also made it an important site. A gradual decline at Spiro set in after 1250, believed to be the result of a drying climate. Population slowly shifted westward toward the bison-filled Plains. The Wichitas' oral tradition describes their similar ancestral journey.

To the north, Oneota culture peoples from the upper Midwest crossed the Missouri River and stepped onto the Plains around A.D. 1300. For centuries Oneota people hunted bison on the prairie, but they did not start to expand their domain until the glory of the metropolitan center of Cahokia in present-day Illinois, located across the Mississippi River from what is now St. Louis, Missouri, faded in the thirteenth century. Oneota peoples displaced indigenous residents by 1600 and sometimes intermixed with them to create new groupings. Oneota expansion matches the oral tradition of the movements of Iowas and Otoe-Missourias (Chiwere-speakers) and of Poncas, Osages, Kansas, and Quapaws (called Dhegiha Siouan–speakers). Ancestral Wichita bands also traveled west and northward and eventually ended up in what is now Kansas. Cycles of wetter climate and abundance followed periods of dryness, hardship, and internecine warfare.

The arrival of more people added to the mixture. Athapaskans came from the far north in pursuit of bison. Over time they moved southwestward after the advent of the Christian era. Out of Wyoming some drifted southward into the southwestern region of America and eventually became the nuclei of the Western Apaches and Navajos. Others separated and drifted onto the central Plains to become the ancestors of the Eastern Apaches, like the Jicarillas. Migrating Southern Athapaskans pushed against their distant linguistic kinfolk, the Lipan Apaches, who were already on the Plains, driving them even farther south. Lipans may have been at the Antelope Creek site in the Oklahoma Panhandle after 1450, although the settlement could also have been inhabited by Teyas, Jumanos, Wichitas, or some other tribal entity. Scientists broadly refer to this time after 1450 as the Village Farming Period.

The coming of Europeans to the continent after 1492 drastically changed American Indian cultures as well as those of the Europeans. Non-native trade goods, including metal knives and cooking pots, and later firearms, brought Native peoples into global commerce and conflicts. The horse transformed certain prairie peoples into some of the finest light cavalry in the world. European diseases radically reduced Native populations by up to 97 percent, because the Indians lacked Europeans' immunity. The Wichita population may have numbered as high as 100,000 at its peak. Following the impact of diseases, disruption, and conflict, the number plummeted to a mere 500. Other groups underwent similar tribulations. But some tribes temporarily prospered. The location of tribes such as the Wichitas and Caddos along prehistoric trade and then historic trade routes gave them an advantage in intertribal trade with the newcomers. Caddos continued to serve as brokers, supplying decorated pottery, bois d'arc wood for bows, salt, hides, dried and plaited pumpkin, and leather pouches to Native neighbors and later firearms (obtained from the French) to the Comanches. A new mixed-blood population (called "métis" from Canadian usage as well as "marginals") arose around missions, trading posts, and forts. Some of the Native peoples took up European-style farming and married non-Indian spouses. Other Indians offered ongoing resistance. Intertribal conflict and European warfare devastated tribes. The Spanish and French allies of some Indians struck against their neighboring tribes to obtain power, territory, and Indian captives. Refugees fled into friendly tribal sanctuaries, adding to their ethnic mixture inside trading posts, forts, missions, and camps.

Other Indians, like the Osages, also lived along prehistoric trade paths and prospered for a time from the new commerce. Even so, as they adjusted to new trade, indigenous peoples lost numbers and territory. Just as it does today, the Oklahoma area sat at the crossroads of major communications routes. To state it too simply but pointedly, Europeans reactivated or seized prehistoric riverine exchange networks, as Neal Salisbury pointed out, and often eliminated the Native participants in the process.

The Spanish traversed the American Southwest to enter the region of Oklahoma. Conquistador Francisco Vásquez de Coronado in 1541 rode on horseback across the state's western reaches when his sun-baked column marched from New Mexico to Kansas in search of the fabled golden city of Cíbola. Instead he entered Quivira, a grass-house ancestral Wichita village, that hot summer in the great bend of the Arkansas River. Coronado found no gold and turned back. Kansa Indians killed the priests he left behind. Juan de Oñate reached the village of Etzanoa in 1601, thought to be a Lower Walnut–phase ancestral Wichita settlement on the bank of the Walnut River near what is now Arkansas City, Kansas. Hernando de Soto also came near the area during his 1539–41 expedition through the Southeast at about the same time as Coronado but is not believed to have entered what is now the state of Oklahoma. The closest he came was his encampment at today's Hot Springs, Arkansas. His men watched earlier as Native traders brokered salt in the Arkansas town of Pacaha near the Mississippi River, while other soldiers brought back not only salt but also copper from their foraging outing.

Spanish missions in Louisiana and Texas, along with presidios (forts) to protect them, brought drastic alterations to the Native peoples' lives. Spanish officials not only sought allies but also tried to change Natives' lifeways to turn them into Spanish Christians. The Spanish arc of missions from the Atlantic Ocean stretched through Florida, Louisiana, and Texas, across the Southwest, and up the Pacific coast. It did not directly include present-day Oklahoma, but Indians in the area felt their effects. Spanish trade goods helped make them dependent on the metal items. Native Americans became vassals of the Spanish king and served not only as allies of the Spanish but often as buffers against hostile neighboring tribes. European trade items like kettles replaced traditional house wares, while Christianity undermined traditionalism and upset internal social relationships. Friars opposed multiple marriages, "superstitious" practices, and the use of tribal languages. Stories about the hairy foreigners spread rapidly along trade routes and helped confirm what Native predictions had foretold for perhaps a half-century.

Wichita raids against San Sabá Mission, established for Lipan Apache and Tonkawa Indians located inside Spanish Texas, provoked a Spanish punitive expedition. In 1759 Colonel Don Diego Ortiz Parilla's troops and Indian allies assaulted a Taovaya-Wichita village at what is now called the Longest site along the Red River in Jefferson County. The fortified Indian defenders repulsed the Spanish soldiers. Over time, however, assaults by the Spanish and their Osage and other Indian allies pressured Taovayas, Tawakonis, and Yscanis in the region to move east and south toward eventual consolidation with the Wichitas during the period from 1760 to 1778.

French *coureurs de bois* (literally, "voyagers or travelers in the woods," that is, mountain men) also brought French trade goods and colonial influence. The French presence tended to have less effect upon Indians, because at first there were fewer French than Spaniards. French firearms briefly led the Osages to assert their influence. The European fur trade also helped undermine American Indian independence and swept tribes into European conflicts. Bénard de La Harpe set up camp on the Red River in 1719 and then across the Arkansas River south of what is now the city of Tulsa. His journal described the lushness of the countryside but expressed regret that Indian conflict blocked further commerce. That same year, La Harpe and Claude Du Tisné established Ferdinandina on Deer Creek where its mouth emptied into the Arkansas River below the present Kansas border. It was the first white settlement in Oklahoma and was for some years a commercial center for the region. Arkansas Post near the mouth of that river in present-day Arkansas served as a magnet for regional Indian trade sporadically after 1683 and more permanently after 1731. The French also set up a post at Nachitoches (1714), to which some of the Caddos moved for easier trading.

After 1700 the Comanches arrived on the southern prairie. They acquired firearms and horses at about the same time and became the finest light cavalry in the world because of their superior mounted skills. Several bands formed alliances with Wichita peoples in the region. For two and a half centuries the Comanches mediated between the villages of the Plains and the Pueblos of Spanish colonial New Mexico. At the end of the eighteenth century a joint migration brought Kiowas and Plains Apaches from the north. Their alliance with the Comanches forged a formidable presence on the grasslands. By the late eighteenth century Comanche served as the trade lingua franca on the Plains in combination with sign language. When someone said *supereyos* in Comanche, traders understood it to mean *sombrero* (Spanish for "hat"). Similarly, Comanche *pijura* was *frijole* ("bean" in Spanish). The later trade in horses and mules helped sustain the fledgling American Republic and continued Comanche influence for some time.

Shortly thereafter, the Cheyennes joined their Arapaho kinfolk along the upper Arkansas River drainage. By the 1820s the Cheyennes and the Arapahos had replaced the Kiowas and Plains Apaches as trade intermediaries in the region. Cheyenne and Arapaho dominance, fed by the establishment of Bent's Fort in southern Colorado, also ended the Comanches' control of trade. Warfare among tribes eventually led to a desire for peace. Meeting in 1840 near Bent's Old Fort, Cheyennes, Arapahos, Kiowas, Comanches, and Plains Apaches concluded their Great Peace alliance.

After the explosive spread of horse culture, trade in horses led to pockets of specialization. Lipan Apaches supplied them to the Caddos, who engaged in major trade with settlers in Texas and later with Americans. A new word entered American English from the role of Comanche and Kiowa intermediaries and their mixed-blood partners in the commerce. Tying the New Mexican Pueblos with the Upper Missouri and Mississippi Valley markets across the southern Plains, "Comancheros" supplied consumers with horses, Indian and Mexican and New Mexican captives, and much more. In 1749 Felipe de Sandoval visited and later described a huge Comanche-sponsored trade fair on the big bend of the Arkansas River, near the confluence of the Arkansas and Purgatoire. He counted well over four hundred tepees and saw Comanches and Kiowas as well as Wichitas bartering with French and even German traders for several days. Firearms, powder horns, ammunition, buffalo robes, and captives were exchanged for horses. Jacob Fowler came upon a large Western Comanche–led fair encampment seventy-two years later at nearly the same location. He estimated that about five hundred Indians, including Kiowas, Plains Apaches, Comanches, Cheyennes, Arapahos, and Indian traders from Taos, were gathered there and busily trading.

Auguste and Pierre Chouteau came from St. Louis and built a mercantile empire from the 1770s into the 1820s that planted deep roots among tribes like the Iowas and Osages. The English also pressed their colonial goals at the same time, however, through traders, soldiers, and settlers as well as missionaries. After 1763 the Spanish and French presence officially but gradually withdrew. In that same year London authorities imposed stringent royal control over the expansion of the American frontier, fueling eventual revolution among the colonials. Although no English colonial settlers ventured into the Oklahoma area, Chickasaws, Caddos, and other Indians carried English trade goods like firearms and sold them in the region. Traders lost no time in setting up their mercantile posts to take advantage of access to Indian customers. Auguste Chouteau's 1839 death ended his trading center at Camp Holmes south of what is today Holdenville. John Shirley and William Shirley's post and James Edwards's trading post were also nearby. Holland Coffee sold his interest in his post on Cache Creek, but it continued. At about the same time Abel Warren opened one in the same vicinity, as Thomas Kavanaugh detailed. The reminiscences of James Mead described his similar commercial experiences.

Jesse Chisholm, a mixed-blood Cherokee, began his trading post in 1858 at Council Grove as a base for his freighting operation. He also sold goods and livestock to westward migrants. A historical marker commemorating his efforts is located near the Tenth Street bridge close to the Lake Overholser dam in western Oklahoma City. After the turmoil of the American Civil War, Chisholm returned to the site. His name is attached to the cattle trail that crossed Oklahoma, linking Texas herds with Kansas markets. U.S. Highway 81, connecting Duncan with Enid, follows the trail to Wichita, Kansas.

American exploration and commercial interaction brought U.S. settlers, soldiers, traders, and policies. Following the Louisiana Purchase in 1803, American explorers like Zebulon M. Pike, Randolph B. Marcy, and Stephen H. Long crisscrossed the region. Adventurers and traders soon opened one of the routes to Santa Fe through the area. Thomas James assumed that his profit from what would become the Santa Fe Trail would only be 100 percent. He was amazed when he reached the town in 1821 and pocketed more than double his estimated return. Traders also eventually brought U.S. soldiers. Josiah Gregg's reminiscences portray the rigors involved in "commerce of the prairie." The removal of tribal peoples from the East, at first voluntarily but later by force, brought new clashes with tribes already in the area that would become Oklahoma. Osage warfare with Cherokees and with Kiowas initiated an official U.S. military presence. Military forts soon followed, bringing roads, settlements, towns, and increasing demands upon Native peoples. One of the main military establishments was Fort Gibson on the Neosho River at its confluence with the Arkansas. Fort Smith on the Arkansas was also nearby.

Indian women were among those who gathered around the hustle and bustle of the forts. Throughout the turmoil of colonial imperial rivalries,

American Indian women played crucial roles in resistance or accommodation. Some led war raids in open defiance of transgressions. Other Native women aided in accommodation to the newcomers through marriage, raising families of mixed-blood children, and learning new technologies like spinning and loom weaving. But women continued to teach their cultural heritage and their mother tongue to their offspring as they had always done.

Federal authorities set up a special agency to deal with American Indians. In 1824 it became a civilian agency, the Office of Indian Affairs. It is now called the Bureau of Indian Affairs (abbreviated BIA), and its staff oversees a wide range of activities among tribes, from courts to oil leasing to education. Indian agencies for selected tribes are arms of the BIA, administered by superintendents. Since the mid-1970s tribes have been able to contract to perform for themselves services and programs that the BIA formerly ran for them. Many tribal contracts must be approved by an area superintendent and then by the U.S. secretary of the interior to become effective. The BIA also looks after land placed into federal trust for tribes and their members.

It is useful to return to the historical background. Bison had played an important role in the diet and lives of prairie Indians for a long time. With the horse, Indians entered their golden age because of increased mobility and efficiency of transport. Buffalo had no natural enemies, so their number grew ever larger on the lush grasses of the Plains. Observers described the Great Herd as containing over 100 million head. One herd along the upper Arkansas River in 1871 was estimated to be fifty miles deep and twenty-five miles wide. When Anglo-American intrusion threatened this resource, Indians reacted fiercely to defend their way of life.

Treaty cessions progressively restricted Indian territories in the Oklahoma area even as more tribes moved into the region after 1830. The Cherokee, Choctaw, Chickasaw, Creek, and, to a lesser extent, Seminole nations in the Southeast altered their governments and ways of life to conform move closely to those of their American neighbors and came to be called the "Five Civilized Tribes." In spite of the changes, over sixty thousand southeastern Indians were forced from their homelands and removed after 1830 along their "Trails of Tears" to Indian Territory. French commentator Alexis de Tocqueville watched as one column of Cherokees forlornly processed by him on a cold, drizzly evening in Arkansas. He was struck by how easily the American nation could deprive Indians of their rights "with singular felicity, without shedding blood, and without violating a single great principle of morality in the eyes of the world." He pointed out the irony: "It is impossible to destroy men with more respect for the laws of humanity." Frontier pressure for Indian lands became legal policy in a series of formative federal court decisions and congressional enactment of a "civilization fund" to transform Indian landholding. The efforts that culminated in passage of the Indian Removal Act (1830) began a long series of forced relocations of Native peoples into the West. When southeastern Indians were marching from their homelands to Arkansas and Indian Territory, Miami and Potawatomi Indians traveled to present-day Iowa, Missouri, and Kansas. After 1830 some thirty-seven tribes and groups numbering ten thousand people journeyed to eastern Kansas. Most of them eventually relocated into Indian Territory.

After the Five Tribes and other Indians had begun their adjustment in their new land, the conflagration of the Civil War burned their homes. The wartime split in tribes resonates into the present. Postwar Reconstruction foretold eventual statehood and legal destruction of their tribal governments. After the war mixed-blood Cherokee attorney and congressional delegate E. C. Boudinot pushed for white settlement and rapid development of the territory. In 1871, for example, he drove the first railroad spike in Indian Territory as a gesture toward bringing in a flood of settlers. He laid out the town of Vinita in northeastern Indian Territory at the junction of two rail lines in the hope of making a real estate fortune. Boudinot advocated breaking up the tribal mass and allotting individual farm plots to Indians.

One of the more contentious issues has been the question of freedmen. Colonists introduced Africans to Indians. The newcomers joined an already existing trade in American Indian captives. Through time, Africans were held as slaves in some tribes, free blacks lived among other tribes, and still other Africans traveled and traded in Indian Country. Sometimes these people intermarried and intermixed (they were also called maroons as well as African-Indians and Black Indians). Following tribal removals, Africans and African-Indians in Indian Territory experienced increasing restrictions upon their lives, especially as the twentieth century dawned, with the rise of land loss and Jim Crow attitudes. Through the nineteenth century, U.S. government policies dictated the definition of tribal citizenship. At the same time tribal governments were under tremendous pressure just to survive, leading tribes increasingly to focus on Indian blood quantum as the qualifier for membership. Toward the end of the nineteenth century the Dawes Commission rolls classified tribal members as either Indians or Africans, exclusively. The former received tribal rights, the latter did not. The Dawes procedure set the tone for the future. That was in spite of Reconstruction treaty pledges of incorporation of freedmen into tribes in the aftermath of the Civil War and federal pledges to aid in providing a postwar solution for the dilemma. Freedmen ultimately became citizens of the United States under allotment agreements, but their political and social rights were restricted, as they were in mainstream American society.

The topic surfaced with renewed interest at the beginning of March 2007. The Seminoles confronted the issue of their freedmen in a 2000 tribal vote and federal court intervention three years later. In 2007 voters in the Cherokee Nation passed a tribal constitutional amendment that ousted perhaps 2,800 descendants of freedmen from the tribe because they were not related genetically to an earlier enrolled Cherokee Indian. The issue roiled not only tribal politics but national racial politics when the Congressional Black Caucus in Washington, D.C., entered the controversy and threatened tribal funding. The subject is pending in litigation, and by mutual agreement between the parties the rights of freedmen were reinstated during the court suit. The intersection of black and Indian issues is contentious for many reasons, including the sting of the potential loss of citizenship by descendants of freedmen and of being stateless exiles should court decisions ultimately uphold the tribal amendment position (see specific tribal freedmen topics in the "Cherokee," "Chickasaw," "Choctaw," "Muscogee [Creek]," and "Seminole" entries). As usual (from the tribal side of the controversy), tribal sovereignty stands to be undermined by an adverse court ruling.

Once again it is necessary to return to history. Advocates of "opening" reserved Indian lands persuaded Congress to enact a series of measures. The Curtis Act (1898) undermined tribal authority to conduct government business, abolished tribal courts, paved the way for eventual statehood, and confirmed the extension of federal court jurisdiction over the territory. The remaining tribal governments were in effect caretaker administrations waiting for more non-Indian settlement and statehood. The legislation authorized the Dawes Commission to privatize Indian landholdings even without Indian cooperation. During the 1890s the Jerome Commission had already secured Indian land cessions from tribes in western Oklahoma, using every fraudulent means available to the federal negotiators.

Allotment of their lands, including many of the thirteen reservations established in the western and central parts of the Indian Territory after the Civil War, left the Indians terribly vulnerable. Tribes suffered not only land and resource losses but repeated assaults on their cultures during the so-called assimilation period after the war, as boarding schools and mission policies took their children away for educational programs. The era from the 1880s to the 1930s is often referred to as the "dark ages" for tribes. Tribal members like the Kiowas saw their land base shrink to a 0.01 percent fragment of its former expanse in two generations. Non-Indians engulfed them. The resulting poverty took a fearful toll on Indian health and longevity. Wholesale land loss added to the dire situation that contributed to impoverishment. Allotment in severalty took away 15.7 million acres of Five Tribes' landholdings and affected 101,500 members who received individual farms. Land loss to their Anglo neighbors quickly followed. For those tribes, allotment left them with only 1.5 million acres under tribal and federal trust control. Before allotment, the land territory of the Five Tribes had equaled the area of the state of South Carolina. Statehood in 1907 incorporated all of the former Indian Territory into the state of Oklahoma. New state officials paid homage to Native heritage when they adopted the design from the Osage war shield for the state flag.

The exploitation, corruption, and mistreatment of Indians and their resources following allotment and statehood served as a lightning rod for Indian discontent after World War I. The call for reform slowly reached a crescendo not only in Oklahoma but throughout the nation. A new period dawned in the 1930s with the enactment of New Deal legislation for Indians. The far-reaching Indian Reorganization Act (IRA, 1934), and the cloned Oklahoma Indian Welfare Act (OIWA), which senator Elmer Thomas and representative Will Rogers successfully pressed for enactment two years later, helped revive tribal governance and cultures. The long devastation of paternalism and allotment policies slowly ended. The act guided tribes in writing tribal constitutions and by-laws. The measure enabled tribal groups to secure a federal charter as cooperative associations. Local associations could market strawberries or sell beadwork. But the legislation left its own legacies. Only a few tribes reorganized under it, and only scattered Indian groups developed credit associations. Another legacy is the current two-tier governmental structure for tribes. The OIWA organized tribes along Western corporate lines with a veneer of popular democracy to smooth the working relationship with the BIA. The other tribal structure was the traditional elders or chiefs' councils, arranged according to time-honored pedigree, clans, and societies, which were responsible for ceremonial activities. The two structures continue side by side, although one usually has little to do with the other.

Tribes experienced further severe setbacks under the termination policy of the 1950s, which ended federal recognition and support for some Indian nations. Additionally, the federal relocation program moved

Indian job-seekers to cities like Dallas and Denver, far away from their homes. That policy copied earlier employment and placement efforts and the World War II trend toward defense plant work and postwar urbanization. A fuller recovery, however, began with the 1960s and the era of Indian activism. Subsequent legislation, like the Indian Self-Determination and Education Assistance Act in 1975 (popularly called Public Law 638 or simply 638), permitted tribes to begin to look after their own affairs. They could take genuine strides toward their own self-governance and self-determination. Eventually tribes could enter into compacts (agreements) with the state on a variety of topics, like law enforcement, tobacco sales, and gaming. Since 1979 special federal courts, called either Code of Federal Regulations (CFR) Courts or Courts of Indian Offenses, have been established for tribal litigation. CFR Courts arose from federal administrative regulations, while tribal court systems arose out of tribal sovereignty. Federal and state legislation took an additional landmark step with the enactment of the Indian Child Welfare Act in 1978 in favor of preserving American Indian families and their cultural legacy through their children.

There have been many bumps along the road toward independence for tribes, and some tribes have made less progress than others. But it has only been about thirty years since lessened federal paternalism unleashed tribal energies. Considering the short span of time, Indian progress has been remarkable. An example of Oklahoma tribal resurgence is the Chickasaw Nation. The federal government appointed Overton James governor of the Chickasaws in 1963, and then his tribe elected him leader in his own right in 1971. When he became leader of the Chickasaw Nation, he had no office and no employees. His office was his kitchen table and his storeroom was the trunk of his car. Through grants and federal government programs, in four years the Chickasaw Nation had a budget of $750, and thirty employees. The tremendous growth continued. By the early 1990s the Chickasaws had an annual budget of over $15 million, with a staff of over three hundred. Today tribal employment in Oklahoma in all sectors of economic activity makes Indian tribes the fourth largest employer in the state. In 2004 the total tribal economic impact on the state amounted to about $8 billion. Tribal income had ripple effects on personal income for employees and suppliers to tribes, which some economists estimate has a multiplier effect of five times on the larger economy but also on health care, housing, bridges, roadways, and taxes paid. Revenue in tribal coffers also sustains Indian families as well as tribal language retention programs and the instruction of a younger generation in the Native heritage and culture. Indians now constitute about 12 percent of the state's population and are its largest minority. The U.S. census in 2000 reported a population of about 400,000 in the state who claimed Indian heritage.

Tribal officials face a host of contemporary issues. Internal disputes revolve around governance, heritage, and development. For some tribes, the determination of tribal membership, which includes the rights of tribal freedmen's descendants, is an ongoing concern. Other groups seek federal recognition. Tribal leaders try to secure gaming revenues, treaty pledges, and resource rights. Tribal members are also vitally concerned with the mainte-

An example of a modern tribal health facility: the Muscogee Nation's Kowetv Clinic in Coweta, Oklahoma

Photograph by Jay Miller

nance of their unique heritage, which includes their languages and cultural practices. Some tribal groups would like to revive long-dormant traditional rituals. Tribal sovereignty has encountered challenges over the use of resources, jurisdiction, fuel and tobacco taxation and sales, and gaming. Tribal claims to water loom as a growing focus in the long-term. Late in 2005 the U.S. Congress enacted Public Law 109-59, arbitrarily taking jurisdiction over environmental issues away from tribes and granting it to the state and thereby diminishing tribal sovereignty. For tribal leaders, the action raised the specter of arbitrary seizures of the past, like removal and allotment.

Tribal responses to assimilation pressures from mainstream society vary widely. Some tribal members cling to ancestral ceremonial traditions. Others reject traditionalism in favor of mainstream society. Some mix tribal rituals, Christianity, and mainstream culture. Education is a realm in which a mixture of old and new takes place. Tribes operate former mission boarding schools like Sequoyah School (Cherokee) and Jones Academy (Choctaw). Tribes infuse the mainstream curriculum with tribal language and culture. Several tribes recently launched their own tribal colleges.

American Indians from Oklahoma have continued to play an influential role on the national scene. In the field of athletics, Pete Houser (Cheyenne) and Albert Exendine (Delaware) pioneered the passing game in football at Carlisle Indian School in 1905. Oklahoma Indian leaders

The historic signing of a tobacco compact between Indian tribes and officials of the state of Oklahoma at the State Capitol, 1992
Photograph by Dick Reed, Capitol photographer

formed the influential National Congress of American Indians in 1944 to serve as a national voice for Indian tribal concerns. Cherokee boarding school product Ruth Muskrat Bronson literally kept the organization going in its infancy, working at her kitchen table. Other Indians from the state, such as Ross Swimmer (Cherokee), Kevin Gover (Pawnee), and Neal McCaleb (Chickasaw), served as assistant secretary for Indian affairs and commissioner of Indian affairs in national political administrations. W. Richard West (Cheyenne) and Gover directed the National Museum of the American Indian in Washington, D.C. Some worked behind the scenes. Herbert Hyde, an Oklahoman of Indian extraction, chaired the committee on resolutions for the 1940 Republican Party national convention held in Philadelphia. He steered the party platform toward supporting the establishment of the Indian Claims Commission (ICC) for the final settlement of Indian claims against the United States. Still others have quietly seen service in noteworthy roles, such as holding national offices in the War Mothers organization, Girl Scouts, and civic groups. Mifaunwy Shunatona Hines (Otoe-Pawnee-Wyandotte and a former Miss Oklahoma) had the idea for the urban American Indian Community House in New York City, located on East 38th Street.

Some with Native heritage shared the spotlight in sports, such as Pirates baseball player Willie Stargell, who was of Seminole descent. In an earlier era Tsianina (Cherokee-Creek) and Te Ata (Chickasaw) entertained audiences worldwide. Comanche LaDonna Harris kept the National Council on Indian Opportunity hearings alive at the end of the 1960s and became a leader in national Indian education, economic opportunity, and sovereignty issues. Native peoples have carried on a proud warrior tradition. American Indians have the highest percentage of military service in the United States relative to the total population. World War II Medal of Honor winners include Jack Montgomery (Cherokee) and Ernest Childers (Creek/Cherokee), among many military heroes from the state.

Because so many ancestors came to Indian Territory from other places, Oklahoma tribes have retained connections with their former homelands and kinfolk. Some Indians still have ties to a sacred spiritual place, such as Bear Butte in South Dakota, a location that is important to the Cheyennes and other tribes. A few tribes seek casino sites in earlier homeland regions. Some tribal members make pilgrimages to out-of-state sites, while more visit festivals, bullfights, and dances.

The rich Native artistic tradition lives. Ancestors chipped images onto rocks in the Panhandle. The Caddos were known for their exceptional ceramics in prehistory. Other tribal groups carried on a flourishing artistic tradition in decorated hides, robes, and tepees. Prisoners held in Florida's Fort Marion during the late 1870s used the transitional medium of ledger-book sheets on which to depict Plains warrior life in scenes including parasols, beaver hats, hunts, and camp life. These prisoners contributed to the start of contemporary Plains Indian painting, and that "Oklahoma" style is ongoing today. Numerous Indian artists maintain their tribal craft and painting heritage. Representational art, paintings, murals, baskets, pottery, sculpture, jewelry, and musical instruments (like flutes) as well as oral and written literary traditions proudly continue.

Since the 1960s and 1970s there has also been a renewal of Indian culture, with a rise in ceremonial life for tribal members and an increase in the awareness that something must be done to preserve tribal languages and heritage. Cultural heritage took different forms for different tribes. For some, the Native American Church with its sacrament of Peyote was their vehicle for preservation of Indianness. Some looked to their Indian Christian church, with its Indian-language hymns and services. For others, the powwow served as the umbrella for keeping specific tribal songs and dances alive. Gatherings perpetuated what Robert Allen Warrior calls "the sweet grass meaning of solidarity." Because various tribes were thrust together in the Indian Territory, they have shared cultural traits (called pan-Indian). The powwow and Gourd Dance, originally Plains phenomena, are now widespread. Delawares, Shawnees, and Quapaws adopted the Caddo Turkey Dance, which the Wichitas also practice. Intertribal sharing continues.

Two examples may help illustrate the continuing American Indian heritage.

At the edge of a powwow ground under the shade of their awning, a niece watches her aunts working their beads into tribal patterns as they discuss the last time they saw an overlay stitch used in beadwork. Children play at their feet. The conversation shifts to one particular dancer's intricate design on his regalia before the niece gets up, places a colorful shawl over her shoulders, and walks to the circle of dancers in the nearby arena to stand behind an aged uncle. He is being honored with a special song, with a line of male friends on either side and a tier of female admirers behind. Crumpled money lies at his feet as an offering. After the song ends, all line up to shake his hand. Some receive a warm hug of mutual long-standing friendship. Some of the males wear silver work and carry beaded rattles with ancient clan designs and colors. Two of his nephews leave the line where they have been standing and after shaking hands return to their chairs at one of the large circular drums in the center of the dance ground. The niece quietly resumes her seat at the camp, listening again to the women's ongoing conversation, this time about a favorite aunt's special recipe for her fry bread. The niece returns to the joking and teasing. Peals of laughter resonate through the camp and accompany the aunt's straight-faced explanation that the secret to her famous recipe is running her fingers through her hair while she is kneading the dough, adding something "special" to the flavorful mix. Colored streamers and vivid items of dance regalia hang from rafters and chair backs and move gently with the breeze. These scenes of family generations, stories, songs, and rituals are played out repeatedly throughout Indian Country.

A second example illustrates the generational role of heritage. A Choctaw grandmother picks up a basket and tells her granddaughter that making the basket puts some of the maker in it through toil and dedication. The basket even gives off its own energy. The basket tells the story of her people, the Creator's People. In an earlier time, Choctaw people used baskets to build earth mounds and to cook their food. Baskets were also used to help bury their dead. Baskets held new babies and served as containers of items for household chores. The Choctaws made baskets to use in trade. Now Choctaw officials give tribal baskets as gifts to visiting dignitaries, to cement alliances. The grandmother carefully explains to her granddaughter that the basket mirrors the life of the People. Her People are intertwined in the spiraling layers of the basket wall. The weaving of the reeds into a basket weaves one generation into another. Through these experiences and others, generations pass along their cultural knowledge.

Participants reinforce their American Indian heritage.

Different generations looked to varied monuments as memorials to the past. Remnants are sprinkled across the Oklahoma landscape. A much older generation visited a stone marker at Fort Gibson recalling the hard work of Andrew Jackson's Indian commissioner Montfort Stokes and his efforts to "civilize" the Indians. He died long ago, in 1842. Caddos continue to visit the Texas grave of Robert S. Neighbors with a mournful nod at the injustice done to him as a result of the help he offered to their people. Some Cherokees still make a pilgrimage to the grave of the Reverend Samuel Austin

Choctaw basket made of river cane, ca. 1920

Museum of the Red River, Idabel, Oklahoma. Gift of Betty Sue Sessions

Worcester and his wife at Park Hill on the outskirts of Tahlequah. International visitors to Fort Sill in southwestern Oklahoma insist on viewing Geronimo's grave.

Some remembrances are sung. A song at a Kiowa powwow dance evokes glories of the past, reminding the Kiowa listeners of the feat of Chief Lone Wolf in his victory over a Texan defiantly waving a repeating rifle:

> *Just because he had eight bullets in his gun,*
> *He felt safe.*
> *But I see he did not come home.*

Again, the generations reinforce their American Indian heritage in Indian Country.

SUGGESTED READING

Bement, Leland C. *Bison Hunting at Cooper Site: Where Lightning Bolts Drew Thundering Herds.* Norman: University of Oklahoma Press, 1999.

Gregg, Josiah. *Commerce of the Prairies.* Edited by Max Moorehead. Norman: University of Oklahoma Press, 1954.

Kavanaugh, Thomas W. *Comanche Political History: An Ethnohistorical Perspective, 1706–1875*. Lincoln: University of Nebraska Press, 1996; repr. 1999.

Mead, James. *Hunting and Trading on the Great Plains, 1859–1875*. Edited by Schuyler Jones. Norman: University of Oklahoma Press, 1986.

Odell, George H. *La Harpe's Post*. Tuscaloosa: University of Alabama Press, 2002.

Salisbury, Neal. "The Indians' Old World: Native Americans and the Coming of the Europeans." *William and Mary Quarterly* 53 (July 1996): 435–58.

Smith, Bruce. "Between Foraging and Farming." *Science* 279, no. 5351 (March 13, 1998): 1651–52.

Tocqueville, Alexis de. *Democracy in America*. 2 vols. New York: Knopf, 1945.

Warrior, Robert Allen. "The Sweetgrass Meaning of Solidarity: 500 Years of Resistance." *Border/lines* 23 (1991–92): 35–37.

Alabama-Quassarte

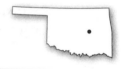

NAME

The Alabamas and Quassartes are separate tribal groups. The word "Alabama" is derived from the Alabamas' designation for themselves, Albamo (meaning unknown). Choctaw speakers claim that "Alabama" or "Alibamu" came from the Choctaw *alba ayamule*, "I open or clear the thicket." It is found in the journals of Pierre Le Moyne, Sieur d'Iberville, describing his visit to Louisiana. Similarly, "Quassarte" is from the Koasatis' designation for themselves, Kowassati. It cannot be translated, although *ati* means "person" in Koasati.

LOCATION AND GOVERNMENT

The "Alabama-Quassarte Tribal Town" is connected culturally to the Muscogee (Creek) Nation, but the tribe is politically separate and free-standing. The tribe's offices are located in an old bank building on Broadway near Main Street in Wetumka in Hughes County. Wetumka is on State Highway 9 about twenty-five miles southwest of Henryetta.

The tribal governmental entity was established under the Oklahoma Indian Welfare Act (OIWA) on June 26, 1936. Members adopted a constitution and by-laws on May 24, 1939. The tribal website is www.alabama-quassarte.org.

BUSINESSES

Revenue is generated from the Alabama-Quassartes' Redhawk Gaming Center in Wetumka and a tribally owned smoke shop.

NUMBER

The tribal town has a certified enrollment of 350 members. The Alabama-Quassartes are related to the 1,000 Alabama-Coushattas in east Texas, located near the town of Livingston about seventy-five miles northeast of Houston. They have a 4,594-acre reservation. The Alabama-Coushattas organized during the Indian New Deal, were terminated from their trust relationship in 1954, and regained federal recognition during the 1980s. Approximately 700 members of the Coushatta Tribe near Elton, Louisiana, also were organized under the IRA, were terminated in 1954, and were again recognized in 1973.

Linguistically the Alabama-Quassartes are part of the Muskoghean language stock. Linguistic evidence indicates that Alabama separated from Muskoghean proper about 2,000 years ago, from Choctaw about 1,400 years ago, and from Chickasaw around 1,100 years ago. The Alabama-Quassartes are closely related culturally to other Muskoghean-speaking peoples like the Creeks, Choctaws, and Chickasaws and share major cultural characteristics with other southeastern Indians.

There was such affinity between the Alabamas and the Choctaws that scholars like John Swanton speculated that the former originated from the latter. Certainly the Alabamas maintained marriage alliances with the eastern Choctaws. The Inholahta division of the Choctaws (the senior of the two major groups) ranked itself junior to the Alabamas, perhaps because the Choctaws considered the Alabamas of the Coosa-Tallapoosa forks, near the modern city of Montgomery, Alabama, to be the heirs of the old Moundville Mississippian chiefdom, according to scholar Patricia Galloway. Archeologists believe that the Dallas phase, centered in the eastern Tennessee River Valley, was ancestral to the Koasatis. Ceramic remains link early Dallas peoples to Etowah chiefdom pottery of northern Georgia dating to A.D. 1050. Lamar culture came to dominate the Dallas population after the mid-1400s. Perhaps the Dallas/Koasati chiefdom was incorporated into the Lamar/Coosa chiefdom of the upper Coosa River Valley. In the Late Dallas phase people believed to be ancestral Koasatis began to move southward to the Coosa River in the 1540s in the aftermath of the Hernando de Soto expedition then later moved to the Tallapoosa and Chattachoochee rivers. Koasati Muscogee peoples during the eighteenth century occupied the upper level of the old Kulumi site on the south bank of the Tallapoosa River. After the Alabamas departed with the French (1763), the Taskigi Koasatis settled the site near Fort Toulouse. Another Dallas-phase site is Toqua, which was the capital during the time of the Lamar culture in the eastern Tennessee Valley. Scientific investigation has revealed that the largest mound at Toqua is aligned with the winter solstice. Archeologists have found five levels of sociopolitical activity in the earthen record there, corresponding to development from farmstead to multimound capital. Most burials also shared an orientation to the winter solstice.

Interestingly, the so-called Spaghetti style of shell gorgets notable for the Dallas phase was also found at Big Eddy sites along the upper Alabama River in the area that would become the state of the same name. The linkage implies polities connected in some way, whether by alliance, marriage, or closely related languages. The French collectively referred to the peoples at the junction of the Coosa and the Tallapoosa rivers as Alibamaux (Alabamas). Ned Jenkins, an archeologist, believed that all those migrants from the Moundville Variant ceramic chiefdom were speakers of a language closely related to historic Alabama. He suggested that these people arrived about 100 years after the Soto expedition. The Koasatis spoke the Alabama language yet derived from the Dallas phase, while the Alabamas came from Moundville. They shared technology and a ceramic style (that is, vessel shapes and handle styles, according to Jenkins), implying a sustained interaction over a long period.

The Spaniards of the Soto expedition first encountered the Alabamas in northern Mississippi in 1540 and the Koasatis in their island town (Coste or Acoste) on the Tennessee River. To the Spanish ear, the Indians' designation for that river was Caskinampo, from the Koasati *kaski*, "warriors," and *nampon*, "to be so many," meaning "their warriors are many," according to scholar Charles Hudson. Spanish chroniclers for the Juan Pardo expedition described their visit twenty-five years later to Chiaha and Olamico, which was the same town. It may have derived its names from the Koasati word *cayha*, "tall," and perhaps from *mico*, "chief or head of town." The settlement that the Spaniards entered was on Zimmerman's Island in the French Broad River. The inference is that most of the residents of the town were Koasatis. Members of the Soto expedition also found Alabamas residing in the vicinity of what is now Starkville, Mississippi. As a result of later European-led changes and population shifts, the Alabamas were living on the river of the same name just below the meeting of the Coosa and Tallapoosa rivers during the following century, which was part of Upper Creek territory. Some also resided among the Lower Creeks.

European intrusion fragmented the Alabamas through warfare, disease, and political intrigue. After France relinquished the area to the English, some of the Alabamas emigrated to present-day Mississippi. Some of them moved nearer French trade sources. Other Alabamas joined the Creeks then fought in the Creek War of 1813–14. Wherever they resided, Alabama and Quassarte villagers relied on male hunting and female gardening and farming. They traced their membership through matrilineal clans. Women made baskets from river cane and pine needles as well as many other products. Among their descendants in Louisiana and Texas, contemporary basketry is tied to tourism.

Many of the Alabamas removed from the Southeast with the Creeks during the 1830s. Like their tribal companions from the trek, the Alabamas gradually established farms in their new homeland. An example of Alabama-Quassarte influence in Indian Territory is Ward Coachman, who served as principal chief of the Creek Nation during the 1880s. He was of mixed Creek and Alabama heritage.

During the 1930s the U.S. Congress enacted legislation permitting tribal groups to form governments and federally chartered corporations to engage in economic activities. The Alabamas and Quassartes merged and took steps toward recognition. They organized as a tribal town separate from the Creek Nation and maintained a traditional tribal town political structure. Alabama-Quassartes in Oklahoma rely upon the Mvskoke language today. Members have worked diligently over the past two decades to build an economic base upon which future members can continue to develop their organization. For the Alabama-Quassartes, religion is a private matter, not to be discussed in public; at the request of their civil leadership, the topic of ceremony is excluded here.

SUGGESTED READING

Galloway, Patricia. *Choctaw Genesis*, 1500–1700. Lincoln: University of Nebraska Press, 1995.

Hudson, Charles. "The Hernando de Soto Expedition, 1539–1543." In Charles Hudson and Carmen Chaves Tesser, eds., *The Forgotten Centuries*, 74–103. Athens: University of Georgia Press, 1994.

Jenkins, Ned. "Early Creek Origins: Moundville Connection." Paper presented to Southeastern Archaeological Conference, St. Louis, Missouri, October 2004.

Swanton, John R. *The Indians of the Southeastern United States.* Bulletin 137. Washington, D.C.: Bureau of American Ethnology, 1946; repr. Washington, D.C.: Smithsonian Institution Press, 1979.

Apache (Plains Apache)

NAME

"Apache" means "enemy" or "not Athapaskan," from the Zuni word *apachu*. Apaches refer to themselves as Naishadena (or shortened to Na-I-Sha), "our People." They have been erroneously referred to in the past as Prairie Apaches and Kiowa-Apaches as a result of their historic close association with the Kiowas. They prefer to be called the Apache Tribe of Oklahoma.

LOCATION AND GOVERNMENT

The "Apache Tribe of Oklahoma" headquarters is located in Anadarko in Caddo County, in southwestern Oklahoma. Tribal members reside in and around Anadarko and Fort Cobb. There are many other Apachean groups through the American Southwest, however, as well as the Fort Sill Apaches of Geronimo, outside Lawton, Oklahoma. The Apache Tribe of Oklahoma is not organized under the OIWA. The tribe's constitution and by-laws (drafted by Houston Klinecole under the direction of tribal elders and approved by the BIA) were adopted in 1972 and amended in 1976 and 1987. The Tribal Council is made up of all tribal members over the age of eighteen, with a chair, a vice chair, and a secretary-treasurer as officers. The annual meeting takes place on the third Saturday in June. The tribe is governed by a business committee of five members that meets monthly. There is no tribal website yet.

BUSINESSES

The Apaches' major casino, the Silver Buffalo Casino, is across the road from the convenience store at their tribal complex. This was the first Indian casino to be fully compacted, meaning that the tribe and the state achieved a written agreement regarding the terms and division of income from the gaming operation. Two other casinos near the Texas boundary at the Red River are planned.

NUMBER

The tribe has about 1,800 members. Enrollment is based on a roll, with a requirement of one-eighth blood quantum and descent from an original allottee.

The Plains Apaches are related linguistically to seven other Southern Athapaskan–speaking peoples, including the Navajos, the Eastern Apaches (such as the Jicarillas), and the Western Apaches (such as the Chiricahuas). Common language ancestry implies a common background. Harry Hoijer, who studied Native American languages, believed that ancestral Apache peoples split from their larger linguistic family in the subarctic forests of the Mackenzie Basin of the Canadian Northwest Territory and gradually moved onto the Plains of Canada perhaps 2,000 years ago. They joined the Sarcees in Saskatchewan province. The Sarcees' language is similar, but the Apaches moved farther south about 1,200 years later. From their central Alaska homeland, their journey took them along the eastern cordillera of the Rocky Mountains, according to James Gunnerson and Waldo Wedel. Morris Opler, Julian Steward, and David Brugge argued for an intermontane route through the Great Basin. Anthropologist William Bittle contended that the Plains Apaches separated from the main group of Apacheans and separated from the Eastern Apaches (Jicarillas and Lipans) around A.D. 1500. Loring Haskell and John Harrington believed that the Plains Apaches departed from the Lipan Apaches as Fremont-Promontory and related peoples entered the northern Plains. Others like Hoijer and Michael Davis argued for a much earlier separation. The debate continues. Oral tradition from the Plains Apaches and from the Kiowas, reported by ethnologist James Mooney, stated that the Plains Apaches merged with the Kiowas in the region of the Black Hills. James and Delores Gunnerson dated the merger about 1700. The two groups became identified as one, with many referring to the Plains Apaches as the Kiowa-Apaches.

The suggested time frame for the entry of Apacheans onto the southern Plains and into the Southwest varies greatly. Dates usually range between A.D. 1300 and 1500. Names used on Spanish documents are notoriously inaccurate and confusing. Scholars believe that the earliest mention in 1541 of bison hunters on foot west of the Pecos River, whom the Spaniards in Coronado's expedition called "Querechos," referred to Apacheans, but they cannot be specific as to tribe. The correspondence of René-Robert Cavelier, Sieur de La Salle, mentioned "Gattacka" camped south of the

Platte River with the "Manrhoet," believed to be the Kiowas. They were trading horses with the Pawnees at the time (the early 1680s).

The Plains Apache origin story shared with other Apacheans the exploits of twin culture heroes Fireboy and Waterboy. The twins destroyed monsters and brought order to the universe. A hand game at the beginning between good and evil determined whether eternal darkness or light would prevail. The Plains Apaches shared with the Kiowas stories about the antics of Coyote that instructed listeners in morality and self-worth. All Apacheans shared a fear of contamination by the spirits of the dead and belief in the vital need for a quick burial and cleansing of the after-effects.

Plains Apaches resided in small family-based camps. Men hunted, while women tended to their camps and gardens. The eldest man served as leader of their extended family or band. Individuals sought spiritual power through a vision quest. It could also be obtained through inheritance from a close relative. Personal medicine bundles, songs, herbs, and shield designs were usually passed on to a close male relative. Bundle keepers tended to be headmen of bands, and individuals addressed sacred bundles as "my grandfather." In the nineteenth century Plains Apaches participated in Kiowa and Cheyenne/Arapaho Sun Dances but did not hold their own. Plains Apache dancing societies involved all prominent adults. Children belonged to the Kasowe or Rabbit Society and learned heritage and traditions in their youth. Leading adult males belonged to the Manitide. The society's dances involved venerated staffs, ceremonies, songs, and lifetime appointments to leadership positions. The Tlinitide or Kintide or Horse Society included the oldest and bravest warriors. It was called the Contraries Society because of members' backward motions and behavior as well as shocking antics. The eldest women joined the secret Izuwe Society, with membership inherited through the female line. If the women prayed for a warrior, he erected a tepee for them upon his return. Ceremonial singing and dancing, as well as use of the sacred Pipe, took place inside the tepee. The women also participated in the Scalp Dance upon the return of a war party.

The Spanish horse transformed the bison hunters into nomads who ventured onto the southern Plains. They took on the characteristics of buffalo nomads, including use of the horse, dependence upon the bison, warrior societies, and medicine bundles. Oddly, the Plains Apaches did not have a girl's puberty ceremony as a major annual event, unlike other Apacheans, including the Navajos. The Kiowas and Plains Apaches allied with the larger Comanche Nation, commonly referred by the acronym "KCA," either just before or just after 1800 to achieve a formidable presence on the southern Plains that served as an integral part of the economy of the region. The KCA used Spanish livestock and trade during this period to maximum advantage to enter into what many consider their golden age. Raids obtained Spanish horses and mules and trade secured other items that increased their value as brokers in Texan, Mexican, and later American commercial activity. The five hundred or so Plains Apaches shifted affiliation to their advantage as circumstances dictated. Of course, the Plains Apaches shared affinity with other Athapaskan-speakers. Historically, the Apaches took in some Lipan and Mescalero kinfolk during perilous times on the frontier. Refugees from attacks, those fleeing destroyed missions like San Sabá, offspring from Spanish soldierly liaisons at presidios, and others sometimes found temporary safe haven among Apache bands.

Walking Bear, One Who Is Surrendered, and Iron Show signed the first treaty of Fort Gibson in 1837 for the Plains Apaches. Intense pressure from the Cheyennes and the Arapahos then led to conflict over hunting ranges until the Great Peace of 1840. Alliances shifted within the region, but the Indians maintained their own peace in the face of the larger threat facing them.

Pioneer pressure increased, game diminished, and smallpox (1839, 1862) and cholera (1849) ravaged tribal families. Eastern tribal intrusion brought enemies closer. Pawnees combined with their allies to inflict a series of defeats on the KCA in the mid-1850s. The Plains Apaches signed the Treaty of Fort Atkinson (1853) in Kansas, led by Poor Wolf, Poor Bear, Prairie Wolf, and The Cigar. The tribe briefly allied with the Arapahos through their 1862 treaty with the United States and added the Cheyennes to their affiliation in the October 1865 Treaty of the Little Arkansas, which Congress did not ratify. The Plains Apaches rejoined the Kiowas and Comanches in the treaty signed at the large council of tribes held at Medicine Lodge in southern Kansas in October 1867. Six years later Pacer, Daho, and Gray Eagle accompanied Captain Henry Alvord and Kiowas and other Indians as part of a delegation to the national capital. Upon his return, Pacer requested the establishment of a school, which was set up by the Quaker teacher A. J. Standing.

The Indians accepted confinement to a smaller reservation under the terms of the 1867 treaty, and the United States began assimilation policies for its wards. Farming was difficult at best on the western prairie, especially without plows, and stock-raising suffered due to inadequate grazing land. Allotment for 214 Apaches between 1901 and 1908 resulted in an influx of white settlers onto the "surplus" land. Plains Apache life depended upon

communal hunting, so individual farming proved disastrous to their social cohesion, while land division and leasing plunged them into poverty.
Boarding school education and missions eventually took their cultural toll,
through diseases, deaths, and conversions, with resulting loss of language
ability and culture. The government effort after the 1880s to ban religious
practices, which scholar William Bittle termed "a religious holocaust," had
devastating consequences for the Sun Dance, medicine bundle use, the
Ghost Dance, and Peyote practices. Returning veterans of the nation's wars
fed Apache nationalism and kept some dances alive. After World War II
men and women participated in powwows attired in full regalia.

At the close of the 1950s the Plains Apaches revived the Manitide or
Blackfeet Dancing Society. It had focused on policing the buffalo hunt
and aiding the poor. Today it holds a four-day gathering each summer.
Participants and visitors set up camps and catch up on people and events
during the past year. Women sometimes perform old Scalp Dances during
the intermissions. In addition, Plains Apaches perform their own dances
as well as war dances derived from the Poncas and Pawnees during their
association in the early reservation era. Of course, Plains Apaches participate in the Gourd Dance and other powwow activities. Their annual
powwow and a culture camp for all ages (since 1992) take place on the
grounds of Apache Park outside Fort Cobb. Some tribal members also
are active in the Native American Church. Almost all Plains Apaches are
members of Christian churches, such as the Baptist, Methodist, and Ho-
liness churches. Whether ceremonialists or Christians, Plains Apaches
continue to sing praises to the Creator, Nuakolahe, "earth he made it."

During confinement to the reservation, Plains Apaches clustered in
five groups termed gonkas (local bands). The geographic area centered
on the communities of Fort Cobb, Boone, Alden, Cement, and Anadarko.
Following pressure for allotment, the Apaches grouped in three communities: Fort Cobb, Boone, and Apache. After 1881 six mission schools and
churches ministered to the Apaches, who also had access to others available to all KCA members.

The Apaches never drew up a charter under the auspices of the federal
government, although the federal authorities treated the tribe as if it had.
From 1936 to 1963 the tribe was a part of the KCA Business Committee.
The Apache Tribe of Oklahoma shares allotted and jointly owned lands
with the Kiowas and the Comanches under terms of the congressional act
of June 24, 1946. The tribe shared in a 1973 Indian Claims Commission
award; a 1998 federal housing loan enabled the construction of housing
and a community center.

SUGGESTED READING

Brant, Charles, ed. *Jim Whitewolf: The Life of a Kiowa Apache Indian*. New York: Dover, 1969.

Haskell, Loring. *Southern Athapaskan Migration, A.D. 200–1750*. Tsaile, Ariz.: Navajo Community College, 1987 (includes discussion of Bittle, Davis, Harrington, and Steward).

Hoijer, Harry. "The Position of the Apachean Languages in the Athapaskan Stock." In Keith Basso and Morris Opler, eds., *Apachean Culture, History, and Ethnology*, 3–6. Tucson: University of Arizona Press, 1971.

Jordan, Julia A. *Plains Apache Ethnobotany*. Norman: University of Oklahoma Press, 2008.

Lockwood, Frank. *The Apache Indians*. New York: Macmillan, 1938; repr. Lincoln: University of Nebraska, 1987.

Melody, Michael E. *The Apache*. New York: Chelsea House, 1988 (for young readers).

Mooney, James. "Calendar History of the Kiowa." In *Seventeenth Annual Report of the Bureau of American Ethnology for 1895–96*, vol. 1, part 1, 141–447. Washington, D.C.: Government Printing Office, 1898; repr. Washington, D.C.: Smithsonian Institution, 1979.

Perry, Richard J. *Western Apache Heritage: People of the Mountain Corridor*. Tucson: University of Arizona Press, 1991 (includes discussion of Brugge, Gunnerson, Opler, and Wedel).

Schweinfurth, Kay Parker. *Prayer on Top of the Earth: The Spiritual Universe of the Plains Apaches*. Boulder: University Press of Colorado, 2002.

Arapaho

The derivation of "Arapaho" is unknown. Perhaps it came from the Pawnee word "Rara-pihu-ru," "one who trades." The Crows referred to them as Arappaho, "many tattoo marks," while Hidatsas called them Arupahu, "many tattoos," possibly from an Indian sign language label. The Arapahos call themselves Inuan-ina (or Hinono Eino), "our People."

LOCATION AND GOVERNMENT

The Arapahos were combined with the separate but linguistically related Cheyennes when placed on their reservation. The two are referred to as one entity, the "Cheyenne-Arapaho Tribes," with headquarters in Concho in Canadian County (about five miles north of El Reno) on a ridge overlooking the old Darlington site. Members who are Arapaho reside throughout seven counties but tend to live in or near the communities of Geary, Watonga, and Canton in Canadian and Blaine counties and in nearby rural areas. The tribes are organized under the OIWA; a tribal constitution and by-laws were adopted in 1937. A rewritten constitution took effect in 1977, requiring all eligible voters to approve business committee actions. The tribes established their own court system during the 1980s. Reforms in 2006 gave them a governor and legislature. The tribal website is www.c-a-tribes.org.

BUSINESSES

Arapahos share proceeds from the Cheyenne-Arapaho–owned Lucky Star Casino not far from the tribal headquarters in Concho, another Lucky Star Casino in Clinton, and the Feather Warrior Casino in Watonga. There is also a small casino operation at Canton Lake. The tribes co-own land, which provides income from leasing, farming, and ranching. Oil and gas leasing also brings in royalty income. Smoke shops provide some revenue. The tribes hold 10,400 acres, although 84,000 acres are in trust (most of which is leased).

Approximately one-third of the combined 12,000 Cheyenne-Arapaho members consider themselves to be Arapahos. The tribes do not divide their figures, and there has been considerable intermarriage through the years, making identification even more of a challenge. Currently individuals must be one-fourth Arapaho or one-fourth Cheyenne-Arapaho for enrollment. There are over 7,000 members of the Northern Arapaho Tribe on the Wind River Reservation at Fort Washakie, near Lander, Wyoming.

Although Arapaho prehistory is clouded in the far past, linguistics can yield clues to peoples' movements. The Arapahos are Algonquian-speakers. Arapaho-Atsinas and Suhtais as Plains Algonquians are closer in language to Proto-Algonquians than are Blackfeet and Cheyennes and even Plains Crees. Therefore linguists assumed that the Arapaho-Atsinas separated from the Proto-Algonquian core later than the others.

Karl Schlesier wrote that by 600 B.C. their ancestors were a part of Laurel culture, which stretched from the Canadian province of Saskatchewan through Manitoba and Ontario and into a part of Quebec and into the upper parts of the United States (present-day Minnesota and Michigan). Perhaps they were descendants of Archaic peoples of the Canadian Shield who had learned to make pottery. These peoples lived on lake shores and along river systems. They fished seasonally on the Great Lakes and hunted for game. Laurel culture eventually became the Blackduck complex, which was ancestral to Central and Western Algonquian–speakers like the Arapaho-Atsinas as well as the Suhtais. Schlesier believed that the Arapaho-Atsinas were western representatives of the Blackduck tradition and that they spread into the prairie of Manitoba around A.D. 800. The Blackduck culture developed in the late Woodland period in the area north of the Great Lakes from Lake Superior to what is now Ontario around A.D. 1000. Prehistorically the Arapahos are believed to have used sweat lodges and tepees and to have lived in mobile bands, east of the Mississippi River. They probably used jumps, arroyo traps, and pounds to hunt buffalo. Some researchers have given the name "Western Shield Archaic" to the culture that developed out of earlier Plano-Arctic and Agate Basin groups. James Wright viewed prehistoric Algonquian peoples across the Canadian Shield as homogeneous. Schlesier saw them as diverging into western and eastern branches.

The Arapahos separated from the Atsinas, usually called the Gros

Ventres, about 1700 or shortly thereafter. Only two of the five major divisions known from earliest contact and earlier survive: the Arapahos (formed from the combination of the Hinanaeina and the Nawathine-hena divisions) and the Gros Ventres. As Plains Indians in the eighteenth and nineteenth centuries, the Arapahos lived much like the Cheyennes in tepees of clusters of extended families. Women tended garden plots and collected various plant foods, nuts, and berries. Men engaged in the hunt. When men killed buffalo, women set about butchering and preparing the carcass. Women also produced decorated buffalo robes for their own use and for intertribal trade.

The Arapaho origin story is known only in part. Four previous worlds preceded the existence of the Flat Pipe medicine bundle. The Flat Pipe story told of a time when water covered the earth. A Flat Pipe Person floated on the water. The Creator thought, and those thoughts caused things to happen. The Pipe Person was given power and sent birds down to retrieve mud, but without success. Finally the turtle brought mud up from the depths and the Pipe Person blew the dried mud in four directions with four songs, to create the earth. The sun, the moon, and a man and a woman were made out of clay, and Pipe Person animated other animal and plant life and taught the Arapaho people how to live. Pipe Person gave the Arapahos a Pipe medicine bundle to convey prayers above. Carved on the side of the Flat Pipe were a turtle and a duck, harkening back to the origin story animals that brought up the first earth in the north. In the nineteenth century the priest performed rites all year long. Priests also cared for men's and women's medicine bundles as well as feathered hoops with feathers in the Offerings Lodge, the Arapaho counterpart of the Sun Dance, in which all adults could participate. There were also curing societies centered on animal spirit-helpers. Men and women belonged to age-graded lodges headed by priests. Arapaho families resided in their separate tepees, with a cluster of them forming an extended family. Related extended families made up a residential band.

In the early nineteenth century the combined Arapahos had an overall council of four chiefs, representing the four major divisions. Before mid-century it is probable that a leading war record and leadership in the Dog Lodge were required for chieftainship. At the Fort Laramie treaty council in 1851 there were two Southern Arapaho chiefs and one Northern Arapaho chief, while during the next decade there were four chiefs. For a time, Little Raven was the main chief of the Southern Arapahos, but in 1863 he insisted on the war chief also being present at negotiations with U.S. officials.

The Cheyenne named Bear Tongue told the story of Cheyenne migration to interpreter Ben Clark in the late 1880s, stating that the Cheyennes joined the Arapahos in the North Platte region. Another Cheyenne named Coyote told the story of a small Cheyenne raiding party in the region of Bear Mountain (that is, Bear Butte, in the vicinity of the Black Hills). The party met a lone Indian. After sign talk, they became friends. That began the alliance with the Arapahos. The Cheyenne bands known as Oivimanas and Hevhaitaneos had special trade and intermarriage relationships with the Arapahos. Although they were separate peoples, the Cheyennes and Arapahos tended to move together. A Northern Cheyenne oral tale credited the Arapahos with first introducing the Cheyennes to horses and leading them to become mounted nomads of the prairies. The Cheyennes moved toward the Black Hills as a result of Sioux and Crow pressures, migrating southwest toward the upper branches of the Platte River. (In the same vicinity of the Black Hills, Cheyennes also met and allied with the Suhtais, the Minnesota Siouan Moiseyos, and the Teton Sioux.) Fur trader Pierre-Antoine Tabeau placed the Arapahos south of the Yellowstone around 1800. By about 1804 they were on either side of the North Platte River, with the Cheyennes farther northward. Meriwether Lewis and William Clark's map of tribal relations on the northern Plains listed the "Kanenavish" (also spelled "Caminanbiche"), assumed to be the Arapahos, south of what are believed to be the Cheyennes.

As early as 1793 French trader Jacques d'Eglise, acting for the Baron Hector de Carondelet of Louisiana, contacted some Arapahos and Cheyennes in an Arikara village on the Missouri River. When Tabeau of the Missouri Fur Company attended a trade fair in the Black Hills sometime around 1800, he marveled at the skill with which the Arapaho buffalo robes were decorated with quillwork and deer hooves. He noted that they also traded prairie turnip flour to the Arikaras for corn. Jean Baptiste de Trudeau described the Arapaho commerce in Spanish goods from the Illinois country and the exchange for corn from the Cheyennes as well as Arapaho pemmican, pelts, and horses. Arapahos transported trade goods from Canada to Wichita Indian fairs on the Red River. The Arapahos also traded in the summer with the Gros Ventres and Crees for Hudson Bay Company goods and in the autumn with the Mandans and the Arikaras. The Arapaho commerce extended across the 800 miles that linked the Middle Missouri River of North Dakota with northern New Mexico. Kit Carson, who was married to an Arapaho woman, later helped supply otter and marten skins and other items to his kinfolk. Trapper and interpreter Thomas Fitzpatrick also married an Arapaho and distributed government presents and rations to her people. By 1811 trader Jean Baptiste Champlain talked to Arapahos on the upper Platte River, who informed him that they visited Spanish traders (Comancheros) on the Arkansas River for guns in exchange for pelts and robes. Manuel Lisa of the Missouri Fur Company dispatched Champlain to deal with the Arapahos; instead of trading, however, they killed Champlain and seized his goods. Lisa built Fort Manuel on the Bighorn River (1812), but Arapaho and Cheyenne attacks led to its abandonment.

Scientist Edwin James chronicled the adventures of Stephen Long's survey party in 1819 and its encounters with Indians. James stopped at an Arapaho and Cheyenne camp on the Arkansas River and observed trade goods out of New Mexico and stolen horses from Mexico. He commented that the Arapahos were part of a trade network that spread from Canada to Mexico and from St. Louis to the Rocky Mountains. A year later journalist John Bell, accompanying the Long expedition's return in late July, encountered Arapahos, Shoshones, Crows, Cheyennes, Kiowas, and Plains Apaches at what is believed to be the Big Timbers of the Arkansas River some thirty miles downstream from what would later become the site of Bent's Fort. Edwin James in late September claimed to have found Arapahos, Cheyennes, Kiowas, and Gros Ventres at nearly the same spot and said that the Arapaho named Bear Tooth was the "grand chief" of the assembled Indians. Jacob Fowler encountered them a year later, still in the same location. The Hugh Glenn/Jacob Fowler party spent the winter of 1821–22 on the upper Arkansas River near what is now Pueblo, Colorado, to trade with the Arapahos, Cheyennes, Kiowas, and Ietans (Comanches).

The Arapahos attacked independent American trappers who operated without Indian approval within their territory. They killed several near Taos (1823) then eight more (with Gros Ventres allies) on the Yellowstone that same year. The opening of the Santa Fe Trail the following year only compounded Arapaho fears of encroachment. Through the decade the Arapahos raided freighters. The trading company of William Bent and Ceran St. Vrain helped stabilize trade for the Arapahos, especially with the construction of Bent's Fort (1832) in eastern Colorado on the Purgatory River near what is now the community of La Junta. (Bent's Fort moved: it had first occupied a site near Pueblo at two locations on Fountain Creek.) The traders located Fort William on the North Platte River and Fort St. Vrain on the South Platte. The Bent brothers and St. Vrain used their contacts in Santa Fe and St. Louis to establish a steady and lucrative trade in horses and mules and in robes and peltry. The Arapahos at first objected to the traders' presence, but gifts soothed relationships.

The marriage of William Bent to a daughter of Cheyenne leader White Thunder helped cement ties to the Arapahos too. According to Captain Lemuel Ford, a member of Henry Dodge's 1835 expedition to the southern Plains tribes, traders bought the buffalo robes for twenty-five cents apiece and, as historian Thomas Schiltz noted, sold them for six dollars each. In 1839 Thomas Farnham visited the fort and was impressed by the crowd of mountain men, New Mexicans, Indians, and U.S. traders. According to him, the Arapahos predominated. The fort hosted nearly twenty thousand Indians of various Native nations in an atmosphere that at times resembled a medieval fair.

When Bent suggested peace among southern Plains Indians, Little Raven and Left Handed Soldier of the Arapahos agreed. The warfare between Cheyenne-Arapahos and Kiowa-Comanche-Apaches was too destructive. The Arapahos persuaded the Cheyennes, and peace was achieved in 1840. The Indians turned their ire to the relentless white encroachments. Tensions increased throughout the 1850s.

Under the onslaught of emigrant trains along the Santa Fe and Oregon trails after 1840, which decreased Arapaho access to bison herds, the Indians signed the 1851 treaty near Fort Laramie. The document pledged peaceful passage of emigrants through the region, and tribes agreed to a large reservation territory. The Arapahos occupied the western portion of the area. In the same decade settlers spilled into the Smoky Hill River Valley and gold-seekers flooded into the Pikes Peak area of Colorado, both prime Arapaho country. Gradually some withdrew north of the Platte into Bighorn country. They became known as the Northern Arapahos (Nenebinenno, "northern men"). Others traveled down the Arkansas River Valley and were called the Southern Arapahos (Nowunenno, "southern men"), linked to the Southern Cheyennes. The Southern Arapahos adopted a contingent of Plains Apaches at their Upper Arkansas Agency.

The Arapahos tried to avoid conflict with the encroaching whites. The Indians signed the 1861 treaty at Fort Wise, agreeing to a smaller reservation on the upper reaches of the Arkansas River at Sand Creek. A smaller number of Arapahos and a larger group of Cheyennes were massacred there in 1864. After war flared, a peace agreement was signed the following year. The Arapahos tried to avoid confrontation by remaining south of the Arkansas River and out of the way. The 1867 Medicine Lodge Treaty placed the Cheyenne-Arapahos on a reservation in Kansas, which was thereafter moved south to the Canadian River of Indian Territory. A presidential executive order two years later created the Cheyenne and Arapaho Reservation there.

Ethnologist James Mooney said that the two major Southern Arapaho bands after the American Civil War were the Waxu'eithis and the Hax-aathinenas, along with three others: the Blackfeet, Wolf Men, and Look-outs. When buffalo were no longer available, Arapahos settled onto farms in clusters of camps, including the Seger colony on the Washita River. The Arapahos tended to live peacefully and tried to avoid conflict. Headmen controlled distribution of annuities and rations, while ritual leader Little Raven and men's lodge leaders Left Hand and Powderface handled po-litical affairs with the federal government into the 1880s. Some Arapahos made use of rail connections to participate in Flat Pipe ceremonies in Wy-oming. After difficulties involving the Sioux and Cheyennes in the hos-tilities of the northern Plains, by 1878 U.S. Indian agency authorities had decided that the Southern Arapahos would remain with the Cheyennes at the Darlington Agency in Oklahoma. The Southern Arapahos would not be permitted to join their relatives the Northern Arapahos in Wyoming. (As a result of Northern Arapaho aid in defeating Sioux and Cheyennes in 1876–77, the U.S. government allowed the Northern Arapahos to settle on the Wind River Reservation in Wyoming the following year.)

After negotiations with the Jerome Commission at Darlington in 1890–91, Arapaho leaders Left Hand and Cloud Chief joined other In-dians to protest congressional ratification of their agreement, to no avail. The evils of allotment came to 1,144 Arapahos the following year. The agreement ended communal property holding and opened their reserve to non-Indian settlement, and Indian allotted lands soon passed to white ownership. Arapaho allottees clustered in band communities: Little Ra-ven at Cantonment, Left Hand in the Red Hills (which became Geary), Powderface in the South Canadian district, and the Seger colony. The fed-eral government set up separate agencies to serve the Arapahos and the Cheyennes. Younger Arapaho and Cheyenne men educated in boarding-schools eventually were elected to a "council" in 1928 to pursue a land claim against the U.S. government for lands taken earlier.

The Cheyenne-Arapaho Tribes were organized under the OIWA. A 28-member business committee governed, with four-year terms for the committee chair and other officers elected for two-year terms. Even though the Cheyenne population was twice the size of the Arapaho population, voting was divided equally. A distribution of a U.S. Claims Commission payment for the 1851 treaty violation as well as an economic development set-aside and the restoration of just under 4,000 acres at Concho moti-vated changes in government structure for the Cheyenne-Arapahos.

Federal and local authorities banned the Sun Dance in the late 1880s.

The Arapahos sent Black Coyote and Washee to investigate the Paiute prophet Wovoka and the Ghost Dance. They returned with a favorable report, and the Arapahos and neighboring tribes participated into 1891 and afterward. Arapaho women played an especially prominent role. Arapaho Ghost Dance prophet Sitting Bull established seven leaders, who spread its influence within the tribe. Shortly after that, Plains Apaches, some of whom were intermarried with the Arapahos, introduced the Peyote ceremony to them.

Today the Arapahos engage in social dances at powwows and benefits, which aid a particular individual (such as a returned soldier). Veterans and other voluntary associations also put on gatherings. Arapahos participated with Cheyennes in larger events in the communities of Canton, Geary, and Colony. Arapahos also continue to be involved in Northern Arapaho ceremonies annually in Wyoming, such as Flat Pipe rituals and the Offerings Lodge (the Arapaho Sun Dance) as well as rituals in Oklahoma. Many Arapahos in Oklahoma also belong to the Native American Church, while there has been an overlap with Christian service activities for some Arapahos (with churches for Arapaho Mennonites in Canton and Arapaho Baptists in Geary). Art, beadwork, and design motifs in crafts carry on the paired tribal color schemes and help convey their cultural heritage. The Arapahos have repatriated human remains from museums and interred them locally. Some of the Arapaho victims of the Sand Creek Massacre were among them.

Notable Arapahos include nineteenth-century leaders Little Raven, Left Hand, and Little Robe. Carl Sweezy, raised in the old way, became an accomplished artist. He was amazed when boyhood chums (who had visited Portland, Oregon, as part of a traveling Indian baseball team) came to him in 1905 and told him that his paintings were on display at the Lewis and Clark Exposition there.

SUGGESTED READING

Bass, Althea, ed. *The Arapaho Way: A Memoir of an Indian Boyhood*. New York: Clarkson N. Potter, 1966 (on Carl Sweezy).

Berthrong, Donald J. *The Cheyenne and Arapaho Ordeal*. Norman: University of Oklahoma Press, 1976.

Coel, Margaret. *Chief Left Hand: Southern Arapaho*. Norman: University of Oklahoma Press, 1981.

———. *The Ghost Walker*. New York: Berkley Prime Crime, 1996 (mystery novel of Northern Arapaho life).

Dorsey, George A., and Alfred L. Kroeber. *Traditions of the Arapaho*. Fairfield, Wash.: Ye Galleon, 1975; repr. Lincoln: University of Nebraska Press, 1983, 1997 (originally published 1902–1903 in four parts in the *Bulletin of the American Museum of Natural History* in New York).

Fowler, Loretta. *The Arapaho*. New York: Chelsea House, 1989 (for young readers).

———. *Arapaho Politics, 1851–1978: Symbols in Crises of Authority*. Lincoln: University of Nebraska Press, 1982.

James, Edwin. "Account of an Expedition from Pittsburgh to the Rocky Mountains, Performed in the Years 1819 and '20." In Reuben Gold Thwaites, ed., *Early Western Travels*, vol. 15. New York: AMS, 1966.

Mooney, James. "Calendar History of the Kiowa." In *Seventeenth Annual Report of the Bureau of American Ethnology for 1895–96*, vol. 1, part 1, 141–447. Washington, D.C.: Government Printing Office, 1898; repr. Washington, D.C.: Smithsonian Institution, 1979.

Schiltz, Thomas. "Ponies, Pelts, and Pemmican: The Arapahoes and Early Western Trade." *Red River Valley Historical Review* 7 (Spring 1982): 28–38.

Schlesier, Karl. "Rethinking the Midewiwin and the Plains Ceremonial Called the Sun Dance." *Plains Anthropologist* 35, no. 127 (1990): 1–27.

———. *The Wolves of Heaven: Cheyenne Shamanism, Ceremonies, and Prehistoric Origins*. Norman: University of Oklahoma Press, 1987.

Trenholm, Virginia Cole. *The Arapahoes, Our People*. Norman: University of Oklahoma Press, 1970; repr. 1973, 1986.

Wright, James V. "Prehistory of the Canadian Shield." In vol. 6, *Subarctic*, of the *Handbook of North American Indians*, 86–96. Washington, D.C.: Smithsonian Institution, 1986.

Caddo

NAME

The tribal name was shortened from Kadohadacho, "the real or main chief" or "true chief," originally referring to a large community at the bend of the Red River near the present city of Texarkana, Texas. The root words in the Caddoan language are *caddi*, "chief," and *hadachu*, "sharp pain" (it also means "something real or true"). As now applied, the word "Caddo" refers to descendants of over twenty-five separate tribal groups from the seventeenth century and earlier. The other major group (called Hasinais, from Hasinay, "our People") was situated on the Neches River of east Texas. Today family members continue their kin connections with one of the major divisions (Kadohadacho and Hasinai) as well as with Anadarkos and a few Kichai relatives.

LOCATION AND GOVERNMENT

The headquarters for the "Caddo Tribe" is at the Binger "Y" fork in the highways about two miles east of the community of Binger in Caddo County (approximately twenty miles north of Anadarko and about seven miles north of Gracemont). The tribe is organized under the OIWA and adopted a charter, constitution, and by-laws in 1938. Their new constitution, ratified in 1976, mandates a tribal council made up of a chair, vice chair, secretary, treasurer, and representatives from Anadarko, Fort Cobb, Binger, and Oklahoma City districts, elected every four years. The Heritage Museum is located within the Caddo Tribe complex. The tribal website is www.caddonation-nsn.gov.

BUSINESSES

The Caddos jointly own about 2,600 acres with the Wichitas and the Western Delawares (hence the abbreviation "WCD" in the name "WCD Enterprises," formed during the 1980s). The land is spread across Caddo, Grady, and Canadian counties in southwestern Oklahoma. WCD Enterprises leases most of the land for income from farming. Some leased land yields oil and gas income.

It also leases a 25,000-square-foot building on a site of just over ten acres on U.S. Highway 62. The Game Lodge Casino-Resort is planned to be located north of Anadarko.

NUMBER

The tribe has just over 4,000 members, with many living in towns such as Fort Cobb and Gracemont around Binger. Others are scattered worldwide.

The Caddos share the Caddoan language with their distant linguistic kin, the Wichitas, the Pawnees, and the Arikaras. Wallace Chafe stated that Caddos separated from the parent Proto-Caddoan community perhaps 3,000 to 4,000 years ago. In prehistory the ancestors of the Caddos resided in the four corners region (where the Texas-Oklahoma-Louisiana-Arkansas boundaries meet) and gradually developed earthen mound cultures along major rivers. They had a stratified and highly ranked society and became a vital part of the Mississippian culture during its peak. The Caddos and Kichais were the westernmost examples of that culture, which extended across the Mississippi River to the east. Abundant examples of mounds dot the landscape. The George C. Davis site with three mounds near Alto in east Texas is dated to A.D. 800, but its culture peaked about 1200. Others include Hatchell, Crenshaw, Goben Davis, and Woods mounds. There are also mounds in the vicinity of Shreveport, Louisiana. Battle Mound in southern Arkansas, near present-day Lewisville and the Red River, is believed to be a late Caddoan site never finished. It is thought to be the center of the province that the Soto expedition members called "Naguatex."

The Fourche Maline culture of the Woodland developed out of what are believed to have been small nomadic bands of the Late Archaic period (such as the Wister phase) hunters and foragers and evolved into the more sedentary ancestors of the Caddos along the Arkansas and Ouachita river valleys. Jerome Rose examined their genetic heritage and maintained that the Caddos are descended from Fourche Maline peoples. Identifiable Caddo culture emerged around A.D. 700–900. Strong leadership and highly stratified organization were required for earth-mound construction. In the Red, Arkansas, Ouachita, Sabine, and Neches-Angelina river valleys, the Caddos farmed and prospered about A.D. 1000–1200. After A.D. 1000 large population centers gradually dispersed their residents into farmsteads that dotted the countryside. The former mound centers with their plazas continued to serve ceremonial functions but had few resident populations. They are considered to have been local chiefdoms. Some are believed to have been more highly stratified than others. So-called Southeastern Ceremonial Complex locations tended to be the largest ceremonial centers but gradually spread through the sixteenth century. The George C. Davis site serves as an example of the processes. Residents abandoned its ceremonial center in the thirteenth century and shifted to outlying hamlets with greater independence, presumed more egalitarian societies, and lessened elite material wealth. Populations by A.D. 1400 tended to move back into regional chiefdoms, sometimes with their own fortified villages, as Dan and Phyllis Morse as well as James Brown have shown. At its peak the Caddo population reached perhaps 200,000 around A.D. 1500, according to Henry Dobyns, Timothy Perttula, and Todd Smith.

For five centuries, ceremonies and life flourished at Caddo mound sites in what is today eastern Texas. Change set in after about A.D. 1250 and activity at the site ceased in about 1450, with treasures recached in the main mound and the ritual capping of the burial mound. Caddo oral tradition indicates that their attention at the time shifted from east to west. Bison hunting increased as an important aspect in people's lives and contact with the Wichitas and the eastern frontier Pueblos markedly increased. The drier period turned some woodland into prairie. People along the Fourche Maline and Petit Jean valleys, in the vicinity of present Fort Smith in Arkansas, were Fort Coffee–phase Kichais who turned to bison hunting and still later became Wichitas.

The Caddo origin tale links the Caddos to emergence onto the surface of the earth from a place called Cha-cah-nee-nah, "place of crying." It is near Caddo Lake in northeastern Texas and Louisiana. The prairie around Battle Mound in southern Arkansas in Lafayette County is called "Crying Place," which may indicate another possible location. From the interior of the earth, the first man brought a Pipe, flint pieces, and a drum. The first woman carried seeds of corn and pumpkin. The outlet closed, causing those on the surface to cry for those left behind (hence the name). The first village, called Tall-Timber-on-the-Hill (Sha'-childi'ni), was believed to be located just north of the present Caddo Lake, which is north of the present city of Shreveport, Louisiana. The traditional Turkey Dance songs of the Caddos include one sequence about two brothers who watched the creation of the lake. Before the emergence at the first council, a man named Ta'sha (Wolf) said a lone Hasinai man should be called Neesh (Moon). Neesh selected the first *caddi* (leader).

The prehistoric Caddos farmed, making use of the trinity of corn, beans, and squash. Pumpkins, gourds, melons, and other plant foods supplemented their diet. Their men also hunted and fished. They were primarily Southeastern Woodlands people but also made forays onto the Plains to seek buffalo. Preston Holder pointed out that ancient Caddoan-speakers held the river bottoms from the eastern Plains extending from Texas all the way north to the Dakotas for their horticulture. The Caddos resided in dispersed hamlets, which their fields surrounded. They lived in high circular log-framed houses thatched with hay. The structures' beehive appearance in the eighteenth century was similar to Wichita grass homes. Caddos also made use of hide tepees when hunting on the prairie. Prehistoric Caddos engaged in trade, utilizing their skill in selecting and bartering bois d'arc wood for bows and their fine pottery. Highly prized Caddo-decorated pottery reached all the way to the Gulf Coast in the south and into the Illinois country in the north. Caddoan velvety dark deer hides were similarly regarded.

Caddo government was highly stratified. At its head was a priestly ruler, called the *chinesi* (also spelled xinesi, from *tsa*, a male title like "Mister," and *nish* or *neesh*, "moon"), who held elaborate ceremonies in a temple atop a platform mound. Second in the hierarchy was the governor of each community. The *caddi* (also spelled *kahdi*) used the assistance of aides (*tamas* or town criers) in governing, relaying decisions, and announcing visiting dignitaries and returning war parties. The Caddo social structure was among the most complex for Native nations north of Mexico. The ranked layers, priestly class, and mound structures made the Caddos worthy heirs of prehistoric Mississippian cultures. Even after drought and other changes led the Caddos to abandon temple mounds, they retained their hierarchical political structure.

The Caddos held an interesting mix of cultural traditions. Their woodland residence gave them strong southeastern traits like dual red (perhaps Kadohadacho) and white (perhaps Hasinai) moieties for war and peace as well as double divisions for east-west and upper-lower, although this is subject to controversy. They used temple mounds and had guilds like some Plains tribes. Today the Caddo stomp dance. They also have Plains traits, however, such as the contemporary Gourd Dance among youths. In a social organization resembling that of the Natchez, individuals and social groups were ranked in terms of seniority and strength. Caddos ensured health and prosperity through a number of rituals and ceremonies. Henri Joutel in May 1687 watched a Hasinai ceremony: "They kept a kind of cadence which they marked with their feet and with fans made of turkey feathers."

His description is similar to the present-day women's Turkey Dance. A Green Corn Ceremony celebrated "first fruits," while a harvest ceremony renewed their world. It also inspired their Native American Church rites. Among the most noteworthy Caddo ceremonies were their regal Calumet displays to honor, welcome, and ritually adopt visitors.

The Caddo peoples already experienced change in their lives as a result of drier climate, bison-hunting dispersal, and tribal conflicts. The coming of Europeans accelerated developments already underway. One firm example of the direct impact of European presence upon the Caddos is the creation of the Natchitoches confederacy as a response to French settlement on the Red River after 1700, when Yatasis and Doustionis joined Ouachita Caddos and Natchitoches ("pawpaw eaters" in Caddo) there. Martha McCollough argued that instead of collapsing in the 1780s the Hasinai chiefdom decentralized for its own safety. She pointed out that this response was a traditional accommodation to outside influences. The religious chiefdom became more secularized and democratic even as the Hasinais became incorporated into the Kadohadacho chiefdom. David La Vere demonstrated that a lengthy series of events transformed the powerful eighth-century stratified chiefdoms into a shattered nation, forced repeatedly to cede lands to the United States government in the nineteenth century. In spite of enormous difficulties, the Caddo people endured because they adhered to ancient Mississippian cultural traditions. They used intermarriage to incorporate outsiders and to create a profitable role as intermediaries while adapting to changing circumstances.

The impact of early Spanish expeditions like Soto's is hotly debated among scholars. Most believe that the effect was minor, even though Soto's men under Luis de Moscoso traversed considerable Caddo territory (in 1541–42) of the Nasonis (whom the Spanish called the "Amaye"), the Kadohadachos (called the "Naguatex"), and the Hasinais (especially at the town of Guasco), destroying towns as they went.

Domingo Terán de los Ríos led the first Spanish expedition out of Mexico City and met the *chinesi* (priestly ruler) in 1591 at a mound town believed to be the George C. Davis site. The Hasinai Caddos repeated their greeting, *tejas* (pronounced "tay-has"), "friends," to such an extent that the Spanish ultimately adopted it as the name for the province. The word became "Texas." The first Spanish mission established in the region (in 1690 near the Neches River) was San Francisco de los Tejas.

Spanish missions between 1690 and 1773 greatly affected the Hasinais of east Texas. European diseases had taken a heavy toll on the Caddo population by the end of the eighteenth century. Missions have attracted considerable scholarly attention because of what they represented and as a result of their impact. Recent archeological investigation has revealed a softer image. Caddo women left their huts and lived in European-styled houses at Mission Los Adaes in Louisiana but continued to use Indian pottery in everyday domestic life through the forty years of the mission's existence. Kathleen Gilmore found evidence at the Roseborough Lake site, which was the French post of St. Louis de Cadohadacho, that also supported a peaceful integration of Native women into the daily life of the French post. The Frenchman Louis Juchereau de St. Denis helped set up the Los Adaes mission and presidio for the Spaniards (1716) just twenty miles from the French trading post at Natchitoches. (The commanders of the fort and the post were related by marriage and religion, even though one was Spanish and the other was French and their two countries officially were enemies.) The French experience in dealing with the Caddos was similar to that of the Spaniards. French traders had lived among the Caddos for years, forever altering the Indians' society as well as that of the French in North America.

The disposition of the Caddo residents at Los Adaes illustrated the complexity of events in the whole region. The mission and fort officially closed in 1773 in the wake of the conclusion of the French and Indian War. H. F. Gregory and George Avery delved into life at the mission and into the aftermath. The Adaes emigrated to San Antonio, with many dying from destitution. Some former residents quietly slipped away from the column before it reached San Antonio and returned to Louisiana. Shortly afterward the survivors founded the towns of Bucareli then Nacogdoches ("persimmon eaters" in Caddo) in Texas. Some probably remained near the old mission, while other refugees melted into Caddo populations in northwestern Louisiana.

The French claim to the region stemmed not just from royal demands but from the ill-fated La Salle expeditions in 1682–84 and the 1699 presence of Pierre Le Moyne, Sieur d'Iberville, and his construction of a fort just above the mouth of the Mississippi River in 1700. Robert Cavalier, Sieur de La Salle, had traveled down the Mississippi from Canada to the Gulf of Mexico in 1686. The remnant of his unfortunate colonizing expedition walked overland across east Texas through Caddo territory. After some of La Salle's men murdered him three years later, his trusted lieutenant Henri Joutel made contact with the Hasinais. His journal described a Caddo victory dance that he observed in May of that same year. It resonated with contemporary practices among today's Caddos: an orator or speaker who made announcements, three days of dancing, feasting, women using turkey feathers (and motions patterned after the turkey) during their dance, gifts given, and ritually offered tobacco. This is reminiscent of the contemporary Turkey Dance.

French fur trade interests came to Louisiana with St. Denis at Natchitoches in 1699. The French built a fort there in 1713. St. Denis (whom the Caddos called "Big Leg") maintained a close relationship with the Natchitoches Indians, who were Caddo-speakers. (In response to the French presence, Spaniards three years later organized an expedition to establish missions and forts to secure their frontier in northeast Texas.) St. Denis joined d'Iberville's brother (Jean Baptiste Le Moyne, Sieur de Bienville) and Canadians to visit tribes up the Red River in 1700. He arranged for the relocation of Natchitoches Indians, to leave their flooded homes in 1702 and live near the Acolapissa Indians on Lake Ponchartrain (until 1713). St. Denis became a trader out of St. John's Bayou, later setting up Natchitoches Post as a depot. Bénard de La Harpe established Nasonnite Post in 1719, reanimating the French alliance with the Kadohadachos. The post was on the site of a former Nanatsoho village on the Red River in northeast Texas.

Just prior to 1700 there were two distinct Caddo confederacies. David La Vere has described the Kadohadachos (made up of four major towns and their satellites), who dominated the great bend of the Red River north of what is now Texarkana. To the west were the nine tribes of the Hasinai chiefdom along the upper reaches of the Sabine, Angelina, and Neches rivers. Below the Hasinais were the Adaes and Aises, who occupied the Sabine Valley. They had earlier been a part of the Hasinais.

The Treaty of Paris in 1763 transferred Louisiana Territory west of the Mississippi to Spain. A son-in-law of St. Denis, Athanase de Mézières, became a Spanish agent. Caddo leaders in the 1770s obtained formal alliances for Spain with tribes to the west and north in an effort to block Osage aggression, which exploded after 1770. Smallpox epidemics attendant upon dislocation led the Kadohadachos to move down the Red River nearer to today's city of Shreveport during the 1790s. The Caddo population shrank, and so did their influence. Disparate groups consolidated for their survival. The Nanatsohos, Nasonis, and Natchitoches became the Grand and Petit Caddos, then the Caddos, during this time. Following the 1714 death of St. Denis, his son Louis and son-in-law de Mézières assumed influential roles among the Kadohadachos out of Natchitoches Post.

Caddos also brought the first Cherokees into Texas that year and arranged a peace with the Choctaws, with whom they had been warring since 1792. Coushattas settled on the Red River the following year. A trickle of other Indians entering Caddo territory slowly grew into a stream. The Quapaws removed to the Caddo Agency in 1826. Kickapoo, Choctaw, Cherokee, Delaware, Shawnee, Quapaw, and Coushatta villages dotted the Caddo Texas landscape by the late 1820s.

The United States acquired the Louisiana Territory in 1803. American officials planned to secure control over the new region. In 1805 the U.S. government began a factory (an American trading post) at Natchitoches. Indian agent John Sibley led a first major council with tribes there during the summer of 1807. Americans renamed the post Fort Claiborne. Caddo, Anadarko, Hainai, Nacogdoches, Nabedache, Kichai, Waco, Taovaya, Tawakoni, and Comanche Indians attended.

Louisiana entered the Union as a state in 1812. The trickle of whites into the region increased after the conclusion of the War of 1812. The founding of Arkansas Territory followed shortly thereafter in 1819. Encroachment on Caddo lands increased, with whites and Indian nations coming from the East. The location of the Indian agent's headquarters shifted from Natchitoches up the Red River to Sulphur Fork (1821), on to Caddo Prairie (1825), then to new buildings nearer Shreveport (1831). Removal of the log-jams (called rafts) on the Red River during that decade created a real-estate boom along the river. The Caddos were forced to relinquish their claim to their territory.

After their last great chief, Dehahuit, died in 1833, the Kadohadachos ceded their Louisiana territory of about 1 million acres through their 1835 treaty and removed to join their Hasinai kin in Texas. Years of loyal, peaceful service to the United States gained the Caddos nothing. Tarshar led a group to east Texas. A second group of Caddos traveled into Mexico and resided briefly near San Antonio. The third group under Whitebead migrated southward and lived among the Kiamichis but later moved back. White squatters held the Indians' former lands and forced the Caddos of east Texas westward. Some Caddos lived among the Anadarkos under Jose Maria as they moved ever westward in Texas.

Over twenty separate tribal groups (such as the Caddos, Cherokees, and Choctaws) resided south of the Red River when Texas gained its independence from Mexico (1836). Texas pressure against American Indians dispersed the Caddos after 1839. They scattered to temporary residences in Indian Territory, west Texas, and Mexico. The time of their removal was also a period of great turmoil. The Texas Revolution and the formation of volunteer militia, called the Texas Rangers, fed fears of Indian hostilities and led to isolated outrages against Indian camps. President Mirabeau Lamar's expulsion policy scattered American Indian bands at the end of the decade. Texas joined the United States in 1846, and the

U.S. government slowly set about trying to provide for the Indians. The Caddos ended up on the Lower Brazos Reserve in Texas (1854). Some fourteen separate Caddo tribes had shrunk to three (the Caddos proper, the Hainais, and the Anadarkos) by 1850. The Southeastern Woodland peoples were forced onto a semiarid prairie.

In 1854 Captain Randolph B. Marcy and Major Robert S. Neighbors selected a lower reserve on the Brazos River of 37,152 acres for the Caddos, Anadarkos, Delawares, and affiliated Wichita tribes. It was just below the confluence of the Clear Fork with the Brazos in what would become Young County, near Fort Belknap. Teacher Z. E. Coombes began elementary instruction in a schoolhouse in mid-1858.

Increasing harassment by settlers, Comanche raids, and rising violence all contributed to a highly volatile situation. Following whites' slaughter of seven sleeping Caddos, agent Robert Neighbors on August 1, 1859, led the Brazos Reserve Indians on a hasty retreat across the Red River to refuge in Indian Territory. They settled on the south side of the Washita River, about eight miles west of today's city of Anadarko in Caddo County, on Leeper Creek. They were on western land leased from the Choctaws and the Chickasaws and intended for the ultimate settlement of Wichita bands. The estimated five hundred refugees walked the nearly two hundred miles, bringing only what they could carry. The Caddos started anew. Upon his return to Belknap in Texas, Neighbors was murdered by an angry white man.

The Civil War split the Caddos. Some signed the Pike Treaty, allying with the Confederacy. Others fled to Colorado. Some sought refuge in Kansas. Most warily remained where they lived. George Washington (Show-e-tat, Little Boy) of the Caddos served the Confederates as a scout. Union-armed Indians including the Caddos and the Wichitas burned the Wichita-Caddo Agency (October 1862).

The federal government moved former enemies, the Kiowas, Comanches, Plains Apaches, and Cheyennes and Arapahos, onto the reservation after the Civil War. In 1871 the Wichita Agency was reestablished across the Washita River from Anadarko. The following year all Caddos were assigned to a reservation north of that river, which they shared with the remnant of the Anadarkos, and became affiliated with the Wichita and Delaware tribes. The federal government created a school in the valley in 1871, and Quaker Thomas C. Battey started what would become Riverside Indian School in 1892. American Baptist and Methodist missionaries opened outposts. Roman Catholics came in 1894. The government combined the Wichita, Kiowa, Comanche, and Plains Apache agencies in

1878 at Anadarko. The Ghost Dance came in the fall of 1890, and John Wilson (Nish Kantu, "Moonhead") and Squirrel were noted leaders. An 1891 Caddo delegation returned from visiting Wovoka, the Ghost Dance prophet, with a favorable report. John Wilson, who was also a Roman Catholic, later carried the Peyote way of the Big Moon to other tribes like the Quapaws and the Osages. As noted, the moon played an important role in Caddo myth and life. In Caddo mythology the moon led the Caddo people into this world and served as their first leader, so anyone associated with the moon would carry great weight among them.

Federal government interference intensified. The government appointed Guadalupe in 1874 as the first chief of all the Caddos. Caddo Jake led them from 1890 to 1902. In 1902 lands of the Caddos, Wichitas, and Delawares were divided under terms of allotment in severalty, and each Caddo received a 160-acre allotment. The federal government opened the remaining land to white settlement. In spite of the allotment of their lands, unlike most tribal nations, the Caddos still occupy their original historic territory, albeit greatly constricted in area. Similarly, descendants of the Tejas in Texas still range between their winter and summer encampment regions (in the summertime they can be found near the town of Snyder).

Caddos organized under the OIWA in 1938. All adult members of the tribe within the agency jurisdiction made up the Caddo Council. Voters selected Harry Guy as chairman in 1973 and again under the new constitution in 1976. Tragically, he died the following year. They elected Doyle Edge, active in the Native American Church, to replace Guy. (Edge also played baseball with the Oklahoma intertribal team that won the North American Indian championship in 1978.)

During the period of self-determination the Caddos have worked to maintain their language. In 1975 they established the Whitebead Hasinai Cultural Center to preserve their cultural heritage. Their Caddo Culture Club and their Hasinai Society keep alive music and dance traditions. The Caddos still have a large repertoire of songs. They hold a series of dances throughout the year as well as traveling to participate in dances in Arkansas, Texas, and Louisiana, all of which are portions of their homelands. The Caddos maintain their ancient traditions, although within a modern context. They still hold an annual round of ceremonial dances, including the Turkey Dance, at their pavilion outside Binger, Oklahoma. Their Turkey Dance features women wearing the distinctive *dastuh* (an elaborate silver hairpiece with a long decorated banner that hangs to the ground behind the dancer). Outsiders such as the Shawnees and the Creeks assist in their stomp dancing.

Human remains throughout prehistoric Caddo territory have been an ongoing concern for the tribe. Tribal members have been involved in repatriation and preservation endeavors. The tribe supervised reburial of remains turned over by the U.S. Army Corps of Engineers, which were discovered during the creation of lakes. In 2003 the tribe filed suit over treatment of remains when Hugo, Broken Bow, and Sardis lakes were created, demanding $44 million in compensation. The Caddos have also voiced claims to Spiro artifacts.

Notable Caddos include potter Jeri Redcorn. Author Cecile Elkins Carter has written an engaging account of her people. Dan Medrano was elected the first secretary of the National Congress of American Indians in the 1940s. Michael Sheyahshe is an animator and digital artist. The Reverend Carol Hampton served as a canon in the Episcopal Church. Fait Elkins set track and field records in the 1927 decathlon. Rabbit Weller played football at Haskell Indian University and professionally in the 1930s.

SUGGESTED READING

Avery, George. "More Friend Than Foe: Eighteenth Century Spanish, French, and Caddoan Interaction at Los Adaes, a Capital of Texas Located in Northwestern Louisiana." *Louisiana Archaeology* 22 (1995): 163–93.

Brown, James A. "Arkansas Valley Caddoan: The Spiro Phase." In Robert E. Bell, ed., *Prehistory of Oklahoma*, 241–63. New York: Academic Press, 1984.

Carter, Cecile Elkins. *Caddo Indians: Where We Come From.* Norman: University of Oklahoma Press, 1995.

Chafe, Wallace. "The Caddo Language, Its Relatives, and Its Neighbors." In James S. Thayer, ed., *North American Indians: Humanistic Perspectives*, 243–50. Papers in Anthropology 24, No. 2. Norman: University of Oklahoma, 1983.

Dobyns, Henry. *Their Number Became Thinned.* Knoxville: University of Tennessee Press, 1983.

Gilmore, Kathleen. *French-Indian Interaction at an 18th Century Frontier Post: The Roseborough Lake Site, Bowie County, Texas.* Contributions to Archaeology No. 3. Denton: Institute of Applied Sciences, North Texas State University, 1986.

Gregory, H. F. *Historical and Archaeological Background of Los Adaes*. Baton Rouge: Louisiana State Parks, 1980.

Holder, Preston. *The Hoe and the Horse on the Plains*. Lincoln: University of Nebraska Press, 1970; repr. 1991.

Joutel, Henri. *A Journal of La Salle's Last Voyage* (originally published 1713). New York: Corinth Books, 1962.

La Vere, David. *The Caddo Chiefdoms: Caddo Economics and Politics, 700–1835*. Lincoln: University of Nebraska Press, 1998.

McCullough, Martha. *Three Nations, One Place: A Comparative Ethnohistory of Social Change among the Comanches and Hasinais during Spain's Colonial Era, 1689–1821*. New York: Routledge, 2004.

Morse, Dan, and Phyllis Morse. "Emergent Mississippian in the Central Mississippi Valley." In Bruce D. Smith, ed., *The Mississippian Emergence*, 153–73. Washington, D.C.: Smithsonian Institution Press, 1990.

Newkumet, Vynola Beaver, and Howard L. Meredith. *Hasinai: A Traditional History of the Caddo Confederacy*. College Station: Texas A&M University Press, 1988.

Perttula, Timothy. *The Caddo Nation*. Rev. ed. Austin: University of Texas Press, 1997.

Rose, Jerome. "Skeletal Biology of the Prehistoric Caddo." In Timothy Perttula and James Bruseth, eds., *The Native History of the Caddo*, 113–26. Austin: University of Texas, 1998.

Smith, F. Todd. *The Caddo Indians: Tribes at the Confluence of Empires, 1542–1854*. College Station: Texas A&M University Press, 1995.

Swanton, John R. *Source Material on the History and Ethnology of the Caddo Indians*. Bulletin 132. Washington, D.C.: Bureau of American Ethnology, 1942; repr. Norman: University of Oklahoma Press, 1996.

Tanner, Helen Hornbeck. "The Territory of the Caddo Tribe of Oklahoma." In David Agee Horr, ed., *Caddoan Indians IV, American Indian Ethnohistory: Plains Indians*, 9–144. New York: Garland, 1974.

Cayuga

The tribal name derives from the Iroquoian name "Kwenio Gwe," "the place where the locusts were taken out." The Oklahoma Cayugas designate themselves as either Hodinqh Syq:ni', "Iroquois," or Kayohkhonq, "Cayuga." They also translate Guyohkohnyoh as "people of the great swamp."

LOCATION AND GOVERNMENT

The "Seneca-Cayuga Tribe of Oklahoma" has its headquarters in Miami, Ottawa County, in far northeastern Oklahoma (about twenty miles from Joplin, Missouri). The Seneca-Cayugas were the first tribe in Oklahoma to reorganize under the OIWA, with their constitution approved in April 1937 and a revision in 1973. A seven-member council, with a chief, serves as the governing body. Members have staggered two-year terms. An annual tribal meeting elects officers. The Dobson Museum in Miami contains information on the Cayugas. The tribal website is www.sctribe.com.

BUSINESSES

Revenue arises from their Grand Lake Casino; two smoke shops; and their Tobacco Company, all shared with the Seneca Tribe. All are located within the area of Grove, Oklahoma, on the east side of the Grand Lake O' the Cherokees. The Seneca-Cayugas co-own about 4,000 acres, of which under 3,000 acres are held as individually allotted land.

NUMBER

The combined tribes number just over 4,200 members. They do not separately designate numbers for each tribe. Many tribal members reside in northeastern Oklahoma, but some reside throughout the world, due to military service, intermarriage, and job opportunities. Cayugas also live in New York and Canada, with the largest number of descendants on the Cattaraugus Reserve there and some at the Allegheny Reserve in western New York, while a large group can also be found on the Six Nations Reserve in Ontario, Canada. Cayugas moved into Canada as early as the beginning of the American Revolution.

The Cayugas speak an Iroquoian language and are active members of the Five Nations of the Iroquois League. The Cayugas are considered Younger Brothers in the league and lived between the Senecas on the west and the Onondagas on the east in what is known as the Finger Lakes region of New York. The league abolished the practice of the blood feud and determined to work as a unit, especially out of their home base in central New York. The French used the label "Iroquois" to designate a variety of Native languages spoken on either side of the St. Lawrence River in the Northeast. According to linguists Wallace Chafe and Michael Foster, Cayugas separated early from the main core language family but encountered ancestral Senecas more than once and were influenced by those episodes.

Theories abound for the origin of Iroquoian peoples. The current hypothesis is local in-place development, although migration stories are prevalent. Archeologists call the stages through the centuries prior to the emergence of Iroquois tribes "Owasco." Paleo-Indian and Archaic Native ancestors lived in small camps. They moved across the landscape in small kin-based bands as they hunted and gathered their food. Pottery appeared during the Late Archaic, followed in 700 B.C. by manufactured tubular tobacco pipes. Domesticated plant use marked the Woodland period, which eventually included corn, beans, and squash. Cayuga village locations have been found on both sides of Cayuga Lake in New York. After about A.D. 1000 population drifted away from riverine and lake sites to stockaded villages on defensible hilltops. By 1400 those fortified villages commanded the surrounding valley corn fields. There was increasing warfare after 1300, as Iroquois oral tradition attests. By about 1450 Seneca and Cayuga tribes had emerged from consolidated villages. Longhouse residence, ceramics, and other features characteristic of the Iroquois had appeared by then. Matrilineal clans dominated civil affairs, conducted inside longhouses as well as throughout the community. The Cayugas probably had hereditary leaders, but the evidence is unclear. From first contact with Europeans into the seventeenth century the Cayugas were about as numerous as the Mohawks and the Onondagas.

The Cayugas have a rich oral tradition. According to their origin story, people lived in the sky realm. One day the chief laid his sick daughter next to an apple tree. The chief dug up the tree, but his daughter fell through the hole toward the water below. The torn earth closed over her. Two birds swam by as she fell. The birds called a council of all the water animals. Volunteers offered to dive for mud to make earth for the girl. Many tried, but finally the toad surfaced with wet dirt, from which turtle made a Great Island. Life began on the land.

In 1653 Pierre Esprint Radisson visited the three major Cayuga settlements and described them. Jesuits set up missions among them around 1668, called St. Joseph, St. Estienne, and St. René. The European presence shortly engulfed the Cayugas in a series of wars that left them devastated. After Iroquois conflict with the French (ending in 1653) and the Susquehannock war in the following decade, the Cayugas chose neutrality during later colonial rivalries. As a result of the conflicts, the Cayugas moved into the Ohio area. The Ohio Valley was a natural extension of the Ohio River out of western Pennsylvania. People and commerce followed the watercourse into Ohio. The mixed Iroquois tribal remnants in the Ohio region by the eighteenth century were called Mingos. They were a group of allied bands (Iroquois, Cayuga, Mohawk, Oneida, Tuscarora, Onondaga, Erie, and Conestoga Indians as well as refugees like Siouan-speaking Tutelos and Saponis among the Cayugas). Further adding to the confusion were Delaware, Shawnee, and Wyandotte peoples in the same vicinity.

The Cayugas tried to remain neutral during the American Revolution, but events drew them into that warfare on the British side. American forces laid waste to Cayuga villages in 1779. Some Cayugas and Tutelos moved to the Six Nations Reserve on the Grand River in Canada, where other Cayugas subsequently joined them after forced sale of their old homeland. A series of treaties from 1789 to 1795 sold nearly all of their New York lands. Through an 1817 treaty, the Mingos who had allied with the Americans obtained a 40,000-acre reserve on the eastern side of the Sandusky River in northern Ohio. It formerly had been Wyandotte territory. The Mingos became known as the "Senecas of Sandusky." Their numbers included many Cayugas. An 1818 treaty added 10,000 acres to their reserve. Additional Cayugas moved to Ohio. On the Sandusky they were joined by other Iroquois League members as well as Shawnees. Their success at farming eventually led to demands for their removal.

In February 1831 the tribe sold its land in Ohio and agreed to relocate to a reservation within the Cherokee Nation in northeastern Indian Territory. Their removal journey took eight miserable months, during which perhaps a third of the 400 died from exposure, malnutrition, and illnesses. When they finally arrived in Indian Territory, they realized that their lands overlapped those of the Cherokee Nation. The newcomers first settled on Cowskin or Elk River. Senecas arrived and also realized they had no territory. United States commissioners, including Montfort Stokes, in a late 1832 treaty adjusted the boundaries for a new Seneca Agency and recognized the United Nations of the Senecas and Shawnees in the first U.S. treaty made with emigrant tribes inside what would become Oklahoma. Their new reserve lay to the east of the Grand or Neosho River and was called the Neosho Reservation. Seneca-Cayugas (the Senecas of Sandusky) occupied the southern portion, while their Mixed Band (Seneca and Shawnee) kin took the northern half.

Some Cayugas shifted their residence from New York to Indian Territory to Kansas, with a few returning to their former homeland. Ties to Kansas kinfolk provided a safe haven during the Civil War era. Most Seneca-Cayugas fled to Kansas and resided on the Ottawa Reserve. Federal authorities in early 1867 made a treaty that sold part of the Seneca-Cayuga lands for use by other Kansas tribes, such as Ottawas, Peorias, and Wyandottes. The document also separated the Shawnees into the Eastern and Western Shawnees and combined the Mixed Band and Senecas of Sandusky into simply the Seneca Tribe. The agreement's terms took effect in 1869.

Missionaries operated schools for the mix of tribal peoples in northeastern Indian Territory in the postwar period. Roman Catholics, Methodists, and Quakers opened schools. Mathias Splitlog, a Catholic, supported the erection of Cayuga Mission Church (west of Grove), which was restored in the 1950s and is now a Baptist church. Over a hundred Cayugas journeyed from Canada in 1881 to settle in Indian Territory; but the Indian agent blocked any further emigration, and some of those who returned northward walked amid incredible hardships. Allotment of the reservation later devastated the Indians' land base. (See the "Seneca-Cayuga" entry for more history.)

Cayuga members participate in a wide range of Iroquoian and other Indian ceremonies. They maintain connections with their New York and Canadian kinfolk. In addition, because of the proximity to other tribes nearby, the Cayugas also take part in neighboring powwows in their region. The Cayugas continue their Green Corn Ceremonial annually, including a ritual football game at their cultural ground called Turkey Ford, which they share with the Senecas. In their ceremonies they offer songs for the thunders, the sun, the moon, and the earth, as well as honoring the start of the ritual season and the first fruits of springtime. Some Cayugas are active in Iroquoian Medicine Societies, in cyclical rituals like the

Strawberry and Blackberry ceremonies, in False Face Society meetings, and in Native American Church events. They also include their rituals in wakes and funerals. The waters of Grand Lake inundated about half of the Seneca-Cayuga ceremonial area in 1940.

More recently the Cayugas have been concerned with the hazards of downstream contamination from Tar Creek runoff. The Tar Creek site of the federal Environmental Protection Agency (EPA) has been a focus of concern for many years as a result of tailing waste from mining activity. Lead, zinc, and other heavy metals invaded the groundwater, and residents in the region are worried about the pollution of air, water, soil, and plant life and the effect on their lives.

Cayuga tribal members have sought land in New York in the vicinity of Cayuga Lake west of the city of Syracuse for the purpose of establishing a lucrative casino operation. The state's governor in late 2004 agreed to their claim, but a year later a court overturned the deal.

Notable Cayugas include Gary Dale Farmer, from the Six Nations Reserve in Canada. He acted in many films, including *Powwow Highway* (1988) and *Dark Wind* (1992). Poet Barney Bush is Cayuga-Shawnee.

SUGGESTED READING

Chafe, Wallace, and Michael Foster. "Prehistoric Divergences and Recontacts between Cayuga, Seneca, and the Other Northern Iroquoian Languages." *International Journal of American Linguistics* 47, no. 2 (1981): 121–42.

Foreman, Grant. *The Last Trek of the Indians.* Chicago: University of Chicago, 1946; repr. New York: Russell and Russell, 1972.

Nieberding, Velma. "Seneca-Cayuga Green Corn Ceremonial Feast." *Chronicles of Oklahoma* 34 (Summer 1956): 231–34.

Cherokee

The tribal name derived from Tsa-La-Gi (CWY in the Sequoyah syllabary), "principal People" or "cave People." It was corrupted to "Chalaque" (in Portuguese and Spanish), "Cheraqui" (in French), and finally "Cherokee" in English by the late 1600s. Their designation for themselves is Ani-yunwi-ya, "real People."

LOCATION AND GOVERNMENT

The "Cherokee Nation of Oklahoma" headquarters is just south of the city of Tahlequah in Cherokee County, in northeastern Oklahoma. It is sixty-five miles from Tulsa and twenty-eight miles from Muskogee. The tribe is not organized under the OIWA, but members wrote and approved a constitution in 1975–76, which set up a principal chief, a deputy chief, and a fifteen-member council, elected every four years. Tribal members voted and amended their constitution in 2003, creating the position of council speaker, increasing council membership, and making other legal and court changes. The tribal website is www.cherokee.org.

BUSINESSES

The success of the Cherokee Nation's economic development has offered a model for other tribes. Some consider the Cherokee Nation to be the most economically successful tribe in the United States. The tribe has engaged in a wide range of economic activities for a long time.

Cherokee Nation Enterprises obtains most of its income from gaming, with over $400 million in annual net revenue. The tribe opened its large Cherokee Casino and Resort in the northeast Tulsa suburb of Catoosa in 2004 (at www.cherokeecasino.com). Following expansion in 2009, it will be the largest casino in the state (with a new name, the Hard Rock Casino Tulsa). The tribe also operates seven other casinos at West Siloam Springs (also with a hotel), Fort Gibson, Roland, Sallisaw, Claremore, Tahlequah, and Will Rogers Downs pari-mutuel horse-racing track in

Claremore (which it purchased in 2004). The casinos operate in conjunction with golf courses, hotels, convenience stores, tobacco outlets, and gift shops.

The Cherokee Nation engages in a wide range of business activities aside from gaming. The tribe entered the high-speed wireless Internet industry in 2005. Forestry and wood products (such as manufacturing pallets and charcoal) offer tribal employment and revenue. The umbrella Cherokee Nation Industries (the manufacturing and services arm of the nation, begun in 1969) provides aerospace equipment to multinational corporations and the National Aeronautics and Space Administration (NASA), cable assemblies and wiring harnesses for military controls, parts distribution to aircraft companies, and medical personnel services. Tribal enterprises continue to expand. Oil and gas production furnishes revenue as well, and subsurface coal is still an available resource. The nation operates a sanitary landfill in Adair County.

Tribal gift shops in Tahlequah, in gaming facilities, and in highway rest stops offer Indian-made items. Recreational opportunities for tourists abound in the region. The tribe's Cherokee Heritage Center in Tahlequah (with a museum, Cherokee Ancient Village, and gift shop) offers numerous exhibits and events.

The tribe possesses 168,000 total acres held in trust as well as just under 100 miles of the Arkansas Riverbed.

NUMBER

The Cherokee Nation of Oklahoma has 265,000 members, with twice that number self-described as Cherokees. There is no blood quantum requirement, just citizenship descendancy based on the Dawes Roll. The 2000 U.S. Census identified over 700,000 who claimed Cherokee heritage nationwide. Northeastern Oklahoma has some 100 Cherokee communities. Perhaps 100,000 tribal members reside within the fourteen-county area. Cherokees are also scattered across the globe, with large enclaves in many major U.S. cities. The Cherokees are one of the largest tribes in the United States.

Over 300 groups clamor for federal recognition as Cherokee tribal entities, but the U.S. government acknowledges only three to date: the Cherokee Nation of Oklahoma, the Eastern Band of Cherokees in North Carolina, and the United Keetoowah Band of Cherokee Indians in Oklahoma. The 13,500 members of the Eastern Band reside today on the Qualla Boundary Reserve, with their headquarters in Cherokee, North Carolina (see www.cherokee-nc.com). The United Keetoowah Band with some 12,000 members is headquartered in Tahlequah (see the "United Keetoowah Band of Cherokee Indians" entry). There are also state-recognized groups. An example is the Georgia Tribe of Eastern Cherokees in Dahlonega in Lumpkin County, Georgia, which claims about 3,500 members.

Linguistics provides some insight into Cherokee origins. Scholars view Cherokee as an Iroquoian language that branched off some 3,500 to 3,800 years ago. Six distinguishable dialects of Cherokee may have been spoken prehistorically, but only two survive. The third dialect to survive into the historic period, Elati or Lower Cherokee, was spoken in a portion of South Carolina and nearby Georgia but has vanished. Kituhwa or Middle Cherokee is spoken among the Eastern Band in North Carolina, while Otali or Overhill or now Western Cherokee is used in Oklahoma. Because of the larger Oklahoma Cherokee numbers, Western Cherokee predominates as the major form today.

Archeologists differ over the origins of the Cherokees in the southeastern portion of the United States. Most point to an Appalachian homeland prior to A.D. 1000. Some Cherokees claim South American origin and a northward migration; others point to a Great Lakes origin among Iroquois and a southward movement. Most Western-trained scientists, however, point to Cherokee expansion out of Pisgah-phase peoples from 1000 to 1500. In other words, most archeologists believe that the Cherokees emerged out of South Appalachian Mississippian chiefdoms. The Cherokees spread outward after the collapse of chiefdoms, displacing the Muscogees from the Little Tennessee River Valley and northern Georgia.

In the beginning, according to a Cherokee origin story, water covered the earth. Creatures lived in the sky vault, the heavens above. It became crowded, so the animals called a council. The water spider volunteered to go down to the water realm, dived to the bottom of the ocean, and brought up mud. The dirt grew and became the earth, a great island suspended over the sea by four cords hanging from the sky vault. Next came the Great Buzzard to swoop down and see the new land. His flapping wings made deep valleys in the wet land as well as forming ridges and mountains. This was Cherokee country. Conjurors placed the sun tracking east to west underneath the dome of the sky vault. Animals and plants sprang forth. Humans were created. The water spider brought a piece of the sun to provide the first fire. Later Lucky Hunter and First Woman (Selu) originated game and corn. It should be pointed out that some Cherokees favor a migration story in which ancestors traveled from South America northward, then turned southeastward, battling the Delawares, before settling in the U.S. Southeast.

Traditional Cherokee cosmology, like that of most southeastern Indians, held that there were two realms, upper and lower. The earth hung on cords precariously between the two realms. The upper world was one of spirits, order, and peace. The lower world was one of water, chaos, and monsters. Contending forces had to be balanced to achieve harmony. The sun was the apportioner of day and night. The sun's manifestation on earth was the sacred fire. Through rituals, the sacred fire was extinguished and rekindled. Major ceremonial observances involved lighting the new fire, ritual sacrifice, purification go-to-water rites, and what are called all-night stomp dances. Cherokees celebrated the bounty of the harvest annually in their Green Corn Ceremony. After the 1750s they also turned to their Booger Dance, in which dancers parodied their traditional Indian enemies and adapted the masked dancers to represent the European threat as lewd and menacing.

The Cherokees resided in villages with plazas and earthen mounds. A priestly class maintained temples with perpetual fires atop platform mounds. By the time Europeans arrived, however, the Cherokees had abandoned mound culture. Women in Cherokee villages tended fields of corn, beans, squash, and melons. Extended families lived in dwellings that were arranged around a central council house and a plaza. The plaza hosted games of stickball as well as ceremonies. A protective stockade enclosed the town. Men hunted for abundant game like deer, bear, turkey, and many other animals.

Membership in the seven clans was matrilineal. Women of each clan selected their own women's council leaders, who could intervene in men's affairs when the cause arose. The head of the women's council was the Beloved Woman (Ghigau). Each town had a local council of elder men who oversaw civil affairs. There was no higher political authority or organization above the town prior to the arrival of Europeans. Like many other Indians in the Southeast, the Cherokees had a dual division for their society of white (peace) and red (war). A peace chief or high priest headed the white division, while a war chief led the red division.

Demographers point to a Cherokee population of 30,000 residing in fifty to eighty towns through 40,000 square miles of the Southeast on the eve of first contact with Europeans. The tribe had the largest population in the Southeast. The Cherokee name the ancient northern town of Kituwah (or Keetoowah) near what is now Bryson City, North Carolina, as their mother town. Their territory embraced all or parts of the contemporary states of North and South Carolina, Kentucky, Tennessee, Georgia, Alabama, Virginia, and West Virginia.

The Cherokees briefly encountered the Spanish expeditions of Hernando de Soto (1540s) and Juan Pardo (1560s), but the English brought lasting impact after 1650. English traders from Virginia and South Carolina by the late 1600s had altered the Indians' economy, while English settlers led to political change. In 1721, under pressure from the British, the Cherokees selected a trade commissioner (whom the British called the Cherokee emperor), from which their first principal chief evolved, establishing a united Cherokee Nation. The Cherokees also agreed that year to their first cession of land to the English. They would sign nine more treaties with the British.

During the French and Indian War (1754–63) the Cherokees at first sided with the British; but the alliance fell apart in mutual attacks that devastated Cherokee towns. Further Indian land cessions followed in the period from 1770 to 1776, when the Cherokees ceded 50,000 square miles to the American colonists. Subsequent Revolutionary War activities laid waste to the Cherokee Lower Towns. In the face of additional cessions in 1777, Dragging Canoe (Tsiya-gunsini) led his Lower Town followers in migrating to Chickamauga Creek near present-day Chattanooga, Tennessee.

In 1785 at Hopewell, South Carolina, the United States signed the first of a series of treaties with the Cherokees. Cherokee historian Emmet Starr detailed the intermixture of European and Cherokee bloodlines, implying the beginnings of acculturation, in the early period. Cherokee society gradually began to shift from matrilineal clans to European-style families, with the male as the head of the household. A mixed-blood population emerged in the eighteenth century to dominate national political life. The early era also saw the beginnings of major population movements. Some Chickamauga Cherokees ventured westward after 1794 and settled in the Arkansas-Missouri area. Others gradually followed. They are referred to as the Old Settlers. By 1800 as many as a thousand Cherokees resided along the St. Francis River in southeastern Missouri and northeastern Arkansas, which ran parallel to the Mississippi River Valley. Historian William McLoughlin detailed how 1794 was the turning point year for the Cherokees. With the loss of much of their hunting grounds, they turned to European trade goods and toward acculturation. The disintegration of towns shifted the population to residence on isolated farmsteads like whites. Naturalist Thomas Nuttall visited 1,500 Cherokee settlers in Arkansas and observed approvingly in 1819 that in outward demeanor they "imitate the whites" and "appeared to be progressing towards civilization" in their scattered farmsteads. He speculated that one day they just might "increase . . . and become a powerful and independent nation."

Perhaps 1,200 Lower Town Cherokees followed their leader The Bowl across the Mississippi River, eventually settling in Arkansas between the Arkansas and White rivers. Others joined them after 1817, the year the federal government created an Arkansas reservation for them, forming what was known as the Western Cherokee Nation. Among the emigrants was the mixed-blood Sequoyah, who also is known as George Guess. Three years later a missionary arrived and established the famous Dwight Mission. In 1819–20 some of the Western Cherokees traveled farther southward into Texas, where they resided below the Sabine River near present Tyler until Texas independence nullified their Spanish land grant. For a time they lived on the Brazos Reserve.

Missionaries had no success among the Cherokees in their homeland until Moravians established a mission school at Springplace in northern Georgia in 1801. Baptists and Methodists followed in 1817. Brainerd Mission began 1817 near what is now Chattanooga, Tennessee, and drew eager workers to spread the gospel. Christianity won converts, especially among the mixed-bloods and Lower Town residents.

The 1802 agreement between the federal government and Georgia officials pledged that the U.S. government would extinguish Indian land claims inside Georgia as soon as possible. Mounting pressure from the outside led in 1810 to the Cherokee formation of a national committee, a precursor of a national government for the tribe a decade later. Assimilationists solidified their control over Cherokee

Sequoyah, the inventor of the Cherokee syllabary

Print of hand-colored lithograph by McKenney and Hall. Library of Congress, Prints and Photographs Division, Washington, D.C., cph 3g02566.

government. By 1821 Sequoyah had perfected his syllabary for writing Cherokee, and their national newspaper the *Cherokee Phoenix*—a first for American Indians—appeared in 1828. The Cherokees gave up their traditional clan system of governance in 1827. They adopted a constitution and formed the Cherokee Nation with John Ross (Kooweeskoowee) as principal chief (served 1828–66). They selected New Echota, formerly Newtown, located in present Gordon County near what is now Interstate Highway 75 in northern Georgia, as their capital.

Encroachment on Cherokee territory and sovereignty reached a crisis in the late 1820s. The discovery of gold inside the Cherokee Nation hastened the wholesale violation of Indian rights. When state laws denied protection to tribal activities and nullified tribal jurisdiction, the executive branch of the federal government failed to come to their aid. Two early 1830s court decisions, *Cherokee Nation* and *Worcester v. Georgia*, became the foundation of the modern legal system today governing the relations of the federal, state, and tribal governments. The fiery debate over removal of the Indians divided missionary societies too. Moravians and Methodists generally fa-

Cherokee principal chief John Ross
Print of colored lithograph by McKenney and Hall. Library of Congress, Prints and Photographs Division, Washington, D.C., cph 3g03156.

vored removal, while Baptists, Presbyterians, and the American Board of Commissioners for Foreign Missions (ABCFM) opposed it to varying degrees. Friends of the Indians like ABCFM board member Jeremiah Evarts led the opposition to removal. U.S. negotiator John Schermerhorn played an infamous role in the removal talks. Support for the Cherokee cause ultimately evaporated. After a cruel federal attempt to move people westward, Chief John Ross, resigned to their fate, organized thirteen detachments for the journey west. Some missionaries like Evan Jones trod the Trail of Tears with their flock. Others, like Samuel A. Worcester, who came to Brainerd Mission in 1826 and New Echota two years afterward and became a legal martyr in the Native cause with Elizur Butler, later journeyed to join his charges.

Finally, a small group under Major Ridge signed a removal treaty on December 29, 1835, in the home of Cherokee editor Elias Boudinot that included generous terms for the signers. At New Echota they relinquished Cherokee territory east of the Mississippi for $5 million and agreed to depart. Congress quickly accepted the treaty. U.S. troops eventually forced out the Cherokees, who traveled across various routes in seventeen detachments along their Trail of Tears (Nunna Daul Tsuny, "trail where they cried") to Indian Territory in 1838–39. Cherokees collected for the last time at Red Clay near Chattanooga, where they had moved their capital in 1832 to escape Georgia, before they began their fateful trek. One church group dismantled their church, labeled the pieces of lumber, and lovingly carried it with them on their journey. They reconstructed their church at the end of their odyssey. It stands today refurbished as the Old Baptist Mission near Westville, Oklahoma. Historians debate the numbers, but some 4,000 out of 17,000 perished on the 800-mile Trail of Tears. Perhaps 1,000–4,000 escaped into the mountains and avoided removal. Beginning in 1819 some in the East had started settling on tracts along the Oconaluftee River purchased through the efforts of Will Thomas. They resided in North Carolina outside the influence of Georgia's removal push and became the nucleus of the later Eastern Band of Cherokees of North Carolina. Some of the Texas Cherokees fled into Indian Territory in 1839.

Cherokee chief Major Ridge

Print of colored lithograph by McKenney and Hall. Library of Congress, Prints and Photographs Division, Washington, D.C., cph 3g03158.

In spite of retributive murders of the 1835 treaty signers in 1839 and the resultant strife, the Cherokee Nation gradually began to function in its new home with a new constitution and government. John Ross dominated the politics. Prosperity slowly returned, especially for the mixed-bloods. Tahlequah served as the new capital. Their Supreme Court building, built in 1844, is the oldest structure in Oklahoma today. Missionaries renewed their evangelization with modest success. Eastern missionary education served as the model and was the reality for influential Cherokee families. The Reverend Worcester's daughter Ann Eliza attended a

Vermont school and his daughter Sarah graduated from Mount Holyoke. Their mother, Ann Orr, had been a classmate of Mary Lyon, founder of Mount Holyoke Female Seminary (1836). In 1851 the Cherokee Female Seminary became the first secondary school for girls west of the Mississippi River. The Cherokees stressed education. By statehood there were 317 day schools in the Cherokee Nation. The Cherokees had a higher level of literacy than surrounding states. Indian academies became the basis for later state higher education endeavors. The Female Seminary in Park Hill became Northeastern State University just after statehood. The Cherokee Orphans' Home became the Sequoyah Orphan Training School for the Five Tribes upon statehood. It is now Sequoyah High School in Tahlequah, which the tribe operates.

Students at the Cherokee Female Seminary, ca. March 1892

J. D. Wilson Collection, Research Division of the Oklahoma Historical Society, #700

Pre–Civil War factions divided the Cherokees. Baptist minister Evan Jones and his son helped form the shadowy Pins, the full-blood Keetoowah Society, in the 1850s to oppose the policies of slave-owning mixed-bloods. When U.S. troops withdrew at the start of Civil War hostilities, Chief John Ross at Park Hill reluctantly signed a treaty with the Confederates in 1861. He spent much of the war in Washington, D.C., however, lobbying for improved relations with the Union government. In his absence, Confederate brigadier general Stand Watie, one of the Ridge Party leaders who escaped assassination in 1839, became principal chief of the Confederate Cherokee Nation. He was the last Confederate general to surrender at the conclusion of the war (on June 23, 1865). Perhaps a quarter of the Cherokee population perished in Indian Territory as a result of the war.

At the end of the fighting, the federal government punished the Five Tribes for siding with the Confederacy, confiscating lands, opening the region to other tribes, creating Indian Territory, granting rights-of-way to railroads, and freeing slaves. Again the Cherokee Nation rose painfully from the ashes. Lewis Downing, a full-blood leader of the Keetoowah Society and a Baptist minister, was elected principal chief in 1867. He oversaw a revived nation in the postwar years and the slow return of prosperity. By 1871 there were about 18,000 Cherokees. Railroads brought settlers who demanded more land, culminating in the 1889 creation of Oklahoma Territory to the west of Indian Territory. A series of land runs saw a flood of claimants enter the region (such as in September 1893, for the 8-million acre western Cherokee Outlet). The Cherokee Nation covered a land area of about 25,000 square miles, three times the size of the state of Massachusetts. A steady influx of people, many of whom married Cherokee enrollees, added to the Indian Territory population. The outcry to open Cherokee lands continued. Following lengthy negotiations, 42,000 Cherokees received a 110-acre allotment of the 4-million-acre reservation. Some others were granted cash payments, because there was not enough land for equal distribution. Mixed-bloods favored allotment, while full-bloods bitterly opposed it. In the words of historian Angie Debo, an "orgy of plunder" quickly divested the Cherokees of their allotted lands. They were plunged into poverty. By the 1920s about 90 percent of those lands had passed to white control.

There were an estimated 2,500 freedmen within the Cherokee Nation in 1867. The postwar threat to remove the freedmen, as pledged in the Reconstruction treaty, led to the awful dilemma of evicting them from their homes, leaving behind the remains of their loved ones, just like the 1830s removal from the Southeast. The federal government's denial of Cherokee Nation authority over the freedmen issue during the postwar period foretold its intrusion into other tribal affairs as the twentieth century approached. As Daniel F. Littlefield, Jr., demonstrated, the issue ultimately subverted Cherokee Nation autonomy. Today there may be as many as 25,000 freedmen descendants of the Cherokees.

In response to growing assimilationist pressures and the pernicious allotment onslaught, Redbird Smith was asked to foster a renewal of ceremonialism among Cherokee full-bloods. After Oklahoma statehood (1907) the twenty-two ceremonial grounds became known as Nighthawk Keetoowahs and the revival was called the Redbird Smith movement. Through their central sacred fires, they kept Cherokee ceremonialism alive. They had representation in the Four Mothers Society, which fostered traditionalism throughout eastern Oklahoma. Littlefield described the futile attempt by the full-bloods under Redbird Smith to set up a utopian community.

Commercial activity continued, however. Attorney E. C. Boudinot served as the brains of the Boomer movement to open Cherokee lands to whites. He helped compile the ordinances for the new town of Tahlequah, the Cherokee capital, and laid out the railroad town of Vinita. The Cherokee Nation paid for the first commercial telephone lines in Oklahoma. As the population grew, commercial activity expanded.

The grinding poverty of the Great Depression forced many Cherokees off their land in search of jobs. An estimated one-half of the Cherokee population left eastern Oklahoma as a part of the new diaspora. Bartley Milam served as the chairman of the Cherokee council beginning in 1938 and was appointed principal chief by president Franklin D. Roosevelt in 1941. He helped restore Cherokee government. Upon Milam's death in 1949, president Harry Truman appointed businessman William W. Keeler chief of the Cherokees. Keeler prepared the Cherokee Nation for self-government in the following years.

Cherokees have served with distinction in the wars of the country. Admiral Joseph Clark served in World War II as the highest-ranking officer of American Indian heritage in the U.S. armed services. Jack Montgomery won the Medal of Honor in the European theater.

After the mid-twentieth century, the Cherokees experienced a new diaspora, resulting from the federal relocation program. Family members sought employment in scattered cities like San Francisco, Los Angeles, Dallas, and Chicago. During the 1950s the family of Charley Mankiller moved to the San Francisco Bay area, where his daughter Wilma grew up.

BIA bureaucratic imperialism dominated Cherokee political affairs until Congress enacted legislation returning self-government to the Cherokees in 1970. The Cherokee Nation could not take advantage of the OIWA in the 1930s, but an Indian Claims Commission settlement in 1961 provided $14.7 million as compensation for the transfer of the Cherokee Outlet. Tribal counsel Earl Boyd Pierce was instrumental in obtaining the judgment. The reinvigorated tribal structure under Keeler adopted a new constitution in 1976. By 1980 tribal members (232,000) and self-identified Cherokees (1.4 million) made the Cherokees the largest Indian tribe in the United States, surpassing the Navajos of Arizona.

The Cherokees reached out to preserve their heritage. The tribe started popular homecoming events called the Cherokee National Holiday during the 1950s and founded the Cherokee National Historical Society in the following decade. The holiday currently draws nearly 100,000 visitors for a mix of culture, history, and dancing. The renewed life of the tribe in the 1960s–70s attracted many home to Oklahoma, including Wilma Mankiller, who was elected in 1987 as principal chief and served until 1995. She was the first female elected to lead a major Indian tribe in the United States. In 1984, for the first time since removal, the Eastern Band and the Western Cherokees met at Red Clay, Tennessee, to address common concerns. They also gathered to celebrate the 1996 purchase of Kituwah and engaged in a series of projects to restore the one-time capital of New Echota in Georgia. For the first time in 162 years, the Cherokee National Council met at New Echota in 1992 as part of the dedication ceremonies. In 2006 Cherokee Nation and Eastern Band members held a joint council meeting at the ancient town site of Kituwah. Tribal members of both groups have also been involved in the National Park Service Trail of Tears National Historic Trail, which Congress established in 1987. Eastern and Western Cherokees annually sponsor mutual events, such as the summertime Trail of Tears Gospel Sing.

Cherokee principal chief Wilma Mankiller (left)

C. R. Cowen Collection, Research Division of the Oklahoma Historical Society, #19687.IN.5C1.2.24

The tribe entered into a self-governance agreement with the United States in 1993. The compact enabled the tribe to take the first steps toward eventually standing on its own feet fiscally and severing many of its ties to the BIA. In 1992 the tribe passed the first bond issue secured by Indian gaming revenues to support construction of an expansion of the tribal headquarters. This was a first in Indian Country across the United States. In 2003 the Cherokee Nation oversaw 150 programs and employed 2,000 people. By 2007 it had an annual budget of $350 million. The tribe's economic impact annually amounted to over $500 million within the state. It contributed to local communities in a variety of ways. One example was revenue from vehicle tag sales, which averaged about $100 per pupil within the tribal region, contributed to public schools in lieu of state tax revenue. During 2004 the nation disbursed over $2 million to Cherokee college students for their education.

Today Cherokee Nation members reside through fourteen counties

(7,000 square miles) in northeastern Oklahoma. Cherokees live in about seventy communities, where the Cherokee language often predominates. Cherokee ritualism continues at a series of ceremonial grounds. The annual Labor Day weekend at Stokes Smith ground outside Vian brings a large number of participants and spectators to feast and dance through the night. Some ceremonial grounds perform the old Green Corn Ceremony. Cherokee traditionalists participate in a wide range of rituals. In many ways the Cherokees in isolated rural communities continue ancient kin-based lifeways, utilizing sharing and reciprocity, while at the same time engaging in subsistence economies and wage-labor. Community names reflect the original Cherokee homeland. Throughout the Cherokee Nation, Baptist and Methodist churches celebrate a unique Cherokee brand of Christianity. They incorporate Cherokee concepts and language into their services. Many Christian materials have been published in the Cherokee syllabary. There are about 10,000 fluent Cherokee-speakers today. In the 1990s the tribe responded to a grass-roots demand and made a conscious effort to teach the tribal language, intended to foster a fluent and all-Cherokee-speaking community in northeastern Oklahoma in twenty-five years. In 2002 the Cherokee National Children's Choir reintroduced tribal youth and an international audience to Native-language hymns.

A 2007 vote amended the tribal constitution and ousted 2,800 descendants of freedmen from tribal membership because they were not related to a Cherokee Indian in their ancestry. The issue created a firestorm of controversy. Bitterness left from the earlier conflict over treaty rights of Loyal Shawnees and Eastern Delaware Indians who desired to separate from the Cherokee Nation but were prevented from doing so aggravated the issue. While freedmen were made tribal citizens under Reconstruction treaty terms if they met certain qualifications, Dawes Commission rules during the allotment era robbed them of any rights, and swindlers often took their lands. Tribal membership of freedmen in the Cherokee Nation is under litigation.

Because of the tribe's large size, there are many notable Cherokees. Little Carpenter, although small in stature, was upheld as the most influential Indian leader of his era prior to the American Revolution. His niece Nancy Ward became a Beloved Woman among her people. Junaluska fought alongside Andrew Jackson and saved the general's life during battle, an act of bravery that the Cherokee later regretted. Stand Watie, a member of the Ridge Party or Treaty faction in the 1830s, represented slave-owning Cherokees as the Civil War loomed and served as a Confederate general during the war. His nephew John Rollin Ridge, eldest son of John Ridge, lived in California and wrote the first novel by an American Indian (the 1854 *Life and Adventures of Joaquin Murietta*). Famous Cherokee outlaws include Henry Starr, Ned Christie, Zeke Proctor, and Charles Arthur "Pretty Boy" Floyd.

Writer, actor, and humorist Will Rogers
Photograph by Underwood and Underwood. Library of Congress, Prints and Photographs Division, Washington, D.C., cph 3a21749.

Will Rogers was one of the greatest entertainers of the early twentieth century, who starred on stage and screen, made radio broadcasts, and was an eagerly read newspaper columnist during the 1920s and 1930s. His childhood chum John Oskisson became a well-known journalist and author. Andy Payne won the grueling 1928 Transcontinental Footrace. Dorothea Lange's photograph of an exhausted Florence Owens Thompson, with children clinging to her in a California migrant labor camp in the 1930s, created the iconic image of a migrant mother of the Great Depression.

Musicians and singers with Cherokee heritage are legion: Rita Coolidge, Douglas Blue Feather, Karen Dalton, Johnny and June Carter Cash, Litefoot, Loretta Lynn, Dottie West, GaWaNi Pony Boy, country musician Ricky Lynn Gregg, Micki Free, Cherokee Rose (Moore) and Silena, opera star Barbara McAlister, jazz singer Keely Smith, songwriter John Loudermilk, Tommy Wildcat, and ethnomusicologist Charlotte Heth. Stage actress and storyteller Iva Rider (known as Princess Atalia) entertained troops with the Young Men's Christian Association (YMCA) during World War I.

Cherokee writers include Barbara Kingsolver, Thomas King, Sara Hoklotubbe, Jean Hager, Daniel Heath Justice, Robert J. Conley, Diane Glancy, poet Gladys Cardiff, journalist and visual artist Kade Twist, and poet and playwright Lynn Riggs (who wrote "Green Grow the Lilacs," immortalized by Richard Rodgers and Oscar Hammerstein II as the Broadway musical *Oklahoma!*).

Ron Lewis was the first Indian in the United States to earn a doctorate in social work and taught for many years at the university level. Homer

Noley is an educator. Author and public radio voice Sarah Vowell is a "cast-off Cherokee," in her own words. Legal scholar Rennard Strickland (also Osage) helped found the modern analysis of federal-Indian law. Attorney Fern Holland worked with Iraqi women for constitutional rights until March 2004, when she was among the first civilian casualties of the Iraq war.

Cherokee athletes include outfielder Robert Lee Johnson, who played for the Philadelphia Phillies; his brother Roy, who played in the outfield for major league teams in the 1930s; Detroit first baseman Rudy York; Philadelphia Phillies pitcher Austin Tincup; Yankee short-stop Bucky Dent; and Colorado Rockies catcher Jayhawk Owens. Gene Conley wore professional championship rings in both baseball and basketball in the late 1950s. Baseball great Hank Aaron also has Cherokee ancestry, as does golfing sensation Tiger Woods. Bud Adams, owner of the Tennessee Titans, is an enrolled member of the Cherokee Nation.

Actor Orvel Baldridge appeared in *The Doe Boy,* a 2001 film directed by fellow Cherokee Randy Redroad. Among Cherokees in the media are actors Wes Studi, Delanna Studi, Yvonne Fisher, Tommy Lee Jones, Lou Diamond Phillips (star of the movie *La Bamba*), and Valerie Red-Horse (in *Naturally Native* and *True Whispers* [on Navajo code talkers]) as well as television reporters Cherokee Ballard (in Oklahoma City) and Janis Walkingstick (anchoring in Little Rock, Arkansas). Victor Daniels (under the name Chief Thundercloud) portrayed the first film Tonto in the series in which Bob Livingston played the Lone Ranger. Miss America 2002, Erika Harold, is of Cherokee (and Choctaw) heritage. Norma Smallwood, the first American Indian to win that title (in 1926), was also Cherokee. She married oilman Thomas Gilcrease.

Cherokee principal chief Ross Swimmer and his wife, Margaret

C. R. Cowen Collection, Research Division of the Oklahoma Historical Society, #19687.IN.FCi.7.8

Actor James Earl Jones's mother was part Cherokee. Activists Al Sharpton and Jesse Jackson; singers Jimi Hendrix, Diana Ross, and Della Reese; and author Alice Walker are of Cherokee freedmen heritage. President Barack Obama's attorney general, Eric Holder, is also of Cherokee heritage.

Ruth Muskrat Bronson represented the boarding school generation (she graduated from Mount Holyoke) and was pivotal in nurturing the National Congress of American Indians in that organization's infancy. Cherokee politicians include Robert L. Owen in the U.S. Senate, congressmen William W. Hastings and Brad Carson, and Finis Smith and Larry Adair in the state legislature. Ross Swimmer and Wilma Mankiller are among recent tribal leaders of note who have played national roles. Dr. Charles Grim headed the U.S. Indian Health Service.

Don Smith, of Cherokee background, was adopted by the Sewid family of the Kwakiutl (KwaKwa Ka'wakw) in the Pacific Northwest. Smith became the Kwakiutl artist Lelooska, who preserved Northwest Coast art and presented it to many audiences. Well-known Cherokee painters include Cecil Dick, who trained briefly in Santa Fe under Dorothy Dunn then at Bacone College before becoming the founder of a revived Cherokee artistic tradition. Other painters of Cherokee heritage include Bert and Connie Seabourn, Kay Walkingstick, Murv Jacob, Dorothy Sullivan, Bill Rabbit, Franklin Gritts, Mary Adair Horse Chief, Donald Vann, Monica Hansen, Raymond Nordwall (who is also Pawnee and Chippewa), and Virginia Stroud. Shan Goshorn is a computer graphics artist. Basket artists include Mavis Doering, Lena Blackbird, Peggy Sanders Brennan, and Ella Mae Blackbear. Bill Glass, Jr., is a sculptor. Jane Osti, Crystal Hanna, Anna Mitchell and Victoria Mitchell Vazquez, and Mel Cornshucker are potters. Lloyd Kiva New served as the director of the Institute of American Indian Arts in Santa Fe from 1967 to 1978.

Business leaders from Cherokee families include Michael Harding, founder of Krispy Kreme Donuts; Conoco chief executive officer Archie Dunham; and Phillips Petroleum chief executive officer W. W. Keeler.

SUGGESTED READING

Confer, Clarissa W. *The Cherokee Nation in the Civil War.* Norman: University of Oklahoma Press, 2007.

Conley, Robert J. *Cherokee Encyclopedia.* Albuquerque: University of New Mexico Press, 2007.

———. *The Cherokee Nation: A History.* Albuquerque: University of New Mexico Press, 2005.

———. *Mountain Windsong.* Norman: University of Oklahoma Press, 1992.

Conley, Robert J., and David G. Fitzgerald. *Cherokee*. Portland, Ore.: Graphic Arts Center, 2002.

Debo, Angie. *And Still the Waters Run*. Princeton: Princeton University Press, 1940; repr. Norman: University of Oklahoma Press, 1984.

Fogelson, Raymond D. *The Cherokees: A Critical Bibliography*. Bloomington: Indiana University Press, 1978.

Glancy, Diane. *Pushing the Bear: A Novel of the Trail of Tears*. New York: Harcourt Brace, 1996.

Littlefield, Daniel F., Jr. *The Cherokee Freedmen: From Emancipation to American Citizenship*. Westport, Conn.: Greenwood, 1978.

Mankiller, Wilma, with Michael Wallis. *Mankiller: A Chief and Her People*. New York: St. Martin's, 1993.

McLoughlin, William G. *After the Trail of Tears: The Cherokees' Struggle for Sovereignty, 1839–1880*. Chapel Hill: University of North Carolina Press, 1993.

———. *The Cherokee Ghost Dance and Other Essays on Southeastern Indians*. Macon, Ga.: Mercer University, 1984.

———. *Cherokees and Missionaries, 1789–1839*. New Haven: Yale University Press, 1984; repr. Norman: University of Oklahoma Press, 1995.

Mooney, James. *Myths of the Cherokee*. Washington, D.C.: 19th Annual Report of the Bureau of American Ethnology, 1900; repr. Nashville, Tenn.: Elder Booksellers, 1982; Cherokee, N.C.: Cherokee Heritage Books, 1982.

Naylor, Celia E. *African Cherokees in Indian Territory*. Chapel Hill: University of North Carolina Press, 2008.

Norman, Geoffrey. "The Cherokee: Two Nations, One People." *National Geographic Magazine* 187 (May 1995): 72–97.

Nuttall, Thomas. *A Journal of Travels into the Arkansas Territory during the Year 1819*. Edited by Savoie Lottinville. Norman: University of Oklahoma Press, 1980.

Parins, James W. *Elias Cornelius Boudinot: A Life on the Cherokee Border*. Lincoln: University of Nebraska Press, 2006.

Perdue, Theda. *Cherokee Women: Gender and Culture, 1700–1830*. Lincoln: University of Nebraska Press, 1998.

Perdue, Theda, and Michael D. Green. *The Cherokee Nation and the Trail of Tears*. New York: Viking/Penguin, 2008.

Power, Susan C. *Art of the Cherokee: Prehistory to the Present*. Athens: University of Georgia Press, 2007.

Starr, Emmet. *History of the Cherokee Indians and Their Legends and Folk Lore*. Oklahoma City: Warden Company, 1922; repr. New York: Kraus Reprint Corp., 1969.

Steeler, C. William. *Improving American Indian Health Care: The Western Cherokee Experience*. Edited by Rashid Bashur and Gary Shannon. Norman: University of Oklahoma Press, 2001.

Sturm, Circe. *Blood Politics: Race, Culture and Identity in the Cherokee Nation of Oklahoma*. Berkeley: University of California Press, 2000.

Trail of Tears: Cherokee Legacy. Dallas: Rich Heape Films, 2006 (DVD).

Wilkins, Thurman. *Cherokee Tragedy*. New York: Macmillan, 1970; 2nd ed. Norman: University of Oklahoma Press, 1986; repr. 1998.

Woodward, Grace Steele. *The Cherokees*. Norman: University of Oklahoma Press, 1963.

Cheyenne

NAME

The tribal name comes from the Dakota Sioux word "Shah'ela" or "Shahi'ena" (or "Saiyena"), "red speech," meaning speaking a foreign tongue although not an enemy and not related to the Sioux like the Dakotas, Nakotas, or Lakotas, whose languages were designated "white speech." The Cheyennes have referred to themselves since the eighteenth century as Tsistsistas, "like-hearted," "the original People," or simply "the People."

LOCATION AND GOVERNMENT

The headquarters for the "Cheyenne-Arapaho Tribes" is located in Concho in Canadian County, about five miles north of the city of El Reno. The Cheyennes were combined with their separate but linguistically related kin the Arapahos on the reservation (see the "Arapaho" entry). The Cheyenne-Arapaho Tribes officially organized a business committee under the OIWA in 1937 and rewrote their constitution in 1975. Tribal members voted overwhelmingly in April 2006 to reorganize their government, putting into place a system of checks and balances. Their tribal government has four branches: the three branches of the United States government plus "The People" with the power of petition as the fourth branch. The governor and lieutenant governor have two-year terms. Members of the legislature are elected for four-year terms. A tribal courts system began in 1988. The tribal website is www.c-a-tribes.org.

BUSINESSES

The Lucky Star Casino, which opened in 1994, is on tribal grounds near the tribal headquarters in Concho; another Lucky Star Casino is located in Clinton. The Feather Warrior Bingo facility is in the southern part of the community of Watonga, with another Feather Warrior operation on Canton Lake. These facilities provide the bulk of tribal income. Four new casinos are planned, along with proposed expansion of the existing casinos. In addition, the Cheyenne-Arapaho Tribes hold some 10,400 acres in trust, used for leasing, farming, and ranching activities. A tribally owned segment of land near Elk City in far western Oklahoma may become a truck stop if plans develop. About 70,000 acres remain allotted in individual tribal trust landholding. Issues of multiple heirship cloud ownership of land parcels. Smoke shops and fuel stops also provide some income. The tribal buffalo herd has about 300 head. Some individuals receive royalties from oil and gas production. The tribal tax commission levies a severance tax on oil and gas extracted from tribal land and allotments.

NUMBER

The tribe has about 12,000 members, most of whom reside throughout the eight counties in the vicinity of the tribal head-quarters, in Clinton, Colony, Canton, Hammon, and Watonga, among other towns. Members are scattered worldwide, however, for work, military service, and other reasons. About two-thirds of the total number are Cheyennes, and the rest are Arapahos. Approximately 7,000 Cheyennes are enrolled in the north at their headquarters in Lame Deer, Montana.

The Cheyennes are a Woodland people who moved onto and adapted to the Plains. They are identified as Plains Indians who followed the buffalo way of life, yet they retain ties to their forest heritage. They were the westernmost Algonquian-speakers in the Woodlands of the Great Lakes region. Linguistically the Cheyennes are more closely related to the Sac, Fox, and Kickapoo Indians than they are to the Crees and Chippewas, all of whom derived from ancestral Algonquian roots. The prehistoric background of the Cheyennes is subject to much debate because it lies so far back in the past. Because they greatly extended the Algonquian range, however, it is assumed that they were among the first to separate from the Proto-Algonquian core and migrate. Archeologist James Wright viewed the Shield Archaic peoples as occupying a giant swath of what is now Canada. They built upon even earlier hunting traditions south and east of Hudson Bay. Frank Siebert's linguistic studies placed the Proto-Algonquian homeland northeast of Lake Superior in the vicinity of Georgian Bay until about 900 B.C. James Tuck labeled these nomadic people Lake Forest Archaic and later Glacial Kame.

Karl Schlesier speculated that prehistoric ancestral Algonquian groups headed eastward from the western edge of Hudson Bay and perhaps became part of the Arvilla culture before they became part of a Woodland tradition. Nancy Ossenberg's skeletal analyses tied the Proto-Cheyennes to Arvilla (along the Red and Minnesota rivers) and Laurel cultures. Climatic change and pre-Dorset Eskimo populations pushed the Proto-Cheyennes into the boreal forest of the north. Schlesier preferred the view that the later Cheyennes as eastern Algonquian-speakers were the first to split off from the core of what became the eastern Besant Valley people in the Canadian province of Saskatchewan. They used the atlatl but were neighbors of bow and arrow–using peoples termed the Blackduck complex (which Schlesier believed were western Algonquian-speakers ancestral to the Suhtais). Brian Reeves, Robert Neuman, and Leigh Syms studied the eastern Besant people and found sites spread from Manitoba through Saskatchewan into Alberta and southward to Montana, Wyoming, North Dakota, and into eastern South Dakota, perhaps as early as 250 B.C. Over time the ancestral Cheyennes arrived on the prairies of Manitoba and Saskatchewan and then moved south into Minnesota and later southwestward toward the Black Hills. Their movement pressed those who could have been Nez Perces and others farther south. Anthropologist John Moore named the original residents of Minnesota the Chianetons, Chongasketons, and Oudebatons, who crossed the Mississippi River separately and then coalesced as the early Cheyenne Nation as they approached the Black Hills region.

Proto-Mandans entered the same Missouri River region and after A.D. 800 pushed against the Cheyennes. Archeologists term this the Initial Middle Missouri Tradition. The Mandans established sedentary earthlodge villages, allied with the Hidatsas, and fought the Cheyennes for three centuries. Schlesier intriguingly argued that around this same time the residents of the Black Hills region made use of unique ceremonial stone spirit wheels such as at Moose Mountain and Big Horn. He said that they represented the Cheyenne Massaum rite, an earth-giving ceremony granting them the right to occupy that region. The structures are popularly called medicine wheels. Schlesier dated them as early as 500–300 B.C., although others have placed them later. He noted that the stone cairn alignments were not for solstices for agricultural purposes but marked the risings of stars important to the Massaum rite. Ancestral Cheyenne conflict with the Proto-Mandans continued until perhaps A.D. 1100. Schlesier contended that the Cheyennes remained east of the Missouri River until about 1680 and that a devastating attack by either Chippewas or Assiniboines on the Cheyenne village of Biesterfeldt (on the Sheyenne River near present-day Lisbon, North Dakota) about 1790 led the Cheyennes onto the Plains as bison nomads. Cheyenne oral tradition maintains that the Rees stole their corn, forcing them onto the bison Plains.

Early ethnologist George Grinnell recorded the Cheyenne origin story. The world was once covered by water from a deluge. A person floating on the surface called out for waterfowl to help. He persuaded them to dive under the water for mud. Swans and geese tried but failed. A mud hen finally came up with mud in its bill. From the mud the earth was created, then the first man and woman. They were the Cheyennes.

While in Minnesota, the Cheyennes were typical Woodland Indians, residing southwest of the Great Lakes. They were sedentary horticulturalists who lived in villages of bark-covered lodges and ate wild rice and other plant foods. Hunters ventured onto the prairie west of the lakes as well as onto the Plains for game. The Cheyennes eventually moved along the Minnesota River and crossed the Mississippi River into North Dakota. They moved as a result of pressure from the Crees and Sioux, although the Cheyennes also fought Dhegiha Siouans who entered the same region. Hudson Bay Company traders had provided firearms to the Crees before that date. The Crees attacked their enemies the Assiniboines, who in turn assaulted the Cheyennes. Once the Cheyennes entered the area that is now North Dakota, they resided along the Sheyenne River. Some built fortified villages, protected by walls and defensive moats. They lived in earth lodges and used mound burials. Excavations revealed that one of those villages, Biesterfeldt, held less than a thousand Cheyennes residing in earth lodges after 1750. John Moore speculated that historic-era southern Cheyenne bands arose from Biesterfeldt residents. Other Cheyenne villages were farther south along the Missouri River, at first on the east side then later on the west side. The Cheyennes also allied with the Mandan-Hidatsa-Arikaras in the region.

Near the Missouri River the Cheyennes made some important contacts. They first met the Moiseyus, a Siouan band from northwest Minnesota's lake district. The two groups hunted together and lived near each other, and eventually there was a Cheyenne band named Moiseyu. The Cheyennes also met the Suhtais, who spoke a dialect of Cheyenne, around 1720 near the Black Hills. The two groups allied, then the Cheyennes incorporated the Suhtais in 1833. Cheyenne oral tradition tells of the struggle between Sweet Medicine (Motsiiyoev) and the ancient leader of the Suhtais (called Lime) and the outcome: the uniting of the two groups. The Suhtais gave the Cheyennes the Sun Dance as well as the Sacred Buffalo Cap (Sacred Hat) medicine (Is'siwun), which was the great legacy of the

Suhtai hero Erect Horns. In the Timber Mountains of Minnesota north of the pipestone quarry, the Buffalo Hat and the associated ceremony, the Sun Dance, were given to Erect Horns and his female companion. Moore dated the Suhtai merger with the Cheyennes about A.D. 1740 and their gifts to the Cheyennes during the following decade. At nearby Bear Butte (Novavose or Nowah'wus, "where the people are taught" in Tsistsistas) near Sturgis, South Dakota, the culture hero Sweet Medicine brought ceremonies and rituals to the Cheyennes, restructuring them into a Plains people. Moore's research has detailed how the Cheyennes proper (the Tsistsistas, "arrow people"), the hunting Omisis, the Masikotas/Fox People, and the Suhtais came together to form the historic Cheyennes.

Sioux and Crow pressure drove the Cheyennes toward the Black Hills, where they became allies of the Arapahos. The Arapahos were also Algonquian-speakers but of a different language. They had preceded the Cheyennes onto the Plains. In the same vicinity the Cheyennes made lasting peace with the Teton Lakotas. Long neighbors, the two peoples continued amicable relations, especially between the Cheyennes and the Oglala and Brule bands. The Masikota band had intermarried into the Lakotas and brought close Siouan ties to the Cheyennes.

Cheyenne religious life focused on renewal of the universe in cyclical fashion. Four major ceremonies engaged tribal members annually in their nineteenth-century life on the Plains. Supernatural beings inside Bear Butte delivered four Sacred Arrows (Maahotse) to Sweet Medicine: two Human Arrows for warfare and two Buffalo Arrows for hunting prowess. The Sacred Arrows are unique to the Cheyennes and had to be renewed in the most important of all Cheyenne ceremonies. After the renewal, the Cheyennes then held their summertime Sun Dance (Hoxeheome, Sun Dance Lodge, or New Life Lodge or Life Generator Lodge) to renew the universe and to ensure prosperity for the tribe.

The rituals of the Massaum (Masehaome, "crazy lodge") reenacted the lessons of Yellow-Haired Girl (Heovestseahe), who taught the Cheyennes how to obtain animals for food, clothing, and shelter. The fourth major ceremony focused on the Sacred Hat (Esevone), a buffalo headdress, as well as its medicine bundle. Various personal medicine and healing rituals complemented Cheyenne religious practices.

The Cheyennes were organized according to bands, which were under the leadership of a respected chief and his council. Each of the ten bands contained several hundred people, who all belonged to an extended family. Sweet Medicine ended the old paramount chiefdom and set up a new system with a chiefs' society and six men's warrior societies. Each of the ten bands could elect four chiefs for ten-year terms to a governing peace Council of Forty-four, or Chiefs' Council, along with four leaders held over from the previous term, including a Sweet Medicine Chief. Men's societies were patrilineal. Women belonged to guilds noted for their products, such as tepee covers, beadwork, or toys.

François and Louis Joseph La Verendrye visited the northern Plains in 1742 and found what are presumed to be the Cheyennes along the river of the same name. French contact with tribes in the region stretched back to the 1680s, leading to later fur trade involvement with Pierre Chouteau and John Jacob Astor's American Fur Company. In 1804 the Cheyennes lived at the mouth of the White River just below the Sheyenne River west of the Missouri River. A Lewis and Clark expedition map showed the Cheyennes in the vicinity of the Black Hills. After about 1806 they lived on the Grand River. They continued to raise corn and traded with riverine tribes and with Plains nomads as well as with Mexican traders. Around that same time, led by the Arapahos, the Cheyennes began a slow movement southward. Most of the Cheyennes were then in today's eastern Wyoming and western South Dakota and on both sides of the North Platte River. Pressure from a long-term enemy, the Crows, and from Shoshone, Pawnee, and Siouan groups to their north contributed to the migration. Some of the Cheyennes and Arapahos slowly moved onto the southern Plains in the region of the upper Arkansas River. Over time the two tribes divided into northern and southern divisions. The use of Bent's Fort aided the formation of the southern group, as tribespeople utilized its trade goods. (The location of the fort within Colorado shifted over the years: see the "Arapaho" entry.) The attraction of trade goods available from Fort Laramie, initially called Fort William, on the North Platte River after 1834 also contributed to the division. Northern Cheyennes depended on its ready supply of goods. The Oregon Trail cut a channel through the Platte River heart of Cheyenne territory after 1840, further encouraging the tribal split.

The Cheyennes and Arapahos had traded with the Kiowas and Comanches near the Arkansas River for years, and by the second decade of the nineteenth century the Cheyennes and Arapahos remained near that river. In late July 1820 journalist John Bell (who was accompanying Major Stephen Long toward the Rocky Mountains) met a mixed group of Indians, which included Cheyennes and Arapahos, along the upper Arkansas River drainage. A week later he encountered a small Cheyenne war party just west of what is now Garden City, Kansas. Before 1830 the western reaches of the Arkansas Valley had become a part of Cheyenne territory. Some Cheyennes, however, remained in their villages on the Missouri into the late 1830s. For a time their tactics and their alliances gave the Cheyennes and Arapahos dominance of the central Plains and its lucrative trade.

Under Yellow Wolf, the Hevhaitaneos (Hair Rope People) band went south to trade with the Bent brothers near the headwaters of the Arkansas River and its tributaries. Before long, the Oivimana ("scabby") band joined them, as well as the Siouan-affiliated Wotapios, who were already present as an outlaw band. They were attracted by the possibilities of the horse trade. William Bent married a daughter of the Arrow Keeper White Thunder about 1835. Bent's Fort in eastern Colorado on the Purgatory River became a focal point for Indian trade on the southern Plains from its initial construction in 1832 until its destruction at the hands of Cheyennes and Arapahos in 1849. The Tsistsistas group called the Heviksnipahis remained in the north between the forks of the Platte River.

About 1826 the Cheyennes and Arapahos began warfare with the Kiowas and Comanches. Following a climactic battle at Wolf Creek in 1838, all sides concluded a famous peace two years later. After that date, however, the Cheyenne Dog Soldiers (Hotamhetaneo) became increasingly militant in the face of ongoing white encroachments, formed separate bands, and ultimately considered themselves a separate nation. They led attacks against the expanding Kansas frontier and U.S. military presence. Some of the Cheyennes entered into treaties with the United States during this period. Members of some Cheyenne groups signed the tribe's friendship treaty with General Henry Atkinson in 1825 in Wyoming. The agreement focused on trade. The influential 1851 treaty at Fort Laramie officially recognized two divisions of the Cheyennes and Arapahos. The document also established tribal territories and authorized U.S. penetration by way of military posts and roads. The United States concluded the Treaty of Fort Wise in 1861 as an attempt to provide a reservation in Colorado. Unfortunately, it became the site of the Sand Creek Massacre in 1864. The 1865 Treaty of the Little Arkansas apologized for the slaughter and pledged compensation. Chief Black Kettle addressed the council and advocated peace. Because the Anglo-American frontier clashed on the central Plains with Cheyenne and Arapaho claims to the same region, the Indians engaged in repeated conflict with U.S. forces. Among the more notable are the Sand Creek Massacre; the annihilation of Captain William Fetterman's troops (1866); the 1868 battle of the Washita, where Black Kettle died; the 1869 battle at Summit Springs; and the famous pursuit of Cheyennes returning from Indian Territory toward Montana in 1878.

Nineteenth-century reformer Helen Hunt Jackson called Sand Creek among the most atrocious acts in all of U.S. history. In the aftermath of the fighting at Summit Springs in Colorado, a U.S. trooper picked up a ledger book from the battlefield. To his amazement, it was filled with colored drawings, called ledger art, depicting Cheyenne life. The ledger book ended up in the Colorado Historical Society and was published in 1999.

Incursions along the Bozeman Trail and gold miners entering the Black Hills further fed Northern Cheyenne animosities. Cheyenne warriors participated in the destruction of George A. Custer's regiment in 1876. U.S. retaliation forced Northern Cheyenne removal to Indian Territory (1877). In the 1879 aftermath of the escape of Little Wolf, Morning Star, and Dull Knife's bands and the massacre of a portion of Dull Knife's band, however, they were returned to Montana in the early 1880s. Some ten thousand U.S. troops chased the bands of men, women, and children, who twice broke out of their confinement. Some others found refuge among the Sioux. This formally separated the Cheyennes, although the split was not agreed to until an 1895 council.

Under the terms of the 1867 Medicine Lodge Treaty, the Cheyennes accepted a reduced reservation in western Oklahoma. President Ulysses S. Grant assigned them their own reservation on an executive-order reserve in 1869. The reservation period began in 1868 for the Southern Cheyennes and in 1880 for the Northern Cheyennes. Tragedy and struggle marked Cheyenne adaptation to reservation life. The 2,151 Cheyennes were among the first reserve tribes in Indian Territory to experience allotment in severalty following the Jerome Commission negotiations in 1890 at the Darlington Agency. Commissioners simply forged signatures and added names at will to secure the agreement. Indians lost most of their allotted land in the immediate aftermath. Three million acres passed from Indian control to non-Indian ownership. Robert Nespor and Donald Berthrong have demonstrated that—despite the claim that allotment would help to produce Cheyenne farmers—in reality it destroyed and undercut Cheyenne farming and ranching and tore the land base from them. The Indians' experiences with allotment poisoned the process and hardened the attitudes of subsequent negotiations with tribes.

John Moore studied settlement patterns. Under allotment selections the Dog Soldiers of Little Robe and the Kit Foxes settled along the North Canadian River in the northern portion of the Cheyenne Reservation, between the contemporary communities of Seiling and Longdale. Bowstring Society families made their camps in the Deer Creek and Watonga vicinity, while those of the Elk Society resided in the area of what is now

Clinton. The Red Moon/White Shield band lived in the Hammon region, while the Siouan-affiliated Masikotas lived near Fonda. Heviksnipahis, Omisis, and Oktogonas took their allotments north of Watonga. Whirlwind's band of Hevhaitaneos settled near the family members of George Bent along the North Canadian River west of Watonga.

The U.S. Army clamped down on Indians who rebelled in 1874–75 and exiled thirty-four of the alleged participants to imprisonment at old Fort Marion in St. Augustine, Florida. Some of the prisoners returned after their education in the East. Among them was David Pendleton, a deacon in the Episcopal Church, who served his people for nearly a half-century in western Oklahoma. As a prisoner called Making Medicine, he created ledger drawings that helped set the stage for contemporary Plains Indian painting. Roman Nose returned from Fort Marion, Hampton Institute, and Carlisle Indian School to aid his people.

Missionaries also came to the reservation. Quakers set up a school in 1876, while Mennonites arrived in 1882 and established their own school. Roman Catholics worked in the northern part of the reservation, with Mennonites in the south. John Seger, a Quaker, began a colony of Cheyenne and Arapaho farmers (1886) on Cobb Creek in the southern part of the reservation. He set up an Indian school in 1892, and a Dutch Reformed Mission began there in 1895. The Seger colony became today's community of Colony. Other schools included Darlington, Hammon, Red Moon, Concho, and Canton. Presbyterian missionary Walter Roe and his wife, along with the humanitarian reform group that met annually in upstate New York at Lake Mohonk, sponsored the Indian Industries League, which fostered traditional crafts in an effort to encourage assimilation of Cheyenne women into the Anglo-American marketplace. Ironically, it encouraged the continuation of women's traditional guilds within tribal society and helped Indian culture survive. Just before allotment, a Southern Cheyenne delegation visited Wovoka and returned in 1889 with word about the Ghost Dance. Followers dwindled after 1891. Some Cheyennes took up the practices of Peyote. Two Cheyennes were among the original incorporators of the Native American Church in 1918 at El Reno. Southern Cheyennes introduced it to their northern kin, as well as the Yuchis, Shawnees, Creeks of Oklahoma, and Taos Pueblo members in New Mexico.

Throughout the early twentieth century the BIA manipulated Cheyenne and Arapaho groups and exploited divisions and families to keep chiefs and their bands in turmoil, weakening tribal resolve. Various New Deal projects, however, encouraged revived tribal arts and tribal organization. Military service and war industries' work took some tribal members to cities, where relatives joined them for urban jobs in the postwar period. These migrations helped break up extended family camps where the Cheyennes had resided after allotment. Wartime service led to the revival of tribal military societies as well as the start of veterans' and War Mothers' groups.

In 1928 a General Council began. Elections were held according to voting districts, which roughly corresponded in the 1930s to district communities. Each district elected a representative to a joint business committee with eight members (later fourteen members), evenly divided between the two tribes.

Patrick Spotted Wolf (foreground) and Robert Woods, Sr. (background) in headdress during the procession for the installation of the president of the Cheyenne-Arapaho Tribal College, 2008

Courtesy Robert Woods and Patrick Spotted Wolf

Before the 1970s, when mechanization came, Cheyenne men found work as agricultural laborers. Cheyenne women continued to make beadwork items for sale to tourists, first along U.S. Route 66 (which passed through their reservation) and later in shops along Interstate 40 (south of the reservation boundary). Leasing of ranchland brought in some income. Some people earned royalties from oil and gas production, while others found jobs in neighboring cities and towns. Tribal men worked during the summertime in the national forests of the nation as firefighters (called "hot shots"). A settlement with the federal government of a claim for land illegally taken in Colorado, in violation of the Treaty of Fort Laramie, enabled some of the Red Moon band in the community of Hammon to move from their tents into town homes in 1968.

In a 1980 court decision (*Cheyenne & Arapaho Tribes v. Oklahoma*), the legal system recognized the right of Cheyenne and Arapaho tribal members to hunt and fish within the boundary of their former reservation without interference from the regulations of state wildlife authorities.

There have been concerted efforts at reconciliation for past wrongs.

Cheyenne descendants of victims of the Sand Creek Massacre in 1864 point to the terms of the 1865 Treaty of the Little Arkansas pledging redress for losses. Cheyennes have been involved in memorial ceremonies held for the victims of the Sand Creek and Washita tragedies. Indian people have been actively involved in repatriating human remains seized in the aftermath of both historical events. Cheyennes participated in a reconciliation ceremony with family descendants of Catherine German in 1990. She had been taken captive during raids in September 1874 and her parents and many of her siblings killed along the Smoky Hill River in northwestern Kansas. She and a sister were rescued in November of the same year when U.S. troops surprised Gray Beard's camp in the battle of McClellan Creek in Texas.

The Cheyennes today celebrate their cosmology and continue to maintain their traditions. The Sacred Arrows are usually renewed annually and the Sun Dance (the Life Generator Lodge) is held each year at two locations in Oklahoma and two in Montana. The conduct of the Sun Dance today replicates the description of the ceremony in George Dorsey's 1905 account. Some make pilgrimages to Bear Butte to offer prayers. Northern and Southern Cheyennes participate in each others' ceremonies, enriching the pool of knowledge. Additionally, most

Cheyenne artist Nathan Hart
Photograph by Kimberly Rodriguez

tribal members take part in a variety of spiritual practices, ranging from Sun Dances to sweat lodges to Peyote to Christian church services. Many also attend one or more of the frequent powwows with giveaways held during the summertime dance season, including the Cheyenne-Arapaho Labor Day Powwow at Colony. The Oklahoma Cheyennes and the Montana Cheyennes share ownership of land on different sides of Bear Butte in South Dakota for religious usage. Both are vitally concerned about ongoing non-Indian encroachments on the site. The Oklahoma Cheyennes also own land in Colorado surrounding the Sand Creek Massacre site. The Council of Forty-four Chiefs continues to meet, separate from the tribal government political structure. Intermarriage increases the ties linking the northern and southern groups. The Cheyennes now refer to themselves as one Cheyenne Nation, without the designation "Northern" or "Southern." Ceremonies in Montana are not performed until the Arrow Renewal has been accomplished in Oklahoma.

Among notable Cheyennes were numerous nineteenth-century chiefs such as Roman Nose, Black Kettle, Making Medicine, and others. Dick West, who was born at the Darlington Agency, went on to head the school of art at Bacone College for years and influenced countless Native artisans. One of his children, the attorney W. Richard West, was the founding head of the National Museum of the American Indian, situated on the Mall in the nation's capital. John Levi was an All-American football player at Haskell in the 1920s and served as a mentor to Jim Thorpe. Henrietta Whiteman Mann headed the Native American Studies Department at the University of Montana. In the late 1970s she led the national lobbying effort on behalf of Indian religious freedom that resulted in the enactment of the American Indian Religious Freedom Amendment. In 2006 she returned to Oklahoma to become the founding president of the Cheyenne/Arapaho Tribal College. The Reverend Lawrence Hart is a Mennonite minister as well as a member of the Council of Forty-four. He served on the repatriation oversight committee for the Smithsonian Institution. Cheyenne deacon David Pendleton was made a saint in the Episcopal Church in 1985. Independent filmmaker Chris Eyre directed *Smoke Signals*, *Edge of America*, and *A Thousand Roads*, which is shown to visitors to the National Museum of the American Indian in Washington, D.C. Artists include Archie Blackowl, Benjamin Buffalo, Merlin Littlethunder, Alfred Whiteman, Jr., Randy Lee White, Nathan Hart, Gordon Yellowman, brothers Charley Pratt and Harvey Pratt, and Edgar Heap of Birds.

SUGGESTED READING

Berthrong, Donald J. *The Cheyenne and Arapaho Ordeal.* Norman: University of Oklahoma Press, 1976.

———. *The Southern Cheyennes.* Norman: University of Oklahoma Press, 1963.

Chalfant, William Y. *Cheyennes and Horse Soldiers: The 1857 Expedition and the Battle of Solomon's Fork.* Norman: University of Oklahoma Press, 2002.

Cheyenne Dog Soldiers: A Courageous Warrior History. Niwot: University Press of Colorado, 1999 (CD-ROM to accompany Jean Afton et al., *Cheyenne Dog Soldiers: A Ledgerbook History of Coups and Combat*).

Fowler, Loretta. *Tribal Sovereignty and the Historical Imagination: Cheyenne-Arapaho Politics*. Lincoln: University of Nebraska Press, 2002.

Giglio, Virginia. *Southern Cheyenne Women's Songs*. Norman: University of Oklahoma Press, 1994.

Grinnell, George B. *The Fighting Cheyennes*. Norman: University of Oklahoma Press, 1956.

Halas, David Fridtjof, and Andrew E. Masich. *Halfbreed: The Remarkable True Story of George Bent Caught between the Worlds of the Indian and the White Man*. Cambridge, Mass.: Da Capo, 2004.

Hardoff, Richard G. *Washita Memories: Eyewitness Views of Custer's Attack on Black Kettle's Village*. Norman: University of Oklahoma Press, 2006.

Hatch, Thom. *Black Kettle: The Cheyenne Chief Who Sought Peace But Found War*. Hoboken, N.J.: John Wiley, 2004.

Hoig, Stan. *People of the Sacred Arrow: The Southern Cheyenne Today*. New York: Cobblehill Dutton, 1992; repr. Norman: Levite of Apache Publishers, 1993.

Mann, Henrietta. *Cheyenne-Arapaho Education, 1871–1982*. Niwot: University Press of Colorado, 1997.

Moore, John H. *The Cheyenne Nation*. Lincoln: University of Nebraska Press, 1987.

———. *The Cheyennes*. Cambridge, Mass.: Blackwell, 1996 (includes Nespor citation).

Schlesier, Karl H. *The Wolves of Heaven: Cheyenne Shamans, Ceremonies, and Prehistoric Origins*. Norman: University of Oklahoma Press, 1987; repr. 1993 (includes discussion of Dorsey, Neuman, Ossenberg, Reeves, Syms, Tuck, and Wright).

Siebert, Frank. "The Original Home of the Proto-Algonquian People." In *Contributions to Anthropology: Linguistics I (Algonquian)*, 13–47. Ottawa: National Museum of Canada, 1967.

Sonneborn, Liz. *Cheyenne Indians.* New York: Chelsea House, 1991 (for young readers).

Chickasaw

NAME

Historically the Chickasaws' name for themselves was Chikasha or Cikassa, "he who walks ahead." The word was anglicized as "Chickasaw." The popular translation is "the People." Southeastern tales portray the Chickasaws as "the people of one fire." They are considered kin of the Choctaws.

LOCATION AND GOVERNMENT

The "Chickasaw Nation" headquarters is in Ada, in Pontotoc County, in south-central Oklahoma. (Before 1997 it was in Sulphur, Oklahoma.) The Chickasaw Nation is not organized under the OIWA but operates under a constitution adopted in 1979 and revised and approved by tribal voters and the BIA in 1983 and again in 1988. A governor, lieutenant governor, and a thirteen-member tribal legislature as well as a judiciary form the government. Elections are held every four years for officers and every three years for legislative members. The tribal website is www.chickasaw.net.

BUSINESSES

The Chickasaw Nation has been in the forefront of economic development among tribes. The nation operates about ninety businesses. Major revenue comes from eighteen casinos and gaming centers: Thackerville's WinStar World Casinos (at winstarcasinos.com), one of the largest in the state, with over 500,000 square feet of gaming area, includes a restaurant, gift shop, theater, golf course, and hotel. The tribe funded the revamping of the exit on Interstate 35 and widening of the roadway to the casino just north of the Red River and the Texas border. The Lazer Zone Family Fun Center, an entertainment center, is located southwest of Ada. Near it is the Travel Plaza, which includes a trading post and smoke shop as well as a gaming center. The Texoma Gaming Center is two miles east of Kingston near Lake Texoma. Other gaming centers are located in Ardmore, Duncan, Newcastle, Paoli (with the Washita Gaming Center, fuel stop, and convenience store), Davis (the Treasure Valley Casino Conference Center), Madill, Marlow (the Chisholm Trail Casino), and Goldsby (the Riverwind Casino just south of Norman, with 219,000 square feet). In 1972 the tribe purchased the Chickasaw Motor Inn in Sulphur and replaced it with its Artesian Hotel, which is adjacent to the Chickasaw National Recreation Area (the former Platt National Park). The tribe owns two other motels. Two trading posts associated with fuel stops and convenience stores are located in Davis and Ada. The nation also operates seven travel plazas along major highways as well as seven tobacco stores. The magisterial Chickasaw Cultural Center sits adjacent to the Chickasaw National Recreation Area near Sulphur. Reconstructed historical structures are found on their Kullihoma Reservation east of Ada.

In 2000 the tribe bought the Bedré Chocolate Factory in Pauls Valley, which sells premier chocolates globally through mail order. Chickasaw Nation members are involved in agricultural and ranching activities on the tribal cattle ranch near Davis. The Chickasaw and Choctaw nations jointly own forest lands, supervised by the BIA. There is some income from oil and gas production leased on tribal land. The tribe has a manufacturing arm that produces horse and stock trailers, a construction company, a computer company that provides information services, and two radio stations. In 2002 the nation started Bank2, with its headquarters in Oklahoma City. The tribe retains just under 3,000 acres in federal trust. About 74,000 acres are held in individual allotments. The nation pioneered in offering its members low-down-payment home mortgages throughout the United States. These economic enterprises have brought the Chickasaw Nation unprecedented financial growth. Its net revenues from gaming in 2006 tripled those from three years earlier. In 2003 the nation contributed over $1.5 million to the region's public schools and universities.

NUMBER

The Chickasaw Nation has 40,000 members, largely concentrated within the thirteen-county area of about 7,650 square miles across south-central Oklahoma that constituted their nineteenth-century reservation. The Chickasaws are the thirteenth largest tribe in the United States. Tribal members are scattered worldwide as a result of family ties, jobs, and military service.

Linguistics provides some information on Chickasaw origins. The Chickasaws and the Choctaws speak a language called Western Muskoghean. They are connected through language to Muscogee/Creeks and other Muskoghean speakers. Written Chickasaw and Choctaw are identical, although there are marked phonological and dialectical differences for the spoken languages. Because of their variations, linguists consider them separate languages. Their close language affinity implies a common origin for the Chickasaws and Choctaws.

The archeological record is unclear about specific Chickasaw origins because of the lengthy passage of time. The Moundville paramount chiefdom (A.D. 1300–1450) spread its influence across the Southeast. As it collapsed its population migrated to new locales. During the fifteenth century Proto-Chickasaws moved out of the Tombigbee Valley into the black prairie rolling hills of what is now eastern Mississippi. They occupied the uplands in the vicinity of the upper Yazoo and Pearl rivers. Other remnant peoples later left collapsed chiefdoms or fled European conflicts to join the Chickasaws. The refugees included the Chakchiumas, Natchez, and others. John Swanton and Arrell Gibson placed the original Chickasaw Old Fields in Madison County, Alabama, near the Tennessee River.

Chickasaw legend tells that long ago Ababinilli, the Creator, directed elders to leave their land in the West for a lengthy migration in which the people followed a sacred pole, which they set upright each night. It leaned eastward daily. When the pole no longer tilted, just after they had crossed the raging current of a mighty river in their rafts, they remained in that location. Later a raven delivered an ear of corn, which Ababinilli told them to plant in this new homeland. Leaders split the people into two tribal groups. The Chactas (Choctaws) moved south and west and the Chiksas (Chickasaws) remained in the north and east.

The Chickasaws resided in towns. Matrilineal groups dominated civil affairs. Women tended common fields of corn, beans, and squash and also gathered berries and nuts. Men hunted abundant game (such as deer) and fished. Chickasaw towns were fortified and protected by a palisade. Each town also had a council house, a ceremonial plaza, and a ball ground. Summer dwellings were open-sided arbors; winter homes were wattle-and-daub structures. Each group had an elder's council that guided civil affairs of the village. Each clan had a chief (*minko*). Chickasaw villages formed a loose confederation with a national council. The tribe was divided into two major groups, the Impsaktcas, who provided the principal chief, and the Intcukwalipas.

Ababinilli oversaw the Chickasaw universe. The Creator made the

Chickasaws out of dust. The sun represented supreme power, and each town tended a sacred fire as a symbol of the sun. Pashofa dances were healing ceremonies held for those who were ill. Annual Green Corn Ceremonies in the town plazas renewed their world. There was a dual division into red/war and white/peace. Men and women played stickball as an athletic contest (men used sticks and women used their hands). Hottuck Ishtohoollo were good spirits, while Hottuk Ookproose were bad spirits. Two holy men (*hopoye*) directed religious rituals. Early ethnographer-trader James Adair described in detail a Chickasaw town he visited near what is now Tupelo, Mississippi.

Spanish explorers under Hernando de Soto found the Chickasaws in what the Spaniards called the province of Chicaza in the Tombigbee highlands, now the northern part of Mississippi. It would remain their homeland into the nineteenth century. Soto's expedition wintered in a Chickasaw town near today's Morgan's Ferry on the Tombigbee River from late 1540 into early 1541. As the Spaniards prepared to depart from Chickasaw territory, those Indians attacked. The Europeans repulsed the assaults then left the area.

Ethnographers still debate the ultimate impact of the Spaniards upon the Chickasaws. Charles Hudson argued that the devastation resulting from the Spanish expeditions collapsed the Native population and led directly to the formation of the Chickasaw Tribe. Others like Jay Johnson saw tribal formation prior to the presence of Europeans in the transition from riverine mound-building to dispersed upland residence for the tribe. Johnson interpreted the Spanish chroniclers' descriptions of the Indian province of Chicaza as referring to the upland prairie Chickasaws.

Their geographic location made the Chickasaws pivotal players in any European power conflict. Although numbering only about six thousand, the Chickasaws influenced traffic up and down the Mississippi River between Canada and New Orleans. The struggle to control the Lower Mississippi River Valley would repeatedly embroil them in imperial activities. A century and a half elapsed after Soto's departure before other Europeans made serious contact with the Chickasaws. In 1673 Jacques Marquette and Louis Joliet traveled down the Mississippi. Nine years later more French from Canada sailed down the river under La Salle. The Frenchmen erected a stockade post on the western edge of Chickasaw territory. To thwart feared English designs on the region, France set up settlements along the Gulf Coast after 1699. But British traders had already come westward. In 1698 Thomas Welch and Anthony Dodsworth had led pack trains of European goods that dazzled the Chickasaws. Chickasaw trade with Britain through the following years infuriated the Catholic French. The Chickasaws became increasingly dependent upon European trade items such as guns, knives, and metal cooking pots. They aligned with the Protestant English.

Conflict with the French and their Indian allies over territory, power, and the Indian slave trade exploded in 1720 in open warfare between the Chickasaws and the French. After an interlude of peace, the Chickasaws persuaded the Natchez to join hostilities against the French in 1729. That turned European fury against the Natchez, who were defeated and became refugees among the Chickasaws. The French decided to punish the inhabitants of two Natchez villages located among the Chickasaws. The French column came upon the Chickasaw peace chief Imayatabee le Borgne's home, the town of Ackia. The battle took place around a hill that is now the location of the high school in Tupelo, Mississippi. Because of the Chickasaws' decisive victory over the French in 1736, some historians credit them with making the United States an English-speaking nation. Chickasaw hostility, they pointed out, prevented the French from consolidating their Great Lakes domain with their base along the Gulf Coast. Of course, the French loss was cemented at the conclusion of the French and Indian War. Chickasaw enmity and raiding against the French and their Indian allies continued throughout that war, which concluded in 1763. The negotiations ending that struggle ceded control of much of the continent to the British, but France relinquished possession of the Mississippi Valley to Spain.

While a few Chickasaws were tied to the French, most of them sided with the English in Pontiac's Rebellion and during the American Revolution. Although unsuccessful, the Chickasaw siege of George Rogers Clark's Fort Jefferson near the confluence of the Ohio and the Mississippi rivers in 1781 led to the fort's abandonment the following year. James Colbert led British partisans and Chickasaw warriors in the final engagement of the war on American soil when he unsuccessfully attacked a Quapaw and Spanish force at Arkansas Post on the other side of the river from Chickasaw home territory. American victory in the Revolutionary War in 1783 presented new challenges to the Chickasaws. The choices split the tribe. Piomingo favored the Americans, while Wolf's Friend maintained ties with the Spaniards. Payamataha advocated peace with both. Some Chickasaws signed a treaty with Spain at Mobile in 1784. Piomingo signed the Treaty of Hopewell two years later in Virginia with the Americans. Some Chickasaws fought on the side of the Americans at the battle of Fallen Timbers. Many Chickasaws were unsure about their future because of the absence of their old ally, Britain. Mixed-blood Chickasaw families vied to assert their commercial success and to seize tribal political power.

The new American Republic sought Indian concessions. After a congressional act in 1796 authorizing trading posts (called factories) in Indian Country, the first was set up at Chickasaw Bluffs at present-day Memphis (1802). Between 1801 and 1818 the United States obtained a series of Chickasaw land cessions totaling almost 20 million acres. Many of the appropriated payments for land went to pay the Indians' indebtedness at the government trading posts. A small number of Chickasaws moved west of the Mississippi River around 1800. After 1801 the Natchez Trace connected what would become Vicksburg to Nashville and opened the door to an influx of white settlers and commercial activity. Sixteen years later Mississippi became a state, and neighboring Alabama joined the Union two years afterward.

Presbyterian Joseph Bullen became the first missionary to the Chickasaws in 1779 and again in 1800–1803. Near the home of Levi Colbert at Cotton Gin Port in Monroe County, Mississippi, Robert Bell of the Cumberland Presbyterian Church in 1820 set up Charity Hall School for the Chickasaws. In 1821 David Humphries and Thomas Stuart started Monroe School near Pontotoc. Before the removal era the Chickasaws had taken on many Euroamerican socioeconomic traits. They were heavily acculturated, leading to their designation as one the "Five Civilized Tribes."

Litigation over control of the so-called Yazoo fraudulent land claims would shape later federal-Indian law in the United States. Yazoo companies illegally claimed a vast expanse of land through Chickasaw territory and bribed legislators for approval. The new nation's highest court under Chief Justice John Marshall in *Fletcher* v. *Peck* (1810) upheld Alexander Hamilton's sanctity of contract in spite of clear corruption and stated that the "exclusive right to purchase [land] from the Indians resided in the [federal] government" without state interference, foreshadowing pronouncements in the Cherokee cases two decades later.

The Chickasaws were the last of the Five Tribes to be removed from the Southeast to Indian Territory. State pressure and federal insistence precipitated repeated negotiations for cession of the Chickasaw homeland. In 1830 Congress passed the Indian Removal Act, and the state of Mississippi enacted laws abolishing the Chickasaw tribal government and opening their land to squatters. President Andrew Jackson personally attended the August 1830 treaty negotiations at Franklin, Tennessee, along with John Eaton and John Coffee for the United States. The resulting treaty exchanged Chickasaw land in Mississippi for a tract west of the Mississippi River. A new treaty a year later at Pontotoc reaffirmed the tribe's emigration. Amendments three years later corrected some glaring shortcomings in the 1831 agreement.

Finally, at the invitation of the Choctaws, the Chickasaws prepared to move. Through the terms of the Treaty of Doaksville in 1837 in the Choctaw Nation, the Chickasaws agreed to settle amid the Choctaws in Indian Territory and to pay $530,000 to the Choctaws for a portion of the new land. Approximately 4,900 Chickasaws with 1,100 slaves trekked to Indian Territory and settled within the Choctaw Nation between the Canadian and Red rivers. Most of the Chickasaws emigrated in 1837–38, but others straggled into Indian Territory up to 1850. Complaints of scandals and maltreatment led to an investigation by Major Ethan Allen Hitchcock, which revealed flagrant frauds in subsistence contracts. (The secretary of war, J. C. Spencer, "lost" the report; Congress investigated on its own a decade later and was scandalized. A claims suit ultimately paid the Chickasaws a paltry $240,000 in 1887.)

Removal dispersed the Chickasaws in five widely scattered emigrant camps. Wealthier mixed-blood families settled in the river valleys. The Chickasaws had gradually resumed the routine of their lives by the 1850s. Archeological evidence from postremoval campsites revealed that the Chickasaws relied more on Native-made pottery and on cattle for their meat, in contrast to the Choctaws, who utilized Euroamerican china, hog meat, and wild game. The Chickasaws historically relied more on hunting and less on agriculture than neighboring tribes. In spite of being taken under the wing by the Choctaws, the Chickasaws chafed at being only one of four districts within the larger Choctaw Nation structure. In 1855 the two tribes separated through a treaty. In 1856 the Chickasaws formed their own government, with Tishomingo (formerly Good Spring) as their capital, including their own constitution and three government branches. Cyrus Harris, a planter born in Mississippi, served as the first Chickasaw governor in their new homeland.

The Chickasaws set about restoring their ancient glory. Chickasaw academies advanced educational achievement. Just east of Tishomingo the tribe opened its first school, Chickasaw Manual Labor Academy, in 1851. (The renamed Chickasaw Male Academy was popularly called Harley Institute by the 1890s to commemorate a beloved teacher and administrator.) Others followed. The expansive Bloomfield Academy opened in 1853 near Achille in Bryan County. It became a female seminary in 1876. In 1917, after a fire, the school was moved to Ardmore and reopened in Carter County. It was named Carter Seminary (1934) in honor of Chickasaw politician Charles D. Carter, whose mother was a sister of the Chickasaw Nation's governor, William M. Guy. Carter served as a U.S. congressman from 1907 to 1927. The Chickasaw Nation took over Carter Seminary in 1984 and continues to operate it after relocating it to Kingston as the Chickasaw Children's Village. The changed name reflects the twentieth century's different approach to education in contrast to the nineteenth century's emphasis on manual labor. The University of Science and Arts of Oklahoma is located in the city of Chickasha on a donated portion of the Chickasaw allotment of Nellie Sparks.

At the start of the Civil War the Chickasaws allied with the Confederacy. The Choctaw/Chickasaw Mounted Regiment out of Fort Washita served with distinction and fought some of the last battles of the war. Chickasaw governor Winchester Colbert was the last Confederate Indian leader to surrender (on July 14, 1865). The Chickasaws were the final Confederate entity to surrender, concluding the Civil War. In April of the following year the Chickasaws and Choctaws signed a Reconstruction treaty with the United States, which freed the Indians' slaves. The terms included the cession of the Leased District to the United States, which wanted to relocate Plains Indian tribes to the region, and permission to establish rail lines. Two major railroads served the Chickasaw region by the 1880s, bringing non-Indian population and creating demands to "open" more Indian lands. The town of Ardmore sprang up in 1880. It became an oil boomtown before World War I. The creation of Oklahoma Territory out of the western half of Indian Territory in 1890 had further increased the number of non-Indians in the area.

Bloomfield Academy, near Achilee, Oklahoma, in 1908

Chickasaw Council House Collection, Research Division of the Oklahoma Historical Society, #20288.75.39.54

The 1897 Atoka Agreement involving the Chickasaws was rejected by tribal voters. The document was resubmitted in the Curtis Act a year later and supplemented in 1902, instituting allotment among the Chickasaws. The ravages of allotment dominated the twentieth century for the Chickasaw Nation. The total of 4,707,904 acres of the tribal domain was allotted to 10,944 citizens of the tribe (including 6,337 Indians by blood and

4,607 freedmen) between 1902 and 1910. Indians got 320 acres, freedmen 40 acres. The U.S. Supreme Court ruled in 1904 (*Chickasaw Freedmen* v. *Chickasaw Nation*) that freedmen had no rights to Chickasaw allotted lands because they had never been made citizens of the Chickasaw Nation. Unbridled exploitation and rapaciousness led to the transfer of land ownership to whites in subsequent years. By the 1920s a mere 300 acres remained in tribal control. The tribe struggled to survive under federal bureaucratic imperialism for almost seventy years afterward.

Old Chickasaw Capitol in Tishomingo
Author's photograph

Under the allotment agreements, the United States sold Chickasaw timberland just before World War I and sold coal and asphalt reserves just after the war. The proceeds of over $19 million were to be distributed to enrollees under the terms of the Atoka Agreement. Fraudulent claimants anticipating a share in the windfall rushed to cash in on the deal. Vigorous Chickasaw opposition in the court system prevented nearly 4,000 claimants from plundering the tribal trust fund. Legitimate enrollees between 1916 and 1925 received about $1,075 each.

During the 1930s, while the tribe bypassed the OIWA, some Indians formed county credit associations in the hopes of furthering their local economies. Some started or expanded farming or poultry operations, while others received aid during the 1936 drought. Tribal members met periodically to continue their tribal political traditions, especially in Seeley Chapel near Connerville before World War II. Chickasaw leadership launched claims litigation in the 1920s that would ultimately yield awards. Congress appropriated $8.5 million in 1949 as compensation for coal and asphalt land then an additional $3.5 million for the tribal Indian Claims Commission award. The Leased District, jointly claimed by the Chickasaw and the Choctaw nations, yielded an Indian Claims Commission judgment (under Public Law 222 in 1924) of $902,000 in the 1950s, of which the Chickasaws received one-quarter. Most of the sums were distributed on a per capita basis. Other groups like the Chickasaw Treaty Rights Association sought to block state taxation (seizure) of allotted land and dilution of tribal rolls.

A grass-roots insistence on democratic forms of tribal government arose in the 1950s. One of its advocates was an educator and salesman named Overton James. The tribal administration created a series of initiatives, one of which was the establishment of the Chickasaw Advisory Council. It served as the forerunner of the Tribal Council. In the 1970s the tribe set up community councils for further improvement in local communication. The Chickasaw governor was instrumental in persuading the federal government to set up an Indian Housing Authority in Oklahoma and a specific one for the Chickasaws (1966).

In 1970 Public Law 91-495 permitted the Five Tribes to select their own leadership. The president of the United States had previously appointed the governor of the Chickasaw Nation. Overton James was appointed governor in 1963 then chosen by voters in the 1971 election. He retired in 1987 and was replaced by his lieutenant governor, Bill Anoatubby, who entered his sixth term in 2007. The growth of tribal budgets illustrated the rise of tribal activities. The annual tribal budget of $50,000 in 1963 had skyrocketed to over $15 million by 1990. Under tribal economic development, health, housing, and heritage initiatives, the Chickasaw Nation made significant strides. From two salaried tribal employees in 1971 employment rose to nearly eleven thousand in 2006. In 1994 the tribe became the first in the United States to negotiate a compact with the federal government to manage its own health care system. In 2005 the tribe announced plans to build a $135 million hospital facility south of Ada.

The tribe obtained a favorable decision in mid-1995 when the U.S. Supreme Court upheld Chickasaw exemption from the state excise taxation of tribal fuel sales. The justices hinted that the state should have levied a tax on the consumer (distributor), in a situation similar to tobacco sales taxation. At the end of 2002 congressional enactment of Public Law 107-331 concluded long-running litigation over claims to the oil resources beneath and ownership of the Arkansas River bed. The Chickasaws reaped a portion of the settlement.

The Chickasaw Nation has been involved in the repatriation and reburial of ancestral remains through their southeastern aboriginal homeland. Examples are the marble markers in Tupelo on the grounds of the North Mississippi Medical Center, which denote the 1997 unearthing and reinterment of remains from a portion of the late-seventeenth-century Chickasaw settlement of Tchoukafalaya (Longtown). A year later the state of Mississippi and the University of Mississippi returned burial objects to the tribe.

The Chickasaws also foster traditional songs. Their stomp dance group offered demonstrations throughout the United States as the Chickasaw

Nation Dance Troupe. The group formed in 1992 to foster tribal knowledge of ceremonial music, dance, and ball play. Former Chickasaw Nation cultural resources director Gary White Deer and others continue ceremonial songs at the cultural ground at Kullihoma, east of Ada. The tribe bought the land (1936) and later built historic structures on it. During the 1970s there was also a resurgence of interest in the stomp dance. It is concentrated in the Ardmore-Mannsville region as well as at Kullihoma. Since 1995 the annual Chi Kash Sha Reunion festival held at the site has brought tribal members and visitors together for an opportunity for a cultural re-

Actress and storyteller Te Ata
(Chickasaw)

*Mary Te Ata Thompson Collection,
Research Division of the Oklahoma
Historical Society, #4275*

naissance of traditional song, dance, and crafts. The annual Chickasaw Festival is held at the old Chickasaw Capitol in Tishomingo. It attracts large crowds for sports, heritage events, culture, rodeo, and other activities. The festival usually commences with leaders' speeches, invoking the tribal motto about the "unconquered and unconquerable" Chickasaw Nation. Favorite festival features are the Chickasaw foods like *pashofa* (their national dish of cracked corn and pork), *tuchie shafut puska* (gritted corn), and *tosher* (poke greens). The tribe sponsors language classes and cultural heritage courses in various communities.

Notable Chickasaws include members of the influential Colbert family, who engaged in business ventures as well as tribal politics. Intermarried white men wielded considerable power in early state politics. William H. Murray, wed to a niece of the Chickasaw governor Douglas Johnston, helped shape the single-statehood movement and form Oklahoma's constitution and then served as governor of the state, 1931–35. Lee Cruce, second governor of the state, was also an intermarried citizen. Johnston Murray, the state's fourteenth governor; Oklahoma Supreme Court Justice Earl Welch; and National Bar Association president William G. Paul were all of Chickasaw heritage. Tom Cole is the representative for the fourth district in the U.S. Congress. His late mother, Helen Cole, was also a politician. Attorney Natalie Landreth worked with the Native American Rights Fund. Neal McCaleb served as assistant secretary for American Indian Affairs for the Interior Department.

Lawyer Charles W. Blackwell in 1995 became the first Chickasaw Nation ambassador to the United States. Tribal member Olin Jones became the first head of the Office of Native American Affairs within the Department of Justice for the state of California in 2000.

Captain Otis Leader, a Chickasaw who was an enrolled Choctaw, was a hero during World War I in the second battle of the Marne, for his Sergeant York–like capture of German soldiers. His gallantry is commemorated with a statue in the U.S. Capitol. Raymond Harvey was awarded the Medal of Honor during the Korean War. Navy Lieutenant Commander John B. Herrington became the nation's first American Indian astronaut aboard the space shuttle *Endeavor* (2002).

Educators include famed University of Chicago historian John Hope Franklin (who is of Chickasaw freedman heritage) and professor Gary Sandefur, dean of the College of Letters and Science at the University of Wisconsin (Madison). Tom Love founded the regional chain of Love's Country Stores and fuel stops. Tommy Thompson, banker, headed the American Indian Cultural Center project in Oklahoma City. Physician James W. Hampton served as president of the American Indian Physicians Association.

Chickasaw member Euell Moore played baseball in the 1930s. Performers include famed storytellers Te Ata (Bearer of the Dawn, Mary Frances Thompson) and Ataloa (Little Song, Mary Stone McClendon), actor Dale Robertson, and singer Anita Bryant. Poet and novelist Linda Hogan, sculptor Clayburn Straughn, potter Joanne Underwood, painters Mike Larsen, Brent Greenwood (also Ponca), and Tom Phillips, and museum curator Towana Spivey are all of Chickasaw heritage. Harold Sheffer Tate and Jerod Tate are composers. Chad Burris is a film producer.

Left to right: Chickasaw leader Overton James, U.S. representative Carl Albert, BIA area director Virgil Harrington, commissioner of Indian affairs Robert Bennett, Choctaw chief Harry Belvin, and assistant U.S. surgeon general E. S. Rabeau, Tuskahoma, Oklahoma, 1967

E. N. Martel Collection, Research Division of the Oklahoma Historical Society, #11628

SUGGESTED READING

Adair, James. *The History of the American Indians* (originally published 1775). Edited by Samuel C. Williams. Johnson City, Tenn.: Watauga Press, 1930.

Atkinson, James R. *Splendid Land, Splendid People: The Chickasaw Indians to Removal.* Tuscaloosa: University of Alabama Press, 2004.

Baird, W. David. *The Chickasaw People.* Phoenix: Indian Tribal Series, 1974 (for young readers).

Cushman, Horatio B. *History of the Choctaw, Chickasaw, and Natchez Indians.* Greenville, Tex.: Headlight Printers, 1899; repr. in abridged ed. Stillwater: Redlands, 1962; repr. Norman: University of Oklahoma Press, 2001.

Fitzgerald, David, et al. *Chickasaw: Unconquered and Unconquerable.* Ada, Okla.: Chickasaw Nation, 2006.

Gibson, Arrell M. *The Chickasaws.* Norman: University of Oklahoma Press, 1971.

Hale, Duane K., and Arrell M. Gibson. *The Chickasaw.* New York: Chelsea House, 1991 (for young readers).

Hoyt, Anne Kelley. *Bibliography of the Chickasaw.* Metuchen, N.J.: Scarecrow, 1987.

Hudson, Charles. *The Southeastern Indians.* Knoxville: University of Tennessee Press, 1976; repr. 1992.

Johnson, Jay. "From Chiefdom to Tribe in Northeast Mississippi." In Patricia Galloway, ed., *The Hernando de Soto Expedition*, 295–312. Lincoln: University of Nebraska Press, 1997.

Littlefield, Daniel F., Jr. *The Chickasaw Freedmen: A People without a Country.* Westport, Conn.: Greenwood, 1980.

Nairne, Thomas. *Nairne's Muskhogean Journals: The 1708 Expedition to the Mississippi River.* Edited by Alexander Moore. Jackson: University Press of Mississippi, 2005.

Swanton, John R. *Chickasaw Society and Religion*. Lincoln: University of Nebraska Press, 2006 (first published in Bureau of American Ethnology Forty-fourth Annual Report, 1928).

Taliaferro, Velma Leftwich. *Memoirs of a Chickasaw Squaw*. Norman: Levite of Apache, 1987.

Choctaw

"Choctaw" may have derived from the Mvskoke/Creek word *cate*, "red." Another possibility is that the name came from the Spanish word *chato*, "flat" or "flat heads," because of the Choctaw custom of flattening infants' foreheads. Creek neighbors called the Choctaws "Chahta" in their own language. The Choctaws also call themselves "Chahta." The word is of unknown origin. The Choctaws are considered to be kin of the Chickasaws.

LOCATION AND GOVERNMENT

The headquarters for the "Choctaw Nation" is in Durant in Bryan County, in southeastern Oklahoma (about ninety miles north of the Dallas metroplex). Their traditional capital is Tuskahoma. Enactment of termination legislation (Public Law 86-192) in 1959 awakened successful Choctaw opposition to its implementation. Public Law 91-495 in October 1970 finally authorized the Choctaws to select their officers through popular election. The national government is ruled not under the OIWA but according to a constitution adopted in 1983. It revived their 1860 constitution with updated modifications. The Choctaws are guided by an elected twelve-member council with a chief. The tribal website is www.choctawnation.com.

BUSINESSES

Major revenue for tribal government is derived from thirteen gaming operations located in the communities of Broken Bow, Idabel, Pocola, McAlester, Stringtown, and Hugo (called the Grant Casino because it is near that community). The casino and hotel complex in Durant (108,000 square feet of gaming area at the Choctaw Casino Resort) offers a hotel, restaurant, conference center, gift shop, and more (at www.choctawcasinos.com). An entertainment complex with a mega-casino, coliseum, hotel, and rodeo arena is being developed on fifty acres along Highway 69 near the headquarters in Calera, south of Durant. The casino complex, less than two hours' travel from Dallas, includes two restaurants, a Chahta gift shop, and a Starbucks coffee shop. The nation invested $35 million to upgrade its Pocola gaming facility. Wagering is also offered at the tribe's Blue Ribbon Downs horse-racing track in Sallisaw. The Choctaws had one of the earliest tribal bingo halls. The tribe runs thirteen travel plazas, most of which serve traffic on interstate highways. It also maintains a large agricultural and livestock presence. About 5,000 acres are under agricultural lease.

Corporate manufacturing is located in industrial parks within the nation. Tribal businesses provide substance-abuse testing for employers. Tribal enterprises in Hugo, Atoka, and McAlester manufacture aeronautical and other metal parts. Through federal contracts the tribe supplies personnel and offers management expertise on military bases for the U.S. government worldwide. The Choctaw Management/Services Enterprise oversees those operations, which include electronic satellite medical transcription services. Modular homes are produced in facilities in Hugo, McAlester, Stigler, and Atoka for Choctaw Manufacturing Development Corporation. The tribe also owns a shopping mall purchased in 1990 in Idabel as well as restaurants, a motel, gift shops, and other businesses. Major tribal revenue derives from nongaming sources. About 130,000 acres under tribal control are mostly individually allotted lands. The tribe and individual allottees also own pine and hardwood forests.

NUMBER

With about 150,000 members, the Choctaw Nation of Oklahoma is the third largest tribe in the United States after the Cherokees and the Navajos. While its people are scattered throughout the world, they are concentrated in the ten and a half counties that formed their reservation in what is now southeastern Oklahoma. Those counties include McCurtain, Pittsburg, LeFlore, Pushmataha, and Choctaw.

Approximately 9,000 Choctaws in Mississippi are clustered in eight rural communities within the vicinity of the town of Philadelphia. The Mowa Band of Choctaws near Mount Vernon is recognized by the state of Alabama (1980) and the Louisiana Band of Choctaws is also state-recognized. About 200 members in the Jena Band of Choctaws in central Louisiana near the town of Jena were federally recognized in 1995. The Houmas of southeastern Louisiana are state-recognized. Of course, Choctaws have intermarried into a wide range of Indian tribes and other ethnic groups. Mestizo families married Choctaws of Louisiana during the eighteenth and nineteenth centuries to create the Choctaw-Apache of Ebarb communities in Sabine Parish.

The Choctaws speak a language that is directly related to the languages of other Muskhogean speakers in the southeastern United States. Choctaw and Chickasaw are called Western Muskhogean languages. Linguists estimate that Choctaw and Chickasaw broke away from the Muskhogean parent language stock about A.D. 800, when Europe was in the early Middle Ages.

There are many Choctaw origin stories. One tells of a great red man who descended from above. He made a sacred mountain out of the mud on a plain. The mountain was called Nanih Waiya. It is located northwest of Philadelphia, Mississippi, on the Pearl River near the town of Noxapter. When his creative work was completed, he called the "red people" from inside the hill. Archeological information revealed that the Proto-Choctaws occupied the fortified oblong mound after 500 B.C. Another Choctaw origin story told of two brothers, Chahtah and Chickasah, who fled enemies. During their flight they followed a leaning pole, crossed a great river, and camped on the banks of Yazoo River. The pole remained erect, indicating their final destination. The two brothers, however, quarreled and separated. One group, the Chahtahs (Choctaws) remained where they were. The pole directed the Chicasahs (Chickasaws) to the north, to northern Mississippi and western Tennessee.

A unique aspect of their culture was the existence of multiple groups termed phratries (the Choctaw word is *iksa*), which had genealogical, kinship, ethnic, and diplomatic implications for their members. The most widely known was the older division (the Inholahta, "beloved people"), which was in a junior relationship to the Alabamas, implying a long-standing connection. The other Choctaw moiety was the Imoklasha, "their people are there." Matrilineal kinship and the levels of social standing were ranked. Individuals could attain rank through great deeds as well.

Archeologists and ethnographers Patricia Galloway, Vernon Knight, Jr., and Christopher Peebles, as well as James Milligan, painted a diverse background to the formation of the historic Choctaws in the eighteenth century.

The core perhaps built the Nanih Waiya mound and resided in the region. Western upland prairie people, termed Plaquemine culture, joined others to form the Chickchiumas and Chickasaws. Some Choctaws came out of the east from the ancient Mississippian mound center called Moundville, the chiefdom in north-central Alabama, which fragmented when it collapsed after A.D. 1400. Survivors of Moundville Variant people journeyed to the Noxubee and Sucarnoochee valleys to become the Proto-Choctaws. Natchez-related peoples who were survivors of a chiefdom on the lower Pearl River came from the southwest and added to the Choctaw group.

Different districts developed among the Choctaws, reflecting geographic and cultural variations. Archeologists believe that the Moundville chiefdom culture collapsed and dispersed before the Europeans came. Survivors became the Burial Urn culture in the region then later moved southward and resided along the Tombigbee River. They made up the eastern group that helped form the Proto-Choctaws and were called Okla Tannap, "people over there from the other side." In the west lived various groups along the Pearl River and its northern headwaters, who were close to the neighboring Chickasaws and also contributed to the Choctaw confederacy. They were referred to as Okla Falaya, "people who were widely dispersed" (Long People). They shared the language of the Long People and were predecessors of the Imoklasha moiety. To the south were people originally also from west of the Mississippi River who now lived along the Pascagoula River and its tributaries. Some of them spoke a different dialect and came to be called Okla Hannali, "people of the Sixtowns." Mobile delta people came from the Gulf Coast to join the confederacy as well. After population loss and dislocations, the speech of the Long People of the north (which is also called the Okla Falaya or Large People) became the standard form of the spoken Choctaw language.

Choctaws resided in sedentary villages near streams. In the early 1800s they may have had as many as fifty towns. The women tended fields of corn, melons, pumpkins, and sunflowers and readily adopted cultivation of French-introduced vegetables later. They also tended livestock. Men hunted and served as warriors. Each Choctaw member belonged to the matrilineal kinship group called an *iksa* (this was the word for clan but is now used as the word for church). Elders of the clan regulated civil and religious affairs. When necessity arose, a district chief (*minko*) convened a national council to deliberate over important issues. Choctaws participated in a seasonal cycle of ceremonies. Their annual Green Corn rituals acknowledged the supremacy of the sun and the sacred fire. The ceremony preceded the corn harvest. Other community-wide dances recognized animal spirits, were offered to protect warriors, and preceded the ball game (called *ishtaboli*). Feasting formed an important part of these activities.

Spanish explorers found the historic Choctaws in the current states of Louisiana, Alabama, and Mississippi. War leader Tascalusa lured Hernando de Soto's Spaniards into an ambush. In 1540 his force punished Choctaw defenders of Maubila (near present-day Selma, Alabama) in an all-day battle, killing a large number of the Indians. The 3,000 casualties represented the greatest single-day loss in battle in America until the American Civil War. The victorious Spaniards remained while they recovered and reprovisioned. Soto himself was among the wounded. The European expedition left the burned-out town a month later. For a century and a half thereafter the Choctaws were largely left alone. The Choctaw Confederacy began to form during this period. Trade goods gradually filtered into the region from the increasing European presence along the coast, which slowly moved inland. The Choctaws left their early imprint on the landscape in several ways. The Appalachian eastern mountain chain, which the Choctaws named, in their language means "people who are allies."

The French dominated the lower Mississippi Valley due to their explorers' claims along the length of the river and settlements that extended along the Gulf Coast. They set up outposts at Mobile on the coast (1702), at New Orleans (1718) at the mouth of the Mississippi River, at Yazoo (1719) on that river, and elsewhere. Colonial conflicts fed Choctaw warfare against their rivals the Chickasaws. Brief periods of peace interrupted nearly constant warfare. The Choctaws liked French trade goods and presents given to mark their allegiance. After 1763, however, the Choctaws had to deal with the English, who dominated the region in the aftermath of the French and Indian War, in which many Choctaws had sided with the French. Choctaws divided their loyalties during the American Revolutionary War between the British and the Americans.

Some Choctaws fought with the Americans in the War of 1812. Choctaw chiefs expelled Tecumseh when he met with them in 1811 and exhorted the Choctaws to join him against the Americans. By the start of the 1800s the century of warfare with external and internal adversaries had reduced the Choctaw population. Intermarriage had begun to alter the old kinship system. Trade also helped change the nature of Choctaw society. The Choctaws were so heavily involved in trade that their language became the basis for the Mobilian trade jargon utilized along the Lower Mississippi River and into the Gulf Coast region.

Missionaries began their efforts with the arrival of French Jesuits in

1726, but they had little success at conversion. English-speaking missionaries followed in 1818–19. John Ficklin and Stuart Dupuy started their preaching in 1819. Thomas Stuart began his work in 1820–21, near Pontotoc, later founding Monroe Mission. He was assisted by Hugh Wilson, who began Tokshish Mission in 1823 then established another mission at Caney Creek. William Blair opened Martin Mission near Holly Springs. Methodists dispatched Alexander Deavers in 1821 and Alexander Tolley six years later. Baptists set up Choctaw Academy (1825). Churches and schools changed Choctaw culture: the Indians adopted a new way of life that favored private property. Elliott, located at Yello Busha in the western district near present Grenada, was the first school established (1818) by ABCFM missionary Cyrus Kingsbury (lovingly called Limping Wolf) for the Choctaws under the guidance of the Presbyterians. Kingsbury established Mayhew Mission in 1820 in the lower district west of today's Columbus, Mississippi. Nine years later he moved to Yok-nok-cha-ya to continue his fifty-year ministry. Mixed-blood David Folsom and intermarried member John Pitchlynn attended. Later Allen Wright was also a pupil. Cyrus Byington with the help of Alfred Wright published the first Choctaw-language book in 1825. Thirteen mission schools operated in Choctaw territory by that year, and over forty missionaries labored in the nation by 1828.

The changes within Choctaw society continued. In 1826 David Folsom, Greenwood LeFlore, and John Garland, all mixed-bloods, altered the Choctaw government. They unseated full-blood chiefs and adopted a written constitution. The Choctaw leaders signed nine treaties with the United States between 1786 and their removal. The nation was the first of the Five Tribes in the Southeast to sign a removal treaty with the United States and thus the first in that region to move to new land in what is now Oklahoma. Mississippi became a state in 1817, and Alabama entered the Union two years later. White settlement in Choctaw territory increased in both states. Pressure mounted on the Indians to remove. A few Choctaws like John and James Pitchlynn, as well as Edmond Folsom, agitated for emigration to a new land. U.S. negotiators Andrew Jackson and Thomas Hinds met reluctant Choctaws for discussions in October 1820 at Doaks Stand in central Mississippi on the Pearl River.

A treaty was signed after troubled negotiations, and the U.S. Congress quickly ratified it at the start of the following year. The Choctaws ceded 5 million acres on the western edge of their domain in exchange for 13 million acres in Arkansas Territory in the west. The United States had purchased the region two years earlier from the Quapaws. This was not a removal document: it permitted white settlers to enter the region and rapidly fill the upper Pearl drainage area. Their presence fed further demands for Indian lands. James Monroe's first major statement of a removal policy arose out of negotiations for an additional cession from the Choctaws in early 1825. Federal authorities used treaty terms to pressure the Choctaws to remove. Some Choctaws had moved before and during the 1820s. By the end of that decade a small but thriving Choctaw settlement called Skullyville existed near present-day Fort Smith, Arkansas. A Choctaw Agency was officially set up in the area in 1827. But demands for complete expulsion of the Indians increased.

Mississippi enacted laws in 1829 extending state jurisdiction over the Choctaws and early the following year abolished the tribal government, making the Choctaws citizens of the state. The U.S. government sent negotiators John Eaton, secretary of state for President Jackson, and Colonel John Coffee to obtain a new treaty with the Choctaws. In September 1830 they met with about 6,000 Choctaws under Moshulatubbee, Nitakechi, and Greenwood LeFlore between two tributaries of Dancing Rabbit Creek (Chunkfiahihlabok) in what is now Noxubee County near Macon in eastern Mississippi. With the help of LeFlore, an advocate of emigration, a removal treaty was signed on September 27, 1830, by LeFlore and Moshulatubbee. Most of the Choctaws had already departed. The treaty permitted Choctaws to elect to remain in Mississippi as U.S. citizens but provided for cession of remaining Choctaw land in the state and removal to Indian Territory. The bulk of the 18,000 Choctaws emigrated in a journey of 550 miles in three parties between 1830 and 1834. Perhaps 6,000 Choctaws remained, landless, in Mississippi.

In Indian Territory the Choctaws set about reestablishing their lives. They settled along the eastern boundary of their new territory according to historic divisions in districts named after their leaders: Pushmataha to the west of the Kiamichi River (for Nitakechi's band); Apunshunnubbee east of that river (for LeFlore's group); and Moshulatubbee south of the Canadian and Arkansas rivers. Greenwood LeFlore opted to stay in Mississippi on his plantation after the generous reward he received in the removal document. The Choctaws adopted a new constitution in their new homeland in 1834. It was the first written constitution west of the great river. The document created a national council made up of nine elected members from each of the three districts as well as the three district chiefs. Many remnant Choctaws in Mississippi joined their kin in the west between 1845 and 1854. Still others came by rail in 1902–1903.

The Choctaws also renewed their educational endeavors. Presbyterian

Alfred Wright founded Wheelock, near Durant, in 1831. Two years later Choctaw annuity payments supported their own school system. The Presbyterians' Spencer Academy, north of Sawyer and Doaksville, educated boys after 1841. In 1843 the nation began Armstrong Academy, located northeast of Bokchito in what is now Bryan County. The Choctaws had a remarkable commitment to public education: in 1836 they founded the first national free public school system in the United States. That commitment extended to higher education. They established Jones Academy near Hartshorne in 1891 and Calvin Institute in Durant in 1894. It became Oklahoma Presbyterian College with tribal support. In 1975 the Choctaw Nation began steps to set up its administrative offices in that structure. Today the Choctaw Nation's headquarters in the building recalls its national commitment to religious education.

The Treaty of Doaksville, north of what was Fort Towson, in 1837 merged the Choctaws with their close linguistic kinfolk the Chickasaws, who paid them $530,000. Neither side was satisfied with the politically forced marriage, however, and an 1855 treaty separated them again. Citizens of one nation had membership in the other. The Choctaws agreed to lease their land west of the new Chickasaw Nation to the United States for $800,000. Half of that amount went to the Chickasaws.

Rival Choctaw groups compromised on a new constitution in 1860. The new guiding document used district chiefs and courts but also included a two-house national council, a principal chief, and a supreme court. The three districts were subdivided into counties.

Spencer Academy, near Caddo, Indian Territory, Choctaw Nation, ca. 1892

Photograph by William M. Caldwell, Paris Texas, Research Division of the Oklahoma Historical Society, #592

Long-standing family, church, and business ties to the South aligned the Choctaws with the Confederacy during the Civil War. Confederate commander Douglas H. Cooper had served as Choctaw agent, and in July 1861 the Choctaws signed a treaty allying themselves with the South. Some Choctaws served in the Confederate armed forces. Battles within the Choctaw Nation, refugees, and carnage brought the direct ravages of warfare to the Choctaws. In the postwar treaty negotiations, the diplomatic skills of Peter Pitchlynn (Hatchootucknee or Snapping Turtle) prevented loss of Choctaw territory beyond their leased district. The Reconstruction treaty permitted railroads to lay track crisscrossing the Indian republics. Towns sprang up along the rail lines. During the postwar period abundant natural resources in the Choctaw Nation attracted business interests and settlement. Intermarried citizen and entrepreneur J. J. McAlester led development of coal deposits within the nation. The railroads also fueled the growth of the lumber industry. Non-Indian laborers in the mines and forest tracts (especially immigrants) fed population growth. During negotiations for Reconstruction, the Reverend Allen Wright suggested that the proposed new postwar territory be called Oklahoma. The name came from two Choctaw words, okla, "people," and humma or homma, "red."

Congress expressed its intention to open the Choctaw domain to white settlement. Tribal delaying tactics forestalled the effects of the Dawes Act for a decade, until the late 1890s. The first allotment agreement with the Dawes Commission, made by principal chief Green McCurtain, ended when the Chickasaws vetoed it. The second negotiation resulted in the 1897 Atoka Agreement, which was ratified by a vote in 1898 under terms of the Curtis Act. This was the commission's first major success. It was basically the same document as earlier. As in the removal era, the Choctaws were the first of the Five Tribes to be allotted. Some 38,000 Choctaws and Chickasaws received allotments from the nearly 7 million acres in the two nations. Chickasaw-Choctaw freedmen and their descendants received forty-acre allotments. Many rapidly lost their allotted lands to their white neighbors in ensuing years through privatization.

Allotment in the area that would become Oklahoma created an opening for Mississippi Choctaw claimants. A legal feeding frenzy occurred. Federal legislation encouraged a migration of Mississippi Choctaws to Indian Territory, and over 400 moved officially in 1903. Similarities to the 1830s in that removal brought charges of speculation, manipulation, and chicanery. Only 1,640 Mississippi Choctaws were officially enrolled out of 24,634 applicants. (As a result of this the federal government recognized the impoverished Mississippi Choctaws in 1918.) Deliberations of the Choctaw citizenship commission served as one of the models for the later establishment of the nationwide Indian Claims Commission in the 1940s.

Two former slaves in the Choctaw Nation, Uncle Wallace and his wife, Minerva, who worked during the winter at Spencer Academy, were discovered singing old spirituals such as "Swing Low, Sweet Chariot," "Steal Away to Jesus," and "Roll Jordan, Roll." The songs became internationally popular and are still widely sung. At the close of the Civil War slaves in the nation were left in political limbo; the Choctaw Nation finally adopted them in 1883, although few rights were attached. Allotment offered freedmen forty acres and U.S. citizenship. There were about 6,000 freedmen in the Choctaw Nation in 1903.

Allotment legislation and subsequent congressional measures provided that the president of the United States would appoint the chief of the Choctaws. The Indians were eager to achieve renewed federal recognition during the Indian New Deal. A tribal convention in 1934 endorsed the Indian Reorganization Act, but that legislation excluded Oklahoma tribes. The Choctaw Nation refused to recognize the OIWA and continued to operate under its traditional government, using an advisory council. The existence of the communal mineral estate after the 1902 supplementary agreement contributed to tribal identity. Congress distributed $8.3 million in 1949 from the sale of a portion of coal and oil reserves on a per capita basis. In 1951 the Choctaws obtained the first tribal decision in the history of the Indian Claims Commission for their Leased District for $3.5 million. Tribal leaders actively participated in the National Congress of American Indians (NCAI), founded in 1944 as a voice for Indian tribal aspirations. Former Choctaw chief and attorney Ben Dwight gave the keynote address to the founding meeting of the NCAI in Denver, Colorado.

Choctaws served in United States wars with distinction. Speaking their Native language to confuse the enemy eavesdropping on communications, Choctaw code talkers relayed vital battlefield information during both world wars. Their success in World War I set the stage for other tribal code talking units during World War II. Perhaps the most famous Choctaw soldiers included Joseph Oklahombi ("People Killer"), who was twice awarded the Croix de Guerre by the French government in World War I, and Van Barfoot, who was awarded the Congressional Medal of Honor during World War II. Edward McClish, a member of the 45th Infantry Division, helped organize Philippine Island guerrilla operations against the Japanese during World War II. Other Choctaws worked in war industries that supported the nation's efforts, underscoring the ongoing urbanization of many tribal members.

Some contact with Mississippi kin kept memories of old dances alive among Oklahoma Choctaws. During the early 1970s the Reverend Eugene Wilson fostered a Choctaw youth group to learn and perpetuate Choctaw dances. His group traveled extensively to perform in public before Choctaws and other audiences in Oklahoma, Mississippi, and Louisiana. Those interested in perpetuating dances formed the Choctaw-

Chickasaw Heritage Committee in 1975. The annual Choctaw Festival held through the Labor Day weekend in Tuskahoma draws more than ten thousand visitors. Over four days they learn about Choctaw heritage, feast on traditional foods, and participate in athletic and other tribal activities. Additionally, Choctaw churches host athletic events, all-night sings, and services using their Native language. Language training is offered to in-

Pushmataha, Choctaw chief
Print of colored lithograph by McKenney and Hall. Courtesy Creek Council House Museum.

terested persons at several sites through forty teachers as well as over the Internet (launched in 2000: the School of Choctaw Language on the Choctaw Nation website). There are currently about five thousand speakers of the Choctaw language.

In June 1999 the Choctaw Nation became the first tribe in the United States to construct its own hospital, the 37-bed Choctaw Nation Health Care Center outside the community of Talihina. The tribe also operates four health centers in other towns. The Choctaw Nation contracted in 1985 to operate Jones Academy, which became a tribally controlled school in late 1988 (Public Law 100-297).

Among distinguished Choctaws were the well-respected nineteenth-century leaders Pushmataha and Moshulatubbee. Marjory Griffin Leake and her husband, KTUL-TV founder James Leake, were in the wholesale grocery business. Tulsa filmmaker Ian Skorodin made the film *Tushka*. Mark Williams and Phil Lucas are also filmmakers. Actor Mark Abbott appeared in the films *Unbowed* and *Naturally Native* as well as *Squanto*.

Ron Anderson's artwork *Killing of an XR-7*, which symbolizes the Plains scaffold burial of a loved one, in this instance his favorite car, a 1969 Cougar
Author's photograph

The acclaimed poet Ai is of mixed Choctaw heritage. Choctaw writers include LeAnne Howe (who is also part Cherokee), Don Birchfield, and Rilla Askew. Attorney Scott Kayla Morrison Standefur was an activist for many years. Gena Timberman headed the state Indian Cultural Center Authority in the state's capital. Clodus Smith served in higher education as president of several colleges. Erika Harold, Miss America in 2002, is of Choctaw (and Cherokee) heritage. Former assistant secretary for Indian affairs Dave Anderson, Famous Dave's restaurant magnate, was of Choctaw (and Ojibwe) ancestry. Oklahoma congressman William G. Stigler introduced an early version of a bill that ultimately became the 1946 Indian Claims Commission Act. Patrick J. Hurley became Herbert Hoover's secretary of war and a roving emissary for Franklin Roosevelt. Historian Anna Lewis was the first female tribal member to earn a Ph.D. degree from the University of Oklahoma (1930). Muriel Hazel Wright was also a historian. Clara Sue Kidwell headed American Indian Studies programs across the United States. Tribal member Cal McLish was a starting pitcher in the 1940s and 1950s. Johnny Bench was a catcher for the Cincinnati Reds and was elected to the Baseball Hall of Fame in 1989. Painters include Norman Howard, Terry Saul (who is also Chickasaw), Jerry Ingram, sisters Valjean Hessing and Jane Mauldin, and Ron Anderson (who is also Chickasaw). The beadwork designs of Roger Amerman and Elena Carol Pate have won repeated awards. Chris Tarpley (also Chickasaw) was an accomplished glass blower. Architect Johnpaul Jones helped design the National Museum of the American Indian in Washington, D.C. Actor James Earl Jones, the voice of Darth Vader in the Star Wars films, is of Choctaw-Cherokee freedmen heritage from rural Mississippi. Choctaw freedwoman Rachel Brown helped preserve the Spiro Mounds. University of Oklahoma college football stars Lucious, Dewey, and Lee Roy Selmon are her descendants.

SUGGESTED READING

Baird, W. David. *The Choctaw People*. Phoenix: Indian Tribal Series, 1973 (for young readers).

———. *Peter Pitchlynn: Chief of the Choctaws*. Norman: University of Oklahoma Press, 1972; repr. 1986.

Birchfield, Don L. *How Choctaws Invented Civilization and Why Choctaws Will Conquer the World*. Albuquerque: University of New Mexico Press, 2007.

Debo, Angie. *The Rise and Fall of the Choctaw Republic*. Norman: University of Oklahoma Press, 1934; 2nd ed. 1961; repr. 1967, 1972, 1982, 1986.

DeRosier, Arthur H., Jr. *The Removal of the Choctaw Indians*. Knoxville: University of Tennessee Press, 1970; repr. New York: Harper and Row, 1972; repr. Knoxville: University of Tennessee Press, 1981.

Faiman-Silva, Sandra. *Choctaws at the Crossroads: The Political Economy of Class and Culture in the Oklahoma Timber Region*. Lincoln: University of Nebraska Press, 1997; repr. 2000.

Galloway, Patricia. *Choctaw Genesis, 1500–1700*. Lincoln: University of Nebraska Press, 1995.

Haag, Marcia, and Henry Willis. *Choctaw Language and Culture: Chahta Anumpa*. 2 vols. Norman: University of Oklahoma Press, 2001–2007.

Howard, James H., and Victoria Lindsey Levine. *Choctaw Music and Dance*. Norman: University of Oklahoma Press, 1990; repr. 1997.

Howe, Le Anne. *Shell Shaker*. San Francisco: Aunt Lute Books, 2001.

Kidwell, Clara Sue. *The Choctaws in Oklahoma: From Tribe to Nation, 1855–1870*. Norman: University of Oklahoma Press, 2007.

Kidwell, Clara Sue, and Charles Roberts. *The Choctaws: A Critical Bibliography*. Bloomington: Indiana University Press, 1980.

Knight, Vernon James, Jr., and Vincas Steponaitis, eds. *Archaeology of the Moundville Chiefdom*. Washington, D.C.: Smithsonian Institution Press, 1998.

Lambert, Valerie. *Choctaw Nation: A Study of American Indian Resurgence*. Lincoln: University of Nebraska Press, 2007.

Lewis, Anna. *Chief Pushmataha: American Patriot*. New York: Exposition, 1960.

Lincecum, Jerry, and Edward Phillips, eds. *Adventures of a Frontier Naturalist: The Life and Times of Dr. Gideon Lincecum.* College Station: Texas A&M University Press, 1994.

McKee, Jesse O. *The Choctaw.* New York: Chelsea House, 1989 (for young readers).

Milligan, James. *The Choctaw of Oklahoma.* Abilene, Tex.: Chapman and Sons, 2003.

O'Brien, Greg, ed. *Pre-Removal Choctaw History: Exploring New Paths.* Norman: University of Oklahoma Press, 2008.

Peebles, Christopher. "Determinants of Settlement Size and Location in the Moundville Phase." In Bruce D. Smith, *Mississippian Settlement Patterns*, 369–413. New York: Academic Press, 1978.

Spring, Joel H. *The Cultural Transformation of a Native American Family and Its Tribe, 1763–1995: A Basket of Apples.* Mahwah, N.J.: Lawrence Erlbaum Associates, 1996.

Trimble, Victor H. *Choctaw Kisses, Bullets & Blood.* N.p.: Market Tech Books, 2007.

Comanche

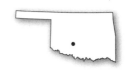

NAME

The Utes' word for their enemies was "Komantcia" (or "Kimaci"), "one who fights me all the time" or "enemy." The label was used by the Spanish and anglicized to "Comanche." The members refer to themselves as Numunah or Nuhmuhnuh, "the People."

LOCATION AND GOVERNMENT

The tribal headquarters of the "Comanche Nation" is located about nine miles north of Lawton in Comanche County. Most tribal members reside in nearby Caddo, Comanche, Cotton, and Kiowa counties. Comanches ended their joint KCA business committee relationship in 1963, and the BIA in 1966 recognized a separate "Comanche Indian Tribe." The Comanche Tribe is not organized under the OIWA, but voters accepted a constitution and by-laws in 1966 and the tribe incorporated in 1972. The tribal council is the governing body. All Comanches who are twenty-one and older elect a seven-member business committee with a chair, vice chair, secretary-treasurer, and four council members. They are elected annually for staggered three-year terms. The Comanche National Museum is in Lawton. The tribal website is www.comanchenation.com.

BUSINESSES

The Comanche Tribe derives revenue from four casinos. The Comanche Nation Casino in Lawton features a convention center and hotel and has 45,000 square feet (at www.comanchenation-games.com). The others are the Red River Casino at Devol north of the Red River near Interstate 44 (at www.comancheredriver-casino.com) and two small casinos: Comanche Star Casino east of Walters and Comanche Spur Casino near Elgin. Enlargements of the casinos are planned. The Comanche Tribe also operates a Water Park on Interstate 44 in Lawton. There are smoke shops and convenience stores inside the casinos. A Comanche Visitors'

Center is adjacent to the Lawton Casino on Interstate 44. The Comanches also own a funeral home in Lawton and the Clean Sweep Company. Individual tribal members have 201,000 allotted acres. The tribe owns about 7,500 acres of trust land dotted throughout six counties of southwestern Oklahoma. The lands are jointly held with the Kiowas and the Plains Apaches and yield lease income from farming, ranching, and oil and gas production. Some tribal revenue is used to aid tribal small business ventures. The tribe also has buffalo and horse herds.

NUMBER

The tribe has about 14,000 members, about half of whom reside in the nearby six-county area. The blood quantum for membership is one-eighth.

The Comanche language is Shoshonean (Central Numic), closely related to the language of the Wyoming Shoshones and still mutually intelligible. Sometime in the far past Shoshone, Hopi, Ute, and Nahua broke off from the Uto-Aztecan language stock. Archeologists trace the origins of the prehistoric Shoshoneans to the western Great Basin of the far western United States. Perhaps around A.D. 1000 Shoshoneans moved from the area of present-day Nevada and Utah into the eastern Great Basin area. They reached Idaho by about A.D. 1250 and arrived on the front range of the Rocky Mountains of Wyoming around A.D. 1450.

Sometime during the seventeenth century Shoshones of present-day Wyoming separated from the main body and entered eastern Colorado. Comanche oral tradition credited either an argument over a hunt or illness for the departure. Much discussion has focused on the time frame: some maintain that the Comanches split from the main body of the Shoshones and were on the Plains much earlier, by the 1550s. The Comanches are considered to be "recent" arrivals on the Plains. Whenever the move occurred, various writers have speculated about the causes. Some claimed that Sioux pressure forced the Comanches onto the Plains, while others pointed to their pursuit of horses and bison. Still others stressed the lure of kinship ties as the motivation for migration and argued that many bands probably moved gradually rather than as a sudden mass exodus. Additionally, writers have expended much energy discussing whether the Comanches were members of one tribe or independent bands. Frenchman

Athanase de Mézières, who aided the Spanish penetration of Comancheria, described the Comanches in 1772 as being divided "into an infinite number of little bands." The Comanches are discussed here as a unified tribe for purposes of brevity, although there were shifting allegiances among widespread and disparate kin-based bands.

Comanche families lived in hide-covered tepees. Sometimes extended families resided alone, while at other times many gathered in a large nucleated encampment. The Spaniards referred to isolated Comanche villages as estancias. Local bands could come together into a division linked through kinship and warrior societies. The later reservation confinement in effect brought all the Comanches together, thereby creating the Comanche Tribe.

Comanches were patrilineal. Males joined men's societies and gained prestige and political influence through war honors. Men hunted game, primarily buffalo. But the members of the bands supplemented their diet with a variety of plant foods. They also traded with neighboring tribes for food products. Women tended the camp and their small garden plots.

For the Comanches, religion was a personal concern. They referred to the Creator as Niatpo (or Ni'ahpi'), "father," sometimes personified in the sun. Each individual strove to obtain personal "power" (puha) from the supernatural forces. Young people could seek power on a vision quest, by visiting a location of particular power, and in dreams or during ceremonies. An individual could establish a medicine society through rituals. Other dances were held for men's societies before and after war parties, for curing, and on other occasions.

At first the Comanches moved into present-day Wyoming and Montana on the northwestern edge of the Plains. They maintained contact with the Shoshonean kin they left behind. The Comanches were among the first to acquire horses and become mounted nomads on the Plains. That was just before or early in the 1700s. At about the same time, Comanches who had intermarried among their cousins the Utes went to visit the Spaniards in New Mexico. The Comanches began to trade with and to raid the Spaniards there as well as the Puebloan peoples. The Plains Apaches referred to the Comanches as the Padoucas, a designation that occasionally appeared in documents as late as the nineteenth century. The Comanches maintained a relationship with the Spanish, sometimes peaceful and other times violent, through the eighteenth century. After they became mounted, the Comanches gradually entered more deeply into trade with Europeans and eventually abandoned their hunting and gathering subsistence for trade. Trade, of course, tied them to the Europeans' political economy. Frenchman Etienne

Venyard de Bourgmont left Fort Orléans on the Missouri River and made contact with the Comanches in 1724. He cemented an alliance.

The Comanche presence blocked Spanish and French advances into the southern Plains and the Southwest. Comanche power postponed American expansion as well. As one example of their influence on events, the Shoshonean dialect became the trade language in the upper Arkansas River region.

After 1719 Caddo and Wichita commerce provided French firearms to the Comanches. They used those weapons to drive the Plains Apaches southward by the 1740s, enabling the Comanches to trade directly with the French. The Comanches continued their own southward movement. They joined with Indian allies in 1758 to destroy the San Sabá Mission, which had been built for the Lipan Apaches near present-day Menard. The strike forced the Lipans to keep migrating farther south. Comanche and Indian allies smashed a retaliatory Spanish punitive expedition the following year.

Reeling from Spanish military attacks and from the ravages of small-pox, the Eastern Comanche Cuchanec leader Ecueracapa made peace in early 1786 with the governor of New Mexico, Juan Bautista de Anza. The agreement inaugurated an era of long-lasting amicable relations between the Spanish and the Comanches. The Spanish policy of opening Comanche access to New Mexico only succeeded in fostering Comanche raiding into Texas, however, to seize additional goods to trade in New Mexico. Intermediary merchants, at first called viageros, "travelers," were called Comancheros in the nineteenth century. The Comancheros continued a profitable commerce in horses and captives, which served as a mainstay for the demands of the expanding American market. French botanist François Michaux toured the Ohio-Kentucky-Louisiana area in 1802 and reported seeing "wild horses" from New Mexico fetching $50 each in New Orleans.

Eventually the Comanches participated in a trade network that connected the Mississippi River Valley with the Rockies and Texas with the Missouri River. They dominated commerce on the southern Plains. Comanche forays through the 1850s sometimes extended all the way to the Gulf of Mexico. James Webb, a Missouri–Santa Fe trader who was in Durango in 1846, watched transfixed from a rooftop as Comanche warriors swept through the town on a raid. He described the experience in his reminiscences.

The Comanches and their trading partners the Wichitas slowly moved southward even as their commerce continued into the late eighteenth century. By the 1750s the Comanches had divided into the eastern group

(Kotsoteka, from kuhcutihka, "buffalo eater"), who raided and traded out of New Mexico; and the western group (Yamparika, from yaparihka, "yama root eater," for the yap root, which was the ancient Shoshone staple food; and Jupe, from hupi, "wood" or "timber"), who maintained their commercial network. This network redistributed eastern manufactured goods toward New Mexico, fulfilling a role similar to that of the Missouri River villagers in the north. Felipe de Sandoval, mentioned in José Pichardo's account of the Southwest, attended a Comanche trade fair in 1749 held on the Big Timbers of the Arkansas River. He described a teeming commercial bazaar filled with people from four hundred tepees in the camp. They bartered all sorts of goods and human cargo. Seventy-two years later Jacob Fowler found in nearly the same spot a huge Comanche-led trade fair that included a mix of varied tribes, even former Comanche enemies like the Plains Apaches, among the five hundred people eagerly engaged in trading. In the 1760s British goods began to trickle into Comancheria, and three decades later Americans appeared to barter

Comanche Village, Women Dressing Robes and Drying Meat (1834–35)

Painted by George Catlin. Smithsonian American Art Museum, Gift of Mrs. Joseph Harrison, Jr., 1985.66.346.

for horses. It was Comanche chief Tabba-quena (Big Eagle) who advised trader Josiah Gregg to take the more direct Canadian River Valley route to his commercial destination in Santa Fe. Comanche bands included the Penetakas, Noconis, Kwahadis, and others.

Around 1800 (most accounts said 1790, while others extended the time frame to 1820) the Comanches made their alliance with the Kiowas. In subsequent years observers often viewed the two tribes as one. Lewis and Clark's 1805 map placed the Comanches and Kiowas in the vicinity of the Black Hills. By 1855 Cheyenne and Pawnee pressure, as well as the desire for pasturage for their horses and raiding opportunities, pushed the Comanches south from the upper Platte to the upper Arkansas and below it.

Captain Randolph B. Marcy and Major Robert S. Neighbors established an upper reserve of 18,576 acres for the southern branch of the Comanches on the Clear Fork of the Brazos River. The reservation ultimately became Shackelford and Throckmorton counties in northern Texas. The U.S. Army set up Fort Belknap nearby. Their first agent, John Baylor, was dismissed and became a rabble rouser who incited Texas prejudices against the Indians. Throughout 1858 John S. "Rip" Ford and L. S. "Sul" Ross led Texas Rangers, Indian allies, and U.S. troops against Comanche villages on the Plains. Locals refused to arrest the murderers of an innocent family, blamed the reservation Indians for any troubles, and demanded that the Indians be forced out of Texas.

The federal government turned its attention to the Plains Indians after the end of the Civil War. Treaty councils, greatly reduced ranges, assignment to reservation confinement, and finally Indian resort to raiding and American military force across the southern Plains (1868–75) combined to bring a draconian peace to the region. Military pressure, economic collapse, and subsistence needs forced Comanche bands onto their reservation during the winter of 1874–75 during the Red River War. The 1867 Medicine Lodge Treaty council pointed to future confinement. This was the first time in their history that the Comanches had come together as a tribe, although periodic ceremonies had also brought most bands together. Their population by then had fallen to about 1,600.

Quakers Josiah and Elizabeth Butler began Fort Sill Indian School with six pupils in 1871 near the agency. When the agency moved to Anadarko in 1879, the school was abandoned. Comanche students were then sent

Quanah Parker, Comanche chief
Muriel Hazel Wright Collection, Research Division of the Oklahoma Historical Society, #14609

to a school in Anadarko until 1890, when a new Fort Sill Indian School was established. Christian missions dotted the reservation after 1881, with Roman Catholic, Baptist, Methodist, Reformed Church, Mennonite, and Presbyterian churches established. Hymns in the Comanche language and summer camp meetings kept the faiths alive among tribal members. Quanah Parker and Kwahada band members aided the Post Oak Mennonite mission. Peyote arrived from the Lipan Apaches in New Mexico around 1890. Quanah Parker was among its leading advocates, even lobbying the later state legislature on behalf of religious freedom for its practitioners.

The reservation experience led to drastic changes in Indian culture. Texas cattle roaming the grasslands of the reserve in the 1880s led to leases that yielded income, called "grass money," and some ranch-hand employment. Agent manipulation and assimilation pressure undermined band and division chiefs' influence and helped spur the emergence of Quanah Parker as principal chief of the Comanches. Although their duties were loosely defined, leaders of the three tribes, the Kiowas, the Comanches, and the Plains Apaches (or Kiowa-Apaches), met periodically as the KCA business committee after 1890 to discuss local concerns.

In 1901 the reservation lands were allotted under the terms of the Jerome Agreement: 1,450 Comanches selected parcels of 160 acres, most along Cache, Beaver, and Medicine creeks. Allotment devastated the tribe. By the time of the Indian New Deal half the Comanches were landless. From 1936 to 1963 the Comanche Tribe shared a joint constitution and business committee with the Kiowas and the Plains Apaches. The revived body had been sanctioned by the federal government during the early 1920s. The group pressed claims against the U.S. government with modest success, but voters rejected IRA-OIWA constitutions during the 1930s. A constitution was accepted in 1940, but it also was not an OIWA document. The BIA arbitrarily recognized a Comanche tribal government in 1940 without tribal consent, using a previously rejected document as the basis. That same year the KCA tribes agreed to remain allied and re-created their 1935 mutual government. It met sporadically.

The Plains soldier tradition of the Comanches surfaced even during the early reservation period. Some worked as scouts at Fort Sill, and others later saw service in America's military wars overseas. Comanche men's society dances sent tribal members off for armed forces service and welcomed returned veterans. The 1952 celebration of Korean conflict veterans became the annual Comanche Homecoming Powwow, which takes place on the third weekend of July in Walters, Oklahoma. The Comanche Nation Fair is held at the end of September.

A variety of dance associations support the Comanche heritage and identity. Early in their twentieth-century reservation experience, tribal members participated in the dances at Craterville Fair, the Caddo County Fair, and the Indian Fair in Anadarko. They revived the Little Ponies in 1972 to welcome Vietnam veterans home. In 1976 they resurrected the Black Knives as a Yamparika group. The Comanche Indian Veterans Association, Comanche Little Ponies, Comanche War Dance Society, War Scouts, Gourd Clan, and War Mothers' associations all sponsor and participate in ceremonies, which feature giveaways and feasts. Comanches travel widely both in groups and as individuals to take part in other tribes' dances. Among links to the older times, some Comanches still travel to Mexico to watch bullfights, as their ancestors had done. Hispanic and Indian community fiestas through the American Southwest and in northern Mexico include Los Comanches folklore performances, dances, and music that commemorate mutual encounters from their past. The Comanches left their imprint on the landscape across the southern Plains, especially in Texas: the town of Comanche in the county of the same name and the towns of Nocona and Quanah in the northern part of the state. There is also a Comanche County in western Oklahoma.

The Comanche Nation in 2002 became the first tribe in the state to open a tribal college, Comanche Nation College in Lawton. It offers courses toward a two-year associate degree. In 1993 the tribe formed the Comanche Language and Cultural Preservation Committee to teach the tribal language.

Prominent nineteenth-century Comanche leaders include Ten Bears, Quanah Parker, Tabananaca (Hears the Sun), and many others. Quanah Parker was perhaps the most famous Comanche. A son of captive Cynthia Ann Parker, he was involved in the abortive raid on the hide hunters' camp at Adobe Walls then later became a leader of accommodation to reservation life. A 50-mile stretch of State Highway 62 from Lawton to Altus was named for him in 1992.

Distinguished Comanches include LaDonna Harris, the former wife of Oklahoma senator Fred Harris. She pressed for employment and educational opportunities for Indian people and kept the National Council on Indian Opportunity hearings afloat in 1968–70 in the aftermath of the assassination of Robert Kennedy. The hearings aired national urban Indian concerns and helped underscore the need for national legislation addressing Native issues. Her own organization, Americans for Indian Opportunity, worked for economic growth for Indian people. Dr. Edwin Chappabitty served many years as a physician and administrator for the Indian Health Service. Paulette Tallchief (also Eastern Delaware) worked in Indian health services and was an educator and a life-long advocate of Indian cultural practices. Linda Warner served as president of Haskell Indian University in Kansas. Cornel Pewewardy was an educator. Lance Keltner was a musician who sang the blues. Paula Smith founded and led the Women's Commission in Ohio. Marvin (Tom) Tahmakera owned Comanche Steel Company in Chicago, Illinois. He was a great-grandson of Quanah Parker and was sent to Chicago as part of the BIA relocation program.

Charles Chibitty of Tulsa was much celebrated in his later life. He was widely acknowledged as the last surviving Comanche code talker from World War II. Organized by William Karty, the code talkers relayed military orders and information in their Native languages, which the Germans could not translate. Chibitty landed at Normandy on D-Day plus one in June 1944 and moved with Allied forces toward Germany. Comanche writers include poets Nita Pahdopony and Stuart Hoahwah. Doc Tate Nevaquaya was a world-renowned painter and flute player, who led a resurgence in the use of the cedar flute. Joe Dale Tate

LaDonna Harris (Comanche)
Courtesy LaDonna Harris

Nevaquaya (also Yuchi) is an artist. The late George "Woogie" Watchetaker was an award-winning fancy dancer, spiritual leader, and widely recognized Indian painter. Other Comanche artists include Leonard Riddles, Rance Hood, Nocona and Quanah Burgess, and Diane Chaat Smith. Kit Fox was a well-known professional wrestler during the 1950s and 1960s. He portrayed a medicine man in the film *The Last of the Mohicans*. Boxer George "Comanche Boy" Tahdooahnippah (who is also Choctaw) is in contention to be middleweight world champion. Rudy Youngblood portrayed Jaguar Paw in the 2006 movie *Apocalypto*. The Red Rhythm Band members are Comanche and Kiowa.

SUGGESTED READING

Bolton, Herbert E., ed. *Athanase de Mézières and the Louisiana-Texas Frontier*. 2 vols. Cleveland: Arthur H. Clark, 1914; repr. New York: Kraus, 1970.

Brashear, Charles. *Killing Cynthia Ann*. Fort Worth: Texas Christian University, 1999 (novel about Quanah Parker's mother by a Cherokee creative writing professor).

Chalfant, William Y. *Without Quarter: The Wichita Expedition and the Fight on Crooked Creek*. Norman: University of Oklahoma Press, 1991.

Comanche Code Talkers. Mannford, Okla.: Hidden Path Productions, n.d. (film on Charles Chibitty).

Fehrenbach, T. R. *Comanches: Destruction of a People.* New York: Alfred Knopf, 1974.

Foster, Morris W. *Being Comanche.* Tucson: University of Arizona Press, 1991.

Fowler, Jacob. *Journal.* Edited by Elliott Coues. New York: Francis Harper, 1898; repr. Lincoln: University of Nebraska Press, 1970.

Hagan, William T. *Quanah Parker, Comanche Chief.* Norman: University of Oklahoma Press, 1993.

———. *United States–Comanche Relations.* New Haven: Yale University Press, 1976.

Hämäläinen, Pekka. *The Comanche Empire.* New Haven: Yale University Press, 2008.

Harris, LaDonna. *LaDonna Harris: A Comanche Life.* Lincoln: University of Nebraska Press, 2001.

Kavanagh, Thomas W. *Comanche Political History.* Lincoln: University of Nebraska, 1996.

———. *The Comanches: A History, 1706–1875.* Lincoln: University of Nebraska Press, 1999.

Keith, Harold. *Komantcia.* Norman: Levite of Apache, 1991 (novel for young readers by the former University of Oklahoma sports information officer; originally published in 1965).

Kershen, L. Michael. *Why Buffalo Roam.* Owings Mills, Md.: Stemmer House, 1993 (for young readers).

Meadows, William C. *The Comanche Code Talkers of World War II.* Austin: University of Texas Press, 2002.

Michaux, François. "Travels to the West of the Allegheny Mountains." In Reuben Gold Thwaites, ed., *Early Western Travels,* vol. 3, 105–306. New York: AMS, 1966.

Pichardo, José Antonio. *Pichardo's Treatise on the Limits of Louisiana and Texas*. Translated by Charles Hackett and Charmion Shelby. Edited by Charles Hackett. 4 vols. Austin: University of Texas Press, 1931–46; repr. New York: Books for Libraries, 1971.

Rollings, Willard H. *The Comanche*. New York: Chelsea House, 1989 (for young readers).

Wallace, Ernest, and E. Adamson Hoebel. *The Comanches: Lords of the Southern Plains*. Norman: University of Oklahoma Press, 1952; repr. 1976.

Webb, James. *Adventures in the Santa Fe Trade*. Edited by Robert Bieber. Lincoln: University of Nebraska Press, 1995.

Delaware Nation

(Western Delaware)

The tribe refers to itself as Lena'pe or Leni-lena'pe, "original People." These Delawares resided at one time in Texas and were associated with the Caddo and the Wichita tribes there until 1859 and afterward when they were forced into Indian Territory. The Delawares referred to themselves as the Absentee Delawares as well as the Western Delawares and now the Delaware Nation (see also the "Delaware Tribe of Indians [Eastern Delaware]" entry).

LOCATION AND GOVERNMENT

The headquarters for the "Delaware Nation" is two miles north of Anadarko in Caddo County, in southwestern Oklahoma. It is on U.S. Highway 281. The Delaware Nation has not organized under the OIWA. Its government operates according to a tribal resolution adopted in 1958, with a constitution and by-laws approved in 1973. The executive committee is made up of a president and five other members, who are elected to staggered four-year terms. The tribal complex contains a small museum, library, and tribal archives. The tribal website is www.delawarenation.com.

BUSINESSES

Revenue comes from the 20,000-square-foot Gold River Casino (at www.goldriverok.com) at the tribal headquarters. A second casino is planned for Hinton, Oklahoma. The tribe's share of an Indian Claims Commission settlement of 1969 through the appropriations measure enacted in October 1972 provided a small sum under Public Law 92-456. The Western Delawares jointly own about 500 acres of trust land with the Wichita and Caddo tribes in Caddo County; hence the popular designation "WCD" for joint enterprises. Some revenue derives from oil and gas leases and the sale of tribal license plates. Individual tribal members gain some income from livestock and agriculture. About 80,000 acres are individually allotted.

NUMBER

___

The tribe has about 1,400 members in and around Anadarko and in Caddo County. Counting all of the descendants, there are perhaps 13,000 Delawares today internationally.

Linguistically the Delawares are Eastern Algonquian-speakers whose language is related to the more northern Munsee and to the southern Unami or Delaware proper. Prehistoric Paleo-Indian and Archaic peoples lived in the Atlantic coastal region that much later became Delaware territory. But no clearly identifiable connection can be made between prehistoric peoples and the contemporary Delawares. During the Woodland period, prior to European arrival, closely related cultures developed markedly different traits upstream along inland rivers from their downstream kinfolk along the same river as it emptied into the ocean. The Woodland era variations were roughly similar to Munsee peoples upstream related by language but differing in cultural traits from downstream Unami-speaking Delaware peoples in the historic period. The Delaware Indians were respected by neighboring tribes, who referred to them in honorific terms as either their "grandfathers" or their "uncles."

The Delawares who met the first Europeans in the 1600s resided on the Pennsylvania side of the Delaware River across from what is now Trenton, New Jersey. Their territory extended northward through present-day New Jersey and into lower Long Island and Manhattan in New York. The exact tribal makeup is not clearly known because of the lapse of time since their disappearance.

Dutch settlers in the seventeenth century pushed Delaware peoples out of the New Amsterdam coastal regions and steadily inland. The Dutch fur trade entangled the Delawares in European material culture and altered their economic and social worlds. Immigrant Europeans pressed varied Delaware-speaking groups ever inland. The diverse groups eventually merged in the upper Ohio River Valley to form the Delaware tribe around 1750 or afterward. They were joined by Munsees, Shawnees, Nanticokes, Mahicans, and other refugee Indians. Three subclans made up the Delawares: the Minsi group, often called Ptuksit, "round foot" (Wolf, for the shape of the paw); the Unami group, usually referred to as Pakoango, "the crawler" (for the Turtle); and the Unalachtigo group, often called Pullaeu, "he who does not chew" (for the Turkey, which swallows its food). Most of the Delaware Nation is made up of Turtle group members.

Because of their long association with Europeans and with Americans, the confederacy of the Delawares with its three branches could have served as a model for the American Founding Fathers during the formation of concepts for the new American Republic. Some Delawares abandoned contacts with the eastern region, broke off in 1793, and moved to what is now the southeastern corner of Missouri near Cape Girardeau on the Mississippi River. Delaware mixed-bloods participated in the fur trade up the river systems that led to St. Louis. Louis Lorimer (or Lorimier), the founder of Cape Girardeau in southwestern Missouri, according to historian Tanis Thorne, married a French-Delaware woman. She became the first woman of that thriving frontier community. Spanish authorities lured some Delawares and Shawnees to their side of the Mississippi River during the 1780s so that the Indian residents could act as a buffer against the Osages. Thriving small riverine communities of Indians, Canadians, Creoles, and blacks dotted the landscape before the War of 1812. Enterprising merchants set up Kawsmouth as a trading center where the Kansas River met the Missouri River. In the 1820s the influential Pierre Menard persuaded a few Delaware and Shawnee Indians to migrate to the Kansa River Valley. Younger brothers of François Chouteau established their own posts to trade with the new arrivals. Dissatisfied tribal members moved anew to the Red River around 1817. A decade later they migrated again to the Sabine and Neches rivers and then deeper into east Texas to join the Cherokees. They received a Spanish land grant in 1820.

Black Beaver led a small contingent of Delawares that separated from the Cherokee Nation in northeastern Indian Territory and traveled to south-central Oklahoma. Fort Arbuckle was established in their vicinity. Black Beaver served as a guide and hunter for several noteworthy U.S. expeditions into the Far West. Delawares from Texas joined the Black Beaver group in 1839 and 1853.

Delawares in Texas served with distinction as interpreters and intermediaries. Delaware and Wichita assistance helped collect tribes for the March 1843 Tehuacani Creek Council with Texas authorities. Delawares were also prominent in the preliminaries leading to the treaty at Bird's Fort that same year and other Texas councils in 1844–45. Delawares came into Indian Territory from the Brazos Reserve in Texas in August 1859. They settled at the Wichita Agency near Fort Cobb. Some one hundred Delawares formally united with the Caddos and Wichitas (1874); other Delawares resided on the Kiowa-Comanche Reservation. The federal government united the two reserves in 1878 for administrative purposes, with an agency in Anadarko.

All of the Delawares in western Oklahoma were collectively called the Absentee Delawares. Most of the Delawares fled to Kansas during the violence of the Civil War. Some intermarried with their Kansas kinfolk, but most returned to Caddo County after the war ended. The reserve that they shared with the Caddos and the Wichitas was allotted under terms of the Jerome Commission agreement signed in 1890. Absentee Delawares took allotments there as either Caddo or Wichita Indians. The remaining land was opened to white settlement in a 1901 lottery. Many of the Indian allotted lands passed out of Native ownership in subsequent years as assimilation pressures increased.

A new opportunity arose for the Absentee Delawares when Congress passed Indian New Deal legislation. The Delawares could assert their tribalism even though they had not done so from 1895 into the 1930s. The Absentee Delawares chose not to organize under the OIWA but gradually worked toward separate tribal existence once again.

The Delawares look to the East for their roots and for their heritage. A retired couple donated 11.5 acres of land located west of Philadelphia, Pennsylvania, to the tribe in 2000. It was land that historically had belonged to the tribe at one time. The tribe sought land in that state and in New Jersey for development, beginning in the late 1990s.

The Western Delawares participate in Caddo and Wichita dances. Delaware women at those dances wear the *dastuh* (the elaborate hairpiece that Caddo women also wear). The Western Delawares maintain ties with their kinfolk in eastern Oklahoma. They too play Indian football to open their spring ceremonial season. Representatives of all Delawares in the state met in 1999 to discuss repatriation issues. It was their first official meeting since 1821.

Today Delawares and their descendants live in recognized groups in the United States and Canada. The Delawares of Western Oklahoma represent those Delawares who emigrated from Texas to the Caddo-Wichita Reserve. Contemporary Delaware Nation president Terry Horton is the great-great-great-grandson of Black Beaver.

SUGGESTED READING

Bierhorst, John. *Mythology of the Lenape: Guide and Texts.* Tucson: University of Arizona Press, 1995.

Chapman, Berlin B. "Establishment of the Wichita Reservation." *Chronicles of Oklahoma* 11 (December 1933): 1044–55.

Hale, Duane K., ed. *Cooley's Traditional Stories of the Delaware.* Anadarko: Delaware Tribe of Western Oklahoma, 1984.

———. *Peacemakers on the Frontier: A History of the Delaware Tribe of Western Oklahoma.* Anadarko: Delaware Tribe of Western Oklahoma, 1987.

———, ed. *Turtle Tales: Oral Traditions of the Delaware Tribe of Western Oklahoma.* Anadarko: Delaware Tribe of Western Oklahoma, 1984.

Thorne, Tanis. "The Chouteau Family and the Osage Trade: A Generational Study." In Thomas Buckley, ed., *Rendezvous: Selected Papers of the 4th North American Fur Trade Conference, 1981,* 109–20. St. Paul: North American Fur Trade Conference, 1983.

Delaware Tribe of Indians
(Eastern Delaware)

English settlers in the early seventeenth century who lived along the bay and the river named for Virginia governor Sir Thomas West, Lord de la Warr, gave his name to local Indians, referring to them as Delawares. The valley or bay stretched through or touched the colonies of New York, Pennsylvania, New Jersey, and Delaware. Because these Indians came from Kansas after 1867 to settle among the Cherokees of Indian Territory, they are sometimes also referred to as the Registered Delawares because they registered among the Cherokees as Delawares for annuities, allotment, and other purposes. Often they are simply called the Eastern Delawares to distinguish them from their western kinfolk in Oklahoma. The Delawares call themselves Lenape, meaning in their Unami dialect "standard," "original," "real," or usually "common People" (*len*, "real" or "original" plus *ape*, "person"). They prefer to call themselves the Delaware Tribe of Indians.

LOCATION AND GOVERNMENT

The "Delaware Tribe of Indians" has its headquarters in the city of Bartlesville in Washington County, in far north-central Oklahoma (forty-five miles north of Tulsa). The tribe is governed by its Business Committee. A lengthy dispute with the Cherokee Nation over sovereign rights culminated in a shocking appellate court opinion in late 2004, ending the tribe's separate recognition as an independent tribe and returning the Delaware Tribe of Indians under the fold of the Cherokee Nation, according to the interpretation of the terms of their 1867 treaty. In effect, the tribe is in legal limbo. The tribal website is www.delawaretribeofindians.nsn.us.

BUSINESSES

The Delaware Tribe of Indians operated a casino and was involved in a large casino-resort complex plan to be developed in Bonner Springs, Kansas (a suburb of Kansas City). It was in the process of acquiring land in trust in its former reservation in Wyandotte County, Kansas, when the Tenth Circuit Court rendered its opinion. In late 2006 officials of the tribe and the city of Dewey, Oklahoma, entered into an agreement for tribal development of a 17-acre parcel on Highway 75 for a commercial center, including a hotel. Through a subcontractor, members of the tribe participated in airborne radar training at Tinker Air Force Base in Oklahoma City. The tribe's minority status enabled it to bid and to contract with the federal government for business until 2003. The tribe has discussed various uses (including recreation) for Copan Lake, which the U.S. Army Corps of Engineers completed in the region in 1983.

NUMBER

The tribe has about 11,000 members. About 3,000 to 4,000 of them are concentrated in Washington, Nowata, Craig, and Rogers counties as well as in urban North Tulsa. The others reside across America. The tribe maintains an updated tribal roll, issues tribal identification cards, provides a quarterly newsletter to members and a tribal newspaper, holds regular elections, and offers many services to members (including child care, housing, health services, dietary aid, and cultural training).

There are also Delawares in Ontario, Canada, along the Thames River centered around Muncy Town near Melbourne (who are Munsee descendants) and Moraviantown, which is in Kent County. In addition, there are substantial numbers of Delaware descendants among other tribes, such as on the Six Nations Reserve along the Grand River near Hagersville in Brant County, and smaller numbers in New Jersey, Wisconsin, Ohio, Colorado, and Kansas. The Nanticoke–Lenni Lenapes are a small state-recognized (1982) group in New Jersey. Other Delaware groups are the Delaware-Muncies (not federally recognized) near Pomona, Kansas, and the federally recognized Stockbridge-Munsees of Shawano County in Wisconsin west of Green Bay. Some Delawares are found among the Brotherton Indians on the east side of Lake Winnebago in Wisconsin and among the Chippewas of Kansas southwest of the city of Ottawa in Franklin County. Because the Delawares were so pivotal and so widespread through history, their descendants are nearly everywhere.

Linguistics offers insight into Delaware origins. Over time Eastern Algonquian divided into a number of separate languages and dialects. Munsee, a Delaware dialect, was spoken in the northern territory of that language group, while Unami was spoken in the southern part of the Delaware-speaking region. The Unamis themselves divided into northern and southern bodies. Southern Unami survives today among the Delaware Tribe of Indians in Oklahoma. Their immediate Delaware ancestors in the seventeenth century lived on the Pennsylvania side of the Delaware River across from what is now Trenton, New Jersey. Delaware territory extended through the present-day state of New Jersey into New York and across the tip of Manhattan and Long Island.

The prehistory of the Atlantic coastal region where the Europeans first encountered the Delawares is poorly understood because it probably lies submerged under the Atlantic Ocean now. Scholars like Charles Callender and others have delved into the topic deeply. There are Paleo-Indian sites (such as the Shawnee-Minisink site in Pennsylvania, which dates to 8640 B.C.), but any connection to inhabitants of the area during the historic period is pure conjecture. Scientists believe the Indians of the Northeast first made widespread use of marine shellfish as a food source during the Archaic period and began using polished stone woodworking tools (called celts). Their use spread to southeastern peoples. The Indians also made use of red-ocher paint for burials and placed broken pottery with the deceased. Those practices were found throughout the region. During the subsequent Woodland period, cultures speaking similar languages developed marked differences upstream (or inland) from their downstream (coastal) kin. The changes were analogous to later upstream Munsee and downstream Unami. There were Iroquois influences in the upstream regions after A.D. 1200, but they are believed to be parallel social developments among neighbors, not the result of conquest.

The Delawares played important roles in early colonial history along the mid-Atlantic. The Indians living along today's Delaware River and New York shorelines first met Europeans arriving in the late sixteenth and early seventeenth centuries. As a result of their early contact with Europeans, the Delawares established many firsts in the long relationship between Indian and non-Indian cultures. Delawares made the first agreements. For example, in 1629 the Dutch met with a council of Delaware Bay Indians near present Lewes, Delaware. Dutch, Swedish, Finnish, and English settlers arrived between 1609 and the 1640s. Because European settlement spread inland from the coastline, the Delawares were also pushed steadily westward. As a result of their odyssey, the Delawares were widely scattered in a historic diaspora and intermarried among numerous Native peoples.

A lengthy migration tale, called the Walum Olum, details a long journey over time for the Delawares. Bark slabs decorated with markings allegedly relate a migration legend across the Bering Strait, followed by a trek crossing the Mississippi River to their homeland on the Atlantic Coast. It was given great credence into the twentieth century. David Ostreicher and other scholars have discredited the Walum Olum, however, which is now largely ignored.

Delaware villages dotted the coastal and riverine regions of lower New England and the Mid-Atlantic region. Longhouses of bark or reed gave shelter to extended families. Their dwellings were vented in the ceiling, and residents slept inside on mats in colder weather. Village farmers raised corn, beans, and squash and gathered nuts and berries in season. Women and children tended nearby cornfields and gardens, while men hunted, especially during the summer, fall, and winter. They provided deer but also bear, moose, wolves, many varieties of fowl, and fish as well as shellfish. Membership was matrilineal. Villages, led by chiefs, could combine with kinfolk in nearby communities as a "tribe" to defend their territory from outside threat. Village and larger councils addressed important concerns. Political organization was quite loose. Delaware-speaking peoples belonged to distinct ethnic groups but were not part of an organized political unit. That would come later in their history.

Early Delaware spirituality is only poorly grasped, because the earliest observers did not understand what they witnessed. The Creator, Great Manito, surveyed the world covered with water. The supreme god is also called Kee-shay-lum-moo-kawng, "who thought us into being," Our Creator. The Great Manito summoned a turtle from the depths of the water. As the turtle surfaced and water coursed off its shell, a tree grew on it. The tree sent out a root. From the sprout came a man. From a second sprout a woman appeared. They became the ancestors of the Delawares. The turtle symbolized earth, life itself. The Great Manito placed four lesser spirits in each of the four directions and assigned them duties. The sun was given the role of providing light. The sun and moon were addressed as Elder Brothers. Delaware youths participated in varied initiatory rites. The Delawares also practiced a Green Corn Ceremony annually before harvest time. Other rituals were supplemented during their sojourn in Indiana along the White River Valley by a reformed ritual called the Big House Ceremony, named for the location where it took place. Inside the structure a series of spiritual activities occurred; while they are no longer performed, the Big House lingers in the memory of tribespeople. On the contemporary Delaware tribal seal is the black-and-red rendition of Mesingw (the Mask Being). Mesingw is the guardian spirit of game animals and aids hunters to be successful, and his face was carved on the center pole of the Big House lodge.

The first encounters between the Delawares and Europeans were not recorded. At some point they met the Dutch, Swedes, and others. The most famous encounter was the Dutch "purchase" of Manhattan (a Delaware word) Island from Delaware-speaking Indians in 1626. The Dutch built Fort Amsterdam there. It developed into New Amsterdam, which itself was the start of the later New York City. Dutch fur trade activity engaged the Delawares and radically altered their lives. The Indians' material culture changed as they adopted trade goods. There were an estimated 8,000 Delawares at the time. The trade depleted beavers locally within twenty-five years and led to expansion of trapping territory by the mid-1660s. The expanding Dutch population also created increasing conflict, which led to loss of Native population and pushed the Delawares out of the area. That began the splintering of the Delawares. A young David Brainerd was shocked to find that the New Jersey Delawares he had come to preach to "were very much scattered." In subsequent years the Southern Unami–speakers were pressed up the Delaware River to the Susquehanna and farther to the Allegheny (whose name comes from a Delaware word) then on to the upper Ohio Valley. In that valley diverse groups merged to form the Delaware tribe around 1750. It had three major clans: Turkey, Turtle, and Wolf.

Because of their location, the Delawares continued to play a prime role in Indian relations with the European arrivals and then with the new American nation. At Newcomer's Town in 1774, Delawares signed the first treaty with the later United States. On September 15, 1778, at Fort Pitt representatives of the fledging United States signed its first treaty with an Indian tribe—the Delawares. They provided support and warriors for the American Revolutionary War cause in exchange for food and the promise of heading a future Indian state.

Other Delawares in the upper Ohio Valley, including Munsees, gradually joined their kinfolk along that river. It was a "prodigious rich" land in the words of trader George Croghan's journal. Rivalries during the American Revolution forced the Delawares to take sides, further dividing them. Eventually the main body of the Delawares after the Treaty of Greenville (1795) relocated to central Indiana along the West Fork of the White River in the vicinity of the present city of Anderson, named for their chief. Other kin were scattered far and wide. The main group departed under the terms of the Treaty of Saint Mary's (1818, which opened the region around Fort Wayne, Indiana, to non-Indian settlement) and removed to southern Missouri, where they joined earlier Delaware emigrants in the Cape Girardeau region. Delaware settlements had been in the area for some time. New Madrid, Missouri, grew up around a Delaware town. In 1780 two Canadians established a trading post there. Spanish soldiers garrisoned a post there in 1789. The town grew up around the fort. Osage hostility and a desire to tap the western prairie for bison led the Delawares to sign an 1829 treaty. They ceded their Missouri tract in exchange for a reserve in Kansas to the west of what is now Kansas City. The Delawares moved by 1831 and were joined by kinfolk who came from the Sandusky River in Ohio. Delawares who migrated to Kansas included Canadian Munsees, Mahicans, Nanticokes, and Conoys, all Algonquian-speakers. In 1837 more Munsees came from Canada and settled among Ojibwes already in Kansas. U.S. authorities in 1861 appointed Charles Journeycake chief of the Delawares in Kansas. He was a Baptist minister from Ohio, and officials hoped he would prove cooperative.

The Delawares in Kansas came under intense pressure to cede their land. Options were few. Events in Kansas engulfed the Delawares, who faced intense pressures. Contending sides of the slavery issue clashed around the Indians. Wagon trains heading westward traversed Indian lands. Railroad interests coveted the Delaware reserve, which included a corridor across a portion of the state. Their Indian agent was a stockholder in the railroad company and used his influence to secure agreements. A treaty of April 8, 1867, modified a treaty from a year earlier with the Delawares. The 1867 agreement provided for the Delawares to remove to Indian Territory and select allotments. The Delawares paid the Cherokee Nation $121,824 for full privileges and rights within that nation. Another $157,600 payment purchased a land base in that nation for the Delawares. The payments totaled $279,424, a sum that exceeded what any other tribe paid for land in the Indian Territory.

Late in 1867 the Delawares moved to the Cherokee Nation to what are now Nowata, Rogers, and Craig counties in northeastern Oklahoma. More traditional Delawares paused on Peoria land east of the Neosho River before taking allotments in Washington County in 1873. They were termed the "Neosho Delawares." The larger portion were referred to as the "Cherokee Delawares" or the "Registered Delawares." The 1867 signatories were viewed as a group not representative of the larger Delaware Tribe and had signed without the tribe's knowledge or consent. When Congress ratified the agreement, it also deceived the Delaware Tribe. The Delawares were placed in an untenable position of not being able to go back to Kansas yet not wanting to be absorbed by the Cherokee Nation.

Delawares experienced many missionary endeavors, especially as they moved across the continent. A Swedish Lutheran missionary, John Campanius, began conversion inroads among the tribe in 1643. Anglican and other preachers attempted to gain converts in the East before great dislocations took their heaviest toll. Among the most famous were the efforts of Baptist minister Isaac McCoy in the Midwest. He was an early advocate of Indian removal to preserve Native culture and lives and saw no conflict between Christianity and Indian ceremonies. Among the enduring attempts at missionization of the Delawares were those of Moravians across the centuries. These evangelicals led by example and worked tirelessly among the Delawares and allied peoples. Famous missionaries at Moravian churches among the Delawares include David Zeisberger (who described his flocks in the 1770s) and John Heckwelder (who chronicled the mission effort after 1740). After the French and Indian War, Moravian missionaries removed their converts to the Muskingum River in Ohio and there erected the towns of Salem, Schonbrunn, and Gnadenhutten. Among Moravian converts during their three generations of mission activity was the famous Chief Teedyuscung after the mid-1740s. David Brainerd, whom Jonathan Edwards immortalized in print, zealously evangelized the Delawares in 1744–47 but had brief success.

The relocatees in Indian Territory gradually made adjustments to their new surroundings. But they faced a new threat. The Cherokee Commission brought allotment to northeastern Oklahoma after 1895, and the division began adversely affecting Delaware Tribe members under the Dawes Commission after 1904. The federal government opened the remaining land to non-Indian settlers, increasing assimilation pressures. The U.S. Supreme Court in the 1904 case *Delaware Indians. v. Cherokee Nation* (193 U.S. 127) decreed that the Delawares "should be given equal rights in the lands and funds of the Cherokee Nation." That full inclusion would be used against the Delaware Tribe in its later bid to separate from the Cherokee Nation.

The U.S. Supreme Court in February 1977 made available Indian Claims Commission awards from 1963 and 1969, providing a share of $15 million to the Delawares through a 1972 appropriations measure (Public Law 92-456). The tribe set aside a portion for health and educational expenses for tribespeople. Tribal members approved an investment plan in 1991 for about $4 million awarded the year before under Public Law 92-456, as compensation for lands in Indiana that the Delawares gave up when removed in 1830. A tribal trust board oversees the funds.

Delawares' desire for their own tribal identity continued to burn within them. In early 1979 the BIA quashed that hope when it abolished the tribal business committee and cut off operating funds, maintaining that the Delawares were subject to the terms of the 1867 treaty and under the control of the Cherokee Nation. BIA officials suggested a per capita division of judgment funds as part of tribal termination, although the BIA had not released the funds. The Delaware struggle for autonomy had been a long one. In 1995 interior secretary Bruce Babbitt and in 1996 assistant secretary of the interior for Indian affairs Ada Deer recognized the Delawares as a separate tribe. The Cherokee Nation claimed that the normal recognition process had been bypassed and immediately filed litigation, but an appellate court in 2004 held for the Delawares until the Tenth Circuit Court of Appeals later that year ruled in favor of the Cherokee Nation.

Beginning in 1993 the tribe sponsored an annual symposium on Delaware history and culture. It was part of a conscious effort to restore interest in the Delaware heritage. That interest has led to the production of language CDs. The Delawares of Oklahoma participated in the formation of the Delaware Nation Grand Council of North America in 1992 in Ohio. The tribal council guided the restoration of damaged gravestones that mark the resting places of former tribal leaders in a cemetery in Kansas City, Kansas. The Delawares had a reservation there before they removed to Oklahoma. They dedicated the reconditioned cemetery in April 1997. The following year a tribal representative attended the dedication ceremony for a monument commemorating the 1843 sale of Delaware land to the homeless Wyandotte Indians. The monument is on the campus of Kansas City Community College. For the first time since 1821 leaders of the Delaware tribes of Oklahoma met in early 1999. Their purpose was to address repatriation cultural issues. It was a preliminary step toward the formation of a joint Native American Graves Protection and Repatriation Act (NAGPRA) committee.

Delawares return to Indiana for tribal celebrations and to recall their ancestral presence there. Delaware chief William Anderson helped found Anderson, Indiana, on the White River in the late eighteenth century. Contemporary tribespeople also return to the Connor Prairie Museum in Fisher (an Indianapolis suburb), where tribal members teach Delaware history, culture, and customs to elementary school children. Connor Prairie is the site of the home of William Connor, who was married to Chief Anderson's daughter, Mekinzes. They founded a line of Delaware leaders.

Small communities in the vicinity of the Kansas Motor Speedway expressed interest in a tribal gaming project. But the decision of the Tenth

Circuit Court quashed any effort to acquire trust land status.

Tribal members also maintain ties to their heritage through rituals, dance, and song. They gather for funeral feasts like their ancestors and offer certain rituals. Delaware descendants also share their heritage and culture in many private and individual ways. Some tribal members are Peyotists. John Wilson (Moonhead), a Caddo-Delaware, introduced the Peyote sacrament around 1880. A form of the Native American Church called the Fish Moon rituals was practiced on the north side of the communities of Little Caney and Cotton Creek on the reserve; Wilson's Big Moon adherents gathered on the south side in the communities of Coon Creek, Blue Mound, and Hogshooter. Charlie Elkhair later led a splinter group. Tribal members sponsor an annual powwow (in early June) and other dances that draw participants and visitors from afar to the tribal ground, called Fall-Leaf Dance Grounds. Eagle Ridge on Copan Lake is another dance ground maintained by the tribe since the mid-1990s for gatherings. Some Delaware women wear the elaborate hair decoration (the *dastuh*) associated with the Caddos. Around the dance circle observers will see traditional dance clothes that are still decorated with the old Delaware curvilinear Woodland designs. The floral patterns of the beadwork designs harken back to ancient ancestral usages. Although Delaware ceremonialism has changed through the centuries, it has not disappeared. Green Corn ceremonies and Big House rituals are no longer performed. But public ceremonies continue, in which participants assemble for a feast and name giving, listen to prayers and addresses, and dress in regalia for dances. Some Delawares visit neighboring tribes for powwows and stomp dances. Some attend the Shawnee Bread Dance. Like the Shawnees and Yuchis, the Delawares play an Indian version of football as an opening event for their spring ceremonial season.

The Delaware legacy also exists on maps and in politics. Numerous place names record their presence on the Atlantic seaboard, such as the cities of Hoboken and Passaic in New Jersey. The state of Delaware as well as the bay and river of the same name are the most visible signs of the Delaware imprint upon the map. The city of Leavenworth, Kansas, arose on land that the Delawares ceded, which military authorities colluded to open even before the treaty had been announced. Bartlesville grew into a city on the Oklahoma land of a Delaware woman. In politics, the Delaware chief Tamanend signed the Treaty of Shakamaxon with William Penn in Philadelphia in 1682. Tamanend's name was immortalized when New York City officials created Tammany Hall as their political club. The Tammany Society began in the 1780s as an artistic fraternal organization but evolved into a political machine in the hands of adroit politicians. The names of the Oklahoma communities of Nowata and Lenapah derive from Delaware words. A national Delaware Heritage Trail, commemorating the Delaware experience across the eastern United States, is planned.

Among notable Delaware Tribe members was the Delaware Prophet (Neolin) during the 1760s. Neolin was one in a series of Delaware shamans whose visions influenced Pontiac to lead his 1763 rebellion against English colonial encroachments. Delaware guides led Zebulon Pike and John C. Frémont across the western American landscape. John Kilbuck, a descendant of Delaware chiefs, was ordained a Moravian missionary in 1884. He and his wife, Edith, founded the famous Bethel Mission on the Kuskokwim River among the Yup'ik Eskimos. James Chrysostom Bouchard (Watomika, born in 1823 in what is now Kansas and raised partly among the Comanches) converted to the Catholic faith and became a Jesuit in 1855, making him the first Indian ordained in the Roman Catholic priesthood in the United States. A more recent notable member was Roberta Campbell (Mrs. E. B.) Lawson, who was president of the national General Federation of Women's Clubs from 1935 to 1938. Tribal member Steve Rodenberg won the 242-pound open division in 1997 at the World Powerlifting Championship held in England. Jacob Parks depicted Delaware ceremonies in art. Ruthe Blalock Jones (who is also of Loyal Shawnee and Peoria descent) is a noted painter. She is a former student of Dick West and head of the art department at Bacone University. Banker, attorney, and businessman Phil Busey of Oklahoma City is a tribal descendant.

SUGGESTED READING

Bierhorst, John. *Mythology of the Lenape: Guide and Texts.* Tucson: University of Arizona Press, 1995.

Brown, James W., and Rita Kohn, eds. *Long Journey Home.* Bloomington: Indiana University Press, 2008.

Callender, Charles. "Great Lakes-Riverine Sociopolitical Organization." In vol. 15, *Northeast,* of the *Handbook of North American Indians*, 610–21. Washington, D.C.: Smithsonian Institution, 1978.

Croghan, George. "A Selection of George Croghan's Letters and Journals Relating to Tours in the Western Country." In Reuben Gold Thwaites, ed., *Early Western Travels*, vol. 1, 45–173. New York: AMS, 1966.

Edwards, Jonathan. *The Life of David Brainerd* (originally published 1822 *as Memoirs of David Brainerd).* Edited by Norman Pettit. New Haven: Yale University Press, 1985.

Grumet, Robert S. *Voices from the Delaware Big House.* Norman: University of Oklahoma Press, 2001.

Harrington, Mark. *Indians of New Jersey: Dickon among the Lenape.* New Brunswick, N.J.: Rutgers University Press, 1963 (for young readers).

Heckwelder, John. *A Narrative of the Mission of the United Brethren among the Delaware and Mohegan Indians* (originally published 1820). Cleveland: Burrows Company, 1907.

Miller, Jay. *The Delaware.* Chicago: Children's Press, 1994 (for young readers).

Ostreicher, David. "The Anatomy of the Walam Olum: The Dissection of a 19th-Century Anthropological Hoax." Ph.D. dissertation, Rutgers University, 1995.

Perry, Lynette, and Manny Skolnick. *Keeper of the Delaware Dolls.* Lincoln: University of Nebraska Press, 2000.

Schutt, Amy C. *Peoples of the River Valleys: The Odyssey of the Delaware Indians.* Philadelphia: University of Pennsylvania Press, 2007.

Wallace, Anthony F. C. *King of the Delawares: Teedyuscung, 1700–1763.* Philadelphia: University of Pennsylvania Press, 1949.

Weslager, C. A. *The Delaware Indians: A History.* New Brunswick, N.J.: Rutgers University Press, 1972.

———. *The Delawares: A Critical Bibliography.* Bloomington: Indiana University Press, 1978.

Wilker, Josh. *The Lenape.* New York: Chelsea House, 1994 (for young readers).

Zeisberger, David. *The Moravian Mission Diaries of David Zeisberger.* Translated by Julie Weber. University Park: Pennsylvania State University Press, 2005.

Fort Sill Apache

NAME

The designation "Fort Sill Apaches" is derived from the twentieth-century confinement of Warm Springs (Ojo Caliente in Spanish) and Chiricahua Apaches identified with the leader Geronimo who resided at the U.S. Army fort on the northern edge of Lawton, Oklahoma. The Fort Sill Apaches identify themselves as one of the four divisions of Chiricahua Apaches. Their tribal name comes from the Chiricahua Mountains of their homeland. They call themselves Nd'e, "the People." Earlier they referred to themselves as Chogunan, "great mountain" or "mountain People." "Apache" may have come from a Zuni term meaning "enemy."

LOCATION AND GOVERNMENT

The headquarters for the "Fort Sill Apache Tribe" is in Apache in Caddo County, in southwestern Oklahoma north of the city of Lawton. The tribe operates under the terms of a 1976 constitution. Members erected a four-building complex on 2.5 acres in the early 1980s. The landholding grew to about 270 acres in Oklahoma by 2007 (with another 30 acres for a restaurant in Deming, New Mexico, and 4 acres in Arizona). The tribal headquarters has an Allan Houser sculpture of a family facing the complex to remind viewers not to forget the past. There is no tribal website.

BUSINESSES

Major revenue derives from the tribe's one gaming operation, Fort Sill Apache Casino and Smoke Shop, located on Gore Boulevard in Lawton near Interstate 44.

NUMBER

The tribe has about 650 members, based on a descendancy roll.

The Chiricahuas share linguistic connections with other Indians, such as the Chippewas, but especially with Southern Athapaskan–speaking peoples, usually referred to as Apaches and Navajos. The language connection implies a common origin at some time in the dim past, normally believed to have been in the far North sometime around A.D. 1200. Origin stories focus on twin heroes, Fireboy and Waterboy. The twins in oral tradition slew monsters threatening this world and established order for the universe. Oral tradition that focuses on the Southwest and northern Mexico lends credence to long residence there instead of the much more recent arrival that scholars often claim.

Chiricahuas lived in widely dispersed kin-based bands. Their society was matrilineal and relied on hunting and gathering. They engaged in almost no cultivation. Members of their closely knit group remained largely autonomous. Not until the mid-nineteenth century did outside forces foster the rise of leaders of whole bands, like Cochise of the Central Band.

By about A.D. 1500 or even much earlier the Apaches had established themselves in the American Southwest. The Chiricahuas occupied the region of what is now southwestern New Mexico, southeastern Arizona, and northern Mexico. Their home territory consisted of the Dos Cabezas, Chiricahua, and Dragoon mountains of the far southeastern corner of Arizona. After 1500 the Spanish pressured the Apaches to hispanicize, but the Chiricahuas offered continual resistance. Antonio de Espejo's desire to explore a part of New Mexico in 1583 was thwarted by what Spaniards termed "Querechos," believed by ethnographers to have been Eastern Chiricahuas.

Although the Chiricahua population originally numbered about 3,000, constant warfare and deprivation drastically reduced its size. The Chiricahuas' bitter enemies the Mexicans in the state of Sonora in 1835 offered a bounty of $100 (or 100 pesos) for each adult Chiricahua Apache scalp, with a lesser amount for the scalps of women and children. The bounty did not slow Chiricahua raiding, and Mexican rancheros provided them with an ongoing supply of foodstuffs and captives. Remnants of the Nednai Apaches from northern Mexico joined the Chiricahuas.

Mangas Coloradas (Spanish for "red sleeves"), a giant man who also had an immense reputation, served as the acknowledged leader of the Eastern Band of the Chiricahuas from 1842 to 1863 in their opposition to the Mexicans. He led the Bedonkohes and Chihennes bands. At first he welcomed the friendly Americans into the region, but their increasing numbers and demands led him into opposition. He and his son-in-law Cochise led raids in Apacheria that made them a byword for fear. In 1863 Mangas Coloradas tried to make peace with U.S. soldiers who were bearing a false white flag of truce but was seized and beheaded by angry miners and members of General James H. Carleton's troop column from California. That act, of course, only fueled more warfare.

Finally, the tactics of General George Crook in the early 1870s and the peace efforts of Tom Jeffords brought an end to the Apache wars. The model Indian agent John P. Clum worked diligently to settle his new charges into a routine at the San Carlos Agency after 1874 following Cochise's death. Forced consolidation of Apache bands there led to the first Chiricahua breakout and subsequent renewed warfare. Some surrendered and were shackled at San Carlos, only to break out again. Victorio led forty warriors in an escape to protest removal to San Carlos and abandonment of their homeland. He was killed in an 1880 fight with Mexican troops at Tres Castillos in the state of Chihuahua. The medicine man Geronimo was one of those who assumed command. After the 1850s he made war against Mexicans to avenge the murder of his family at Janos in northern Chihuahua. Following another breakout from the reservation, General Crook was recalled to take up the pursuit of Geronimo. Al Sieber, chief of scouts, was a part of the U.S. Army entourage as well as New York Herald reporter Frank Randall, who offered his readers eyewitness accounts. After Geronimo again escaped from confinement, Crook was relieved of his command. The tactics of General Nelson A. Miles, who ultimately used one-fourth of the whole U.S. Army in pursuit, helped force the surrender. Some five thousand U.S. soldiers, three thousand Mexican troops, and hundreds of scouts and volunteers chased about thirty members of the

Geronimo, ca. 1898

Photograph by Adolph F. Muir. Library of Congress, Prints and Photographs Division, Washington, D.C., cph 3c24560.

Apache band. Leonard Wood, who later gained fame in the Cuban and Philippine campaigns, was a member of the troop. Author John G. Bourke, who wrote vividly of the chase, was a military aide. The terror across the Southwest resulted less from conflict than from journalistic hysteria. But Geronimo became famous and his name (from the Spanish Jerónimo, Jerome) entered the American vocabulary. Well after he returned to farming, he rode in Theodore Roosevelt's inaugural parade in 1905. In 1909 Geronimo fell from his horse, became ill, and died of pneumonia. He is buried in the

Fort Sill Apache Cemetery. After twenty-four years as a prisoner of war, he was not permitted to return to his beloved Arizona homeland.

As a result of the Treaty of Guadalupe Hidalgo in 1848 and the Mexican Cession, the United States laid claim to a large segment of Chiricahua Apache territory. Miners, ranchers, and farmers flooded the region, under the protection of U.S. Army troops. Military force (some of the officers were also investors) pressured the Apaches until they reluctantly agreed to move to a reservation. Many of the Chiricahuas lived peacefully on first one reservation then another. Upon Geronimo's 1886 surrender, General Miles lied and promised the hostiles fertile lands after a mere two-year imprisonment. Instead, all 498 men, women, and children were collected at San Carlos and shipped aboard railroad cattle cars to exile at Fort Marion in Florida. A public outcry had fed the pressure to remove the Chiricahuas. Male leaders like Geronimo were sent to Fort Pickens on the opposite side of Florida. Miles had promised that the families would remain together. Instead they were separated. Peaceful, noncombatant Apaches as well as cooperative army scouts like Chatto were also herded together and sent away. Two years later the exiles were moved to Mount Vernon Barracks just north of Mobile, Alabama. There a young Walter Reed served as post surgeon. (He would go on to glory as a professor of medicine at the Army Medical College: his experiments connected the deadly yellow fever to a virus transmitted in the bite of mosquitoes and his abatement procedures helped residents of Cuba and canal laborers in Panama.) A few other Apaches were added to the number in 1891.

Tragically, ultimately nearly one-third of the Apache children sent to Carlisle Indian School in Pennsylvania died there. Geronimo's son Chappa briefly attended Carlisle and is one of those buried in the National Cemetery portion of Magnolia Cemetery in Mobile. After seven years the 296 Apaches were moved again in 1894 to Fort Sill, where they established twelve hamlets. That base was their prisoner of war camp for twenty years. President Grover Cleveland established a reservation there for them early in 1897 by executive order. Dislocation, malnutrition, and damp climate—the Apaches claimed that they had to climb to the tops of trees in the woodland of Alabama just to glimpse the sun—led to continual loss of life.

Frank Hill Wright and Walter Roe Cloud established a Dutch Reformed Church of America mission school in 1899, and in 1903 Geronimo became their most famous convert. Today the Apache Reformed Church in Apache, Oklahoma, serves as a community center, meeting place, and location for socializing for tribal members. Lawton school superintendent Stephen Barrett obtained President Roosevelt's permission (despite army staff objections) to take down, transcribe, and publish Geronimo's memoirs, aided by returned Carlisle student Asa Daklugie.

As the close of the frontier and very distant rumblings of world war loomed for the American military, the U.S. Army wanted to turn Fort Sill into an artillery school in 1910. Geronimo's death the year before helped clear the path by eliminating an icon. Chiricahua farms, unfulfilled allotment pledges, and a very successful cattle operation, however, blocked the development. Politicians hastily appended to the end of the annual Indian appropriation bill for 1912 a provision (Public Law 335) that granted the Apache prisoners their freedom. The federal government sold Chiricahua cattle at a loss and closed that operation. The Apaches could not be moved back to Arizona because of lingering memories of the recent past, so the Mescalero Reservation located west of Roswell, New Mexico, was selected as their destination. The Chiricahua prisoners were forced to take 80-acre allotments or choose to return to New Mexico. Of the remaining Chiricahua Apaches, 163 of them who were more traditional left for New Mexico and 76 who were more acculturated to their farms remained on their allotted land scattered around the towns of Apache and Fletcher in southwestern Oklahoma. After twenty-eight years of imprisonment they were officially freed from prisoner of war status in 1914. The removal of members to New Mexico further divided the former prisoners. It was a sad ending to a flagrant example of unfair confinement and malicious abuse of a group for the sake of mining and ranching profits in Arizona. It remains one of the most blatant injustices in U.S. history.

The Fort Sill Apaches never formally organized under the federal government's guidelines such as the OIWA. In the mid-1970s the tribe finally underwent a reorganization and received an Indian Claims Commission award for lands lost. They formally linked with their Warm Springs kinfolk in New Mexico under the long-time leadership of Mildred Cleghorn. She accompanied

Artist Allan Houser and Chief Mildred Cleghorn (Fort Sill Apaches), by Houser's sculpture *As Long as the Waters Flow* (1988) at the State Capitol, 1989

© *Anna Marie Houser*

some Chiricahua Apaches who returned to Arizona in 1986 for a centennial commemoration of Geronimo's surrender at Skeleton Canyon north of Fort Bowie. One of the picnic observers, shocked at the sudden appearance of the Indians, later gave four acres to the tribe. The Fort Sill Tribe once owned the land near their ancestral Dragoon Mountains in Cochise County, Arizona. Now the Dragoon Mountains lie mostly within Coronado National Forest. The Apaches had occupied a reservation in the vicinity of the town of Benson in the 1870s and unsuccessfully sought a casino location there in the 1990s.

The tribe maintains some of its traditional ceremonies. Although the major event is the girl's puberty ceremony among other Apache groups in the Southwest, it is not emphasized among the Fort Sill Apaches. Most notable are the Apache Fire Dancers, whose nighttime effects of fire, shadows, and movements evoke mountain spirits. They paint the top part of their bodies and wear a kilt skirt with a belt and boots. On their heads they wear a U-shaped wooden slat crown and a mask. The four dancers (for four directions and four seasons) give thanks for crops and prosperity. Their steps enthrall spectators, while the antics of the clown alarm some. The Fort Sill Tribe sponsors a Ceremonial Dance weekend in late September, which brings many people to the gathering. A tribal princess in traditional regalia is a part of the events.

Among notable Fort Sill Apache members was long-time chairwoman Mildred Cleghorn (1910–97). She was born a prisoner of war but went on to receive the Ellis Island Medal of Honor from president Ronald Reagan and was considered a National Treasure. She exhibited her dolls twice at the Smithsonian Institution's Folklife Festival. Cleghorn was elected chair of the newly consolidated Fort Sill Chiricahua–Warm Springs Apache Tribe in 1976 and served in that capacity for eighteen years. She is buried in Fort Sill's Apache Cemetery.

Cleghorn's cousin Allan C. Houser (1914–94) changed the family last name from Haozous, "pulling root," to Americanize it. He was the first baby born to a Fort Sill family after the end of their captivity and grew up to become a teacher and a world-renowned sculptor. He studied with Dorothy Dunn in Santa Fe then became a painter and muralist (the inside of the Department of the Interior building in Washington, D.C., contains his series of murals) before turning to sculpture. Houser went on to found the sculpture curriculum at the Institute of American Indian Art in Santa Fe. President George H. W. Bush awarded him the National Medal of Arts at the White House in 1992. Houser is considered "the patriarch of Native American contemporary fine art." His personal all-time favorite sculpture was *As Long as the Waters Flow,* a fourteen-foot-tall black bronze statue on the south side of the Capitol in Oklahoma City. Painter Carol Soatikee was Fort Sill Apache and Pima. Carlisle-educated Jason Betzinez as an elderly man stumped the cast on the popular television game show *What's My Line?* in 1958. Panelists failed to guess that as a young man he had followed Geronimo on the warpath. Inman Cloyde Gooday, a respected medicine man, was recognized as the Outstanding Indian of the Year at the Anadarko American Indian Exposition in 2000. He was the patriarch of the Fire Dance. The grave of Geronimo continues to serve as a pilgrimage site for visitors to Fort Sill because of his legendary status in American history.

SUGGESTED READING

"Allan Houser: An American Treasure." *News from Indian Country,* April 17, 2006, 19 ("patriarch" quotation).

Ball, Eve, et al. *Indeh: An Apache Odyssey.* Provo, Utah: Brigham Young University Press, 1980; repr. Norman: University of Oklahoma Press, 1988.

Barrett, Stephen M., ed. *Geronimo's Story of His Life.* New York: Duffield, 1906; repr., edited by Frederick W. Turner, New York: Dutton, 1970.

Betzinez, Jason, with Wilbur Nye. *I Fought with Geronimo.* Harrisburg, Pa.: Stackpole, 1959.

Chamberlain, Kathleen. *Victorio: Apache Warrior and Chief.* Norman: University of Oklahoma Press, 2007.

Debo, Angie. *Geronimo: The Man, His Time, His Place.* Norman: University of Oklahoma Press, 1976.

Geronimo and the Apache Resistance. Los Angeles: Peace River Films, 1988 (part of the American Experience series on PBS).

Haley, James L. *Apaches: A History and Culture Portrait.* Norman: University of Oklahoma Press, 1999.

Johze, Benedick. "The Fort Sill Apache." *Chronicles of Oklahoma* 39 (Winter 1961–62): 427–32.

Lieder, Michael, and Jake Page. *Wild Justice: The People of Geronimo vs. the United States.* New York: Random House, 1997.

Sladen, Joseph Alton. *Making Peace with Cochise: The 1872 Journal of Captain Joseph Alton Sladen.* Edited by Edwin R. Sweeney. Norman: University of Oklahoma Press, 1997.

Sneve, Virginia Driving Hawk. *The Apaches: A First Americans Book.* New York: Holiday House, 1997 (for very young readers).

Stockel, H. Henrietta. "An Annotated Chiricahua Apache Bibliography: Selected Books." *American Indian Quarterly* 25 (Winter 2001): 153–76.

———. *On the Bloody Road to Jesus: Christianity and the Chiricahua Apaches.* Albuquerque: University of New Mexico, 2004.

———. *Survival of the Spirit: Chiricahua Apaches in Captivity.* Reno: University Press of Nevada, 1993.

Turcheneske, John A., Jr. *The Chiricahua Apache Prisoners of War: Fort Sill, 1894–1914.* Niwot: University Press of Colorado, 1997.

Fox

See the "Sac and Fox" *entry.*

Iowa

NAME

The Iowas call themselves Paxoche or Pahodje (also spelled Bah-kho-Je), "gray snow." The name "Iowa" or "Ioway" is from the French name "Ayouais."

LOCATION AND GOVERNMENT

The "Iowa Tribe of Oklahoma" headquarters is three miles south of the town of Perkins in Lincoln County. Their tribal form of government was established under the 1936 OIWA, with a tribal business committee of five members, a constitution, by-laws, and a charter. Elections are held every two years, with officers serving staggered terms. The tribal website is www.iowanation.org.

BUSINESSES

Revenue derives from the Cimarron Bingo Casino in the former Veterans' Hall on trust land in the town of Perkins, smoke shops, a Minimart in the community of Carney, and Bah-kho-Je Gallery in Coyle. The tribe has a nonprofit aviary for injured eagles.

NUMBER

There are about 500 Iowas in the vicinity of Perkins, although most Iowas live throughout the United States, with some scattered overseas. Approximately 3,000 northern Iowa members are enrolled on their reservation in Kansas, south of the towns of Falls City and Rulo in Nebraska, and scattered across the United States. The northern Iowa Tribe has its headquarters in White Cloud, a community on the Missouri River in Brown County, Kansas.

The Iowas are Chiwere Siouan–speakers, which means that they are related by language to the Otoes and Missourias and distantly related to the Winnebagos (Ho-Chunks). Archeologists trace their prehistoric antecedents, like those of other Chiwere Siouan–speakers, to the Oneota culture after A.D. 900 west of the Mississippi and Missouri river valleys, especially to the upper Iowa River during the centuries preceding European occupation. "Oneota" is the name that archeologists gave the Upper Mississippian prehistoric culture found on that river and spread across many states in the region. Archeologist R. F. Sasso placed the Iowas near the present Twin Cities of Minnesota in 1100. The Chiweres are all believed to have been at one time Proto-Winnebagos who resided in the Great Lakes region. The main body moved westward to the Iowa River Valley, where the Iowas split from the main group and the Otoe-Missourias continued southwestward to the mouth of the Grand River in what is now Missouri before they became separate tribal groups. The ancestral Iowas resided in villages on terraces above rivers. Women grew crops of corn, pumpkins, beans, and other produce in the rich soil of the floodplain. Hunters supplemented their diet with game, such as buffalo, antelope, and fowl. Streams offered fish, mussels, and clams. Clay mixed with ground mussel shell was used to produce pottery bowls and other decorated containers. Extended families, arranged according to clans, resided in a village. Like their kindred Otoes, the Iowas had seven chiefs and seven clans. By the nineteenth century the Iowas had dual clan divisions, which were made up of several subclans. The Black Bear clan dominated the clans in one division (called a phratry) that was responsible for the winter and early spring activities of the tribe. The second major segment, the Buffalo clan, oversaw agriculture and spring and summer activities. Leadership was hereditary.

Stories of the mythic origin of the Iowas point to Red Earth, on the Wisconsin shore of Lake Michigan. The Great Spirit created all things. After putting into place the universe and all its forms, the Great Spirit sent clan heads to the Iowas. The black bear came out of the ground and brought the canoe and the sacred Pipe. The bear taught the people how to farm. In other versions the bear, pigeon, and buffalo came from above.

The Iowas also shared a legacy with their Oneota forbears in their use of medicine bundles and shamanistic societies. They utilized tattooing as a sign of high rank. Scholar David Blakeslee believed that the Dhegiha Siouans, very distant relatives of Chiwere-speakers, well after A.D. 1300 passed the Calumet ceremony (the use of the sacred Pipe in adoptions) from one group to another. Perhaps the Iowas served as the ritual's conduit to the Winnebagos, who in turn passed it on to Algonquian and Iroquois peoples to the north and east. As the Iowa bands migrated, their ancestors lived for a time with Omaha and Ponca bands. They rejoined around 1700 at the Big Sioux River (on the current boundary between South Dakota and Iowa) for defensive and trade advantages. Scholar Dale

Henning speculated that the Iowas/Otoes and Omahas/Poncas were key residents at Blood Run village on that river as they traded with Plains Indians like the Dakotas and other Native settlements in eastern Wisconsin. Blood Run is located about fifteen miles southeast of present-day Sioux Falls, South Dakota. It has hundreds of earthen mounds. Later the Iowas brought red pipestone and hides to trade in the east for European manufactured goods. During this period the Native residents used mounds for burials and a serpent effigy, perhaps as a revitalization movement. Residents abandoned Blood Run after 1714.

The Iowas gradually shifted their residence. French *coureurs de bois* traded with the Iowas starting in the late 1670s as René-Robert Cavelier, Sieur de La Salle, sought to expand French imperial influence. The Iowa villages then were near Lake Pepin and Green Bay in what is now Wisconsin. European trade items such as metal kettles, knives, beads, and cloth and later muskets gradually filtered into Iowa households. The Iowas allied with the Dakota Sioux after 1685 for attacks on Native enemies, especially against the Miamis and their French allies, who sought slaves. The Iowa Indians slowly migrated and resided in various villages in the state that now bears their name. They moved southward and settled near present-day Council Bluffs, where after 1757 they engaged in a flourishing horse trade through the Missouri River Valley region. After about 1700 trade successes led to a golden age for the Iowas. The wealth increased caste, nobility, rank, and status within Iowa society. The Iowas moved to the Des Moines River Valley and on to the Mississippi Valley by the end of the eighteenth century.

European colonial rivalries swept the Iowa Indians into conflicts for European control of people, territory, and commerce through the central and northern Mississippi River region. Although small in number, the Iowas wielded greater influence than might be expected as a result of colonial rivalries and their strategic location between the Mississippi and Missouri rivers. Their warriors fought for the French in the French and Indian War in New York, in the War of 1812 against the Americans, and in the American Civil War on the side of the Union. Iowas joined Sac and Fox Indians in a 1780 assault on St. Louis and in raids on the Osages through the following decade. Although largely loyal to the British at the beginning of the nineteenth century, the Iowas were cultivated by Americans with modest success. The efforts of Manuel Lisa made some headway. Other frontier influences also had long-term impacts. Chief White Cloud married a daughter of French trader Joseph Robidoux, who founded the Blacksnake Hills trading post that later became the community of St. Joseph, Missouri.

Their marriage produced a long-time line of Iowa leaders. Members of the famed Lewis and Clark expedition watched a foray of Iowas, Sacs, and Sioux wade across a river near the mouth of Moreau Creek as they traveled to attack the Osages.

The Louisiana Purchase included lands of the Iowas and other Indian nations. Their incorporation led to radical change. European and American diseases took their toll on the Iowa population and reduced their already small numbers. American frontier expansion at the start of the nineteenth century pressured the Sacs and Foxes to move across the Missouri River into Iowa territory, further restricting Indian hunting territory. Iowa leader Voi-Ri-Gran signed a friendship treaty with the United States in St. Louis in October 1805, and a delegation of Iowas visited Washington, D.C., the following January. The federal government wanted to impress the Native chiefs with urban sights and sounds. That April the Iowas and Sacs and Foxes received their first Indian agent, Nicholas Boilvin. He brought U.S. Indian policies and demands. Federal officials set up trading factories to lure Indians away from Spanish and English influences and to make the Indians indebted to the U.S. government. The authorities also bestowed a peace medal on Indian leader Hard Heart, recognizing him officially as Iowa chief. He and other leaders signed a treaty at Portage des Sioux in September 1815.

Movement of other Indians and white settlement pressured the Iowas to move south and west. Sporadic violence involving Iowas and militias fed tensions. A series of treaties between 1824 and 1838 ceded land to the United States, including portions of today's Missouri and Iowa. Beginning in the 1820s a few Iowa youths were sent for American education near St. Louis. Big Neck (also called Great Walker) and White Cloud sent their children to the Jesuit St. Regis Academy in nearby Florrisant. The United States started efforts to "civilize" the Indians, teaching farming, weaving, and living in log houses. Intermarriage with whites began. By 1838 the Iowas were restricted to a strip of former Kansas Indian land ten miles wide and twenty miles long. It is near present Highland, Kansas, the location of the boarding school that served both Iowa and Sac and Fox pupils under the Reverend Samuel Irwin and the Reverend William Hamilton.

Iowa chiefs attended the grand Indian council that the Cherokees hosted in Tahlequah, Indian Territory, for a month in 1843. The Iowas also toured Europe with George Catlin in the 1840s. White Cloud helped select the tribal travelers.

Increasing intrusion onto their lands and the connivance of their agent led the Iowa chiefs to agree to another land cession in 1854. The small remainder of their land had been allotted to tribal members by 1860. The following year the Iowas ceded much remaining land in Kansas and Nebraska (the latter for the Sac and Fox Indians of the Missouri River). They retained an agency at No Heart, Nebraska. Disputes involving advocates of allotment and release from restrictions and those who favored the status quo fed tribal conflict. Perhaps three-fourths of Iowa males residing in Kansas served in the Union Army, seeing action in two major battles at Prairie Grove in Arkansas and at Baxter Springs in Missouri during that conflict.

In the late 1870s Iowa families began to abandon their Kansas homes and leave for Indian Territory, renewing old friendship with the Sac and Fox Indians, who had been there since the Civil War. The Iowas settled to the west of their old friends. An executive order on August 15, 1883, assigned the area to them as their reservation. Two years later Congress provided for the sale of the Iowa and Sac and Fox lands in Kansas and Nebraska, with provision for those who wished to remain (further embedded in law by an 1867 act). There were then only about four hundred Iowas. In the north the old Greater Nemaha Agency merged with the Potawatomi Agency in 1882. The northern Iowas, however, prospered as farmers. Their descendants are now called the Iowa Tribe of Kansas and Nebraska.

In the Indian Territory a Quaker agent served under President Grant's peace policy and established a Quaker mission among the Iowas before the turn of the twentieth century. The Jerome Commission (under David H. Jerome) negotiated its first agreement for the allotment of Iowa land in May 1890. Southern Iowas took allotments just south of today's town of Perkins. The so-called surplus land was opened to whites in the Run of 1891, with eager land-seekers flooding onto the former Iowa, Sac and Fox, and Potawatomi reserve. Some Iowas moved to the Otoe agency and settled there.

The period of allotment for the Iowas was a time of hardship and dissatisfaction. An Interior Department competency commission visit in 1916 hastened the loss of the Iowas' allotted lands. The commission arbitrarily ruled individual Indians competent to sell their allotments to the awaiting buyer, and owners were quickly persuaded to sell their parcels. State attempts to tax Iowa allotments and their improvements, a lack of annuity and land settlement payments, local regulations, encroachments on Indian customs, diseases and deaths, and the Ghost Dance turmoil affected the Iowas deeply. Some wanted to find new land elsewhere, while others wanted to return to the North. But ceremonies brought the Iowas into close contact with nearby tribes on their allotted reserves, friends who had once been tribal enemies. Those Indians introduced some Iowas to Native American Church practices. Others shared Christian beliefs.

Both southern and northern Iowas shared in Indian Claims Commission payments received in the 1970s (under the terms of Public Law 92-29 in 1971) as partial compensation for unfilled treaty obligations and unpaid land purchases. In 1986 the Oklahoma tribe halted BIA police services from the Shawnee Agency. The tribe contracted with the federal government for tribal policing and signed a compact in October 1991 with the state's governor, providing for cross-deputization with Lincoln County for law enforcement jurisdiction and services.

Although in outward appearance the Iowas resemble their white neighbors, they continue to practice selected aspects of their Indian culture. Families still gather for a funeral feast for the deceased and a memorial feast a year later. The annual Iowa Powwow, held in July, honors veterans, elders, and participants. They may Gourd Dance in the afternoon and powwow dance in the evening. Families sponsor giveaways to acknowledge individuals and organizations important in their lives. Iowas also take part in the dances of neighboring tribes. Some tribal members participate in the activities of the Native American Church.

Marvin Franklin, a northern Iowa, served as commissioner of Indian affairs in the 1970s. *Native America Calling* public radio host Harlan McKosato was raised on Iowa lands in Perkins. James Two Guns (an Iowa-Seneca) served as a stuntman for the film *The Last of the Mohicans*. Saginaw Grant (also Sac and Fox) is an actor. Buck Cheadle was an athlete and coach.

SUGGESTED READING

Blaine, Martha Royce. *The Ioway Indians.* Norman: University of Oklahoma Press, 1979; repr. 1995.

Blakeslee, David. "The Origin and Spread of the Calumet Ceremony." *American Antiquity* 46 (October 1981): 759–68.

Henning, Dale, and Thomas Thiessen. "Dhegihan and Chiwere Siouans in the Plains." *Plains Anthropologist* 49, no. 192 (November 2004): entire issue, esp. 591–601.

Lost Nation: The Ioway. N.p.: Fourth Wall Productions, 2007 (film).

Sasso, R. F. "La Crosse Region Oneota Adaptation." *Wisconsin Archaeologist* 74 (1993): 246–90.

Kansa/Kaw

Early French traders recorded *ak'a* from the Siouan dialects as
"south wind." It was abbreviated to "Kaw." The "wind" connection
may also be from the tribal role in an Omaha Indian war ceremony
that paid homage to the power of the wind in assisting warriors. The
tribe has also been referred to as Kansa, Kansas, Kanza, Ko'za, and
Konza. The Kansas/Kaws claim to have undergone more changes
in spelling of their tribal name than any other tribe west of the Mississippi River. The name of the state, the river, and the largest city
in the state are derived from the tribal name. Other Kansa words
dot the Kansas landscape. For example, the name of the Neosho
River derived from the Kansa word *ne*, "water." The tribal members
call themselves Kka-ze, which is also the name of a clan. They were
known as the Kaw Nation through the twentieth century. "Kaw"
and "Kansa" are used interchangeably here.

LOCATION AND GOVERNMENT

The "Kaw Nation of Oklahoma" has its headquarters in Kaw City
in eastern Kay County, in north-central Oklahoma. The Kaws are
organized under the OIWA, with a seven-member tribal executive council that governs. They adopted their constitution through
a vote in August 1990. A General Council of all adult members
over the age of eighteen determines the selection of candidates for
elective office. The tribal website is www.kawnation.com.

BUSINESSES

The Kaw Nation's South Wind Casino (at www.southwindcasino.
com) is near the community of Newkirk. Four smoke shops are
located near Highway 77, in Newkirk, Ponca City, Braman, and
close to Lake Ponca. A travel plaza with a motel is on Interstate
Highway 35 at its intersection with Highway 177. The Kanza Phar-
macy is inside the Newkirk tribal clinic. The Kanza Museum offers
tours. Tribal representatives participated in the 2006 dedication
of an earthen dwelling in Atchison, Kansas, at the confluence of

the Missouri River with Independence Creek. It is the site where Lewis and Clark expedition members encountered an uninhabited Kansa village during their travels. A second replica dwelling is found in Allegawahoo Heritage Memorial Park, south of Council Grove, on land that the tribe acquired in 2000, also a part of their reserve before their 1873 removal.

NUMBER

The tribe has about 3,000 members, based on a descendancy roll. There are no Kaw full-bloods. About 25 percent of the members reside near their tribal headquarters in the communities of Kaw City and Fort Oakland and in the vicinity of Newkirk, Braman, and Ponca City. The rest are scattered nationwide.

The Kansas share the Dhegiha Siouan language with the Osages, Quapaws, and Omaha-Poncas, indicating a common origin. Linguists believe that the Quapaws first separated from the main body of the Dhegihas, followed by Osages and Kansas. They also shared the oral story of originating as a single tribe along the Ohio and Wabash rivers south of the Great Lakes. Linguists James Springer and Stanley Witkowski speculated that about A.D. 1000 Proto-Dhegiha broke off from the precursor of the Chiwere-Winnebago language. The Dhegihas were a part of the Oneota culture during Upper Mississippian times. Linguists suggest that around 1300 the Dhegiha Siouans began to separate from each other, although some scholars argue for a much more recent breakup. That is also the date at which Oneota peoples began to filter out onto the Plains in search of buffalo herds. At the mouth of the Ohio River the Quapaws continued in their migration story by drifting downstream, while the rest of the group traveled upriver along the Mississippi to its intersection with the Missouri River. They gradually moved up the Missouri, and the Osages and Kansas separated from the parent body. Kansa oral tradition and linguistic similarity with the Osage language strongly suggest a close relationship between the two. Oral stories of the two tribes maintain that as one people for a time they resided on a peninsula on the Missouri, as ethnologist J. Owen Dorsey reported.

Archeologist Waldo Wedel identified the Doniphan site in eastern Kansas (near the town of the same name) as a Kansa occupation, lacking in pottery even though it was strongly Oneota. He speculated that it may have been the village that Etienne Venyard de Bourgmont visited in 1724.

Wedel also believed that the Fanning (in northeastern Kansas) and King-Hill (in St. Joseph, Missouri) sites were late-seventeenth-century Kansa occupations that were also western Oneota. Material remains showed they had trade contact with Lower Loup (ancestral Pawnee) peoples and not with Dhegiha Siouan (Iowa-Otoe) intruders nearby. The Kansas dominated the area of northern and eastern Kansas at the time. Spaniard Juan de Oñate referred to a group that may have been the Kansas as the "Escansaques," but the designation could have referred to some ancestral Wichita group.

The Kaw origin story tells of their people residing on a small, crowded island created before the rest of the earth. Mothers wanted more room for their children. They asked Wacondah, the Great Spirit, for more space. Animals like beavers, muskrats, and turtles added to the island, ultimately filling out the entire circle of the world's land.

Kansas resided in villages along watercourses. Villages divided into two moieties or halves, Keepers of the Pipe and the Wind People. Further subdivisions denoted lesser groupings down to the extended family unit. Men hunted, while women tended garden plots. The Kansas resided in villages but sent large parties out to hunt the buffalo. Each gens or society had its own sacred bundle.

Father Jacques Marquette and Louis Joliet located the Kansas next to the Missourias on the lower Missouri River in the 1670s. A decade later French traders met Kansas, perhaps in what is now northeastern Kansas or northwestern Missouri. The French quickly developed trade, bringing change to Kansa culture and also pressure to raid the Pawnees and Plains Apaches for the lucrative trade in captives.

In the 1720s Etienne Venyard de Bourgmont led a French commercial delegation from New Orleans seeking trade with the Spaniards in Santa Fe as well as with intervening tribes. He found the main Kansa village on the Missouri River just above Independence Creek in present-day Doniphan County, Kansas, and initiated further peaceful relations. Bourgmont used the Kansa village as his depot for traveling to visit the Plains Apaches. Kansas accompanied the Frenchman westward as the Indians sought bison during their annual summer hunt. Bourgmont turned back because of illness but later completed his trek to the Plains Apaches.

About 1740 Frenchmen returned to the Kansa village to erect Fort de Cavagnial (also spelled Cavagnolle), near the mouth of Salt Creek along the Missouri River. The Kansas moved their village in 1752 to the confluence of the Kansas River with the Missouri to have greater ease in trade. The location opened the riverine highway to French trade with Santa Fe and the intervening tribes. The Kansa tribe had established a long-lasting connection to the French. Intermarriage with the French, as well as with Otoes and Missourias and later the Osages, took place. The Kansas gradually moved westward within what is now the state of Kansas. They came under increasing pressure from other Plains Indians and from emigrant upper Midwest tribes. Those intrusions and other factors at first undermined then severely cut into their traditional way of life.

The Kansas raised seasonal crops in cleared river bottoms and supplemented their food supply with summer and winter buffalo hunts. During the winter they left their main village and scattered to hunt for deer and trap fur-bearing animals. Later they traded peltry to Euro-Americans. In their permanent village (Blue Earth Village on the Kansas River after 1800) they lived in earth lodges. They also lived in circular structures that were covered with bark, matting, or reeds. While on the prairie, they used tepees. Membership in a clan was patrilineal. Kansas shared traits such as medicine bundles, bison nomadism, formalized priesthoods, and the Calumet dance with fellow Dhegian Sioux but also with Chiwere Sioux and Central Algonquians such as the Illinois, Sacs and Foxes, Kickapoos, and Miamis.

Although the members of the Lewis and Clark expedition did not meet the Kansas, they called them the "Kausus." In 1806 Zebulon Pike met with Osage and Kansas Indians and shared the Calumet. He helped initiate peace between the two tribes, which had been warring off and on since 1794. After their truce, they mutually turned their attention to attacking the Iowas and Otoes.

Kansas signed their first agreement with the United States in 1815 for peace and friendship. Four years afterward Major Stephen Long met Kansa leaders and warriors at Cow Island on the Missouri River. A June 1825 treaty ceded about 2 million acres of Kansa land in Kansas to the United States, and a separate agreement in August granted a roadway across tribal territory. It became the Santa Fe Trail, stretching from Missouri to New Mexico. The Kansas also began to depend on government annuities. The U.S. government insisted on an end to Kansa depredations against emigrants on the Santa Fe Trail. Missionaries made no headway, however, in spite of dedicated efforts.

A provision in the 1825 treaty for 640-acre allotments for mixed-blood Kansas included White Plume's grandchildren. The provision inflamed internal Kansa tribal tensions. The land was in the vicinity of present-day Topeka. White Plume was the son of an Osage father and a Kansa mother and led the mixed-blood group within the Kansa tribe. The three full-blood bands under Fool Chief, American Chief, and Hard Chief moved to the Neosho and upper Kansas River valleys. George Catlin visited them in 1831 and painted portraits of residents. The Kansas left Blue Earth Village about 1830–45.

In 1846 a new treaty with the United States ceded most of the reservation in the Kansas River Valley. The Kansas were left with only a small portion of their territory: a reservation near Council Grove on the upper Neosho River about twenty miles by twenty miles in size (256,000 acres). The amount of annuities increased. Whites already at Council Grove refused to leave and did not cease agitating for the complete removal of the Indians. In 1859 the Indians ceded over two-thirds of their reservation, retaining only 80,000 acres near the Neosho River. As a small tribe at the junction of major rivers and occupying territory deemed to be prime lands, the Kansas were doomed. Over two hundred years they were nearly wiped out as a viable entity. Moreover, the United States relocated nearly 100,000 eastern Indians onto Kaw and Osage domains in Kansas.

After the Civil War, pressure rose to remove the last of the Kansas. Kansas City and Lawrence were burgeoning in population. The Kaws underwent continuing losses from confinement, disease, and malnutrition. The population plummeted from 1,700 in 1850 to 533 in 1873, when the Kansas finally removed to Indian Territory under an agreement approved in mid-1872 (the act of May 8, 1872, 17 Stat. 85). Congress provided that the Kansas would pay for the former Osage land out of proceeds from the sale of their Kansas reserve. The Kansas sold the remainder of their Neosho Reserve and bought 100,137 acres from the Osages. Their relocation took place despite the protestations of Chief Allegawaho. After seventeen days of migration, the Kansas settled along the Arkansas and Beaver rivers in their new homeland. Agent Laban J. Miles reported in 1879 that confinement and illnesses had taken the lives of nearly one-half of them in seven years. The tribal population sank to a low point of 193 by 1887.

The Kansas were not only neighbors to the Osages, Quapaws, Poncas, and Otoes on their reservation: they were related to most of them as fellow Dhegiha Sioux. All shared the misery of resettlement and longing for religious fulfillment. In the early 1880s the Kansas took the *ilonshka* dance (probably the Sioux Grass Dance that the Poncas had taught them) to the Osages. The reservation period witnessed excitement over the Ghost Dance and Peyote religious ceremonies. Giveaways and speeches at intertribal dances also helped perpetuate old traditions.

The Kansa reservation adjoined the Cherokee Outlet, and the grasslands of the region appealed to cattle ranchers and to settlers. David Payne established Rock Falls in the far northwest corner of Kay County on the Chikaskia River as one of his Boomer settlements and pushed for opening the land to whites. Federal authorities evicted him and demolished the community because it trespassed on restricted land. Starting in 1883, leases brought some income to the tribe. That year the Kansas formed a tribal government similar to the Osage government so that the tribe could take advantage of leasing. In 1883 tribal members elected Kebothliku as their chief, who was succeeded by Washungah. The Santa Fe Railroad line came within ten miles of the Kansa Reservation on the west. The trains brought eager homesteaders for the opening of the Cherokee Strip in 1893. About 6.5 million acres of Indian land had been opened for settlement. Demand rose for more land to become available. Jerome Commission members met with the Kansas in June 1893 to secure allotments and additional land for an opening to whites for settlement. Mixed-bloods favored an agreement, while full-bloods opposed allotment. The Indians delayed, and the commissioners departed.

U.S. vice president Charles Curtis drafted an allotment bill that the Kansas accepted. A tribal delegation took it to Washington, D.C., in early 1902. Congress quickly approved the measure (Public Law 227) on July 1, and 249 tribal members received about 400 acres each. Curtis and his children and friends received about 400 acres each as members of the tribe. (He had been dropped from the tribal roll when he remained in Kansas after the tribe departed for Indian Territory but used his political influence to gain reinstatement.) Curtis retained his allotted land, but other tribal members received certificates of competency under measures like Public Law 29 in 1926 and hastily sold their lands. Amid the hubbub of allotment, town site promotion, and emigration to new lands, Kaw City was laid out on the Arkansas River across from the agency, which was renamed Washungah.

The tribe had no chief after Washungah died in 1908, so there were no official council meetings to transact business. The federal government gathered Indians at the agency in late 1922 and through an election chose Lucy Tayiah Eads as the first female principal chief of the Kansas and an eight-member council. She had been adopted by the late chief, attended Haskell Indian University in Lawrence, Kansas, and worked in New York City as a nurse before returning to the agency. As principal chief she pressed a claim against the federal government for payment for Kansas lands and for acceptance that oil and gas rights on the reservation were communally owned by the tribe. Oil leasing after 1920 brought some revenue to the tribe, although most leases were on lands opened to whites. The federal government in 1928 consolidated the Kansa Agency with other tribes at Pawnee.

The Depression helped scatter tribal members as they looked for jobs. The tribal council dissolved in 1935. By the end of World War II most Kansa allotted lands had been sold or lost. The mixed-blood Kaw Cemetery Association continued to function, however, and in 1958 its members played a leading role in the writing of a tribal constitution. When mixed-bloods asserted their claim against the U.S. government under terms of the 1825 treaty, the full-bloods announced their own claim.

The federal government through the U.S. Army Corps of Engineers pushed for the construction of Kaw Dam after 1963, and the creation of a lake on the Arkansas River in 1976 inundated the reservation. The lake is a source of water for Stillwater as well as fishing and camping along its 168 miles of shoreline. The government moved Kaw City to higher ground. The council house was dismantled stone by stone and restored on the site of their current powwow grounds on Washunga Bay. The lake swept over the former school, council house, and cemetery, which was relocated to a 15-acre tract in Newkirk. Kahola band members of the Mehojah family began the Kaw Protective Association in the 1950s to pursue full-blood concerns. They challenged mixed-blood chairman Tom Dennison's quantum qualifications (he was one-sixteenth Kaw) to have held office since 1958. The full-blood side won the Pepper court decision in 1975 (over an election held the year before), and the business committee election resulted in full-blood members of the Kahola band holding office.

In the 1980s the tribe gained nearly 1,100 acres and gradually began to prosper. In 1995 it opened the Kanza Museum at its headquarters. The only remaining speaker of the language, sadly, was retired University of Kansas linguist Robert Rankin, but the tribe has held language classes at its headquarters. Rankin worked on a dictionary for the language, and teaching materials were developed from his grammar. Tribal members also continue dance traditions. The Kansa Tribe holds an annual powwow on the first weekend in August at the tribal dance ground on Kaw Lake near Kaw City. Since 1986 it has included contest dancing.

Each year tribal members travel for a powwow to Council Grove, Kansas, and take part in the Wah-shun-gah Days celebration. In 2000 the tribe purchased 150 acres for a commemorative park four miles southeast of the city on Little John Creek. The site contains remains of the old Kaw Agency. In addition, the tribe has favored an American Indian statue atop the Kansas State Capitol.

Notable Kansas include U.S. vice president Charles Curtis, who was a one-eighth descendant of Chief White Plume on his mother's side. Curtis's grandmother raised him at the Kaw Agency until she sent him to Topeka to live with white relatives so he could receive schooling. Curtis was a ward of agent Laban Miles as a youth. In 1929 Curtis became the vice president of Herbert Hoover, ironically a nephew of the very same Miles. Michael McBride III, an attorney in private practice, is a Kansa tribal member and served as an associate justice of the Supreme Court for the tribe. Jim Pepper Henry (who is also Creek) was a Native American jazz trumpet pioneer and served as the assistant director of the National Museum of the American Indian. The last full-blood Kansa Indian, William Mehojah, died in 2000. He served as tribal chairman from 1987 to 1990, during which time the tribe wrote a new constitution to engage in economic development activity.

SUGGESTED READING

Dorsey, J. Owen. "Omaha Sociology." *In Third Annual Report of the Bureau of American Ethnology for 1881–82*, 211–14. Washington, D.C.: Government Printing Office, 1884.

Herring, Joseph B. *The Enduring Indians of Kansas*. Lawrence: University Press of Kansas, 1995.

Johnson, Alfred. "Kansa Origins: An Alternative." *Plains Anthropologist* 36, no. 133 (February 1991): 57–65 (includes Wedel citations).

Springer, James, and Stanley Witkowski. "Siouan Historical Linguistics and Oneota Archaeology." In Guy Gibbon, ed., *Oneota Studies*, 69–83. Minneapolis: University of Minnesota, 1982.

Unrau, William E. *The Kansa Indians: A History of the Wind People, 1673–1873*. Norman: University of Oklahoma Press, 1971, repr. 1986.

———. *Mixed-Bloods and Tribal Dissolution: Charles Curtis and the Quest for Indian Identity*. Lawrence: University Press of Kansas, 1989.

Kialegee

NAME

"Kialegee" derives from *eka-lache,* "head left," the original name for the tribal town in the Mvskoke (Creek) language. The word may have come from the town warriors' practice of taking trophy heads during battle.

LOCATION AND GOVERNMENT

The headquarters for the "Kialegee Tribal Town" is in a storefront on the Main Street of Wetumka in Hughes County in south-central Oklahoma, near the North Canadian River. The town organized in 1941 under the OIWA. Kialegee is therefore separately recognized by the federal government, distinct from the Muscogee (Creek) Nation. Culturally Kialegee Town is a part of the Muscogee people, but politically they constitute separate legal entities. A *meko* (king or chief) serves as the executive officer with a council as the legislature.

BUSINESSES

A fuel stop and convenience store/smoke shop are located on Main Street in Wetumka. A mixture of tobacco sales revenue, farming income, and federal grant funding provides support for town social services.

NUMBER

The tribe has about 400 members.

Linguistics provides only a hint of Kialegee development. The Kialegees speak the Mvskoke (Creek) language. The Muskhogean language family began splitting apart around 3,000 years ago, later than the division of Cherokee from Northern Iroquoian and Caddo from Northern Caddo.

Archeology cannot provide specific information on prehistoric sites directly linked to the Kialegees because too much time has passed to offer conclusive evidence. In general terms, Muskogean peoples spread outward from Moundville Variant chiefdoms after A.D. 1400. Their descendants emigrated eastward, eventually settling along the Tallapoosa River in Alabama. They shared the mound-building and sun-worshipping traits of other Mississippians in the Southeast. After about 1400 that culture began to decline. Ceremonial centers became single-mound sites among separate allied towns. Archeologist Ned Jenkins has pointed out that residents along the Coosa and Tallapoosa rivers were Mvskoke-speakers.

The people who lived in Kialegee Town raised agricultural products in their riverine settlements in Alabama. They were matrilineal in their town and clan relationships. Women and children tended the agricultural fields of corn, beans, and squash. Men hunted for game and defended their town from intruders. A *meko* (chief) presided over council deliberations, while medicine men oversaw rituals and ceremonies. The major Green Corn Ceremony took place to celebrate the fall harvest. Ball play marked the conclusion of the dance cycle for the year.

Loss of life resulting from European diseases led to shifts in southeastern Native populations. Kialegee was one of about fifty towns of the Muscogee (Creek) Confederacy, which may have had a total population of over twenty thousand. Kialegee Town's social and political makeup mirrored the arrangement of the larger Muscogee Nation.

Refugees added to the population movements as American Indians fell back from the devastation in the wake of colonial conflicts like the 1715 Yamassee War. For a time, European rivalries and the Muscogees' strategic position made the Muscogee peoples predominant in the region. They maintained a balance in Spanish, French, and English colonial intrigue until the British emerged victorious in 1763. The Americans inherited the British influence after 1783.

Through the 1790s U.S. Indian agent Benjamin Hawkins pressed an assimilation policy emphasizing missions, education, and individual farms. His policy made inroads among Lower Creeks. Opposition gradually rose to increasing Anglo land cessions. The Red Stick War of 1812–14 climaxed in what is called the battle of Horseshoe Bend among the Upper Creeks. The punitive land cession that followed affected all the Muscogees. William McIntosh of the Lower Creeks rose to prominence as a trader, businessman, and leader.

Kialegee leaders were active participants in colonial and early national events. They signed a treaty of peace with the United States on June 29, 1796. The town's residents joined the Red Stick Upper Creeks in the violent outbursts of the Creek civil war. U.S. troops burned the town in 1813.

Kialegee leaders subsequently agreed to treaties in 1814, 1818, 1825, and 1826. Finally, under pressure for Muscogee removal in the 1830s, 166 Kialegee families trekked from Alabama to Indian Territory. There they began anew in the vicinity of what is now the community of Hanna in McIntosh County. They farmed along the North Canadian River Valley. John Swanton, an ethnologist from the Bureau of American Ethnology, visited the Kialegee ceremonial ground in 1912. He found them a red/ warrior town, but their ceremonial ground was abandoned. Residents told of fierce ball play competition against the neighboring Alabamas in their recent past.

Assimilation pressures took their toll. Mission schools helped convert town members to Christianity. Allotment forced members onto individual farms then over the years led to a transfer of land ownership from Indians to whites. Most of the Kialegees today belong to Indian Baptist churches.

The 1936 OIWA permitted tribal groups to organize credit associations and to form governmental entities. It divided Muscogee tribal towns. Three of the Muscogee Nation communities organized separately. The Thlopthloccos and Alabama-Quassartes formed town governments in the late 1930s. Members of Kialegee Town operated as a separate entity under the OIWA in 1941.

Today the members of Kialegee Town annually celebrate Kialegee Nettv (Day), which attracts members and visitors to celebrate the town's history and heritage. The elders of the town strive to instill the language, culture, and traditions in the younger generation. New stories about contemporary activities join older oral commentaries to chronicle Kialegee heritage.

SUGGESTED READING

Jenkins, Ned. "Early Creek Origins: Moundville Connection." Paper presented at the Southeastern Archaeological Conference, St. Louis, Missouri, October 2004.

Swanton, John R. *Early History of the Creek Indians and Their Neighbors*. Bulletin 73. Washington, D.C.: Bureau of American Ethnology, 1922; repr. New York: Johnson Reprint Corp., 1970; repr. Gainesville: University Press of Florida, 1998.

Kickapoo

NAME

In popular usage, the tribal name is derived from the Central Algonquian word "Kiwigapawa," "he moves about, standing now here, now there." The French labeled them "Kicapoux" and "Quicapoux." Perhaps more accurately the name may come from *kikaapoa*. Although its meaning is uncertain, some interpret it as meaning "people who move about."

LOCATION AND GOVERNMENT

The headquarters for the "Kickapoo Tribe of Oklahoma" is just outside the town of McLoud, north of Interstate Highway 40 in Potawatomi County (about ten miles east of Oklahoma City and ten miles west of Shawnee). The tribe is organized under the OIWA and a 1940 federal charter. The tribe adopted a constitution in 1937 and amended it in 1977. A five-member business committee governs the tribe, including a chair. They are elected every three years. A General Council of all adult tribal members meets annually. There is no tribal website yet.

BUSINESSES

Major revenue comes from the Kickapoo Casino, recently expanded, on State Highway 62 north of McLoud. There also is a tribal smoke shop. The tribe has just under 1,100 acres in trust land and about 5,000 acres in individual allotments. Agriculture has always been an important element of their culture and continues to be a source of income.

NUMBER

The tribe has about 2,500 members. Most reside in the vicinity of McLoud and in rural areas of Potawatomi, Oklahoma, and Lincoln counties. There are also about 1,500 Kickapoos (of the Vermillion band) in the far northeastern corner of Kansas. With headquarters in Horton, they are officially called the Kickapoo Tribe of Kansas. The Mexican Kickapoos, also called the Texas Kickapoos and the Kickapoo Traditional Tribe of Texas because of their residence along the international boundary of the Rio Grande, number about 700. Their focus is the community of Eagle Pass, Texas, on the boundary with Piedras Negras, Mexico, as well as their religious ground and community at Nacimiento in the state of Coahuila. Some Oklahoma Kickapoos reside in Eagle Pass as part of the Texas Kickapoos. It is an indictment of U.S. policies that Great Lakes Indians like the Kickapoos now reside deep inside Mexico.

Linguistics provides some insight into Kickapoo prehistory. Linguist Ives Goddard viewed Kickapoo, Mascouten, and Sac-Fox as four dialects of a single Algonquian language, which implied that all were one group not too far in the past. The Kickapoos eventually absorbed the Mascoutens. Proto-Algonquian was spoken perhaps less than 3,000 years ago in the homeland area extending along Georgian Bay on Lake Ontario. At an early stage it fragmented into ten or more distinct groups that became the Ojibwes, Menominees, Potawatomis, Shawnees, and Illinois. Legend recounts an ancient argument over the disposition of a bear's foot that led to the Kickapoos' separation from the Shawnees.

The archeological background of the Kickapoos is unclear because of movements through time. It also is not possible to connect archeological sites to known tribal groups except for the most recent era. Prehistoric peoples in the western region adjoining Lake Erie and Detroit, where the Kickapoos resided when Europeans arrived, probably survived through a mix of hunting, gathering, and fishing. After A.D. 1000 the Younge culture predominated, with its grit-tempered cord-marked pottery. Longhouses perhaps were charnel houses but also included residences. Large villages had protective palisades. After A.D. 1400 cooler and wetter summers occurred. The population as well as movements increased. Smaller agricultural and fishing villages predominated. Residents made use of the maize-beans-squash trio as well as riverine resources. There was a slow general migration of population out of the region.

Kickapoos resided in autonomous villages during the seventeenth and eighteenth centuries. A headman directed civil activities, while a war chief directed defensive and offensive actions. A council of headmen considered important concerns. The Eagle clan provided the tribal chief, while the Raccoon clan supplied the second chief/speaker. Members of Kickapoo families lived in large brush-covered rectangular houses that utilized reed mats. Women tended gardens and fields of corn, beans, squash, and other plant foods. They also gathered berries and nuts. Men hunted and fished. Following the harvest, residents left their villages for the winter buffalo hunt, pursued west of the Mississippi River in the eighteenth century. They lived in temporary camps during the hunt. The tendency over time was for separate bands to grow more independent as they engaged in different alliances and trade relations. The Kickapoos were patrilineal in their clans and moieties. The moieties were named black (*oskasa*) and white (*kiiskooha*), contrasting dark and light. The Kickapoos shared many cultural attributes with their Central Algonquian linguistic kinfolk: the Sacs, Foxes, Potawatomis, and Shawnees, especially the Shawnees. The Kickapoo moiety division determined teams for competition in races and games as well as the seating arrangement for rituals.

According to the Kickapoos, the Great Manitou, Creator, oversaw the cosmos. Kickapoo religious beliefs were similar to those of the Foxes (see the "Sac and Fox" entry). Assistance to the Great Manitou came from lesser deities: the four winds, the sky, moon, stars, and grandmother earth. The son of the Great Manitou, called Wisaka, created the earth and all life on it. Like other Algonquians, the Kickapoos regard the four winds, the sky, the sun, moon, stars, and the earth as important figures. Wisaka gave life to the Kickapoos and provided them with their sacred bundles or sacred packs. The four major bundles are the basis of tribal ceremonialism for the Oklahoma Kickapoos. Medicine societies that focused on the clan bundles performed annual rituals in spring. Additionally, the societies engaged in their Green Corn Dance and their Buffalo Dance. Other rituals included clan naming ceremonies for infants and burial rituals. Feasting accompanied many activities.

French trader-explorers found the Kickapoos west of Lake Erie in 1640 across an expanse of what is now northwest Ohio and southern Michigan. Shortly thereafter the Kickapoos moved to southern Wisconsin, after Ottawa and Iroquois attacks dislodged them. A Kickapoo-Mascouten force of young warriors attacked and overwhelmed colonial trader George Croghan and his party in 1765 in Ohio and wounded Croghan but eventually released them to the French after seizing their trade wares. The Kickapoos were linked with the French. After the French withdrew, the Kickapoos then allied with Spain, which made it easier for the Kickapoos to move over time to Missouri, Texas, and Mexico. The Kickapoos in Wisconsin began long-lasting contact with

Miami-speaking tribes, which extended to their movement to the Wabash River in what would become Illinois. Kickapoos residing in Illinois established ties with the Potawatomis, which continued after their migration into Kansas. After the mid-1700s the Kickapoos in today's central Illinois near Peoria became known as the Prairie band. They hunted buffalo.

Kickapoos were the first Indians to greet (twice) the Lewis and Clark expedition as it departed St. Louis in 1804. About 400 Kickapoos journeyed in the spring of 1833 from Illinois to a site on the west bank of the Missouri River north of Fort Leavenworth. Because they came from the region between the Wabash and Vermillion rivers, they were called the Vermillion Kickapoos. They occupied the western area of the Wabash drainage. The Vermillion band absorbed the Mascoutens and generally supported Tecumseh's pantribal movement, while the Prairie band opposed it. Each band signed a separate cession of Illinois lands in a treaty with the United States in 1819. They consented to occupy lands in southwest Missouri south of the Osage River, but migration took some fifteen years. U.S. soldiers forcibly removed recalcitrants in 1834. A third group of Kickapoos moved in 1763–65 to the lower Missouri River and operated independently. They supported Pontiac's Rebellion against the English. Some Kickapoos participated in Black Hawk's Sac migration before the Kickapoos moved to Missouri. In 1832 Kickapoos consented to a new Treaty of Castor Hill with the United States that removed them to Kansas, onto a 12-square-mile reserve.

Changing policies and shifting allegiances shaped the world of the Kickapoos. On the eve of the American Civil War the strife of Bleeding Kansas battered the Indians. Kickapoos settled onto diminished lands near the town of Atchison. Railroad promoters after the Civil War secretly utilized political connections to swindle the Kickapoos out of their lands. In disgust, Mokowhat led sixty followers to join Mexico Kickapoos. Other Kickapoos accepted allotments in Kansas and lost them, while still others ended up on the diminished common reservation lands. Kennekuk's band clung to his prophetic and accommodationist preaching and remained where they were. Potawatomi converts officially merged with Kennekuk's Kickapoos in 1851.

The odyssey of Kickapoos in Mexican territory led many to reside on the Sabine River then on the Brazos Reserve in Texas and later in Indian Territory. A few saw service in the Mexican Army. Mothakuck's band on the Brazos engaged in wide-ranging trade. On Wildhorse Creek in the Muscogee Nation of Indian Territory, Kickapoos under Papequah traded lucratively with the Comanches. A third band under Pecan re-sided on the Canadian River.

Many Kickapoos moved into southern Kansas during the American Civil War. A large number moved to Mexico after the war ended, joining kinfolk who had lived there since 1849. They settled in the vicinity of Nacimiento. Approximately half the tribe moved to Indian Territory beginning in 1873 before others emigrated from Mexico and from Kansas to settle among them in 1875. Federal officials established an executive-order reservation in 1883. The Kickapoos' 100,000-acre reservation proved too tempting to assimilationists. The pressure to assimilate under allotment after 1875 led to bitter dissension. In 1891 outright fraud under attorney John T. Hill, who produced an allotment document that sold "surplus" lands (1895), led to permanent tribal division. More Kickapoos migrated to Mexico. The Kickapoos who had come from Kansas in 1875 formed a progressive group that accepted allotment and remained in Oklahoma. Only gradually did dissidents return during the late 1920s. Congress appropriated money (Public Law 178) in 1908 to support the investigation of alleged frauds regarding allotment losses. Allotment took away the Kickapoo land base and added to their impoverishment. The national Meriam Commission in the 1920s was alarmed to find that the average annual income per capita for the Kickapoos was less than half that for all Indians nationwide, which itself was pitifully low.

Most Kickapoos remained engaged in agricultural pursuits. They kept to themselves except for rare public controversies. During a recent discussion of proposed routes for Interstate 40 through Oklahoma City, Kickapoos objected to a path through their former lands that threatened traditional lifeways. They also voiced opposition to the ongoing lure of urban life that crept steadily closer to them from the state's capital.

In July 1997 representatives from three Kickapoo groups (in Kansas, Oklahoma, and Mexico) met in Kansas for a summit. This marked the first time that all three had been together since their division in that state in the nineteenth century.

There is much movement of Kickapoos between Oklahoma and Mexico. Oklahoma Kickapoos bring Mexican kinfolk north for health care at the tribal clinic in McLoud. Oklahoma Kickapoos travel to Mexico in February and March to help open the ceremonial season. The Kickapoos hold a number of seasonal rituals as a part of their spiritual beliefs. Members may participate in ceremonies focused on sacred packs at the beginning and end of the ceremonial season. Family members may sponsor feasts for the departed, naming ceremonies, and adoptions. The

Oklahoma and Mexican Kickapoos are often described as being among the most culturally conservative Indian groups currently in existence. They continue to isolate themselves from the larger society, being highly independent and tied to their customs. They practice their traditional rituals and ways of life. Approximately 80 percent of the Kickapoos speak only their tribal language, not English. But some Kickapoos participate in neighboring powwows.

Among notable Kickapoos are Kennekuk (also called Kanakuk), a prophet who established a tribal religion in Illinois and died in 1852. His teachings advocated virtuous living and combined Christian elements with traditional beliefs as an accommodation to the changing world they faced as they farmed. Historian Joseph Herring credited Kennekuk with preventing Kickapoo expulsion from their Kansas lands, where they had arrived in 1834. Kickapoo girl Myra Frye was adopted by Quaker missionary Elizabeth Test. Frye became an educator and founded Lawansa Tepee, an Indian club in Los Angeles. Cecil Murdock was a painter. Singer Aragon Starr (also Muscogee) produced musical CDs such as *Meet the Diva* and the one-woman play *The Red Road*.

SUGGESTED READING

Chapman, Berlin B. "The Cherokee Commission at Kickapoo Village." *Chronicles of Oklahoma* 17 (March 1939): 62–74.

Gibson, Arrell M. *The Kickapoos: Lords of the Middle Border.* Norman: University of Oklahoma Press, 1963; repr. 2005.

Goddard, Ives. "Central Algonquian Languages." In vol. 15, *Northeast, of the Handbook of North American Indians,* 583–93. Washington, D.C.: Smithsonian Institution, 1978.

Herring, Joseph. *The Enduring Indians of Kansas.* Lawrence: University Press of Kansas, 1995.

———. *Kennekuk, the Kickapoo Prophet.* Lawrence: University Press of Kansas, 1988.

Kiowa

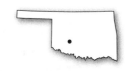

The tribal name has no meaning in the Kiowa language. Perhaps it is derived from the Comanche tribal name for the Kiowas, Ka-i-gwu, "two halves different," designating the warriors' half-shaved head, which left the hair on the other half long and uncut. From that eventually came what some consider the modern meaning: "principal People." The Kiowas refer to themselves as Tepda, "coming out," and Kwu'da, "pulling out," probably recalling their origin stories.

LOCATION AND GOVERNMENT

The headquarters complex for the "Kiowa Tribe" is in Carnegie in Caddo County (moved there in 1979 from the Anadarko Agency), in southwestern Oklahoma. A constitution has governed the tribe since 1970, with an eight-member business committee elected by all eligible voters. The tribal museum, which opened in 1983, is in Carnegie. The tribal website is www.kiowaok.com.

BUSINESSES

The tribe receives revenue from its 63,000-square-feet Kiowa Casino (www.kiowacasino777.com) located near Interstate 44 just north of the Red River. It opened in May 2007. (The Comanche Red River Casino is within sight up the road.) The Kiowas have shared Land Use Committee membership with the Comanches and the Apache Tribe since the 1960s as well as oversight of income from a strip of land lying between Fort Sill and Lawton and a plot of land in Anadarko. The tribe purchased the Indian City USA tourist village area in Anadarko. Income is also derived from leasing and agricultural production on individual allotted land. The BIA administers 282,599 acres of trust land for the Kiowas, Comanches, and Plains Apaches.

NUMBER

The tribe has 7,500 members residing in Oklahoma in Caddo, Comanche, and Kiowa counties and in the communities of Carnegie, Fort Cobb, and Anadarko. There are about 12,000 Kiowas in all, who are scattered worldwide due to jobs, military service, and marriage.

Linguists link Kiowa to the Tanoan language of the Eastern or Rio Grande Pueblos of Taos, Isleta, San Ildefonso, Pecos, and Jemez (especially the latter two) of New Mexico. Arthur Jelinek dated their departure from the Pecos River region after A.D. 1300. Kiowa-speakers maintain that the language is unique and do not connect it to any other language. The Kiowas made their migration toward the southern Plains in the mid-eighteenth century. Kiowa oral tradition points to an origin in the far North (some claim in Canada). Their journey is depicted in the literary work of Pulitzer Prize–winning Kiowa novelist N. Scott Momaday. Years of strife with the Dakotas and the Cheyennes arose from conflicting claims to the Black Hills region. During their odyssey the Kiowas made long-lasting alliances with the Sarcees, Crows, and Arikaras of the North. Kiowa leader Satank's grandmother was Sarcee. Kiowa leader Tauhasen perhaps was of Arikara ancestry. He was a member of the Kata band, closely associated through trade with the Arikaras. While in the North, the Kiowas acquired their sacred thanksgiving ceremony, the medicine lodge Sun Dance. The Plains Apaches, also called the Kiowa-Apaches, merged with the Kiowas in the North. As a group they later came to dominate the region between the Arkansas and Red rivers in the late nineteenth century.

The Kiowa origin story tells of their emergence out of the ground through a hollow cottonwood log. The supernatural being Saynday called them forth and then instructed them in how to hunt and survive. The Kiowas consider their homeland to be south-central Montana in the vicinity of modern Virginia City.

The lifestyle of the nomadic Kiowas matched that of other Plains Indians who followed the buffalo. They made use of medicine bundles, tepees, and vision quests, held an annual Sun Dance near the summer solstice, and had ranked warrior societies. The four top warriors formed their government executive committee. Kiowas unveiled their two-foot-tall Tai-me image during their Sun Dance. They had six men's and two women's societies. The most respected eldest brother led each band or topadoga, an extended family. In the nineteenth century bands divided into a northern group in Kansas and a southern group in the Texas Panhandle. Kiowa status was ranked by social classes, with the wealthiest families operating as an aristocracy.

A chance meeting of a Kiowa named Gui-k'ati (Wolf Lying Down) led to a lasting alliance with a Comanche named Pareiya (Afraid of Water) around 1790. That led in turn to peaceful relations with the Santa Fe authorities after 1806. The Kiowas made peace with the Osages (1834) and then with the Cheyennes and Arapahos in 1840 near Bent's Old Fort. Mutual raids ranged from the American Southwest south into Texas and Mexico.

The first white Americans that the Kiowas encountered were members of Captain John Bell's party in 1820, after the troops had separated from the main body of the column under the command of Major Stephen H. Long. Artist Samuel Seymour sketched the Kiowa encampment while the Indians stood in fascination and examined the horses' shoes. The Indians later briefly met members of the Nathaniel Pryor/Hugh Glenn/Jacob Fowler expedition (1821) then encountered the U.S. Dragoon expedition that came onto the southern Plains in 1834. Painter George Catlin accompanied the Dragoons and did a portrait of the famous Kiowa chief Tauhasen. Three years later Kiowa leaders signed their first treaty (at Fort Gibson) with the Americans, pledging mutual friendship. Montfort Stokes and A. P. Chouteau represented the United States.

In 1853 Kiowas met federal negotiators at Fort Atkinson in Kansas on the Santa Fe Trail. The Indians accepted annuities, forts, and military roads in their territory. Six years later authorities removed some Texas Indians into the Kiowa region. Kiowas did not participate in Confederate activities during the Civil War as some Indians did. Kiowas under Stumbling Bear and Comanches had a day-long running battle with Kit Carson's soldiers in the Texas Panhandle, however, in November 1864. Kiowas attended the parley at the mouth of the Little Arkansas River in 1865 and agreed to a large reservation south of the Arkansas in combination with the Plains Apaches and Comanches. Kiowa leaders talked with federal officials a year later, and Kiowas attended the Peace Commission council (the largest assemblage of Indians in history) on the southern prairie, held on Medicine Lodge Creek in southern Kansas in late 1867. The resultant treaty confined the Kiowas to a reservation reduced from 39 million acres to under 3 million acres in what is now in western Oklahoma and provided gifts and annuities, missionaries, voluntary allotments, and government "civilization" plans. The treaty confederated the Kiowas, Comanches, and Plains Apaches, abbreviated as KCA.

Tribal members resisted confinement to their assigned reservation. It took draconian measures after 1868 to enforce peace on the KCA Indians by 1875. U.S. Army authorities turned Camp Washita (1869) into Fort Sill, making it one of the largest military posts in the nation and underscoring the problem facing the army on the southern Plains. Federal officials recognized Kicking Bird as chief of the Kiowas. Under the Grant peace policy, authorities placed a Quaker agent over the KCA, but the best efforts of Lawrie Tatum ("Baldy" to the Kiowas) and James Haworth (called Senpo Guadal, "Red Beard," by the Kiowas), who succeeded Tatum in 1873, failed to quell discontent. Instead of focusing on civilizing his charges, the agent spent his time negotiating for the return of captives and stolen livestock and arranging to pay depredation claims to aggrieved settlers. In the wake of the 1871 Indian attack on the Warren wagon train teamsters near the town of Jacksboro in northwestern Jack County, Texas, U.S. military authorities tried a new approach to quell Indian opposition. Kiowa leaders Satank, Satanta, and Big Tree were sent to prison in Texas. The Indian leaders had led raiding into Texas that fed other attacks, resulting in the killing of over a hundred whites. The measure only temporarily quieted the frontier.

The most famous battle of the 1874–75 Red River War was the unsuccessful Indian assault on the hated buffalo hunters barricaded at Adobe Walls in the Texas Panhandle. Among the hunters who held off the assault was Bat Masterson, who went on to become a legendary gunfighter and lawman (portrayed later on television), and John Wesley Hardin, who became a gunfighter and outlaw. Military tactics that brought constant pressure against the Indians forced their ultimate submission and return to reservation life. Using the hyperbole of a successful commander reporting to his superiors, General Phil Sheridan termed the prosecution of the war "the most successful of any Indian campaign in this country since the settlement by the whites."

In 1892 the Jerome Commission arrived to dictate terms leading to eventual allotment. Brooking no opposition, commission members forged Indian signatures on their final agreement. Their land opening through lottery of the remaining 2 million acres in 1901 brought a flood of non-Indian settlers, railroads, and towns. Hoping to block the opening, Lone Wolf was stung when the Supreme Court announced in a famous 1903 decision that Indians essentially had no rights in the face of near-total congressional power over them. Allotment and government agents' activities undermined traditional band leaders' authority. The peace group settled the southern portion of the reservation nearer Fort

Sill. The former war group of conservatives, whom the agent derisively labeled the "Implacables," settled across the northern part of the reservation. Lone Wolf reluctantly accepted his allotment, selected for him by the agent, near Carnegie.

Boarding school education and other assimilation policies soon altered Indians' lives. Quaker Thomas Battey set up the first school for Kiowas in 1873. Under agent James Haworth the government built the first houses for the Indians. An Indian police force was created, and in 1888 the first Court of Indian Offenses was established. Lone Wolf (Kiowa), Quanah Parker (Comanche), and Tawakoni Jim (Tawakoni-Wichita) served as the first Indian judges. Episcopal, Methodist, Presbyterian, Baptist, and Roman Catholic missionaries erected churches. The U.S. troops ended the Sun Dance in 1890. That year the Kiowas acquired the Ghost Dance, called the Feather Dance, but the Indian agent suppressed it during World War I. After 1870 some Kiowas joined Native American Church ceremonies. According to their mythology, Devils Tower in Montana was created for the Kiowas and connected them to the Pleiades in the night sky. It became the first U.S. national monument in 1906 and has more recently been involved in litigation over rock climbers' access versus the sanctity of Native religious beliefs.

Federal officials throughout the 1920s manipulated Kiowa governmental decisions. Following the Indian New Deal period in the 1930s, however, after considerable thought, officials created a Kiowa tribal government in 1940. Tribal members in a meeting at Riverside Indian School approved a constitution that established their contemporary government structure.

Kiowas transferred Plains pictographic, hide, and winter count artwork onto canvas near the turn of the twentieth century. Charles Ohettoint instructed his brother Silverhorn, who in turn showed the techniques to Stephen Mopope, while Wohaw directly influenced Monroe Tsatoke, to help create southern Plains Indian painting. The Kiowa Five, along with Lois Smokey, became internationally noteworthy artists in the 1920s under the guidance of Oscar B. Jacobson at the University of Oklahoma. Another member, James Auchiah, and others were heavily influenced by the symbolism of the Ghost Dance and the Native American Church. They converted the skin-painting style into "easel art" sought after by collectors worldwide.

In spite of radical changes in the Kiowas' lives, tribal and intertribal dances kept traditions alive with a variety of clubs, fairs, and festivals, such as at Dietrich Lake and Craterville Park. Returned Kiowa veterans combined with elders of the tribe to revive ceremonial societies in the

1950s. Tribal members founded the resurgent Kiowa Gourd Clan (Tiah-pah or Tia-piah) and the Kiowa Black Leggings Warrior Society (Ton-Kon-Gah). The Ohomah Lodge perpetuates war dancing. The famous Kiowa "49" social songs arose from war journey and raiding songs. Kiowas remain active in southern Plains powwows and identify with them. Additionally, a number of club, society, and family dance events are held to honor memories of past events, focus on community needs, and recall heritage. The Kiowas look to family, songs, places like Devils Tower and Rainy Mountain, and other sources to maintain their identity. Anthropologist Luke Lassiter pointed out that the Kiowa phrase *hohn-day-onh-day*, "everything is good," invokes faith, belief, heritage, and cultural core values, whether in a Flag Song ceremony or a hymn sung in church.

Methodists set up churches after 1887 in Anadarko and elsewhere called Mount Scott, Cedar Creek, Methvin, and Botone. Baptists under J. S. Murrow and his wife helped establish churches at Elk Creek, Rainy Mountain, Redstone, and Saddle Mountain, beginning in the 1890s. Missionary Isabel Crawford is buried in the Saddle Mountain cemetery. The missionaries struggled at first but gradually made converts. Quaker, Roman Catholic, Dutch Reformed, and other denominations also worked in the region. Kiowas worship in their churches with their own brand of Christianity, filling their sanctuaries with Kiowa-language hymns.

Kiowa artists: Monroe Tsatoke, Jack Hokeah, Stephen Mopope, Oscar Jacobson, Spencer Asah, and James Auchiah, ca. spring 1930

Oscar B. Jacobson Scrapbook Collection, Research Division of the Oklahoma Historical Society, #2114.4.53.0

Kiowa women aided their families during the harshness of the assimilation period, when they realized they could no longer tan buffalo hides after confinement to the reservation and loss of the herds. They emphasized beadwork for sale through the local Indian trader, who was also a storekeeper and could extend credit. Kiowa women carry on that beadwork tradition today.

Oklahoma Indian tribal court systems in the modern era rose out of a 1978 court opinion (*Littlechief*) denying that the state had jurisdiction over a murder committed on Kiowa trust land. In response, tribes began to set up their own criminal codes and courts. In 1979 the federal government created the Court of Indian Offenses in Anadarko, now called the Code of Federal Regulations Court, for tribes in the vicinity.

Claudine Davenport and Gus Palmer, Sr. (Kiowas), at the dedication of Cutthroat Gap Monument, January 20, 1995
Cowen Collection, Research Division of the Oklahoma Historical Society, #19687. IN.KIO.EV.12.9

Notable Kiowas include the famous Cozad family of singers. Sharon Ahtone Harjo, an art teacher and painter, as Miss Indian America in 1968 accompanied Gourd Dancers who helped spread that dance style through Indian Country. Author N. Scott Momaday has written eloquently about his heritage. His father, Alfred Momaday, was a painter. Jake Chanate received the Congressional Medal of Honor during World War II. Painters such as Silverhorn and Zotom and the Kiowa Five (Spencer Asah, Monroe Tsatoke, Stephen Mopope, Jack Hokeah, James Auchiah, and the sixth, the lone woman, Lois Smokey) as well as more contemporary artists like Robert Redbird, Jr., T. C. Cannon (also Caddo), Tom Poolaw (also Delaware), David Williams (also Tonkawa), Barthell Little Chief, Blackbear Bosin (also Comanche), Parker Boyiddle, Ted Creepingbear, Dennis Belindo, Kevin Connywerdy (also Comanche), and Sherman Chaddlesone continue Plains artwork traditions. Well-known painter Virginia Stroud is Creek and Cherokee but is an adopted Kiowa. Vanessa Paukeigope Jennings, a granddaughter of Stephen Mopope, is noted for her beadwork.

Harding Big Bow kept one of the medicine bundles and was a leader in the Native American Church. Ethel C. Krepps, an attorney, wrote knowledgeably about her Kiowa background. Kirke Kickingbird is an attorney. Physician Everett Rhoades served as head of the Indian Health Service as assistant surgeon general of the United States. Black Leggings Society founder Allen Quetone worked forty years for the BIA and was the great-grandson of famous leader Stumbling Bear. Parker P. McKenzie was the second Indian (the other being the more famous Sequoyah) to help develop a written orthography for a tribal language. Gus Palmer, Jr., is a poet, writer, translator, and professor. Actor Hanay Geiogamah (also Delaware) taught and wrote drama by and about Indians. He was technical advisor for the film *Dark Wind* (1992). Alyce Sadongei was a poet and a trainer for the Smithsonian's National Museum of the American Indian. In his short life, Russ Saunkeah was a gifted guitar player who performed with national bands. Contemporary Kiowa musicians include Tom Mauchahty-Ware and blues guitarist Jesse Ed Davis. The members of the Red Rhythm Band are Kiowa and Comanche. Phil Walker was the Little Red football mascot at the University of Oklahoma (1957–60 and 1970). Dr. Joseph H. Sahmaunt was an Indian Athletic Hall of Fame basketball player then athletic director and professor at Oklahoma City University.

SUGGESTED READING

Boyd, Maurice, with Lynn Pauahty, eds. *Kiowa Voices*. 2 vols. Fort Worth: Texas Christian University Press, 1981–83.

Haley, James L. *The Buffalo War*. Norman: University of Oklahoma Press, 1985 (Phil Sheridan quotation on viii).

Jelinek, Arthur. *A Prehistoric Sequence in the Middle Pecos Valley, New Mexico*. Museum of Anthropology, Anthropological Papers No. 31. Ann Arbor: University of Michigan, 1967.

Lassiter, Luke E. *The Power of Kiowa Song*. Tucson: University of Arizona Press, 1998.

Mayhall, Mildred. *The Kiowas*. Norman: University of Oklahoma Press, 1962; 2nd ed. 1984.

Medawar, Mardi Oakly. *Death at Rainy Mountain*. New York: St. Martin's, 1996; repr. New York: Berkley Prime Crime, 1998 (a mystery novel).

Momaday, N. Scott. *The Way to Rainy Mountain*. Albuquerque: University of New Mexico Press, 1969.

Mooney, James. "Calendar History of the Kiowa Indians." In *Seventeenth Annual Report of the Bureau of American Ethnology for 1895–96*, vol. 1, part 1, pp. 141–447. Washington, D.C.: Government Printing Office, 1898; repr. Washington, D.C.: Smithsonian Institution, 1979.

Palmer, Gus, Jr. *Telling Stories the Kiowa Way*. Tucson: University of Arizona Press, 2003.

Rand, Jacki Thompson. *Kiowa Humanity and the Invasion of the State*. Lincoln: University of Nebraska Press, 2008.

Miami

NAME

The Miamis refer to themselves as Myaamia, "downstream people," according to tribal linguists. Neighboring tribes had various pronunciations of this term: for instance, the Mesquakies refer to the Miamis as Myaamiiwa and the Ojibwes call them Omaamii. Derived from these varied forms, the name "Miami" is found today throughout the Midwest.

LOCATION AND GOVERNMENT

The headquarters for the "Miami Tribe of Oklahoma" is in the community of the same name in Ottawa County in far northeastern Oklahoma (about fifteen miles west of Seneca, Missouri, and ninety miles northeast of Tulsa). The tribe operated under a 1939 constitution according to the provisions of the OIWA, with revisions approved in 1993. A federal charter was ratified in 1940. Tribal government is a business committee with a chief plus four members, elected for three-year terms. All tribal members eligible to vote constitute the Miami Council. There is a tribal library. The tribal website is www.miaminaion.com.

BUSINESSES

The Miami Tribe operates several small businesses through its Miami Nation Enterprises, including Miami Designs (embroidery and T-shirts), Miami Business Services, Miami Cineplex theater, and Miami Tribe Entertainment, which includes their casino (The Stables) situated in the city of Miami. It is the only gaming facility owned jointly by two tribes, the other being the Modocs. The tribe currently manages just over 2,000 acres of tribal properties in its jurisdictional area of northeastern Oklahoma. It is also purchasing small parcels of land in Ohio, Indiana, and Illinois in order to maintain the Miamis' connection to their ancestral homeland.

NUMBER

The citizenship rolls of the Miami Tribe list just over 3,500 members. There are perhaps over 2,600 Miamis in Indiana, descendants of those excepted from the 1846 forced removal. They are not federally recognized but maintain a headquarters in Peru, Indiana. Historically, the Oklahoma Miamis were referred to as the Western Miamis, while their Indiana kinfolk were called the Eastern Miamis.

The Miamis shared their Central Algonquian language with a large number of Indian tribes across northern North America. The Miami and Illinois people speak different dialects of the same language. Among them were many smaller historical bands, such as the Weas, Kaskaskias, Peorias, and Piankashaws. Sauk, Mesquakie, and Kickapoo are also closely related to the Miami-Illinois language, as are the Ojibwe, Ottawa, and Potawatomi languages.

Archeologists speculate that ancestral Algonquian groups resided prehistorically to the west of Hudson Bay. These people moved southward of the Great Lakes and became the Miami-Illinois, Potawatomis, Menominees, Foxes, Shawnees, and others. Linguist Ives Goddard proposed that at least 2,500 to 3,000 years ago Proto-Algonquian was one group that was spoken in the region of Georgian Bay near Lake Huron and Lake Ontario. Thereafter the language group quickly split into at least ten groups that grew increasingly distinct. The Miami-Illinois–speaking people were among them.

After A.D. 1200 increased Mississippian influences can be found among archeological remains. There is evidence of a spread of Mississippian styles throughout much of the region in subsequent years. The antecedent prehistoric culture of the Miami tribal groups is called Huber. Near the time of European arrival, archeological evidence indicates seasonal movement to exploit marsh environments through small camps then a return to larger fortified summer agricultural villages, making use of corn-beans-squash cultivation and fall-winter elk-bison hunts on the nearby prairie. There are also remains that suggest Oneota influences. Mississippian objects such as disk pipes and gorgets came from the South. Over time the remains show increased contact with western Oneota peoples and more bison hunting during winter.

The Miami origin story is related to that of other Great Lakes tribes. In general, at the origin water covered everything. The Creator asked water animals to dive and bring up mud then placed the wet dirt on a turtle's back, where the earth expanded.

Probably to improve their trade advantage, the Miamis moved in the 1680s to the region between the St. Joseph and the Illinois rivers, approximately where the modern states of Michigan, Ohio, and Indiana meet. Miami-speaking groups along the St. Joseph relocated to the upper Wabash and Maumee rivers (in the region of contemporary Fort Wayne, Indiana) to form the Miami Tribe. Those along the middle Wabash in time became the Weas. The Piankashaws occupied the lower Wabash and Vermillion rivers.

Trying to identify the constituent parts of the Miamis is confusing. Beginning in the seventeenth century, French observers identified six subgroups that constituted the Miamis: the Atchatchakangouens, Kilatikas, Mengakonkias, Pepikokias, Piankashaws, and Weas. By mid-century the independent Weas had absorbed the Pepikokias. At the mid-point of the next century the Weas and Piankashaws merged with the Illinois Confederacy tribes to form the Confederated Peorias. The other Miami subgroups either were absorbed or vanished in the eighteenth century in the chaos of war, relocation, and disease that engulfed the region. As a further complication, the Miamis resided at times in Wisconsin with the Mascoutens, Kickapoos, and Potawatomis and in the late eighteenth century took in refugees such as Delaware and Shawnee Indians fleeing conflict.

Scholar Susan Sleeper-Smith underscored how women of the Miami and Illinois nations intermarried with French fur traders and the impact of those unions. Together they created a distinct mixed-blood Roman Catholic Indian identity in the Great Lakes region for nearly two centuries. Their new religious affiliation enabled Native women to avoid some of the limitations that patrilineal indigenous society placed on them. Additionally, the new couples aided tribal survival during eighteenth and nineteenth centuries with the agricultural surpluses that they produced. Still later, some acculturated to mask their indigenous ancestry. Beginning nearly from the inception of the unions, people crossed ethnic boundaries on a regular basis.

The Miamis shared many religious traits with their Illinois Confederacy kin. The Miamis divided themselves into Sky and Earth divisions or moieties. They were also divided into bands or villages, each of which had a war chief and a village chief. In the eighteenth century the bands were Le Pied Froid, La Demoiselle, and Tepicon. At that time the bands resided at Fort Miami, on the northern Eel River, and at Tippecanoe. Their Creator was the Master of Life, and medicine men intervened for villagers in the affairs of the supernatural. Village residents turned to the performance of the Midewiwin in the nineteenth century as a bridge to traditionalism amid a time of great change. The Midewiwin was adopted from the Ojibwe Grand Medicine Society of the late seventeenth century to foster physical and spiritual healing and to achieve harmony in the individual's life. Much of the rest of traditional Miami religious life was destroyed or lost in the tumult of the seventeenth to nineteenth centuries.

Frenchman Gabriel Druillette encountered the "Oumanik," believed to be the Miamis, in 1658 at the mouth of Green Bay in present-day Wisconsin. Father Jacques Marquette established the mission of the Immaculate Conception among the Kaskaskias, a constituent tribe of the Illinois Confederacy, on the Illinois River in April 1675. Slightly later a mission was set up for the Miamis on the Kalamazoo River in what is today Michigan. French missionaries found the Indians eager for the Christian faith as well as French trade goods. Missionaries claimed that they had good success using hymns to teach about Christianity, building on Native cultural traits. French dreams of domination of New France focused on members of the Illinois Confederacy. For a time the Miamis occupied settlements along the south shore of Lake Michigan and along the St. Joseph River.

Many Indians passed through Miami territory in the wake of the fierce Iroquois attacks in the 1650s. Potawatomis, Kickapoos, and other tribes focused their aggressions on Miami territory. They drove the Miamis out of the region and into Ohio along the Miami River. After securing peace with the Susquehannocks in 1676, the Iroquois turned their attention to western expansion. They attacked the Miamis and Illinois in 1680. The Miamis fought back but also moved.

Eventually the Miamis and Weas joined Pontiac's abortive pan-Indian rebellion on the side of the French. Under the terms of the peace in 1763, the Miamis migrated back to Indiana. It is likely that they had hunted and traveled through Indiana for a long time. The Miamis switched allegiance during the Revolutionary War and supported the British and helped keep the region in turmoil for a decade afterward. Miami chief Little Turtle (Mishakinaquah) aided an American Indian coalition opposed to white encroachments. His skill and the ineptitude of his enemy led to a series of resounding defeats for U.S. forces, the most notable against Josiah Harmar in 1790 and Arthur St. Clair in 1791, which was one of the worst defeats in U.S. military history. Lengthy preparation and training under General Anthony Wayne led to a resounding victory for U.S. forces in the battle of Fallen Timbers in 1794. The punitive Treaty of Greenville was signed the following year. Scholar Bert Anson pointed out that the reluctant Miamis were the last of the Indians to attend the great Greenville council. The Miamis eventually signed thirteen treaties with the United States. Most of them ceded territory. After his 1794 defeat, Little Turtle became an advocate of peace with the United States and an accommodationist. His stance split the Miamis into pro-American and opposition factions, which have been examined by scholars Harvey Carter and Rob Mann.

Most of the Miamis remained neutral during the War of 1812. Little Turtle and mixed-blood leader Jean-Baptiste Richardville persuaded them to stay out of the impending conflict. Little Turtle died aiding the Americans during 1812. But Miami chiefs Pacane and Chapine and their followers sided with Tecumseh and the British (Pacane at Amherstburg, Chapine at Fort Wayne). William Henry Harrison's large American force in 1812 captured Fort Wayne then proceeded to destroy Miami villages, including that of the neutral Little Turtle. The force spared his government-issued house, however, from the conflagration. After the warfare subsided, the United States renewed efforts to remove Indians from the Old Northwest. One focus was the region of the Miamis, the area where the St. Mary's and the St. Joseph rivers met to form the Maumee River, a vital link from the Great Lakes by way of portage to the Wabash-Ohio rivers. A prominent Miami woman named Tacumway, sister of the chief, controlled all trade that passed the portage between the Maumee and Wabash rivers. She was the mother of Jean-Baptiste Richardville.

After the land cession in 1826, the Miamis were restricted to northern Indiana. Indian indebtedness to traders obligated their lands for ultimate payment. By the terms of the 1846 treaty, the U.S. government determined to remove the Miamis, the last Indians remaining in Indiana. The federal authorities divided the tribe into two groups. In 1846 over three hundred Miamis were taken by canal boats and a steamboat—their Trail of Tears—to a new reserve in eastern Kansas located on Sugar Creek near the Peorias and Quapaws. Phyllis Gernhardt showed that Indian traders reaped rewards from the removal and also contracted to handle it, so they profited both ways. Local militia members, creditors, speculators, and U.S. troops collected the Miamis and herded them toward boats. Escapees were tracked down, manacled, and delivered to the boats. Some desperately grabbed fistfuls of dirt as a small piece of their homeland as they departed. A few, such as the Slocum, Richardville, LaFontaine, and Godfroy families, were permitted to remain. Chief Jean-Baptiste Richardville accepted a $30,000 payment and title to 20,000 acres for relinquishing land in Indiana. His inherited wealth and position made him the richest Indian in America in the 1820s and

1830s. Not quite half of the Miamis escaped the removal but were scattered, while some eventually returned to the Indiana area. The Miamis were among the last tribes to be sent to Kansas under the Indian Removal Act. Their departure from Peru, Indiana, split the tribe into western and eastern divisions. Christmas Dagenet served as the conductor for the Miami, Wea, Kaskaskia, and Piankashaw tribes leaving Indiana. He led them to the vicinity of what would become Paola, Kansas. After Dagenet's death in 1848, his widow married Baptiste Peoria (a Wea).

Instead of the pledged 500,000 acres, on their arrival the Miamis discovered that their Kansas reserve was 325,000 acres. Over the ensuing years some landless Miamis migrated from Indiana westward and were adopted or intermarried into neighboring tribes like the Quapaws. In a reverse flow, some Kansas Miamis drifted back to Indiana. In 1848 the western Miamis moved to the eastern side of the Marais des Cygnes (Marsh of the Swans) River. There they remained neutral during the American Civil War. Underlying the tragedy of Bleeding Kansas leading to the Civil War in the United States, however, was the ongoing conflict to possess Indian lands in Kansas.

Some Kansas territorial politicians joined the land-hunger frenzy. The attorney general and a senator speculated in Indian land holdings and represented railroad interests eager to open tribal lands. Governors pressed their own state militias to ignite hostilities with tribes to serve as an excuse to evict the Indians. An 1854 treaty with commissioner of Indian affairs George A. Manypenny reduced the Miamis' 1840 acreage from 325,000 down to about 70,000, with a proviso to allot parcels to individual tribal members. Kansas outrages encroached on Miami rights and lands. White settlers cut their timber, opened farms on Indian land, and even drove the Miamis from their homes. In many ways it was a replay of their earlier treatment in Indiana, with a similar result. Federal authorities pressured the Miamis and other Indians to sign a new treaty in February 1867. Sixty-five Miamis agreed to remove to Indian Territory and to allot there. Thirty-three Miamis chose to remain in Kansas on fee-simple land as citizens. In desperation, in 1868 the Miamis removed to Indian Territory, where they were pressured to confederate with the Peorias, Weas, Piankashaws, and Kaskaskias. Collectively, they were labeled the Five Tribes or the United Peorias and Miamis, but at the last minute the Miamis pulled out of the confederation, remaining a distinct and separate entity. Of the approximately 300 Miamis originally removed to Kansas, only 91 remained by 1868. Another removal push took place in March 1873, after the Kansas congressional delegation gained enactment of laws (acts of January 23 and March 3, 1873, 17 Stat. 417 and 631) fostering the sale of remaining Indian lands and another tribal split: those selecting removal once again and those choosing to remain. Chief Richardville and his family came to Indian Territory in 1882 to land that would become the Robinson-Mayes Dairy.

The Miamis intermingled with other Indians in northeastern Oklahoma. Some received their allotments among the Quapaws. Rich ore was first discovered on the allotment of a Miami woman, Emma Gordon McBee, on the Quapaw reservation. That fostered a mining boom. As with so many other tribes, allotment devastated the Miami Tribe. Individual members sold or lost their land with remarkable speed. By the time of the Indian New Deal, the tribe was landless. In spite of lacking a land base, however, the Miami Tribe squeaked through the period of federal termination with its tribal recognition intact.

Daryl Baldwin, director of the Myaamia Project at Miami University
Courtesy Daryl Baldwin

Ceremonies and gatherings take place in the tribal longhouse. The Miamis' dance ground is located east of their tribal farm, which is the allotment of Isadore Labadie, about one mile west of the city of Miami. An annual fish fry held on the Fourth of July draws many. The annual powwow in the first week of June also attracts many visitors and intertribal singers and dancers. The annual tribal general council meeting has coincided with the annual powwow gathering since 2003. In 1995 a free chili feed with a stomp dance in late January grew into a two-day wintertime art market fest. Miami tribal members also participate in regional Indian festivals in Paola, Kansas, in Kansas City, and elsewhere.

The last fluent speaker of Miami died during the 1960s. The tribe has worked diligently since that decade with the help of Miami University in Oxford, Ohio, on many projects of mutual interest to preserve their culture and language. In 1994 the tribe began an earnest effort to restore its language (see www.myaamiaproject.org and www.myaamiafoundation. org). In July 2001 the tribe and the university launched the Myaamia Project. Faculty, staff, and students from Miami University regularly attend tribal functions. In 2008 there were twenty Miami Tribe students attending Miami University as a result of the Miami Indian Heritage award created by the university. Daryl Baldwin and his family have nearly single-handedly fostered a revival of the language.

One of the most notable Miamis was Little Turtle. As a young warrior, he led the defeat of an American force under Augustin Mottin de la Balme in 1780 and became the Miami war chief. He then joined the coalition that twice humiliated U.S. military expeditions. The catastrophe involving Arthur St. Clair in 1791 emboldened Congress to undertake its first hearings into executive branch actions, including the war department and its field activities. William Wells, an adopted member who married Little Turtle's daughter and died during the War of 1812, is immortalized with a county named for him in Indiana and with prominent thoroughfares named for him in Chicago and Fort Wayne. Wes Leonard is a linguist with a doctorate from the University of California at Berkeley. Catherine Clary Green served on the city council and as mayor (2004–2006) of Huntington Beach, California. Craig and Chris, the Davis Brothers, are a bluegrass duo.

SUGGESTED READING

Anson, Bert. *The Miami Indians.* Norman: University of Oklahoma Press, 1970.

Carter, Harvey Lewis. *The Life and Times of Little Turtle.* Chicago: University of Illinois Press, 1987.

Foreman, Grant. *Last Trek of the Indians.* Chicago: University of Chicago Press, 1946; repr. New York: Russell and Russell, 1972.

Gernhardt, Phyllis. " 'Justice and Public Policy': Indian Trade, Treaties, and Removal from Northern Indiana, 1826–1846." In Daniel H. Barr, ed., *The Boundaries between Us,* 178–95. Kent, Ohio: Kent State University Press, 2006.

Goddard, Ives. "Central Algonquian Languages." In vol. 15, *Northeast,* of the *Handbook of North American Indians,* 583–93. Washington, D.C.: Smithsonian Institution, 1978.

Mann, Rob. "The Silenced Miami: Archaeological and Ethnohistorical Evidence for Miami-British Relations, 1795–1812." *Ethnohistory* 46 (Summer 1999): 399–428.

Rafert, Stewart. *The Miami Indians of Indiana: A Persistent People, 1654–1994.* Bloomington: Indiana Historical Society Press, 1996.

Sleeper-Smith, Susan. *Indian Women and French Men: Rethinking Cultural Encounter in the Western Great Lakes.* Amherst: University of Massachusetts Press, 2001.

Missouria

See the "Otoe-Missouria" *entry.*

Modoc

NAME

The tribal name came from the word *moadokkni*, "southern." The neighboring tribe in their California homeland, the Klamaths, referred to them as Moadlaks or Maklaks, "people of the south." They are both members of the Penutian linguistic family. The Modocs refer to themselves as Maklaks, "the People."

LOCATION AND GOVERNMENT

The headquarters for the "Modoc Tribe" is located downtown in the community of Miami in Ottawa County. The administrative offices are attached to the north end of a casino (The Stables), about twenty miles from Seneca, Missouri. The Modocs are one of the eight tribes located along an avenue called the Turtle's Trail out of the city of Miami in far northeastern Oklahoma. They are led by five council members and a chief. Prior to that the tribe had only a shadow government and no constitution because of federal termination. There is not yet a tribal website.

BUSINESSES

As a result of allotment during the 1890s and termination of federal supervision over property in the 1950s, the reconstituted tribe started with only the acreage of its church and cemetery as a landbase. The tribe owns a bison herd. The Stables casino in Miami is jointly owned by the Modocs and the Miami Tribe. It is one of the largest employers in the region.

NUMBER

The tribe has just under 200 members. It is the smallest federally recognized tribe in Oklahoma.

Archeologists place the Penutian-speaking peoples, the Klamaths and the Modocs, in their homeland in the Northwest since prehistoric times, possibly extending back to 5000 B.C. It is believed that the Klamaths and Modocs made use of a larger region extending farther east than during the historic era.

In the historic period the Modoc homeland was in southwestern Oregon and northwestern California. Their territory straddled what is now the Oregon-California state boundary. It encompassed lands north and east of Mount Shasta, along Lost River, and near the Lower Klamath, Clear, and Tule lakes. The Modocs and the Klamaths probably were originally a single group, since their language and culture are closely related. The Modocs mostly resided on the edge of the Plateau region but also utilized resources and possessed some cultural traits of the Great Basin, of California, and of the Plains.

Scholars argue over where to place the historic Modocs culturally. Some placed them in the Northwest Coast culture. Others classified them in the Great Basin culture region according to their traits. Still others associated them with California tribal cultures, albeit in the farthest northern reaches of that state. Perhaps a slight majority of scholars situated the Modocs among Plateau cultures of the inland Northwest (hence they are included in volume 12 of the *Handbook of North American Indians*). Throughout their history the Modocs took cultural aspects from each of these regions as their own adaptations.

The Modoc origin story is shared with the nearby Klamaths. The world was a disk floating on water. To the west, beyond a distant mountain, lay the afterworld, where spirits dwelled in an existence that was the reverse of earthly life. In ancient mythic times Gmukamps (Mythic Old Man) was the dominant figure. He was a trickster-transformer. Gopher transformed the world so that plants and animals could live on it. Gmukamps peopled it. The people then presided over a council in which mythic beings announced what earthly form they would take.

The Modocs at Klamath Lake celebrated the first fruits of the season of the waka (pond lily) and communally held memorial services and a feast for their departed. The villages controlled areas that yielded products like fish and seeds and were located along rivers or on the shoreline of lakes. The Modocs used the services of a shaman to intercede in the supernatural realm to bring an individual success and health. They had three major band divisions: the people of the west (Gumbatwas), people of the far country (Kokiwas), and people of the river (Paskanwas). The Modocs relied on camas bulbs, pond lily seeds, and tubers as mainstays of their diet, supplemented by other foods like seeds and nuts. Men hunted game and waterfowl and fished. The Modocs migrated through their territory in pursuit of seasonally available foods, such as annually moving to spring fishing camps. Their winter housing was an earth lodge, which was snug against the cold of the higher elevation. In milder climates and different locations, they used smaller mat-covered structures as well as the Great Basin wickiup. The mat house could also be banked with earth to insulate it for cold weather. Both men and women wore woven basket hats.

Trade from the Columbia River Valley by way of neighboring tribes reached the Modocs well before Euro-American fur traders did. Horses, guns, and other items helped transform the Indians' culture. Once U.S. officials designated certain individuals as chiefs, dissension increased and division wracked the tribe. But the Modocs remained isolated from the presence of Euro-Americans along major rivers and the coastline. All of that changed with the discovery of gold in California in 1848. Droves of white miners and supporters entered the region. The community of Yreka sprang up on the edge of the Modoc hunting range. Wagon traffic headed along the Oregon Trail passed through their territory, and the Modocs periodically attacked the emigrant trains.

Grievances accumulated on both sides. Local miners massacred forty Modocs. After the American Civil War more people poured into the region, with increased violations of Indian rights and lands. Under the terms of an October 1864 treaty, Modocs, Klamaths, and the Yahooskin band relinquished their territory and agreed to move to a smaller reservation in Klamath homelands. Modoc leader Captain Jack (Kientpoos or Kintpuash) disapproved of the new reserve and a year later led fifty followers back home. They found that cattle ranchers had taken over their village domain on Lost River near Tule Lake, but they made the best of the situation.

When U.S. troops entered the village in November 1872 to return the Indians forcibly to the reserve, fighting broke out. Captain Jack and followers fled to sanctuary in the forbidding landscape of the Lava Beds south of the lake. Hooker Jim led his band to join Captain Jack. During their journey the Modocs killed eighteen friendly whites. In response, residents of Linkville formed a vigilante mob. Their threat against the nearby innocent Hot Creek band under Shaknasty Jim drove those Modocs to unite with Captain Jack. The Modoc War lasted just over six months and proved to be one of the costliest wars in all U.S. history. It probably could have been prevented even in the white-hot atmosphere of massacres through a quick official U.S. response. The federal government could have created a Modoc reservation out of the Lava Beds and a portion of the southern shoreline of the lake, but it did not.

After attempts to arrange a peace failed and despite the warnings of dire circumstances, General E. R. S. Canby accompanied other peace commissioners to parley with the Modocs. While they were conferring, Captain Jack drew a pistol and shot Canby, mortally wounding him. Canby was the only general to die during the Indian wars. Other commission members were also shot. When informed of the unprovoked attack by the Modocs, commanding General William T. Sherman thundered about "their utter extermination." The Modocs retreated into their stronghold. Constant military pursuit of the Indians kept them on the move (accompanied by artillery barrages), cut them off from water, and led ultimately to their surrender. No more than fifty-seven Modoc warriors had held off over a thousand U.S. troops and had killed forty-five of them.

A few Modoc prisoners were attacked and murdered by whites en route to confinement. After a speedy military trial, four of the Modocs were found guilty of killing Canby and were sentenced to death, including Captain Jack. They were hanged. Captain Jack's skeleton was eventually stored in the Surgeon General's museum in Washington, D.C. Nine days after the execution 155 Modocs (42 men, 59 women, and 54 children) were shipped to exile in Indian Territory. Two Modocs, Barncho and Slolux, were delivered to Alcatraz to serve life sentences for their roles in the attack on the commissioners. The other Modocs arrived in Indian Territory chained together in railcars then in wagons. Military authorities appointed Scarfaced Charley as Modoc leader. They were settled at the Quapaw Agency on the Eastern Shawnee portion of that reserve. Shortly thereafter, 4,040 acres were purchased from the Eastern Shawnees for the Modoc reservation. The Modocs, of course, had arrived with only the clothing on their backs and meager possessions, so they had to start from scratch.

The dead peace commissioners included a minister, which alarmed the church leaders who had advocated reform of American Indian policy. The controversy regarding the causes and consequences of the Modoc War aroused reformers' questions and helped fuel the formation of the Indian reform movement in the United States. One of the surviving commissioners, Alfred Meacham, toured eastern stages giving lectures, accompanied by several Modocs, which added a personal immediacy to the reformers' quest for change in U.S. Indian policies.

Quaker missionaries set up a mission school for the Modocs. Steamboat Frank became the first full-blood Indian minister in the Society of Friends, took the name Frank Modoc, and was the Modoc Church's first pastor. Modoc men found work on nearby farms as laborers and hauled freight. Women made traditional crafts for sale. Many helped to erect the Modoc Friends Church and became active in it. The church and cemetery were placed on the National Register of Historic Places in 1980. The church was restored four years later. Relocation, illness, and infant mortality led to a decline in population, down to ninety-nine in 1879 and only sixty-eight by 1891. About ten Modocs who were ill were permitted to return to Oregon through the 1880s. Upon receiving their allotments in 1891, some Modocs sold or leased their lands and quickly returned to Oregon. By mid-1893 under fifty remained in Indian Territory. The federal government shut down the Quapaw Agency in 1901 and transferred management of Indian affairs to Edgar Allen, the superintendent of the Seneca Indian School. After thirty-six years in exile, the surviving Modocs were added to the Klamath Agency roll in Oregon when Congress passed a measure (Public Law 306) on March 3, 1909. Many Modocs returned there. For all intents and purposes, their tribal government ended in the 1880s with the death of Bogus Charley, the last chief. He had been appointed by Quaker agent Hiram W. Jones, who oversaw the Quapaw Agency, which included the Modocs. The Indian agents served as de facto chiefs. Jones worked in collusion with Quaker superintendent Enoch Hoag to exploit the Modocs and the other Indians at the agency. The Modocs, of course, continued to meet informally and to discuss issues of concern. A historical marker along Highway 10 outside of the city of Miami notes the cemetery in which the Modocs from their diaspora are buried.

Ironically, the Klamath Tribe was also terminated (in 1956). Timber company desire for the fine pine forest on the million-acre Klamath Reservation fed the push for an end to federal protection. Corporate desire successfully combined with efforts by Oregon politicians like the former governor, who by then served as the secretary of the interior, overseeing natural resources and Indians. Public Law 83-587 terminated the Klamath Tribe and provided for a per capita payment. Modocs living in Oklahoma who were enrolled opted for the payment. Many were intermarried among other ethnic groups by then and resided throughout the Midwest.

Fewer Modocs resided in Oklahoma. Most prospered in farming and related work. Congress similarly terminated the Modoc Tribe of Oklahoma as a tribal entity in mid-August 1956 through the same Public Law 83-587. Former members continued to meet informally, however, and took part in the Inter-Tribal Council of Oklahoma tribes. Restoration of tribal recognition eventually took place through congressional enactment in May 1978 (Public Law 95-281). At the time the only remaining tribal land was the Modoc cemetery of four acres. It served as a community focus. (The Klamath Tribe in Oregon was recognized again in 1986 and also underwent the reestablishment of tribal identity.) In 1978 Bill Follis, great-grandson of exiled band leader James Long, became the first Modoc chief in Oklahoma since Bogus Charley in 1880. The Modocs completed their tribal complex in 1983 as a part of their restoration.

There are no more full-blood Modocs in the Oklahoma tribe. Linguists classify the Modoc language in Oklahoma as "resting." The Modocs work in concert with other Northeast Eight tribes in Oklahoma to combat pollution in the area. Long-term mining activity in the Tri-State Region left a legacy of soil and water contamination along Tar Creek that threatened lives and livelihoods in the long term.

Notable Modocs include Captain Jack, who worked to save his old way of life and his people in their homeland. Scarfaced Charley led the exiles during their darkest hours as prisoners of war, as they adjusted to their new homeland. A grandson of Shaknasty Jim, Clyde James, was recognized for his athletic ability in basketball by induction into the American Indian Athletic Hall of Fame in 1977. His daughter, Patricia Easterla, became a noted author and professional speaker.

SUGGESTED READING

Martin, Lucille J. "A History of the Modoc Indians: An Acculturation Study." *Chronicles of Oklahoma* 47 (Winter 1969–70): 398–446 (William T. Sherman quotation on 416).

Murray, Keith A. *The Modocs and Their War.* Norman: University of Oklahoma Press, 1976; repr. 1985.

Quinn, Arthur. *Hell with the Fire Out: A History of the Modoc War.* New York: Faber and Faber, 1998.

Muscogee (Creek)

NAME

"Muscogee" is of unknown origin in spite of being the name for the widely used Muskhogean linguistic family spoken throughout the historic Southeast. Nineteenth-century ethnographer Albert Gatschet proposed that it derived from a Shawnee word for "wet ground" or "swamp" or "marsh" as a description of their surroundings for their Tuckabatchee town hosts. Perhaps because the Muscogee Confederacy was made up of a complex mix of tribal towns, the label was adopted. Gatschet's reasoning is now doubtful, leaving the derivation unknown even though it is their self-designation. There are numerous variations of the spelling (Muscogee, Muskogee, Maskogee, Mvskoke). "Mvskoke" is now preferred for the language, "Muscogee" for the nation. Some prefer Mvskoke Etvlwv, "Muscogee town" or "community." Muscogee people usually also refer to themselves according to their tribal town or tribal community, church, or ceremonial ground (such as Okfuskee, Hanna, or Abeka), then their clan, and finally their family connection or genealogy. "Creek" derived from British traders who referred to local Indians living along the Ocmulgee and Ochesee rivers in Georgia as "Ochesee Creek Indians." It was shortened to "Creek" in everyday usage. ("Ochesee" or "Ochisi" or "Otchisi" is itself a Hitchiti Indian word to designate those who do not speak Hitchiti.) "Creek" is still sometimes used to designate the Mvskokulke, "all the Muscogee people." The word "Creek" was heavily used in the nineteenth century and is used here for that period.

LOCATION AND GOVERNMENT

The "Muscogee (Creek) Nation" headquarters is situated just north of Okmulgee in Creek County. The population is heavily centered in the counties of McIntosh, Tulsa, Creek, and Hughes. The legislative chamber meets in a domed building recalling their ancestral culture, called the Mound. The name of the capital town invokes the Ocmulgee Mississippian mound site in Macon, Georgia, the former ancient capital of the Creeks there. Muscogee Nation tribal towns and communities are scattered throughout eleven counties in the east-central portion of Oklahoma. The Muscogee Nation is organized under the OIWA, operating under a tribal constitution adopted in 1979, and has three separate branches of government. The principal chief and the second chief serve four-year terms. National Council members occupy staggered terms. All adult tribal citizens are eligible to vote. The nation plans to purchase the Creek Council House Museum in the town square of Okmulgee. It once housed the legislature for the tribe following removal. The tribe has a strong court system. The tribal website is www.muscogeenation-nsn.gov.

BUSINESSES

Revenue from casinos in Tulsa (on South Riverside Drive at 81st Street), Okemah, Checotah, Okmulgee, Muskogee, Eufaula, and the Duck Creek community south of Tulsa provides much of the nation's income. Ground-breaking took place in 2007 for a new $200-million casino-entertainment center south of the Tulsa facility on Mackey Sand Bar on the Arkansas River. Three travel plazas (in Muskogee, in Okmulgee, and on Interstate Highway 40 at the Wewoka exit) also contain smoke shops. The nation does not engage in any manufacturing activities at present, but the tribal Business Enterprise entity utilizes Small Business Administration Section 8(a) to do contracting with the federal government and with other tribes. The nation's construction company built expansions for other tribal casinos as well as projects such as housing, aircraft runways, and others. The Muscogee Nation's highway services company provides roadway, runway, and bridge repair and repaving. The tribe's road department works cooperatively with counties to surface rural roadways. The tribal fire suppression company offers smoke alarms as well as electronic security services and personnel security to clients. The tribal information technology contract with the Cherokee Nation supports a call center in Tahlequah. The tribe was the first in the United States to own a building leased to a regional area BIA office, in the city of Muskogee.

Under the umbrella of the Muscogee Nation's Trade and Commerce Authority, a document imaging company saves and stores business records. A neon sign company has a contract to produce public signage. Two thousand acres of farmland near Hanna produce alfalfa and other agricultural products. Cattle and buffalo herds offer both meat and history on the hoof. A local Muscogee Nation and Okmulgee industrial park provides sites for businesses and includes a transit center for the Muscogee Nation bus service.

NUMBER

The tribe has about 65,000 members, based on a descendancy enrollment, making the Creeks the fourth largest tribe in the United States. The 120-member Isle de Jean Charles Bilozi–Chitimacha Confederation of Muskogees of Louisiana (south of Houma) are state-recognized (2004). About 2,600 Poarch Creeks live near Atmore, Alabama. They are descendants of Little River Creek mixed-bloods (kin of Alexander McGillivray) who "won" the Second Creek War and remained on their ancestral lands and are federally recognized (1984). There are unrecognized groups claiming Muscogee heritage in Alabama, Georgia, and Florida.

Linguistic affinity connects the Muscogee Nation's citizens with many ancient and contemporary residents of the southeastern United States. Muscogees are distantly related by language to Choctaws and Chickasaws as well as others. Muscogee ancestors resided in a series of Mississippian-period temple mound centers and satellite communities throughout present-day Georgia and Alabama. Oral tradition recounted a long migration from the Far West, perhaps the Rocky Mountains, crossing a giant river and finally settling in the southeastern portion of what is now the United States. Oral stories also tell of four major foundational towns: Cusseta, Coweta, Abeka, and Tuckabatchee (which is credited with origination of the annual Green Corn Ceremony). Tuckabatchee and Coweta are considered paramount towns. Linguists like Jack Martin contend that the tribal language stock Mvskoke spread eastward out of the Louisiana region in prehistoric times. Archeologists point to local development and link several late Woodland sites like Kolomoki in Georgia to the Proto-Creeks. Tribespeople also assert an ancestral claim to the Mississippian sites of Etowah and Ocmulgee National Monument in the same vicinity ("Ocmulgee" means "bubbling water" in Hitchiti). Near Ocmulgee is the

Lamar mound site, the location of a palisaded ceremonial center after A.D. 950. It is a Proto-Creek site too. De Soto expedition members entered the main village of the province of Ichisi, believed to be the Lamar site, in 1540. During historic times Creeks lived in Georgia, Alabama, and northern Florida and were the strongest Native force in the Deep South during the early part of that time.

Although each town had its own origin story, two basic outlines existed in the confederacy. Tuckabatchee founders descended from the Upper World (sky). Cusseta residents believed that they had originated when their ancestors emerged from the earth out of a cave, perhaps from the navel of the world someplace in the Rocky Mountains. Atop a sacred mountain, the King of the Mountains gave the people the first fire. Prior to that, a dispute among the people had created four divisions. Wherever their ultimate origin, the predecessors of the Muscogee people migrated eastward, according to oral tradition, crossing a mighty river before settling in the Southeast. The Cowetas and Cussetas traveled until they encountered the Coosas and what are believed to be the Abekas along the Chattahoochee River. Coweta and Cusseta became Lower Creek towns. Tuckabatchee represented the Upper Creeks. After a series of events, the four major towns formed the nucleus of the Muscogee Confederacy.

Paramount chiefdoms of the Coosa, Tallapoosa, and Alabama river systems provided the core for what would become the Upper Creeks. Archeologists like Ned Jenkins have studied ceramics made by women and linked them to various prehistoric sites. Their studies connected the Etowah chiefdom to Savannah pottery and through Dallas-phase pots to the Little Egypt site and to the Coosa chiefdom, which appeared about A.D. 1400. Later the Spanish chronicler known as the Gentleman of Elva described the leader of the Coosas when he came out to meet members of Soto's expedition. The Proto-Creek chief was carried aloft on a sedan chair. He was arrayed in a cape of marten skins and a crown of feathers. Scientific explorations of Moundville Variant peoples who departed the Warrior Valley after 1450 showed that they settled in the upper Alabama River Valley, where some became part of the Big Eddy phase. Then they moved into the lower Tallapoosa River Valley in the Atasi phase, contributing by about A.D. 1650 to the rise of what would ultimately become the Upper Creeks.

Some of the Moundville Variant peoples moved into the upper Alabama River Valley and on to the middle Chattahoochee River in the Lamar phase to form the Cusseta and Coweta chiefdoms. These chiefdoms absorbed the Apalachicolas and other mission Indians (also incorporating some Ocutes) and then became the Lower Creeks. The Ocute paramount chiefdom fragmented and later emerged as a Yamassee chiefdom on the Okmulgee and Oconee rivers. (The Yamassees themselves incorporated remnants of the Tama and Guale chiefdoms.) Spanish attacks in the 1680s and the lure of British trade drove Chattachoochee town residents to the Okmulgee and Oconee rivers.

The coming of Europeans changed nearly everything. Hernando de Soto's 1540 expedition fostered warfare and devastation among the Creeks. His chroniclers described visits to large platform-mound villages with spacious plazas and temples that are believed to have been predecessors of the Creek towns of Coosa and Cusseta. The expedition's diseases devastated Native peoples along its path. As an example, the Tristan de Luna expedition visited Coosa, capital of Upper Creek ancestors, twenty years after the earlier conquistador. Luna's men found Coosa deserted, its population allegedly depleted and the remnants scattered. The Spaniards' devastating impact, traced by scholar Marvin Smith, led to shrinking population, loss of control over territory, and steady movement downriver by what became the Muscogee peoples.

In the ensuing years remnants from other devastated Indian nations helped form the Muscogee Confederacy. Scholars disagree on when it started. Some believe the confederacy was a war league long before the arrival of Europeans, while others point to the European presence as the original cause and consider the confederacy to be a result of the 1715 Yamassee War. Tribes came together in a political and diplomatic confederacy that was already well underway by 1700. Most of the members of the more than sixty towns spoke Muskhogean, but others spoke different languages (such as the Yuchis, Shawnees, Natchez, and some Chickasaws). All shared a remarkably similar southeastern Native culture and were for the most part matrilineal in their descent, with residences arranged around a courtyard in clusters near a central ceremonial ground. Muscogee villages relied on corn as the mainstay of their diet. Women tended fields (allocated by clans) and gardens. A portion of each family's harvest was placed in the town's communal storage for a time of need. Muscogee men hunted, fished, and provided protection for their town. Residents identified first with their town, a feature unique to the Muscogees. Towns and clans were divided into red and white halves (moieties). By 1685 the Creeks numbered about 15,000.

European powers contended for almost a century for control of Creek territory and trade. Nearing the end of the seventeenth century the Spanish, French, English, and Creeks jockeyed for both. English trade inroads in Carolina turned that colony into the center of trade in Indian slaves and animal pelts, involving the Lower Creek towns that were located closer to the English. Over time, English trade followed the Creeks who moved from Charlestown to the site where the Oconee and Ocmulgee rivers met. First Spanish then French forces fell before the superior English trade goods and tactics.

Conflicts led refugee tribes to seek protection in English, French, Spanish, and Creek locales in the early eighteenth century. French attempts to secure bastions for influence and commerce led to brief warfare against the Alabama towns of the Upper Creeks just after 1700. The French set up Fort Toulouse to protect their Mobile base after a 1714 treaty. The new fort was in the heart of Creek country on the Tallapoosa River. English influence again ultimately won, despite setbacks such as the disastrous Yamassee War (1715). In its wake, Lower Creeks moved from the Ocmulgee River in central Georgia to the Chattahoochee, with some going all the way to the Tallapoosa River in Alabama. The Spanish struggled with the English for control of Creek trade and territory for another decade before the English were victorious. The British king chartered Georgia as a colony in 1732, encouraging further English encroachment. Governor James Oglethorpe landed with settlers the following year. Shrewd diplomacy, aided by Yamacraw chief Tomochichi and mixed-blood Mary Musgrove Bosomworth, led to gradual expansion of Georgia settlements. The small coastal community of Savannah grew up around the Musgrove trading post. With the 1763 treaty that signaled the withdrawal of Spain and France, the Creeks had to deal exclusively with the aggressive English.

A division of Creeks more clearly developed: Upper Creeks living along the Coosa and Tallapoosa rivers of Alabama and Lower Creeks residing on the Chattahoochee and Flint rivers that in part formed the present lower Alabama-Georgia border. The divisiveness intensified under English influence. Lower Creeks' access to trade goods and to contact

The original Tullahassee Mission building, destroyed by fire on December 19, 1880

Research Division of the Oklahoma Historical Society, #7683

with Indian agent Benjamin Hawkins and his agricultural project in the 1790s, with its emphasis on spinning and weaving for women, tied them more closely to U.S. government policies. A Creek delegation under Alexander McGillivray ventured to meet with George Washington in 1790 and sign a treaty, the first that the new constitutional republic ratified. McGillivray acted as the de facto principal chief of the Muscogees, which was a radical departure from traditional leadership patterns. Before him, *micos* (chiefs) from the four major towns usually had led, with Coweta being primary. McGillivray, a mixed-blood, was of chiefly lineage, descended from Hickory (Ocipofa) in the Upper Creek country, but he was not a *mico*. His death in early 1793 plunged the confederacy into chaos. The split between Upper and Lower Creeks increased, furthered by white squatters on Indian lands, tribal punishment for Creek attacks upon whites, constant frontier expansion, and rising Indian nationalism under the pleas of Shawnee/Creek chief Tecumseh.

Opothleyahola, Creek chief (nicknamed Old Gouge)

Print of colored lithograph by McKenney and Hall. Courtesy Creek Council House Museum.

Under Chief Menawa some Creeks (called Red Sticks for their painted war clubs and bodies) rebelled. Loss in the battle at Horseshoe Bend on the Tallapoosa River in Alabama (1814) during the first Creek War broke Creek power in the Southeast. General Andrew Jackson's punitive cession treaty took from the Creeks three-fifths of present-day Alabama and one-fifth of Georgia, totaling over 23 million acres. Most of the Muscogee signers had been under his command. The war was a turning point, because it sped pressure for eventual removal. In the following decade a few tribal towns decided to remove to Indian Territory. Mixed-blood William McIntosh signed the Treaty of Indian Springs in 1825 agreeing to ultimate removal, but he failed to gain the consent of other Creeks or Cherokees. Although the treaty was nullified, 2,500 of his supporters migrated, beginning in late 1827.

In 1832 all Creeks who remained in Alabama underwent allotment of their lands. The resulting swift and fraudulent loss of those lands helped spawn the Second Creek War (1836), analyzed by John Ellisor. It led to the forcible removal of the remainder of an estimated 20,000 Creeks and their slaves along their Trail of Tears to Indian Territory (1836–37). The Lower Creeks of McIntosh had settled in the region of the Arkansas and Verdigris rivers in their new land, while Upper Creeks established their farms along the Canadian River and its tributaries. Their relative geographic positions in Indian Territory reversed their relative locations in the Southeast. The Upper and Lower Creeks formally reunited in 1840 and experienced something of a brief golden age. Survivors recovered, changed lifeways, prospered, operated under their own laws and court system, and oversaw a model educational system with notable academies like Tullahassee and Coweta. Bacone College in Muskogee and the predecessor of the University of Tulsa grew out of Creek mission educational endeavors. Through the terms of an 1856 treaty, the Muscogees ceded land to the Seminoles for a reservation.

The difficulties of the American Civil War sparked more internal strife among the Creeks. Some joined the Confederacy, while others tried to escape to safety in Kansas. Bloody attacks by Confederates and Muscogee and Cherokee allies in three battles (across the territory north of today's Tulsa) then malnutrition in wintertime Union camps in Kansas took the lives of perhaps five thousand Creeks. Among those lost was respected Upper Creek leader Opothleyahola. African Creeks were the first blacks in the United States to organize within the Union Army against the Confederacy. They were also the first to experience combat by regularly mustered black federal troops during the Civil War and saw much battlefield action. Warfare devastated the Muscogee Nation.

During the postwar Reconstruction period the Muscogee Nation lost 3.2 million acres—the western half of its lands. Although it had been divided in wartime loyalties, the entire Muscogee Nation was treated as disloyal. The postwar treaty in 1866 (the Creeks' fourteenth treaty with the United States) helped set the stage for subsequent territorial status and ultimate statehood for Oklahoma. Creeks established a new constitution with a government based on the U.S. model and set up a new capital at Okmulgee on the Deep Fork of the Canadian River in 1867. Freedmen's towns slowly developed, and the Muscogee Nation established ten schools for them. Freedmen had representation in the tribal legislature. Railroad construction brought with it non-Indian settlements, which in turn demanded territorial organization and protection of their interests. The newcomers' communities developed into American communities, not tribal towns.

Mission societies set up boarding schools within the Muscogee Nation. Pupils studied their lessons at Wetumka, Wealaka, Asbury, Nuyaka, New Tullahassee, Coweta, Muskogee, and Okmulgee (which also served as an orphanage). An example of accommodation with the larger society is the life of Pleasant Porter. He was born in a log cabin but received a boarding school education at Tullahassee school. As an adult he was active in his Eufaula Masonic lodge, the Elks, and the Odd Fellows organizations, was an elder in his Presbyterian church, and served on mission school boards. Porter was acculturated yet identifiably Muscogee. He went on to serve as a chief for the Muscogee Nation in 1899–1907, the era of maximum encroachment into Creek affairs. The Curtis Act (1898) forced allotment in severalty upon the nation after the Dawes Commission enumerated its citizens. Among the Muscogees, 12,000 Indians and 6,800 freedmen received 160-acre allotments, totaling 2,997,114 acres out of their former domain of 3,079,095 acres. The remaining land was opened to whites, who quickly acquired the bulk of Indian and freedmen landholdings. Allotment tore away the tribal land and economic base.

Federal provisions dissolved most of the tribal government in 1906 during the height of the assimilation period of Indian policy. Ongoing land frauds fed other tribal grievances and led to convulsive opposition to those policies, which took the form of the Sands Rebellion (1870s), the Green Peach War (1880s), and the so-called Snake Rebellion in 1909, named after its reputed leader, Chitto Harjo (Crazy Snake). The 1909 rebellion was the last major Indian "uprising" in the United States. There was also localized sporadic violence during World War I. Repeated oil gushers within the nation added to the confusion. In late 1905 a wildcatter struck oil on a family farm that lent its name to the oil field, Glenn Pool. Oil discovered on the allotment of Jackson Barnett in 1912 quickly set records for daily, monthly, and yearly production. The gushers made Barnett fabulously wealthy. So much wealth flowed that it created the fortunes of Thomas Gilcrease and William Skelly as well as petroleum companies. Ida and Robert Glenn and Jackson Barnett moved to California. The litigation and exploitation resulting from Barnett's estate and a few others combined with lurid tales of Osage murders to create a gradually growing desire to reform national Indian policy. From 1906 to 1936 federal paternalism, the expansion of congressional power, and officials' cynical manipulation of tribal government undermined the operation of the tribe. Federal officials appointed chiefs, who in their turn anointed council members. BIA authorities controlled the tribe like puppeteers. After statehood over 2 million acres of Creek allotted land was sold and over $50 billion in petroleum was extracted. From 1934 to 1955 elected officials presided over the tribe's affairs. From 1955 to 1970 the BIA appointed the principal chief.

The contemporary Muscogee Nation attempts to perpetuate traditions while dealing successfully with the challenges of the twenty-first century. Following federal legislation enacted in 1970, the nation in the following year duly elected Claude Cox its first principal chief since the start of the twentieth century. His base of political support within the nation came from Lower Creeks, who dominated the nation's politics. He led the drafting and adoption of a new constitution under the terms of the OIWA and modeled after the U.S. government. Cox revitalized the legislative branch as he started the process of tribal political and economic development. Representatives elected from districts serve in the National Council, the legislative branch of the nation. Muscogee Nation litigation during the 1970s and 1980s helped affirm tribal sovereignty in the areas of constitutional self-governance (the decision of *Harjo v. Kleppe*, 1976), tribal court systems (*Hodel*, 1988), tribal bingo operations exclusive of state interference (*Indian Country, USA*, 1987), and establishing that the tribal court is the proper forum for disputes involving tribal business (*Bank of Oklahoma v. Muscogee Nation*, 1992). Successive chiefs built upon their predecessor's accomplishments to continue the expansion of tribal political and economic activities, including gaming.

The Muscogees have always been a mixture of peoples. Several groups historically within the confederacy sought separate recognition and funding. During the 1930s and 1940s the Alabama-Quassarte, Kialegee, and Thlopthlocco towns obtained federal charters, technically making them federally recognized. They still receive Muscogee Nation funding and services, however, and are considered Creek (see the "Alabama-Quassarte," "Kialegee," and "Thlopthlocco" entries). Natchez refugees found safe haven among Abeka Creeks following the French destruction of the Natchez kingdom in 1730. There were Natchez refugees among the Chickasaw, Cherokee, and Catawba nations. There is an identifiable Natchez community within the Muscogee Nation today (see the "Natchez" entry). The Yuchis reside in several communities outside Tulsa. They currently are members of the Muscogee Nation but seek separate federal recognition (see the "Yuchi/Euchee" entry).

Wider American Indian traditions for the Creeks are maintained through powwows held in school gyms, in public parks, and during festivals. Hymns and Indian services at 140 Indian churches continue the Mvskoke language. In addition, Creek ceremonies are perpetuated at

Ernest Childers (Creek and
Cherokee) with his Congressional
Medal of Honor

Courtesy Elaine Childers

fourteen ceremonial towns (or stomp grounds in popular speech) throughout the Muscogee Nation in addition to three Yuchi grounds, as well as at tribal centers of other groups like the Shawnees and Quapaws. Rituals involved a sacred fire at the center of the towns or square grounds, annual ceremonies combining thanksgiving for the first fruits of the land with renewal of the earth and ritual purification, and acknowledgment of the role of women, commonly called the Ribbon Dance. The all-night dancing attracts members of other towns to lend aid as well as spectators. Those practices mirror ancient rituals focused on a sacred fire at the center of the square ground as described in Spanish chronicles from 1540.

One observer watched through the night as the southeastern Indians performed dances in which they were "violently stamping their feet" on the ground. Hence the label "stomp dance." Annual Green Corn Ceremonies in the summertime are referred to as "the busk," derived from the Mvskoke word *posketv*, "to fast," a part of the ritual. Numerous tribal and private endeavors also strive to preserve and to teach the Mvskoke language. There are about eight thousand Mvskoke-speakers today in Oklahoma. In 1996 the Muscogee Nation set up a committee to oversee revitalization of the language. The College of the Muscogee Nation, established in 2004, offers language and cultural classes along with a mainstream college curriculum. Also supporting traditions are the Redstick Warriors association and the Mvskokulke Etvlwa Etelaketv ("all the Muscogee towns sitting together") organization (established in 1984), which reflected the old tribal town structure as a political group.

Among notable Muscogees are famed leader Opothleyahola and his nemesis William McIntosh, poet and author Alexander Posey, Hollywood producer Bob Hicks, singer Jamie Coon, writers Craig Womack, Lonnie Magee, and Cynthia Smith, and storyteller/actor Will Hill. Roley Haines was a famous preacher of the gospel in Mvskoke. The late actor Will Sampson starred in the 1975 film *One Flew over the Cuckoo's Nest*. Poet and musician Joy Harjo received the Lifetime Achievement Award from the Native Writers Circle of the Americas in 2003 for her contributions to literature.

Creek painters include Solomon McCombs, Fred Beaver, Bobby Martin, Johnny Diacon, and Jackson Narcomey. Painter Acee Blue Eagle (Alexander C. McIntosh, also Pawnee) was a student of Oscar Jacobson at the University of Oklahoma. Kenneth Johnson is an award-winning jeweler. Paul Moore created the massive sculpture of forty-six people, wagons, and horses as a monument to the Land Run in Oklahoma City's Bricktown. Singers include dance club singer Linda Imperial and fourth-season *American Idol* winner Carrie Underwood.

Ernest Childers (also Cherokee) received the Congressional Medal of Honor for action in the European theater in World War II. Allie Reynolds, pitcher for the 1947–53 Yankees when they won six world championships in seven years, was active in Muscogee politics. His total of seven World Series wins is second only to the achievement of Whitey Ford. Outfielder Adair "Paddy" Mayes played with the Philadelphia Phillies. Jack Jacobs quarterbacked the University of Oklahoma team (1939–41) before turning professional. Law professor Anita Hill, who testified against Supreme Court nominee Clarence Thomas during his confirmation hearing, is of Creek freedman heritage. Timothy S. Posey is a leading lawyer. Susanne Barnett Strouvelle was the adopted Indian daughter of Alice M. Robertson, the missionary and congresswoman from Oklahoma (1921–23). Strouvelle was the first Creek citizen to receive an allotment. Alice Robertson's mother, A. E. W. Robertson, supplied the Mvskoke name *hyechka*, "music," for the civic music club in Tulsa, which still sponsors concerts. It is the oldest music organization in the state.

SUGGESTED READING

Chaudhuri, Jean, and Joyotpaul Chaudhuri. *A Sacred Path: The Way of the Muscogee Creeks.* Los Angeles: American Indian Studies Center, University of California, 2001.

Debo, Angie. *The Road to Disappearance: A History of the Creek Indians.* Norman: University of Oklahoma Press, 1941; repr. 1967.

Ellisor, John. "The Second Seminole War: The Unexplored Conflict." Ph.D. dissertation, University of Tennessee, Knoxville, 1996.

Gatschet, Albert. *A Migration Legend of the Creek Indians.* 2 vols. Philadelphia: D. G. Brinton, 1884–88; repr. New York: Kraus, 1969.

Green, Michael D. *The Creeks*. New York: Chelsea House, 1990 (for young readers).

———. *The Politics of Indian Removal: Creek Government and Society in Crisis*. Lincoln: University of Nebraska Press, 1982; paperback 1985.

Hahn, Steven C. *The Invention of the Creek Nation, 1670–1763*. Lincoln: University of Nebraska Press, 2004.

Jenkins, Ned. "Early Creek Origins: Moundville Connection." Paper presented at the Southeastern Archaeological Conference, St. Louis, Missouri, October 2004.

Lawson, John. *A New Voyage to Carolina*. Edited by Hugh Talmage Lefler. Chapel Hill: University of North Carolina Press, 1967; repr. 1984 ("violently stamping their feet" on 45).

Martin, Jack. "Language." In vol. 14, Southeast, of the *Handbook of North American Indians*, 68–86. Washington, D.C.: Smithsonian Institution, 2004.

Piker, Joshua. *Okfuskee: A Creek Town in Colonial America*. Cambridge, Mass.: Harvard University Press, 2004.

Scordato, Ellen. *The Creek Indians*. New York: Chelsea House, 1993 (for young readers).

Smith, Marvin. *Coosa: The Rise and Fall of a Southeastern Mississippian Chiefdom*. Gainesville: University Press of Florida, 2000.

Swanton, John R. *Creek Religion and Medicine* (first published 1928). Lincoln: University of Nebraska Press, 2000.

———. *Early History of the Creek Indians and Their Neighbors*. Bureau of American Ethnology Bulletin 73. Washington, D.C.: Government Printing Office, 1922; repr. New York: Johnson Reprint, 1970; Gainesville: University Press of Florida, 1998.

Zellar, Gary. *African Creeks: Estelvste and the Creek Nation*. Norman: University of Oklahoma Press, 2007.

Natchez

NAME

The origin of "Natchez" is unknown. In the Mvskoke language in Oklahoma it is often rendered "Notchee." The early French pronounced the name "Nahchee."

LOCATION AND GOVERNMENT

The Natchez office is located in Weleetka in southern Creek County, southwest of Henryetta. The Natchez are members of the Muscogee (Creek) Nation. They are not a federally chartered tribal town or a separately recognized tribe but desire to be recognized as such.

NUMBER

In 2002 the Oklahoma Natchez launched a concerted effort to enroll the estimated 7,000 Natchez who are believed to be widely scattered in other tribal groups.

According to linguists, the Natchez language belongs to the Gulf family of languages and is distantly and tangentially related to the main Muskoghean language stock. It is also remotely related to the nearby Tunica language and the Taensa and Avoyel languages in the same area on both sides of the Mississippi River.

The Natchez achieved legendary status because they practiced a full Mississippian lifeway with platform temple mounds, perpetual sacred fires, and a true southeastern chiefdom before the eyes of astounded French chroniclers, who left vivid accounts. The Natchez also loomed large on the historical stage because they commanded the Lower Mississippi River Valley, in the vicinity of the present city of Natchez, a region deemed strategic by a series of European imperial powers. French enmity in concert with Indian allies ended Natchez hegemony in 1730.

It is purely speculative, but the Tunicas and Natchez may have been descendants of the large Archaic-period mound center at Poverty Point that flourished in northeastern Louisiana around 1500 B.C. It was located on a watercourse that connected to the Mississippi River. Archeologists perceive the Natchez Indians as direct descendants of the Natchez Bluffs culture of the Lower Mississippi Valley region. Pottery marking the Bluffs era developed late in the prehistoric period. Archeologists note that the local population drastically declined after the departure of the Spanish under Hernando de Soto. Survivors are believed to have migrated toward the northeast. Ceramics revealed a direct line from the Coles Creek culture to the Plaquemine culture and flowering in the Natchez during the historic period. The pottery design style for the Natchez is called Fatherland Incised, named for their major ceremonial site. Archeologist Kenneth Carleton studied eighteenth-century Choctaw ceramics and found that Addis-like paste for pottery had borrowed elements from Pearl River mound peoples after A.D. 1200, from Plaquemine cultures along the Lower Mississippi Valley, and from Natchez culture of the same region. He determined that motifs on Choctaw pottery were similar to Natchez designs and saw shared imagery as well as shared beliefs and identity.

In the French descriptions, the Natchez lived in ten towns along tributaries of the Mississippi River. The Great Sun was the name of their ruler, and his kinfolk ruled each of the towns in his domain. The Great Sun resided across St. Catherine Creek from the main town, which was termed the Grand Village. The Natchez population shifted residence from nearby Emerald Mound to the Grand Village after European arrival. Although under kin rule, the villages were different matrilineages and ethnicities, especially after Taensas and other refugees swelled their populations. The Great Sun claimed direct descent from the controlling orb in the sky. His ceremonial center is called the Fatherland site, which had three mounds roughly aligned with the winter sunrise and summer sunset at solstices. The hereditary ruler presided over two major annual ceremonies that marked the equinoxes, atop pyramid mounds aligned to the solstices, signaling the yearly shift from the summer farming to the winter hunting season. Archeologists believe that the mounds were built after A.D. 1200 in four successive stages. One of the most impressive of the other mound centers is Emerald Mound (used A.D. 1300–1600), second in size in North America only to Monks Mound at Cahokia.

In the early 1700s the Natchez population numbered only about 3,500. At the top of their main mound sat a temple some thirty feet long, with high mud-plastered walls and a pitched roof. The interior had two rooms, according to the French eyewitnesses. Pierre Le Moyne d'Iberville visited the Natchez in 1700 and described the perpetual fire in their temple. The first room held the sacred fire and a cane basket that contained the bones of the last ruling Great Sun. Sacred relics lined the walls, with images of supernatural beings adorning the roof of the temple. The second room held other ritual objects and coffins containing the remains of earlier rulers. The remains of other leaders' and kin were interred in the floor. Atop the other mound was a house (twenty-five by forty-five feet), the home of the reigning Great Sun. Members of the ruling family resided in eight large houses at the plaza level. Behind them were quarters for others in the village. Scholars once viewed the Natchez as a rigid hierarchical chiefdom along the lines of classic Mississippian era cultures. Ethnologist Karl Lorenz more recently found the Natchez of the early eighteenth century to be a loose confederacy of autonomous villages, albeit under the same leader. Frenchmen attended the impressive burial rites in the south plaza honoring the passing of the Tattooed Serpent, the war leader and brother of the Great Sun. The funeral took place on June 1, 1725. The awed Europeans watched the solemn procession, retainer sacrifices, and elaborate rituals that accompanied the ceremony.

The Natchez origin story mirrors those of other southeastern Indians in its outline. For the Natchez, Coyocopchill, the Infinite Spirit, created a man and woman who descended from the Upper World to earth. He was the younger brother of the sun. He directed the people to build a temple in which he placed a sacred perpetual fire as a piece of the sun brought to earth. The sacred fire became a symbol of the Natchez religion. The keeper of the fire told Antoine Simon Le Page du Pratz, a Dutch member of Jean Baptiste Le Moyne de Bienville's party that established French New Orleans, a different story. He maintained that the Natchez migrated from Mexico along the Gulf to their location on the lower Mississippi River.

In 1542 members of the Soto expedition entered the Indian town of Quigaltam in 1542, located on the east bank of the Mississippi River in the northern portion of what would become Mississippi. Historians and ethnologists differ over whether the town and its province were Natchez. The main town, the Spaniards reported, had five hundred houses. Leaders of the province dispatched a hundred canoes with seventy men in them to attack captain of foot Juan de Guzmán and his small force of twenty-five men from the Spanish expedition, which had been sent out to disperse the canoes. The chronicler described the principal men aboard canoes and underneath awnings. The leaders wore colorful feathered plumes and mantles.

The major presence, however, proved to be the French, who kept traversing the region. French explorers Louis Joliet and Jacques Marquette and later La Salle in their turn came down the mighty river. Sieur d'Iberville established the French settlement at Fort Maurepas on the coast near old Biloxi (now Ocean Springs) in 1699. Still more French outposts followed at Mobile on the coast (1702), Fort Rosalie at Natchez (1716), New Orleans at the mouth of the river (1718), and Fort St. Pierre at Yazoo River north of Natchez (1719). By the end of the 1720s the French were in conflict with the Natchez, who began a series of attacks, the most notable being the 1729 assault on Fort Rosalie, probably with the encouragement of the English-allied Chickasaws. An inept French commander mishandled a plot within the Natchez polity and was too aggressive in response and turned it into a full-blown rebellion. Of course, the French struck back, with a 1730 all-out retaliatory attack that nearly annihilated the Natchez by the following year and forced remnants of the group to flee. The French executed many of the Natchez and sold survivors into slavery in the West Indies, especially on the island of Santo Domingo. Refugees fled to sanctuary among the Chickasaws, Choctaws, Cherokees, Catawbas, and Abeka Creeks. Other enclaves are the Eastern Band of Natchez of the PeeDee River and the Edisto-Kusso Natchez of Charleston, South Carolina. The Natchez among the Abekas represented the royal family. They settled in the Taladega Valley then a generation later among the Ispogoga Creeks. Non-Indian residents entered into the Natchez homeland, which served as the southern terminus of a road (using the Natchez Trace) connected to central Tennessee.

Among the Muscogees, the Natchez sided with the Red Sticks among the Upper Creeks. Under removal in the 1830s, the Natchez trekked to Indian Territory with the Creeks, settling near what is now Eufaula, and with the Cherokees, settling near what is now Braggs. Natchez identified with Abeka and Little Abeka Creeks.

Natchez descendants among the Cherokees in the 1960s established the Medicine Springs ceremonial ground near Gore under the guidance of Archie Sam. They innovated the "milk can" leg shellshakers for nighttime dancing. Natchez-Creek-Cherokee Baptist churches in the southwestern portion of the Cherokee Nation carry on languages, social links, and other conservative cultural patterns. The Natchez continue to participate in ceremonial ground and church activities. Natchez descendants from Oklahoma and the Eastern Band of Natchez from South Carolina came together for the first time in March 2007 at the Grand Village of the Natchez. They participated in a joint powwow, recalling their heritage.

Notable Natchez include George Stiggins, mixed-blood author of a Creek Indian history in the nineteenth century. Cherokee ceremonial leader Redbird Smith was trained by Natchez spiritual leader Creek Sam.

Smith lived in Notchee town in the Illinois District of the Cherokee Nation amid religious conservatives. Archie Sam, *mico* of Medicine Springs Ceremonial Town among the Cherokees, was of Natchez descent and was a source of much ethnographic information, as his uncle Watt Sam had been before him. Archie Sam befriended me.

SUGGESTED READING

Barnett, Jim. *The Natchez: A History to 1735.* Jackson: University Press of Mississippi, 2007.

Brown, Ian W. *Natchez Indian Archaeology: Culture Change and Stability in the Lower Mississippi Valley.* Archaeological Report No. 15. Jackson: Mississippi Department of Archives and History, 1985.

Carleton, Kenneth. "Where Did the Choctaw Come From? An Examination of Pottery in the Areas Adjacent to the Choctaw Homeland." In Patricia Kwachka, ed., *Perspectives on the Southeast,* 80–93. Athens: University of Georgia Press, 1994.

Cushman, Horatio B. *History of the Choctaw, Chickasaw, and Natchez Indians.* Greenville, Tex.: Headlight Printers, 1899; repr. Stillwater: Redlands, 1962, in an abridged edition; repr. Norman: University of Oklahoma Press, 2001.

Lorenz, Karl. "A Re-examination of Natchez Sociopolitical Complexity: A View from the Grand Village and Beyond." *Southeastern Archaeology* 16, no. 2 (1997): 97–112.

Sam, Archie, and Janet Campbell. "The Primal Fire Lingers." *Chronicles of Oklahoma* 53 (Winter 1975–76): 463–75.

Van Tuyl, Charles, with William Walker. *The Natchez: Annotated Translations from "Histoire de la Louisiane," a Short English-Natchez Dictionary.* Oklahoma City: Oklahoma Historical Society, 1979.

Nez Perce

NAME

The tribe's name came from the French *nez percé*, "pierced nose," and was also used by the Lewis and Clark expedition members in 1805. Why the French and the Americans used the term remains a mystery, because the Nez Perces did not practice nose piercing. Perhaps one of them wore a nose pendant. The Nez Perces refer to themselves as Ni Mii Pu (also Numipu or Nimipu), "the People."

LOCATION AND GOVERNMENT

None in Oklahoma. The Nez Perces briefly occupied land in north-central Oklahoma.

BUSINESSES

None in Oklahoma.

NUMBER

The tribe has about 8,500 members, but few in Oklahoma, since the headquarters is in Idaho, east of Lewiston.

The Nez Perces are Sahaptian-speakers linked to the Yakamas, Umatillas, Klickitats, and Wallawallas of the Pacific Northwest. The Nez Perces saved and fed members of the starving Lewis and Clark expedition after they emerged from crossing the Rocky Mountains in 1805. The explorers restored their health and lived among the Nez Perces for months. The Nez Perces played games with the members of the Corps of Discovery, who introduced them to a new game called baseball. The Nez Perces had a long history of never killing white people. They strove to reside at peace with the newcomers. The United States acknowledged the good relations in 1855 with recognition of the land that the Nez Perces lived on. Included was the Wallowa Valley, where the band of old and young Chief Joseph lived for centuries.

The United States pressured the Nez Perces to sign a new treaty in 1863 that reduced their rights to the Wallowa-Imnaha country in southern

Oregon. Their reservation was 7.5 million acres. The agreement breached the treaty of 1855 pledging a large Nez Perce reserve. The 1863 document shrank the reservation to 750,000 acres. The United States wanted that portion ceded because gold had been discovered. Indian religious and cultural differences played a key role in the cession too. The United States favored The Lawyer, a Christian Nez Perce leader, as overall chief. He led the Kamiah group of Nez Perces. In the 1863 treaty he ceded 95 percent of the reservation, almost all of which was occupied by non-Christian Nez Perces. His land base was untouched. The United States set up a reservation under executive order in the Wallowa Valley in 1873, only to revoke it two years later. U.S. officials tried to force the Nez Perces to the Lapwai Reservation.

Steadily crowded by encroaching white settlers and faced with growing violence, Chief Joseph and other leaders for three months led followers toward Canada. They refused to be herded to a smaller reservation in Idaho. The U.S. Army pursuit across 1,600 miles of the Northwest remains one of the epic journeys, filled with human drama. The Indians skillfully engaged and outfoxed army forces chasing them. Nearly at his goal, a trapped Chief Joseph surrendered to Brigadier General Nelson A. Miles, making his famous remark that he would "fight no more forever." There were about 1,500 Nez Perces in 1877.

The following year the United States exiled the destitute band, which included both Nez Perces and neighboring Palouses. In 1878 they resided at the Quapaw Agency in northeastern Indian Territory at what was known as Modoc Spring. When the Nez Perces first arrived at Baxter Springs, Kansas, for their journey to Indian Territory, the sweltering heat prevented the Indians from walking to their destination as planned. The U.S. government hired Modoc Indians, who themselves had been exiled, to haul wagonloads of Nez Perces to Modoc Spring. After a year the government moved the Nez Perces to lands assigned to them just west of the present town of Peoria. Joseph was adamant in his insistence that the federal government uphold Miles's pledge that the Nez Perces could return home if they would only surrender. The commissioner of Indian affairs, E. A. Hayt, visited the Nez Perces in October 1878, heard their complaints about where they resided, and took the Indian leader on a tour of the region to select a new home. The Indian Office purchased land in the Cherokee Outlet for the Nez Perces, just west of the Ponca Reservation where the Chikaskia River met the Salt Fort Creek of the Arkansas River. The reserve had 90,700 acres. The remaining 322 Nez Perces of the 430 who had originally been exiled made the eight-day trek to their new home, called the Oakland Reserve. Pioneer reminiscences credited thick oak trees as the origin of the name. The new agent was not informed about his new charges, so he was ill-equipped to feed and house them. The first winter the Nez Perces suffered terribly from exposure, malnutrition, and illness.

After several months about one-third of the band under Yellow Bull moved up the Salt Fork and began to farm. For a time three youthful educated Nez Perces came from Idaho to serve their kinfolk as missionary teachers. One of them opened a school in 1879. Very gradually the Nez Perces seemed to adjust to their new life and to make some progress. In spite of this limited adjustment, the number of Nez Perces declined to 287 by 1884. Eyewitness cattleman J. C. Henderson described the Nez Perces as "the most dissatisfied people that I had ever seen" because of displacement, chronic homesickness, and illness.

The Indian residents were increasingly plagued by trespassers, both humans and livestock. Tribespeople agreed to cattle leasing in early 1884, which brought some income. Congress in 1880 had purchased the Nez Perce reservation from the Cherokees for $300,000, and the Nez Perces received title to their reservation in June 1883.

Just over thirty Nez Perce widows and orphans were permitted to return to Idaho in the Pacific Northwest in May 1883. A national public outcry arose to allow the remainder to go home, although white settlers in the Wallowa Valley raised strenuous objections. Reform groups advocated for the Indians' return. Among supporters were Presbyterians who operated a small school for the Nez Perces. Congress enacted a measure, which senator Henry L. Dawes secured on July 4, 1884, that left any decision to the interior secretary. The federal government divided the Nez Perces into two groups: 118 who were deemed not under Idaho indictment for conflict and considered progressive could journey to Lapwai under Huses Kutte; the other 110 would be sent with Joseph to the Colville Reservation. None were permitted to return to their beloved Wallowa Valley, because of the animosity of the white settlers who occupied it. Congress in early 1885 appropriated $18,000 to pay for the Indians' moving expenses. In exchange for the federal government paying their expenses to go home, the Nez Perce leaders deeded their Indian Territory reserve to the United States. All of the Indians were eager to return to the cool of the Pacific Northwest and leave behind the "hot place." Finally, in 1884, the Indian agent permitted all Nez Perces except a few with Joseph to travel to the Lapwai Reservation. He died still exiled on the Colville Reserve, in 1905. The former Nez Perce lands in Indian Territory went in 1885 to the

Tonkawas, now near the town of the same name in Kay County.

Nez Perce descendants have held a variety of powwow, rodeo, and horseback rides to commemorate their mistreatment at the hands of the United States and to recall their exile as well as their heritage.

After a six-year diaspora, the Nez Perces left Indian Territory. Little remains of their sojourn. North of the Tonkawa tribal headquarters is a small cemetery with a U.S. military–issued gravestone for a daughter of Chief Joseph: a silent memorial to a great injustice toward her people.

SUGGESTED READING

Blevins, Richard Lowell. "Henry Allen's Use of Historical Sources in 'From Where the Sun Now Stands,' a Novel of the American West (Chief Joseph, Clay Fisher)." Ph.D. dissertation, University of Pittsburgh, 1985 (Chief Joseph quotation).

Chapman, Berlin B. "The Nez Perces in Indian Territory." *Oregon Historical Quarterly* 50 (June 1949): 98–121.

Greenwald, Emily. *Reconfiguring the Reservation: The Nez Perces, Jicarilla Apaches, and the Dawes Act.* Albuquerque: University of New Mexico Press, 2002.

Henderson, James C. "Reminiscences of a Range Rider." *Chronicles of Oklahoma* 3 (December 1925): 253–88 (quotation on 278).

Lavender, David. *Let Me Be Free: The Nez Perce Tragedy.* Norman: University of Oklahoma Press, 2001.

Nieberding, Velma. "The Nez Perce in the Quapaw Agency." *Chronicles of Oklahoma* 44 (Spring 1966): 22–30.

Osborne, Alan. "The Exile of the Nez Perce in Indian Territory, 1878–1885." *Chronicles of Oklahoma* 56 (Winter 1978–79): 450–71.

Pearson, J. Diane. *The Nez Perces in the Indian Territory: Nimiipuu Survival.* Norman: University of Oklahoma Press, 2008.

Osage

The name "Osage" came from *wazaze,* which was anglicized to Wazhazhe, their name for themselves. It is also close to the name for a clan and a personal name in that clan (Wazaze Ska, White Osage). Linguistically related Dhegiha Siouan–speakers like the Omahas, Poncas, Kansas, and Quapaws also used that name for the Osages.

LOCATION AND GOVERNMENT

The headquarters for the "Osage Nation of Oklahoma" is in Pawhuska in Osage County, in north-central Oklahoma. The tribe operates under a constitutional government approved in 1994 and not under the OIWA, with a ten-member National Council. A president heads the government, which has three branches. Elections staggered every four years select membership on the council and a chief officer. The United States Congress in late 2004 enacted a measure (Public Law 108-431) reaffirming the Osages' right to set their own membership criteria. They call the measure their "liberty bill." The tribal website is www.osagetribe.com.

BUSINESSES

The tribe has been known for its fabulous mineral (oil and gas) wealth, which peaked in the 1920s. A principal chief, a vice chief, and eight other members of an elected Osage Mineral Council administer the mineral estate, called the Osage Mineral Trust. Only those who have a direct ownership interest in shares in the oil and gas estate (called a "headright") can vote for council members for at-large four-year terms. Because of the alarming history of exploitation involving the Osage mineral wealth, the tribal government is separate from the oversight of the oil and gas interests. Legislation on tribal governance in 2004 left the mineral estate structure untouched. The Osage Tribe also receives income from ranching, farming, and leasing of pasturage. The tribe leases an industrial park building in Hominy to Southwest Corset Company.

In August 2004 the tribe opened the Million Dollar Elm Casino (with 100,000 square feet) in Tulsa at the junction of the L. L. Tisdale Freeway and 36th Street. Another casino of the same name is located high on a hill overlooking Sand Springs and the Arkansas River Valley below, on Highway 97 (which is called 129th West Avenue). A third casino with the same name is in Bartlesville, with 42,000 square feet of entertainment space on a 132-acre parcel (at www.osagecasino.com and www.milliondollarelm.com). The tribe also operates Oklahoma Bingo in Pawhuska and the Native Frontier in Hominy. Another casino opened in 2008 near Ponca City, with a hotel planned. The Palace of the Osage Grocery store is in Fairfax. In 2005 the tribe founded Osage Data for electronic information systems. Additionally, the tribe owns 100 acres located about twenty-five miles north of Bartlesville in southern Kansas. Osage County constitutes their 1.469-million-acre reservation (2,296 square miles), which the tribe purchased in 1870 from the Cherokees. There are two tribal museums in Pawhuska.

An economic impact study released in 2008 showed that the tribe had grossed $222 million the year before. Tribal commercial ventures, including gaming, generated nearly $140 million, while its mineral interests took in $56 million. Tribal employment of about 1,400 made the Osages among the largest employers in the state, and the Osage Nation purchased $79 million in services and supplies.

NUMBERS

The tribe has just over 18,000 members. About 4,000 reside on the federal reservation in Osage County in the main Osage communities of Hominy, Fairfax, Pawhuska, and Skiatook. About 4,000 of the total membership hold a full or partial headright to mineral wealth. About 6,500 other American Indians also live on the reserve. Under the terms of the more inclusive late 2004 legislation, tribal membership jumped from 4,000 to 18,000.

The Osages speak a Dhegiha Siouan language and are linguistically related to the Quapaws, Kansas, and Omaha-Poncas. They represented one group in prehistory. Linguists believe that Quapaw separated first from the main body, followed by Osage and Kansa. They not only have a common speech but also share cultural traits. Anthropologist Garrick Bailey pointed to an Upper Mississippian origin for those traits. The preservation Osages represented a Mississippian priesthood based on clans, Pipes, bundles, and elaborate rituals. Their great bundle priests' Pipes had shell and copper bead decorations (notable Mississippian traits).

Ethnologist J. Owen Dorsey left a full account of the Dhegiha Siouan migration story, briefly summarized here. A large single group began migrating from the southern Great Lakes region. It may have been Oneota, an Upper Mississippian–era culture. It traveled down the Ohio River Valley to the Mississippi River. At the mouth of the Ohio the Quapaws split off and traveled downstream. The main body went up the Mississippi to the mouth of the Missouri River. The Osages and Kansas were one people who lived for a time on a peninsula on the Missouri River. They continued their journey until the Osages settled at the mouth of the Osage River. After an argument over division of buffalo parts following a hunt, the Kansas separated and left the Osages. Each of the Dhegiha groups adopted customs of the local residents they encountered.

Linguists have provided additional insight into the movement of the Dhegiha-speakers. Central Siouan began splintering about A.D. 700 when the predecessor of Dakota separated. Sometime around 1300 the Dhegiha Siouan language groups separated from each other, according to James Springer and Stanley Witkowski. That is approximately the same time when Upper Mississippian Oneota peoples began to enter the northeastern Plains region in pursuit of increasing bison herds. Other scientists have argued for a later emergence of separate Dhegiha Siouan–speakers. Because cultural practices among Oneota-speakers varied greatly, there continues to be much scholarly discussion about an Osage connection to Oneota.

The major known Osage archeological sites have Euro-American trade items in them. Euro-American metal kettles quickly replaced pottery vessels. Few sites yielded prehistoric remains of an ancient culture. Grand Osage sites in Missouri are Brown, Hayes, and Carrington along the Osage River. Plattner village near Malta Bend on the Missouri River is a Little Osage location. Carl Chapman, who examined Osage archeological remains, believed that they grew out of regional Neosho focus culture and concluded that the Dhegihas developed locally in the region. Many of those who studied the Dhegihan past believed that they arrived late in the area west of the Mississippi River, probably just before their initial contact with Europeans.

According to the Osage origin story, Wakanda (or Wah'kon-Tah), the creative power in the universe, made all bodily forms on earth. The four symbols of Wakanda were earth and sky and night and day. The female power of the moon and stars ruled the night. The male power of the sun dominated the day. The Osages claimed to be the children of the middle waters, which symbolized the universe we know of sky, earth, and water. Wakanda ended chaos (*ga-ni-tha*) by separating the middle waters into the natural elements of air, earth, and water. The Osages of their creation story divided into Sky People and Earth People. Sky People (Tzi-sho) descended from among the stars to the new land. After much wandering, they found the Hun-kah, Earth People, and joined them to form the Osages, the Children of the Middle Waters, Ni-u-ko'n-ska. They represented the unity of sky, earth, land, and water.

Like other Dhegiha Siouans, the Osages shared their dual division of the tribal circle and their functions, rituals conferring war honors, and major religious ceremonies as well as rites for child naming and death customs. The Osages were patrilineal, with each member belonging to one of twenty-four clans. The nine Sky People's clans represented the sky and peace division (also called a moiety). The fifteen Earth People's clans symbolized earth and war. Each division had a hereditary chief. The Osage clan system resembled that of other Central Algonquians. In addition, the clans were further divided into subclans, identified with a specific animal as a totem. The Osages possessed sacred medicine bundles and used them as the Kansas did. Osage villages were similarly divided between Sky and Earth sides. The Osage village was a model of their universe, along an east-west axis that was the main avenue. The path replicated the daily track of the sun. A trend developed in the early nineteenth century as a response to external threats in which separate villages formed around able war leaders even though they were not hereditary chiefs.

In the Osage village men hunted and engaged in raiding. Women raised corn, beans, squash, and melons. They also gathered wild potatoes, berries, and nuts. The Osages had five bands: Little Osage, Big Hill, Hearts Stay, Thorny Thicket, and Upland Forest. Each band at one time probably had its own independent hunting territory and carried out its own ceremonies, separate from the other bands. At their height, the Osages may have numbered 18,000. The Frenchman who authored *Tixier's Travels* described life in a Great Osage village on the Neosho River in Kansas during 1840 as well as delighting in all of the hectic activity of a summer buffalo hunt. Members of the earlier Stephen H. Long expedition in 1820 remarked admiringly on the Osages' "beautiful symmetry."

French traders ventured into the Osage River region from the Missouri River. Gradually the Osages became more deeply tied to French trade goods and became fur trade partners with the French. The French viewed their location as a strategic one dominating the lower Missouri River system. The Osages were placed between the Spanish in the Southwest and the English in the Northeast. French-supplied firearms and horses helped the Osages to dominate neighboring tribes. Osage forays against the Caddos and the Wichitas intensified. Osage pressure helped push Caddoan peoples south of the Red River. In 1712 Osage warriors went to the aid of the besieged French who defended Fort Detroit. There they met its commander, Etienne Venyard, Sieur de Bourgmont, who was impressed by Osage abilities. Eleven years later he was sent to cement alliances with western tribes, which he did. He brought many to New Orleans and selected one member from each of the tribes to accompany him to visit the France of King Louis XV.

French presence and power declined along the Missouri after 1724, because their attention shifted eastward. Trade with Indians continued, and so did an occasional attack on French *coureurs de bois* passing through Osage country. Osage warriors participated in the stunning French defeat of British major general Edward Braddock's force as it approached Fort Duquesne in 1755. Located at the forks of the Ohio River at what is now Pittsburgh, Pennsylvania, the fort commanded the entrance to the Ohio Valley. The war's end, however, brought a treaty in 1763 that transferred control over the area west of the Mississippi River from France to Spain. The Osages largely ignored Spanish regulations on their raiding and were not cowed by Spanish warfare against them. Itinerant merchant Auguste Chouteau obtained a monopoly on Osage trade from the Spanish, built Fort Carondelet (1795), and carried on a profitable trade with the Osages. Pierre Laclède founded St. Louis in April 1764. The Osages referred to St. Louis as Sho'to-To-wo'n, Chouteau's Town. Archeological investigation shows that the Little Osages dominated the fur trade of the lower Mississippi Valley from their settlement at the Plattner site on the Missouri River after 1723; but then their influence diminished, and they moved to the Hayes site at the headwaters of the Osage River after 1790.

Osages were among the first Indians who met Lewis and Clark expedition members soon after the corps departed upstream from St. Louis in 1803. When competition threatened trade profits under Manuel Lisa around 1800, the Chouteau brothers persuaded some Osages to move their village out of Lisa's territory. Auguste's brother Pierre in 1802 persuaded Cashesegra (Big Foot) and deposed chief Claremore (Clermont to the French and Spanish) to lead about half the Great Osages to the region of the Three Forks, where the Verdigris, Neosho, and Arkansas rivers met. The new village (at the site of present Claremore, Oklahoma) was then called Claremore's (Clermont) Town. The Chouteaus began a new trading post there, looking to the river link to New Orleans to improve their profits. They successfully manipulated Osage society and ended Osage unity. After about 1770 the Osages evolved a new seasonal economic cycle that included twice-yearly Plains bison hunts and Arkansas Valley winter peltry trapping to replenish their trade goods.

After the 1803 Louisiana Purchase, the U.S. government used that territory as a new home for eastern emigrant tribes. When the Cherokees, Choctaws, Chickasaws, and Creeks arrived, they joined traditional enemies of the Osages like the Sacs and Foxes in encroaching on Osage hunting territory. Pierre Chouteau, Indian agent for what was termed Upper Louisiana, engineered an 1808 treaty in which the Osages ceded most of what is now Missouri and a portion of Arkansas to the United States. Treaties in 1818 and 1825 obtained more Osage lands. In 1822 the Chouteaus persuaded some Missouri bands of the Osages to move to the large trading post at what is now Salina on the Neosho River in Oklahoma. Followers of Pawhuska flatly refused to relocate.

In 1825 an Osage Reservation was established in extreme southern Kansas. It was 125 miles long and 50 miles wide. The Osages built towns in the eastern portion and welcomed missions in the St. Paul, Kansas, area. To quell Osage warfare with emigrant eastern tribes like the Cherokees and to control the frontier, the United States established Fort Gibson in 1824 on the Neosho River. Several years afterward author Washington Irving, while on a tour of the prairie, met some Osages and described them as "the finest looking Indians I have seen in the West." Epaphras Chapman and Job Vinal in 1821 opened the first missionary outpost in Indian Territory at Union Mission next to Claremore's band.

French influence ran deep among Osage mixed-bloods. In 1847 Jesuit Father John Shoenmakers came and set up a mission near St. Paul on the Neosho River. He established a boys' school. That same year the Sisters of Loreto began a Roman Catholic girls' convent school. Most Osage mixed-bloods attended and were Roman Catholics. They also farmed. The U.S. government sponsored these "civilizing" endeavors.

The American Civil War divided the Osages as it split the United States. All of the Osage leaders except the Little Osages signed the October 1861 treaty with Confederate delegate Albert Pike. Later, during fighting, some Osage bands fled to Confederate sanctuary to the south.

Little Osages enlisted with Union forces. Non-Indian encroachment, squatters, and outright theft of their lands pressured the Osages in Kansas to move to Indian Territory. Treaties in 1865–68 nibbled away at their Kansas reserve, and they finally agreed to remove in an 1870 congressional measure (16 Stat. 362). In the 1870s the Osages bought 1.475 million acres in the Cherokee Outlet (see the act of June 5, 1872, 17 Stat. 228) then gave their kinfolk the Kansas about 102,400 acres in the northwest corner of the Osage reserve. (In the sixty years after 1808 the Osages ceded 88 million acres to the United States.) Mixed-blood Osages settled on bottomland farms along Caney Creek on their Indian Territory reserve. The Big Hill band occupied Salt Creek; the Upland Forest people went to Hominy Creek; the Thorny Thicket and Hearts Stay bands settled on Bird Creek near the Pawhuska Agency; the Little Osages established their camps along Caney Creek. Some Osage mixed-bloods, called Half-Breeds, remained in Kansas. They took allotments in Kansas in June 1870 but were brutalized, burned out, and forced into Indian Territory in 1872–74. In addition, perhaps two-thirds of their linguistic kin the Quapaws resided in the southeastern segment of the Osage Reservation from 1874 to 1889.

On their new reserve the Osages had a difficult time feeding themselves, because the buffalo herds were gone, drought destroyed what crops they planted, and the ration system frustrated them. Agent Cyrus Beede encouraged the formation of an Osage council with a governor, Joseph Paw-ne-no-pashe, in 1878 to handle problems. The tribe created a constitutional government in 1881 under the impetus of James Bigheart. Voters elected Paw-ne-no-pashe their first principal chief in 1882. The Osages were reasonably well off through that decade from annuities paid in cash and money from leasing over 350,000 acres to Texas cattle ranchers. Non-Indians kept moving into the region to carry on commerce, to work, and to intermarry. By the start of the twentieth century the non-Indians numbered just under 15,000, which was far more than the 2,200 Osages.

The BIA chafed at the separate Osage constitutional government and its bitter opposition to allotment. The United States abolished the Osage government in 1900 and in its place set up a fifteen-member council subject to the agent. The Osages were the last tribe in the future state of Oklahoma to relinquish their communal reservation lands. In 1906 they gave up their reserve. The territories of Oklahoma and Indian Territory became the state of Oklahoma the following year. Because the Osage Indians held out against allotment and were the last to accept it, officials of the new state uniquely created the new county entirely out of the reservation. It is larger than the state of Delaware. Under allotment, the surface land was ultimately divided among 2,229 enrolled Osages, each receiving about 660 acres. The 1906 legislation dictated the form of the tribal government and froze the membership of the Osage Tribe as it was for that year. Descendants of those original members were not eligible to be recognized as members of the tribe until the U.S. Congress passed new legislation in late 2004. There was no "surplus" land to be opened to settlement. Osage author John Joseph Mathews recalled that instead of a land run on the reserve there was an "oil run." The profligacy and death of the era was a topic in Edna Ferber's novel *Cimarron* (1930) and in Linda Hogan's *Mean Spirit* (1990).

About a decade prior to their allotment agreement, Henry Foster found oil on the Osage reservation. Derricks spread from east to west across the reservation, replicating the much earlier spread of pioneer settlement across the continent. Mathews termed it "the great frenzy." Twenty-eight boomtowns suddenly sprang into existence. The June 1906 Osage Allotment Act provided for allotment in severalty but also mandated that subsurface mineral wealth would be shared communally among the Osage tribe. Those 2,220 Osages listed on the tribal roll as of 1907 shared in the petroleum bonanza. Royalties peaked in 1925 at $13,200 per headright. Eighteen oil leases on November 11, 1924, auctioned under an elm tree near the Osage tribal building in Pawhuska sold for more than $1 million. That gave the tree its lasting name. The 1906 act divided the tribe into those with headrights and income and those related by blood but with no tribal rights. Osage expenditures on needless luxuries gave rise to numerous stories about excess. Little was done to staunch the flow of money drained through an orgy of ongoing fraud, swindles, and even outright murders extending into the mid-1920s. Congressional legislation in February 1925 tightened inheritance rules. But loss of allotted land continued. By the time of the Indian New Deal two-thirds of Osage land had passed to non-Indians. By the mid-twentieth century one-third of headrights had passed to non-Osages. The research of Garrick Bailey and Terry Wilson demonstrated that the issue of mixed-bloods dominated tribal politics after 1890. One-third of allottees were originally placed fraudulently on the tribal roll. Officials were elected to the tribal council on the basis of headright (allottee) ownership and not on the basis of the tribal roll.

After 1924 Fred Lookout served as principal chief. He was a leader of Peyote ceremonies, and his father had been a band leader. He was widely admired and is still esteemed. During the 1930s the tribe was the first in the nation to build and administer a tribal museum (1938). Other initiatives included changing the blood quantum to one-half or more for tribal membership. Tribal women did not obtain the vote until 1941. Another legacy of the period was that the Osage tribal government operated without a constitution. Local interests lobbied Congress hard and gained the exclusion of the Osages from the IRA and the OIWA because of the lure of mineral wealth. As a result of this exclusion and federal paternalism, the Osages never organized under the OIWA.

Osages served in the U.S. military in World War I and World War II and in subsequent conflicts. Ester Quinton Cheshewalla, a mixed-blood, was one of the first Indian women to join the U.S. Marine Corps after the Japanese attack on Pearl Harbor. Other Osages worked in defense industries during the 1940s.

Dissatisfaction with the tribal government grew during the 1960s. Critics formed a grievance body in 1964, the Osage Nation Organization (ONO). A major part of the opposition derived from the changing mixture of tribal membership and perceived conflicts over headrights. The tribal government functioned under Public Law 192 in 1957, which provided for elected officials and the division of tribal funds. Public Law 605 in 1984 extended the council's existence. The ONO pressed for voting rights for those who were born after 1907 and who held no headrights and won an affirming district court ruling in 1991 (*William Fletcher* v. *U.S.*, which itself ultimately arose out of the 1978 decision in *Logan* v. *Andrus*). The opinion had an immediate practical effect. Following the hard work of the Osage Commission, the tribe wrote a constitution that was put into place in a 1994 referendum. After additional litigation and a decision in 1997, a new election took place in November 2005 under authorizing legislation enacted the year before. The Osages separated their tribal government from the business and mineral council that oversees the mineral trust. The legislation enfranchised those who had no headright. It created a government modeled after that of the United States with three branches. This marked the first time that all Osages were permitted to cast ballots as tribal members.

In 1981 the federal government paid the Osage Tribe $7.4 million to settle tribal claims to lands seized to construct Skiatook Lake, under which petroleum reserves allegedly rested. The Osages have made accusations of federal mismanagement of tribal assets for many years. At any given time several claims suits involving the Osages are nearly always pending.

The reservation experience brought new dance traditions to the Osages from neighboring tribes. In the 1880s the Kansas and the Poncas gave *ilonshka* drums to Osage bands. The new dances quickly helped fill the cultural void when elders who practiced old traditional ritual beliefs died. The Osages built round E-lon-shka dance houses. At about the turn of the twentieth century the Osages also constructed Big Moon Peyote churches. From the Omahas the Osages received the men's and women's Soldier Dance and associations. The Otoes and Cheyennes provided the popular hand game.

The Osages maintain tribal traditions, although in altered forms. The passing of a family member is no longer remembered with an elaborate mourning ceremony, but the family hosts a funeral feast and a memorial feast a year later. In spite of much that has happened to the tribe, Osage traditions continue. Among the Osages many life-changing activities such as marriage made use of traditions (such as wedding outfits) but also included affirmation from their Roman Catholic faith. An elderly Osage was painted with Peyote symbols and colors and dressed in finery but also buried with a Roman Catholic mass. Each June, on three consecutive weekends, the Osages hold their E-lon-shka dances in each of three districts (Hominy, Gray Horse, and Pawhuska). They celebrate the selection of an eldest son of a family to serve as tribal drum keeper, acknowledged with a solemn procession, feasting, dancing, and gift-giving. I'N-Lon-Schka (a variant spelling) means "playground of the eldest son." The Indian-attired participants are called Straight Dancers for their style of dress. The ceremony celebrates annual rebirth, reverence for all life and the drum, and socializing within the tribe. Periodic War Mothers' dances are held too. In spite of their wealth, or because of it, the Osages have tried to remain aloof from other Indians in Oklahoma and have worked to sustain their heritage and language. Their Immaculate Conception Church (called the Cathedral of the Osages) in Pawhuska, with its remarkable stained glass windows, celebrated its one-hundredth anniversary in 1987 as one of the oldest Roman Catholic parishes in Oklahoma. The Osage language is nearly extinct. But the tribe is making a concerted effort to revitalize it and teach it, led by elder Mograin Lookout.

The legacy of the Osages is also manifested throughout their ancient territory. The tribal name can be found in many areas, including the Osage River in Missouri. The Osage word for their linguistic kin, the Kon'za or Kansas, provided the name for the state. Osage City and Osage County mark their Kansas legacy. Topeka, Chetopa, and Neosho are Osage place names there. The Little Osages called a river in what is now Nebraska the Ni-Btha-Ska, "water-flat-white." The French translated it into La Platte, and it was further anglicized into the Platte River. The traveler journeying from Tulsa, Oklahoma, to St. Louis, Missouri, using Interstate Highway 44 passes through much of the heart of historic Osage territory. Osage names were also attached to tribes. The Osage label for the Comanches, Pa-Do'n-Ka, "wet-nose people," was hispanicized into the Spanish and French name for them, Padouca. It is found on numerous historic documents from the era. Osage place names also mark regions outside their domain. Examples include Ki-La-Ma-She ("twin peaks" in Osage), which became the Kiamichi Mountains of southeastern Oklahoma; Marais des Cygnes (Marsh of the Swans or Place-of-the-Many-Swans, from Little Osage) for a river; and Marmonten for a town. The Osages participated with the Missouri Historical Museum and Society in commemorating the centennial of the Lewis and Clark expedition (2003–2006). Their former reservation is a part of the Tallgrass Prairie (over 40,000 acres), which also extends northward and is the largest protected tallgrass prairie preserve in North America.

Notable Osages include John Joseph Mathews, a mixed-blood Osage (one-eighth) educated at Oxford University who wrote classic accounts of tribal life and history. Major General Clarence L. Tinker was in charge of reorganizing the U.S. military air forces after the Pearl Harbor attack. He died during the battle of Midway in 1942. Tinker Air Force Base in Midwest City was named for him. Angela Gorman, a member of the Eagle clan, was a noted opera singer in the 1920s. Maria Tallchief and

Front row (left to right): Colonel Zach Miller (101 Ranch), Gordon "Pawnee Bill" Lillie, Frank Phillips holding Standing Bear's baby, Osage chief Fred Lookout, and Francis Revard

Blanche Garrison Collection, Research Division of the Oklahoma Historical Society, #19160.157

her sister Marjorie (mixed-blood Osages) became fabled ballerinas. Maria was one of the leading female interpreters of George Balanchine's 1950s classic works and also his wife. In 2008 Marjorie's son, George Skibine, became assistant secretary for Indian affairs for the United States. Bob Cannon was a noted high jumper while at Haskell Institute and in later international competitions in the 1950s. "Pepper" Martin, nicknamed the "Wild Horse of the Osage," played baseball for the St. Louis Cardinals in the 1930s. Rosa Hoots's horse Black Gold won the 1924 Kentucky Derby, making her the sole American Indian winner of that race. A young Anglo cowboy grew up in Pawhuska and environs, followed an early visiting film crew as their wrangler, and ended up in Hollywood as the movie star Ben Johnson. Osage member Diane Fraher wrote and directed the film *The Reawakening*. Wendy Ponca was a well-recognized fiber artist who designed fashions. Other Osage artists include Carol Woodring, Ryan Redcorn, Yeffie Kimball, Gina Gray, and Norman Akers. Attorney Jeff Standingbear was a lineal descendant of Chief Fred Lookout. George E. Tinker is a theology professor at Iliff School of Theology in Denver, Colorado. Rennard Strickland is a legal scholar. Carter Revard is a retired professor of English and a renowned poet.

Chickasaw painter Mike Larsen, Indian ballerinas Yvonne Chouteau (Osage), Rosella Hightower (Choctaw), Maria Tallchief (Osage), Marjorie Tallchief (Osage), Moscelyne Larkin Jasinski (Peoria), and Oklahoma State Arts Council director Betty Price, at the dedication of the mural behind them in the Capitol Rotunda, November 1991

Courtesy Oklahoma State Arts Council

SUGGESTED READING

Bailey, Garrick, ed. *The Osage and the Invisible World*. Norman: University of Oklahoma Press, 1995.

Baird, W. David. *The Osage People*. Phoenix: Indian Tribal Series, 1972 (for young readers).

Bell, John. *The Journal of Captain John Bell, Official Journalist for the Stephen H. Long Expedition to the Rocky Mountains, 1820*. Edited by Harlin Fuller and LeRoy Hafen. Glendale, Calif.: Arthur H. Clark Company, 1957.

Burns, Louis F. *A History of the Osage People*. Tuscaloosa: University of Alabama Press, 2004.

———. *Osage Indian Customs and Myths*. Tuscaloosa: University of Alabama Press, 1984.

Callahan, Alice Anne. *The Osage Ceremonial Dance In-Lon-Schka*. Norman: University of Oklahoma Press, 1990.

Chapman, Berlin B. "The Dissolution of the Osage Reservation." *Chronicles of Oklahoma* 20 (September 1942): 244–54; 20 (December 1942): 375–87; 21 (March 1943): 78–88; 21 (June 1943): 171–82.

Chapman, Carl. *The Origin of the Osage Indian Tribe: An Ethnographical, Historical and Archaeological Study*. New York: Garland, 1974.

Christian, Shirley. *Before Lewis and Clark: The Story of the Chouteaus, the French Dynasty That Ruled America's Frontier*. New York: Farrar, Straus and Giroux, 2004.

Din, Gilbert C., and Abraham P. Nasatir. *The Imperial Osages: Spanish-Indian Diplomacy in the Mississippi Valley*. Norman: University of Oklahoma Press, 1983.

Dorsey, J. Owen. "Omaha Sociology." In *Third Annual Report of the Bureau of American Ethnology for 1881–82*, 211–14. Washington, D.C.: Government Printing Office, 1884.

Hogan, Linda. *Mean Spirit*. New York: Macmillan, 1990 (novel about the 1920s murders).

Irving, Washington. *A Tour on the Prairies.* Norman: University of Oklahoma Press, 1956 (quotation on 22).

Mathews, John Joseph. *The Osages: Children of the Middle Waters.* Norman: University of Oklahoma Press, 1961; repr. 4th ed., 1982.

———. *Wah'Kon-Tah: The Osage and the White Man's Road.* Norman: University of Oklahoma Press, 1932.

McAuliffe, Dennis, Jr. *The Deaths of Sybil Bolton.* New York: Times Books/Random House, 1994.

Red Corn, Charles H. *A Pipe for February.* Norman: University of Oklahoma Press, 2002; repr. 2005.

Ribbons of the Osage: The Art and Life of Georgeann Robinson. Tulsa: Full Circle Communications, n.d. (video).

Rollings, Willard Hughes. *Unaffected by the Gospel: Osage Resistance to the Christian Invasion, 1673–1906: A Cultural Victory.* Albuquerque: University of New Mexico Press, 2004.

Springer, James, and Stanley Witkowski. "Siouan Historical Linguistics and Oneota Archaeology." In Guy Gibbon, ed., *Oneota Studies,* 69–83. Minneapolis: University of Minnesota, 1982.

Tixier, Victor. *Tixier's Travels on the Osage Prairies.* Translated by Albert Savan. Edited by John F. McDermott. Norman: University of Oklahoma Press, 1940.

Wilson, Terry Paul. *The Osage.* New York: Chelsea House, 1988 (for young readers).

———. *The Underground Reservation: Osage Oil.* Lincoln: University of Nebraska Press, 1985.

Otoe-Missouria

Historically the Otoes and the Sioux were long-standing enemies. "Otoe" derives from the Sioux word *watoa*, "lechers," a term of contempt from their enemies. "Missouria" came from the Illinois words "Misouri," "people of the dugout," and "Emissourita," "people having dugout canoes." The Otoes left their imprint on the geography of the Plains: Ne-braska, "flat river" (their name for the Platte), became the name for the state through which that river flows. The Otoes and the Missourias were separate peoples at one time but are discussed here as one group because they are combined as one tribe today.

LOCATION AND GOVERNMENT

The headquarters for the "Otoe-Missouria Tribe" lies just outside the town of Red Rock in Noble County, in north-central Oklahoma. In spite of OIWA guidelines, the Otoes governed themselves through their traditional system of clan elders and a tribal council until 1984, when they initiated a formal tribal government with a constitution and by-laws. The tribal website is www.omtribe.com.

BUSINESSES

In the 1980s the Otoes were one of the first American Indian tribes to create a bingo operation to generate tribal revenue. It grew into the Seven Clans Paradise Casino, across the highway from the tribal headquarters in Red Rock. A larger First Council Casino is located on former Chilocco Indian School property near the Kansas border. The tribe also operates two travel marts off Highway 77 near Chilocco and the Kansas border. Each travel mart includes a Little-Bit-o-Paradise Casino. A large Paradise Casino is under development at Chilocco. The Otoes own a gas station and a convenience store, just south of the tribal cultural center.

NUMBER

The tribe has 1,500 enrolled members in Oklahoma.

The Otoes are related by their Chiwere language to other Siouan-speakers like the Winnebagos (now called the Ho-Chunks) and the Iowas. Similarly, Otoe prehistory was in the region north of the Great Lakes as a part of Oneota Upper Mississippian culture. The Otoes have been removed from the Oneotas for so long, however, that their relationship is debated, some saying the Otoes are not derived from Oneotas. There is firm evidence of the Iowas' connection to the Oneotas: because the Otoes are linguistically related to the Iowas it is easily assumed that they had the same origin, which may not be the case. In the distant past the Chiwere Siouans are believed to have been a part of the main body of Siouans, which also included those who would become Dhegiha-speakers. Tribal members gradually moved southwestward after A.D. 1250 or 1300 into what is now central Missouri, placing these Woodland dwellers on the edge of the vast prairie. The archeological sites of the Lake Koshkonong culture in south-central Wisconsin, the Orr phase in southeast Minnesota, the Utz phase in north-central Missouri, and the Correctionville–Blue Earth phase in south-central Minnesota mark the prehistoric movement of the Chiweres. The Otoes and Missourias shared aspects of Woodland culture with their linguistic relations who lived in sedentary villages but also ventured onto the buffalo Plains. They resided in earth lodges, as well as bark lodges like the Iowa Indians. They too held property communally and shared with others of their language the vision quest for guidance through life. Their dances were divided into male and female spheres, with appropriate attendant activities. Elaborate funeral feasts celebrated the life of the departed and are still held as memorials. After the advent of the horse, the Otoes and Missourias were mounted warriors until confinement to a reservation restricted their movements. They appeared on Jacques Marquette's 1763 map in the vicinity of the current Iowa-Minnesota border. Sometime around 1700 they crossed the Missouri River and migrated to the Platte in present-day Nebraska, although they continued to hunt across the Missouri River. After about 1450 Missourias resided in what is now Van Meter State Park in Saline County, Missouri. Pawnee opposition halted the westward progress of the Otoes, who settled in the region.

Each clan and each family within the clan had its own oral narrative of the Otoe origin story. The accounts started in ancient mythological time after the earth was already in existence. Four animal brothers named objects and events as they sought a homeland. The brothers granted sacred knowledge to clans. The animals also began ceremonies that belonged to specific clans as rituals and rites like tattooing and use of the Pipe. The trickster created food for the people from his body with the aid of Rabbit.

The Otoe-Missourias lived in sedentary villages on either side of the Mississippi River, depending upon the century. Women tended fields of corn, beans, squash, and pumpkins. Men hunted animals, including buffalo. Their villages were situated along waterways of the Missouri River drainage. The use of the horse sometime around 1700 to 1730 brought with it cultural traits of the Plains tribes. The residences were earth lodges for several related families but also tepees and bark-covered lodges.

Tribal members belonged to one of seven clans, of which the Bear clan was the largest and most influential. It provided leadership for the tribal council and for the buffalo hunt and other fall-winter activities. The Buffalo clan led spring-summer activities and was identified with corn. Others included the Pigeon, Owl, Elk, and Eagle clans. Secret societies, dance associations, and civic groups also existed. Perhaps the Otoes in the past had a moiety system of Earth and Sky like other Siouans.

A combined Otoe and Pawnee force defeated the Spanish expedition in 1720 led by Don Pedro de Villasur. Estevan Miro, governor-general of the Spanish province of Louisiana, in 1585 described the Otoes on the Platte River and their close relationship with the Iowa Indians, who were then on the Des Moines River. During their sojourn, the Otoes gave the name "Nebraska" to the river, and it later became the name of the state. The Nemaha River derived from the Otoe word for water (*ne*) and for cultivation (*maha*). The Missourias lent their name to the Missouri River and the state of the same name. After about A.D. 1450 Missourias lived at the Utz site along the Missouri River. There they engaged in far-flung trade in bison hides, red catlinite, turquoise, and galena (lead sulphide), as scholar Robert Bray noted. Otoe trade connected the Arikaras to the west with tribes to the east. Some Missourias emigrated in the 1670s to the area of the Grand River in the northern portion of their namesake state. French traders found them there around 1700. Etienne Venyard de Bourgmont visited the Missourias and began to trade with them. He set up Fort Orléans (1723–24) on the Missouri River opposite their main village at the Utz site. Two years later he took some Otoe-Missourias for a visit to France.

Around 1723 a group of Missourias left their ancestral residence at the Utz site and moved to the Gumbo Point site near the Little Osages, who dominated the fur trade. Later members of the Lewis and Clark expedition described the great fertility of the lush countryside when they traversed it in 1804. The Otoe-Missourias were one of the first American Indian tribes to meet the members of the Corps of Discovery during their journey, at a high bank on the Missouri River close to the mouth of the Platte, which led the famous adventurers to name the site Council Bluff. It subsequently became a point of departure for American traders and pioneers heading west. (The tribe participated in planning for the bicentennial events commemorating the expedition in 2004–2006.) At the time of the visit by the Corps of Discovery, the Otoes and Missourias had merged, with some of the Missourias having joined the Osages and the Kansas. After spending time with them, members of the 1819 Stephen Long expedition referred to the Otoes and Missourias "as one nation."

An 1817 document began the treaty period for the tribes. U.S. negotiators responded to the necessity for Indian adjustment to earlier treaty cessions when they signed a treaty with the Otoes and other Indian residents of their region at Cantonment Leavenworth in mid-1828. To quell Indian conflict over territorial claims, federal agents held another council in 1830 at Prairie du Chien, where the Wisconsin River met the Mississippi, and tribes relinquished claims in western Iowa. Otoes sold a tract of ten miles termed the Nemaha Half-Breed Reservation for mixed-blood families. Otoes protested the U.S. treaty terms of 1833, which granted reservation lands that the Otoes claimed as hunting grounds to Potawatomi, Chippewa, and Ottawa Indians. The Potawatomis, in their turn, ceded the tract in 1846 to the federal government, which opened the lands to settlement. An 1836 treaty relinquished the so-called Platte Purchase lands. The Otoes and Missourias were under the jurisdiction of the Council Bluffs, Nebraska, agency, along with Omahas and Pawnees until 1855. Restricted hunting territory, unpaid annuities, and disease took a toll on the Native population. The Otoes and Missourias declined from 1,000 to 600 members during that time, losing an estimated one-third of their number in smallpox and cholera epidemics in 1851.

Frontier expansion led officials to press the Otoes for a further land cession. The commissioner of Indian affairs, George Manypenny, in his annual report remarked on his visit in 1853 with the Otoes and Missourias, during which he urged "their removal to a new home." In March 1864 he had a tribal delegation sign a treaty that ceded to the United States all their territory west of the Missouri River and south of the Platte in eastern Nebraska except for a tract (twenty-five by ten miles) on the Big Blue River. The slight adjustment of the tract necessitated a new agreement in December. That would be their new home, south of today's Beatrice,

Nebraska. The land had been ceded by the Kaw Indians in 1825. Before the 1854 treaty, the Otoes and Missourias were a loose confederation of seven clans. Each of the clans had its own chief. After the treaty, they came under a principal chief (Big Soldier). His son succeeded him as Chief Harragarra and oversaw the acquisition of a new reservation in the Cherokee Outlet of Indian Territory. Upon his death in 1894, his son Moses Harragarra became chief, selected by the Otoe Chiefs Council in late 1899. Moses Harragarra died in 1966.

The Nemaha Half-Breed Reservation Treaty of 1830 was the first congressional authorization of allotment in severalty for Indians. The very first allotments were made to Otoes in present-day Nemaha County, Nebraska. Allotments were farms assigned to or selected by individual Indians, intended to lead them to assimilation into American culture. Allotments could be sold by untutored Indian owners, however, and the policy ultimately led to catastrophic Indian land loss. After contested surveys, allotment patents were issued in fee simple (a deed) in 1860. Lewis Neal received the first one, making him the first Indian allottee. The town of Aspinwall briefly arose on his allotment. To this day, their Oklahoma kin lament the Nebraska residents of the Half-Breed tract as the "lost ones."

After migrating to their reduced reserve on the Big Blue River in 1855, the Otoes resided there until 1881. They were under continual pressure. The Oregon Trail brought emigrant wagon trains across the Indians' lands. Beset by railroad and other frontier interests, they increasingly suffered at the hands of schemers, in spite of Quaker guidance after 1869 under the Grant peace policy. The tribal population fell to under five hundred. Over the years discontented Otoes and Missourias discussed selling out and removing to Indian Territory. A deep division grew between those who favored starting anew in Indian Territory (called the Coyote band under Medicine Horse and Little Pipe) and those who insisted on remaining where they were and even selling more land (called the Quaker band). After lengthy maneuvering, Congress in 1876 authorized the survey of 120,000 acres on the Otoe and Missouria reservation in preparation for sales following intense railroad and public pressure. Scholar Berlin Chapman noted that the 1876 act was the first in U.S. history to provide for the sale of reservation land exclusively to bona fide settlers in a frontier attempt to keep out speculators. An act in 1879 loosened the restrictions.

Some Otoes and Missourias slipped away and settled in Indian Territory at the Sac and Fox Agency in the late 1870s in spite of being pursued by Indian police and military forces for illegally leaving the Nebraska reservation. Under terms of an 1881 act, northern Otoe-Missourias removed to a new 129,000-acre reservation north of today's Stillwater, Oklahoma, along Red Rock Creek and adjacent to the Ponca and Pawnee reservations. For eighteen days they walked beside or rode on seventy wagons carrying their possessions. The tribes reimbursed the United States for their Indian Territory lands, paying $61,000 out of the tribal trust fund from their 1876 land sale. Over time the Otoe-Missourias at the Sac and Fox Agency also filtered onto the Red Rock Reserve. Members of the Coyote band (called the Absentee band), which had come in 1878, had rejoined the tribe by 1890. In 1882 the Otoes and Missourias joined the consolidated agency for the Poncas and Pawnees. The Indian Territory region had previously been part of the Cherokee Nation before the 1866 Reconstruction treaty, under which lands were opened as an outlet to the Great Plains.

Under the terms of the General Allotment (or Dawes) Act of 1887, Indians of the Ponca Agency were allotted land, starting in 1891. When Otoes under William Faw-Faw and George Arkeketa resisted, the Indian agent stopped the overt resistance with the threat of harsh measures. In all 885 allotments were made, with later corrections, patterned after Charles Curtis's agreement with the Kansa Indians. Curtis was a Kansan of Indian heritage who served as vice president and in the U.S. House. Because the entire reserve was allotted to Indians, no surplus lands were opened. Although no white settlers entered the lands, the reservation for the Otoes and Missourias officially ended with the completion of allotment in 1904. It was not long before one-half of the lands were lost from Indian possession. High courts held in 1912 that the federal government administered trust lands and guardians appointed for minor Indians could not arbitrarily sell the lands and drain the accounts, reinforcing in law the trust relationship (upheld in *U.S. Fidelity and Guaranty Co.,* 1940).

Two years after he gave up the state's governorship, Henry S. Johnston became the Otoes' attorney to pursue their land claims case. Two decades later attorney Luther Bohanon successfully took the case to federal court. Otoe elder William Burgess testified to the Indian Claims Commission (ICC) members in 1947 that "[t]he [U.S.] government has never treated the Otoes with justness and fairness." He urged a just settlement of their claims. Six years later the commission held for the Indians, marking the first time that the ICC upheld added compensation for lands under Indian title of Native use and occupancy under the claims act of 1946. It was also the first tribal win for land claims west of the Mississippi River. After years of wrangling, the ICC judgment of $1.2 million was awarded in 1964–67.

A boarding school served Otoe and Missouria students until it closed in 1919, at which time pupils attended a public school at Red Rock or boarding school at Pawnee (which closed in 1958) or Chilocco (which the federal government shut in 1980). The former Otoe boarding school facility serves as a community center.

Aided by attorney Johnston, Otoe-Missourias in November 1914 signed articles of incorporation for their Peyote church. Jonathan Koshiway, Charles White Horn, and others created the Otoe Firstborn Church of Christ, the first legal attempt to safeguard the use of Peyote under the First Amendment of the U.S. Constitution. In the 1930s the statewide Native American Church absorbed Otoe membership. The statewide organization arose from Koshiway's suggestion. The 1997 death of Truman Washington Daily silenced a noted Road Man (priest) of the Native American Church, who was also the last fluent speaker of the Otoe-Missouria language. The University of Missouri had awarded him an honorary doctorate in recognition of his language preservation efforts. The last full-blood Missouria died just after the turn of the twentieth century.

Otoe-Missourias served with distinction in the armed forces of the United States. During World War II the Otoes formed the first all-Indian chapter of the American War Mothers organization in 1942. The women's activities honored tribal members in military service and continued basic Otoe values of supporting the community. Several Otoe women have held offices in the state, regional, and national structure.

The Otoes and Missourias perpetuate tribal traditions. They continue to hold large family-sponsored funeral feasts as memorials to the deceased and feasts for naming ceremonies. Some members belong to the Native American Church, with its sacrament of Peyote. Dance traditions are perpetuated through the annual Otoe Powwow held every July near the tribal headquarters. Giveaways still honor recipients with gifts of blankets, housewares, dance items, and feasting. Song leaders continue lineage, clan, and tribal ties. The dancers wear clothing adorned with Otoe ribbon work and moccasins. Long, close ceremonial ties to the Kiowas gained the Otoes the gift of the use of the Gourd Dance in 1905, and it is still performed.

Notable Otoes include Truman Daily, well-known attorney F. Browning Pipestem, author Anna Lee Walters (who is also Pawnee), and poet and playwright Annette Arkeketa (who is also Muscogee). Pipestem was a mentor to me, as he was to many others. Sanora Babb, an Anglo baby born on the Otoe reserve in 1907, went on to work as a magazine author in Los Angeles and wrote a famous novel of Depression-era America, *Whose Names Are Unknown* (which was eclipsed by John Steinbeck's best-selling *Grapes of Wrath* in 1939).

SUGGESTED READING

Bray, Robert. "The Utz Site." *Missouri Archaeologist* 52 (December 1991): entire issue.

Chapman, Berlin B. *The Otoes and Missourias: A Study of Indian Removal and Its Aftermath.* Norman: University of Oklahoma Press, 1965 (Manypenny quotation on 38).

James, Edwin. "Account of Stephen H. Long's Expedition, 1819–20." In Reuben Gold Thwaites, ed., *Early Western Travels,* vol. 15 (quotation on 134). New York: AMS, 1966.

Walters, Anna Lee. *Talking Indian.* Ithaca, N.Y.: Firebrand, 1992.

——, comp. *The Otoe-Missouria Elders: Centennial Memoirs (1881–1981).* Red Rock, Okla.: Otoe-Missouria Tribe, 1981 (58-page booklet).

Wishart, David J. *An Unspeakable Sadness: The Dispossession of the Nebraska Indians.* Lincoln: University of Nebraska Press, 1995.

Ottawa

NAME

"Ottawa" is derived from *adawe*, "to trade" or "to buy and sell" in the Algonquian language. Tribal members prefer Odawak (singular Odawa; variants: Adawe, Ottawa, etc.). Their name came from their location between the Potawatomis and Ojibwes, favoring their commercial role.

LOCATION AND GOVERNMENT

The "Ottawa Tribe" headquarters is in Miami in Ottawa County, in far northeastern Oklahoma (about twenty-five miles from Joplin, Missouri). The Ottawa Tribe is organized under the OIWA, and its government operated under a 1939 corporate charter then later a 1979 constitution. A business committee of five members, including a chief, meets quarterly. The Tribal Council for elections consists of all eligible members over the age of eighteen. Members of the business committee are elected to staggered three-year terms. There is no tribal website.

BUSINESSES

Major revenue derives from the tribe's HighWinds Casino at the junction of Highways 10 and 137 about four and a half miles east of the city of Miami, which includes an adjacent recreational vehicle (RV) park. The county contains ten Indian gaming facilities, the largest number for any county in the state. The tribe also operates the Otter Stop convenience store, fuel stop, and small casino near town. The tribe steadily built its land base following the ravages of allotment in the 1890s and the termination of federal supervision in the 1950s, which combined to leave it virtually landless.

NUMBER

The tribe has about 1,600 members.

The Ottawa language belongs to the Algonquian family, which covered most of northeastern North America. Archeologists have a challenge trying to pinpoint Ottawa origins. Their historic region contains one of the oldest sites on the continent. The Shaguiandah site on Manitoulin Island, Ontario, if confirmed at 30,000 years of age, could be among the earliest Native population locations. Small fortified subsistence villages in central and western Michigan during the period around A.D. 1200, sometimes termed Peninsular Woodland culture, have left evidence of some trade or interaction (reminding the observer of the historic Ottawas). Historic-period Ottawa occupations have been identified at northern Lake Huron, Fort Michilimackinac, and Gros Gap sites of the immediate region. Archeological finds in the northern Lake Huron region usually are assigned to the Ottawas, whom Europeans encountered there. In the Mackinac area and at Fort Michilimackinac, excavations revealed Ottawa cultural remains intermingled with Fort Ancient–Whittlesey ceramics. According to their language group, the Ottawas were first known in villages in the southern part of the present state of Michigan, along the Grand River, and in portions of Ohio and Indiana.

The origin story for the Ottawas is similar to the Ojibwe (or Chippewa) story. For the Ottawas, the Creative Force in the universe was Gitche-Manitou. The Earth, wife of Gitche-Manitou, was in charge of nature. At the beginning there was water everywhere. Naanabozho asked the animals to dive down and bring up mud, which would then be made into dry land. The otter dove deeply but could not find mud. The muskrat went beneath the surface of the water and came back with earth in its paws. Naanabozho took the earth in his hands and held it up to the sun. When the mud dried, he threw it about, creating a large island for animals to live on.

According to an oral tradition among the Ottawas late in the 1600s, the Fork People and the Otter clan separated, and some settled on the western shore of Lake Huron and the southern shore of Lake Erie in the vicinity of what is now Detroit. They also were along Beaver Creek in Pennsylvania and the Maumee Valley of Ohio at different times. The Ottawas during the late seventeenth century joined the Potawatomis and the Ojibwes in relocating to the western Great Lakes region, responding to French imperial pressures and hoped-for opportunities. Members of the "Three Fires" (Ottawa, Ojibwe, Potawatomi) separated at the Mackinac Straits. A loose association, however, continued. It is likely that in the 1600s some of the Fork People, and perhaps other clan members, lived on Manitoulin Island, which is located adjacent to Ontario on the Canadian side in Lake Huron and is billed as the world's largest freshwater island.

In the late seventeenth century the Ottawas had four or five clan divisions, which included Bear (Kishagon), Gray Squirrel (Sinego), Fish (Keinouche), Fork People (Nassaueketon), and Otter (Ne-gig, also called Sable). Nanabush provided the bridge for the Ottawas to make spiritual contact with the Creator. Medicine men provided a link to the supernatural.

The Ottawas resided in villages and cultivated corn, beans, and pumpkins. They practiced horticulture and agriculture during spring and summer. As winter approached, they journeyed to their wintering grounds along the shore of southern Lake Michigan.

The Ottawas' contact with Europeans began early and accidentally. A large group of Ottawas greeted Samuel de Champlain in 1615 near the mouth of the French River in the region of Georgian Bay on Canada's Atlantic coast. The Ottawas already traveled great distances for trade as well as raiding. In their commerce they would barter tobacco, corn, other plant products, and furs as their part of a lengthy intertribal transaction. The arrival of French traders, however, transformed the Ottawas. By 1634 their role as brokers in the Great Lakes region engaged them more and more deeply in European-Indian politics. Colonial relations eventually involved the Ottawas in Iroquois and Algonquian rivalry. Conflict forced the Ottawas to leave their ancestral lands in Ontario. They joined a portion of the Wyandottes to travel westward until they reached Dakota territory in 1654. Warfare with the Dakotas forced the Ottawas back to Lake Superior on Chequemagong Bay, Keewanaw, Manitoulin Island, and Sault St. Marie. The Ottawas sided with the Hurons and the French during the French and Indian War.

By 1673 Michilimackinac became the center of Ottawa territory. Ottawas resided near present-day Detroit, along with Potawatomis and Wyandottes, before 1754. The period of the French and Indian War (1754–63) brought great destruction and movement of refugee populations into Ottawa territory. As a British colonial aide to Sir William Johnson, trader George Croghan in 1763 helped negotiate with Pontiac for an end to his rebellion. Croghan was personally well acquainted with "the Ottawa sachem" and met him several times. The English trader and interpreter described Pontiac as "a shrewd and sensible Indian of few words." Croghan also opened the western Great Lakes country to British traders and English influence. Incidentally, he had tried unsuccessfully to persuade Pennsylvania authorities starting in 1750 to maintain a presence in that region, but they refused. By the middle of that decade the French had won the Indians to their side in the coming conflict.

Repeated maltreatment from U.S. negotiators and ongoing pressure from Americans later on the frontier fed Ottawa resentments. They joined Native coalitions and sided with the British during the War of 1812. American forces devastated Indian towns along the Wabash. Ottawa warriors fought to protect their Maumee settlements. They were engaged at Niagara and were at Tecumseh's side in the battle at Moraviantown.

As the American frontier swept into the Northwest Territory, however, the Ottawas signed thirty-two different treaties between 1785 and 1862 that involved their homelands. Several bands living in the Sandusky, Ohio, area ceded their land to the United States and migrated to a new 74,000-acre reservation in eastern Kansas in 1832. It was on the Marais des Cygnes (Marsh of the Swans) River near present Ottawa in Franklin County, Kansas. In 1833 the remaining Ottawa holdouts signed an agreement with the United States that relinquished all their land on the western side of Lake Michigan and accepted a reservation in Kansas. Ethnographer Henry Schoolcraft arranged for a contingent to travel to Kansas by canal boat and steamboat in 1837. A final group migrated two years later to Kansas from the Maumee, Ohio, region.

The Reverend Jotham Meeker, a Baptist, was influential for the Ottawas who resided in Kansas. He also served an invaluable ethnographic role, because he avidly recorded information on their customs and published a collection of Ottawa customary law in 1850 titled the *Ottawa First Book*. Even under his umbrella, the Indians were placed under intense pressure to cede lands and move. Finally, after relentless pushing, they signed a treaty in 1857 and agreed to relocate in northeastern Indian Territory. The Ottawas were made up of several bands. Some (from the villages of Blanchard's Fork, Roche de Boeuf, and Oquanoxa in Ohio) had been with the Little Traverse, Michigan, band that had emigrated to the Toledo, Ohio, area to live with the Potawatomis before they too removed to Indian Territory. Others had moved to the Maumee Valley and eventually ended their lives in Oklahoma. Ottawas in Oklahoma primarily descended from Otter and Fork People clan members who migrated from Ohio in 1832–39 to Kansas and then to Indian Territory.

The turmoil of the Civil War era, which for Kansas erupted in the mid-1850s, brought Indian and white refugees into the region, but the postwar period saw an increase in settlers. Members of the Baptist Home Mission Society "engaged in blatant fraud" over Ottawa lands in Kansas, as detailed by William Unrau and H. Craig Miner. These Baptists conspired with Indian agent Clinton Hutchinson to cheat the Ottawas out of their lands. Hutchinson, Kansas, is named for him. They bribed Indian leaders for property. Two years later one-fourth of the reservation (about 20,000 acres) was set aside for a "university" to benefit the Ottawas. By 1864 whites speculated freely in Indian lands of the "Ottawa University." Lots were laid out on it for a town. The federal government ultimately ruled that Hutchinson and his cohorts had acted wrongly, but that did not help the Indians. Surrounded by enemies and torn by internal strife, most Ottawas moved to Indian Territory. Few ever attended "their" university. Today the school still operates under Baptist leadership.

In the 1890s allotment affected the Ottawas in Indian Territory as it did so many other tribes in the United States. Townsite promoters bought 577 acres of choice land on the banks of the Neosho River just north of the agency. The site became the thriving town of Miami. After their allotment in 1892 an Indian Service inspector met with tribal members in 1903 to arrange for the allotment process to conclude so the remaining land could be opened to white settlers in 1908, a year after statehood.

During the post–World War II period congressional conservatives wanted to divest the federal government of costly responsibilities. Terminating federal connections to tribal governments became a priority. Among the 109 tribal entities that were severed, Congress in August 1956 (Public Law 943) terminated the federal trust relationship with the Ottawa Tribe of Oklahoma and its property. Responding to the misdirection of the federal government, tribal members had voted for termination the year before. Many of the individual Ottawas had allotted farms and were acculturated to the surrounding white population, so they were not as devastated as tribal members elsewhere. Still, former tribal holdings (558 acres) quickly passed into non-Indian hands, leaving any reconstituted tribe almost landless in subsequent years. The Ottawa Indian cemetery was their lone surviving land and became the focus of tribal identity and attention. A final roll listed 630 Ottawas. After lobbying and a federal change of heart regarding termination, Congress restored federal recognition to the Ottawa Tribe and its neighbors on May 15, 1978 (Public Law 281).

As a result of the swindles involving the Ottawa University scam as well as fraud perpetrated by the later commissioners appointed to rectify the initial activity, the federal government in 1965 paid the tribe $406,000. The tribal effort to reestablish its land base continues. Ottawa Tribe members also share concerns over mining waste pollution in the eight-tribe region in the wake of lead and zinc mining that was carried out since the dawn of the twentieth century. The issue united the tribes and other local residents to press for a cleanup of what is called the Tar Creek region.

Subsidence of surface land also continues to be a concern. Poultry runoff into the region's water system is a danger as well.

The largest number of Ottawas remain scattered across southern Michigan and also in Canada among the Ojibwes. The federal government periodically recognizes a new tribe, and among them may be various bands or settlements of Ottawas in Michigan. Members of the Little River Band of Ottawas reside in the vicinity of Manistee in the northwestern Lower Peninsula of Michigan. Oklahoma Ottawas maintain contact with their far-flung kin. Several small American Indian reserves for Chippewa and Ottawa descendants remain on Manitoulin Island today. Electronic communication, visiting, and celebrations are among the contacts that continue. Through their kinfolk, Oklahoma Ottawas can tap deeply into their historic roots, drawing from residents still living in their prehistoric and historic territories. Some Michigan Ottawas have taught the tribal language to Oklahoma tribal members through class work at the Northeastern Oklahoma University campus branch in Miami.

The Ottawa Tribe of Oklahoma laid claim in 1998 to 1,281 acres of land near Springfield, Illinois, in DeKalb County. The tribe sought the parcel under terms of the July 1829 Treaty of Prairie du Chien, which transferred 5 million acres to the United States. The tribe claimed that the terms were never fully carried out. In 2005 the tribe also claimed 350-acre North Bass Island in Lake Erie off the Ohio shoreline. The tribe members maintained that it ceded the region in an 1831 treaty before they moved to Kansas. Officials of the state of Ohio contended that the tribe was attempting to gain leverage to force the state to grant permission for the tribe to set up a casino within Ohio.

A major focus of Ottawa cultural activities is the annual Ottawa Powwow held on Labor Day weekend on their tribal dance ground, begun in 1964. Most Ottawas in Oklahoma today are Baptists, a legacy of the efforts of Jotham Meeker in the nineteenth century. But their annual powwow draws tribal members from near and far, as well as visitors, for the food, the spectacle, the fellowship, and the ceremonies. Among the foods they enjoy is their traditional succotash, made from beans and dried corn. Some Ottawas also continue to observe the ten-day mourning period for the deceased.

Perhaps the most notable Ottawa was Pontiac (1720–69), a member of the Otter clan. He led an American Indian alliance in the southern Great Lakes region against the English, called Pontiac's Rebellion. He hoped for French aid and Indian allied help, but the effort failed. Although the rebellion focused on the siege of Detroit, it involved a thousand miles of frontier. Britain won the French and Indian War, though, and in 1763 became dominant in the American colonial frontier. London's centralization attempts in the aftermath of the rebellion upset the American frontier and fueled ultimate desires for American independence. Pontiac signed a peace agreement with the British in 1766, but his murder thereafter sparked furious Ottawa outbursts against Illinois Confederacy tribes. Another famous Ottawa is Enmegahbowh (1810–1902), who was the first Indian priest in the American Episcopal Church. He was born of Ottawa parents who resided with the Rice Lake band of Ojibwes north of Lake Ontario. Enmegahbowh means "one-who-stands-before-his-people." After his schooling in St. Paul, Minnesota, he helped found St. John's in the Wilderness. It is now called St. Columba's and is the oldest surviving Indian Christian church congregation in Minnesota. Bishop Henry Whipple ordained Enmegahbowh as a priest in 1867.

SUGGESTED READING

Cash, Joseph, and Gerald Wolff. *The Ottawa People.* Phoenix: Indian Tribal Series, 1976.

Croghan, George. "A Selection of George Croghan's Letters and Journals Relating to Tours in the Western Country." In Reuben Gold Thwaites, ed., *Early Western Travels,* vol. 1, 45–173. New York: AMS, 1966.

Dixon, David. *Never Come to Peace Again: Pontiac's Uprising and the Fate of the British Empire in North America.* Norman: University of Oklahoma Press, 2005

Unrau, William E., and H. Craig Miner. *Tribal Dispossession and the Ottawa Indian University Fraud.* Norman: University of Oklahoma Press, 1985.

Pawnee

NAME

The origin of the tribe's name is debated, but perhaps it is from the Choctaw words *pana*, a "braid" or "twist," and *mahaia*, "to curve" or "bend up," referring to the distinctive scalp lock of Pawnee warriors. The name could also derive from the Pawnee word *pariki*, "horn," referring to the scalp lock. The spelling "Pani" is increasing in usage.

LOCATION AND GOVERNMENT

The headquarters for the "Pawnee Nation of Oklahoma" is in Pawnee in Pawnee County, in the north-central part of Oklahoma. Under the OIWA, the Pawnees formed a business council, a Chiefs (Nasharo) Council, and a tribal constitution with by-laws and charter. The tribal website is www.pawneenation.org.

BUSINESSES

A tribal service station and a small casino, called the Pawnee Trading Post, are located on the route to Tulsa. There is a slightly larger casino operation near the tribal headquarters. The Pawnees have discussed placing casinos on various other properties, including the land of the former Chilocco Indian School nearer the Kansas border.

NUMBER

The tribe has just over 2,500 members, of whom about 400 reside in Pawnee and Payne counties in the communities of Pawnee, Skedee, Lela Cleveland, Ralston, and Meramec and near Yale.

Archeologist Waldo Wedel traced Pawnee prehistoric residence to the Central Plains tradition for several centuries before the arrival of Europeans. Their homeland during that residence was along the Republican, Loup, and Lower Loup rivers of what is now northern and central Nebraska. Wedel and others divided the Plains traditions into two main segments. The first is called Smoky Hill and dates from about A.D. 900–1500. Patricia O'Brien has ably connected some of the Smoky Hill ritual practices discovered in the site remains with Pawnee spirituality and beliefs. The other tradition is known as Upper Republican and dates from around 1050 to 1350. Both archeological traditions are considered to have played a role in the Lower Loup phase from 1500 to 1700, which is widely considered to be the predecessor to the historic Pawnees. A confederation of ancestral Pawnee bands lived in the thirteenth and fourteenth centuries (during the Upper Republican phase), along the Platte and Loup rivers of Nebraska. At about the time when the first Europeans arrived on the continent, earth lodges of the Proto-Pawnees began to have altars and east-facing entrances. That alignment meant that the first rays of the vernal and autumnal sunrise passed through the entrance and illuminated an altar on the opposite wall. West was the direction of the Evening Star and feminine power, such as Mother Corn. The oral tradition of the Skiri (earlier cited as Skidi and Skedee) division of the Pawnees and linguistic affinity with the Caddos and Wichitas lend credence to Skiri claims of a southern origin and a migration north, leading to a merger with other Pawnees. Localized groups became the basis for the ancestors of what would turn out to be historic Skiri and South Band divisions.

Linguist Douglas Parks dated the separation of Pawnee from Caddo proper about 3,300 years ago. The Pawnees are also closely affiliated with the Arikaras of the northern Plains, who separated from the Pawnees after A.D. 1400. The archeological tradition associated with the Arikaras is called the Coalescent because it merged Eastern Woodlands settled traits with buffalo Plains traits.

Predecessors of the Pawnees took the arrangement of their villages from the brilliant firmament overhead at night. The area on the west side of the earth lodge (*waharu*) was considered sacred, representing the garden of the Evening Star. Rituals maintained the Pawnees' relationship with the Sky Beings in celestial bodies. Other ceremonies perpetuated balance with earth's sacred beings. A wide variety of dances and ceremonies kept alive their universe, all an extension of Tirawahat, the all-encompassing creative force. Tirawahat created star deities like Morning Star and Evening Star when the universe was born. Morning Star was a hunter and warrior (symbolized by eagles and hawks) and the model for Pawnee male behavior. The Evening Star tended a garden and raised Mother Corn. She controlled the powers that never sleep (symbolized by the owl), such as Thunder, Lightning, Wind, and Clouds. Evening Star was the mother of the people and a model for Pawnee women. From the union of male and female forces in the universe came a girl. Sun and Moon united to create a boy. From the union of that boy and girl came the Pawnees.

One of the most noteworthy Pawnee ceremonies was the Hako or adoption ceremony involving the sacred Pipe. Pawnee star priests gazed through the lodge smoke hole to study celestial movements and to determine the proper time for rituals. Ethnologist Clark Wissler said that among all Indians the Pawnees made the most extensive use of sacred medicine bundles, in rituals, in annual ceremonies, and in their personal lives. A Skiri story said that one bundle had been carried across the skies on the shoulders of Morning Star's younger brother.

Tirawahat Aitus, "heaven father who is above," is everything. He is the unseen power who created the universe: intermediaries such as stars, constellations, winds, plants, and animals as well as Evening Star, Morning Star, the Sun, the Moon, and a host of other celestial beings, each responsible for aspects of the world (weather, fertility, etc.). After Tirawahat had created all things, he spoke, and a woman and a man appeared on earth.

Europeans in the late seventeenth century found Pawnees living in large sedentary earth-lodge villages on terraces above the Platte and Loup rivers. Their men hunted buffalo semiannually on the Plains, while women raised beans, squash, pumpkins, and corn and gathered wild vegetal foods. Their leaders, chiefs and priests, oversaw life in villages of earth-domed lodges. Council members deliberated issues of importance. Priests looked after an elaborate round of rituals and ceremonies, which included medicine bundles for each of the villages and the major societies.

The Pawnees had heard tales of soldiers' horses, shiny metal armor, and the hairy appearance of the men of Coronado's Spanish expedition to the Arkansas River in 1541. The conquistador allegedly met a Pawnee chief in a Wichita village (perhaps Quivira) near the great bend of the Arkansas River. Pawnees later participated in the decimation of the Villasur expedition in 1720. It had left Santa Fe and marched northward across the prairie to the Platte River in an unsuccessful attempt to intercept French interlopers. Each of the four major Pawnee bands subsequently maintained its own alliances with European colonial powers contending for regional control. Claude Du Tisné cemented an alliance with the Chaui, Pitahawirate, Kitkahahki, and Skiri bands of the Pawnees on the Arkansas River in 1719. They resided along the Republican, Tappage, and Grand rivers.

The Pawnees were immortalized early in American letters. The novels of the Leatherstocking Tales series by James Fenimore Cooper (the first major author in the hemisphere) were the precursors of the popular "Western." Cooper met the Pawnee chief Pitaresaru (Man Chief), who was touring the East, in the 1820s and interviewed him. Pawnee Indians then played a prominent role in Cooper's favorite novel of his series, *The Prairie* (1827). The Pawnee character, called Hard Heart, portrayed the ideal ally of the white mountain man Hawk-eye. The Indian sidekick as trusty Indian guide was used again and again as a theme in American literature, including Tonto and the Lone Ranger in later years. Members of the Stephen Long expedition were equally impressed by Pitaresaru and believed that he would rise to future leadership of his people and fame.

Beginning in 1806, when two Pawnees visited president Thomas Jefferson in the nation's capital, a stream of U.S. explorers and negotiators visited the Pawnees. Successive treaties after 1818 narrowed Pawnee bands' territories in Nebraska and Kansas until the four bands were restricted to a single reservation in Nebraska in 1857. The classic account of Santa Fe trader Josiah Gregg described a Pawnee attack against his caravan during a stormy New Year's night in 1833. Some Pawnees served as valued scouts in the U.S. Army in the 1860s–70s in campaigns against their Sioux and Cheyenne enemies. From an estimated population of 12,000 in the early nineteenth century, Pawnee numbers plummeted through war, disease, and adverse conditions on their reservation, down to only about 600 by the start of the twentieth century. They removed to Indian Territory in 1875, where allotment ultimately took much of their land base. The opening of the "surplus" land in 1893 brought an influx of white settlers.

During the assimilation period the Pawnees, who were often demoralized and impoverished, turned to the Ghost Dance as well as to the sacramental use of Peyote in the Native American Church for spiritual sustenance. It was in this period of boarding school education that some Pawnees accepted Christianity. Missionaries had begun work among them in the 1830s. During one especially severe winter, with starvation threatening the Pawnees on their reserve, local rancher Gordon W. Lillie fed tribal members. The grateful tribespeople dubbed him their "white chief" and granted him the tribal name "Pawnee Bill." He went on to establish a legendary Wild West Show that employed Pawnees and other Indians. Their performance at the Antwerp World's Fair (1894) enthralled a child who grew up to be the Roman Catholic pioneer priest Urban de Hasque, who had a long and distinguished career in Oklahoma.

Established in 1874, the Pawnee Agency was consolidated in 1928 for five tribes (the Pawnees, Otoe-Missourias, Poncas, Tonkawas, and Kaws). The business council and chiefs' councils were formed under the OIWA. A judgment payment in 1964 from the court of claims for past land cessions provided the tribe a nest egg of $7.3 million.

Traditions are carried on today through a variety of means. Pawnees and their Caddoan-language kin the Wichitas continue their cyclical visiting with tribal, cultural, and social sharing each summer. The Pawnee Veterans' Association sponsors the Pawnee Homecoming Powwow (begun in 1946 for returning veterans), held the first weekend in July. Indian veterans, seasoned dancers, family, relations, and spectators come from far and wide for feasting, dancing, singing, and ceremonies as well as craft shows, camping, and visiting. The Pawnee dancers' regalia are covered with images of Pawnee cosmology: star motifs, celestial designs, and bird imagery. Images of lightning bolts, stars, and crosses within circles elicit memories of the nighttime firmament, creation stories, and Tirawahat's all-encompassing presence. Traditions also continue through the family-sponsored Young Dog, Kitkahahki, Memorial Day, and Veterans Day dance gatherings. On December 25 the Pawnees hold their annual Christmas Day Dance to celebrate Christ's birth and also to honor veterans and give thanks to the Creator. They often play traditional hand game contests. In addition, the tribe members are making strides to teach their language to their younger generation. The Pawnee Nation Academy, begun in 2004, provides a college curriculum for mainstream and cultural education in their former boarding school building.

The Pawnees' long residence in central Plains river bottoms creates a spiritual bond with the prairie landscape. Tribal stories are filled with descriptions of special topographical features such as caves, springs, and hills. The Plains area contains sites of a sacred geography, recalling mythic councils of animals within those natural lodges. Pawnee tribal members have also been involved for some time with repatriation of human remains from repositories such as historical societies, in part as a result of lengthy documented residence in the region. A couple donated sixty acres of farmland to the Pawnees in 2007. The parcel, to be used for repatriation, is near Dannebrog and Grand Island, Nebraska, land ancestral to the Pawnees along the Loup River. The state sued the Environmental Protection Agency over Pawnee tribal land and water regulations (termed treatment-as-state status) in March 2005. Later that year a provision in the national highway transportation funding measure (Public Law 59) granted the state jurisdiction over Indian Country environmental regulations within the state and superseded tribal provisions. The measure was a reminder of the worst aspects of paternalism.

The most well-known Pawnees include the physician Charles Knife Chief and attorney John Echohawk, the executive director of the Native American Rights Fund. His brother Walter is also an attorney for the same organization. Another brother, Larry Echohawk, was the first American Indian elected to serve as attorney general of a state (Idaho in 1991). The tribe includes many other lawyers, accountants, teachers, artists, and professionals.

Moses Yellowhorse (also Yellow Horse) pitched just two seasons for the Pittsburgh Pirates baseball team in the early 1920s. But his speedball was so legendary that he appeared as a character in the "Dick Tracy" comic strip of Chester Gould, who was born in the town of Pawnee in 1900 and reared there. Full-blood Kuruks Pahetu (Richard Allen) was a noted musician in the 1930s, who attended Bacone College and the Julliard School of Music.

Petalesharo (Pawnee)
Print of colored lithograph by McKenney and Hall. Courtesy Creek Council House Museum.

Anna Lee Walters (who is also Otoe/Missouria) is a well-known author. Bruce Caesar (who is also Sac and Fox) is a jeweler in silverwork who is widely exhibited. Acee Blue Eagle (Alexander C. McIntosh, also Creek), Albin Jake, and Daniel Horse Chief (also Cherokee) were well-known painters. Award-winning artist Austin Real Rider is also part Sioux. Kevin Gover, an attorney, served in the Clinton administration as assistant secretary and commissioner of Indian affairs (1997–2000) then became the director of the National Museum of the American Indian in 2007. Brumet Echo-Hawk, now a celebrated painter, met Ernest Childers coming up the other side of the hill when Childers completed his Medal of Honor–winning clearing of the ridge during World War II. Martha Ann Clark served as an aide to Bill Clinton's National Security advisor Sandy Berger. James Riding In is a professor of American Indian Studies. The Native hip-hop duo Culture-ShockCamp (Quese IMC/Marcus Frejo

Attorney John Echohawk (Pawnee)
Courtesy John Echohawk

and DJ InDiviDual and ShOck B/Brian Frejo) are Pawnee-Seminole. They appeared in the 2005 film *New World*. Also part-Pawnee are the Indian hip-hop artists Lil Mike (Jesus Silva II) and Funny Bone (Jesus Silva IV).

SUGGESTED READING

Blaine, Martha Royce. *Some Things Are Not Forgotten: A Pawnee Family Remembers*. Lincoln: University of Nebraska Press, 1997.

Boughter, Judith. *The Pawnee Nation: An Annotated Research Bibliography*. Lanham, Md.: Scarecrow, 2004.

Gregg, Josiah. *Commerce of the Prairies*. Edited by Max Morehead. Norman: University of Oklahoma Press, 1954.

Hyde, George E. *The Pawnee Indians*. Norman: University of Oklahoma Press, 1974; repr. 1988 (1st ed. Denver: University of Denver, 1951).

Murie, James R. *Ceremonies of the Pawnee*. Edited by Douglas R. Parks. 2 vols. Smithsonian Institution, Contributions to Anthropology No. 27. Washington, D.C.: Smithsonian Institution Press, 1979; repr. 1981; repr. Lincoln: University of Nebraska Press, 1989.

O'Brien, Patricia. "Evidence for Antiquity of Women's Roles in Pawnee Society." *Plains Anthropologist* 36, no. 134 (April 1991): 51–64.

Parks, Douglas. "Northern Caddoan Languages." *Nebraska History* 60 (1979): 197–213.

Wedel, Waldo R. *Prehistoric Man on the Great Plains*. Norman: University of Oklahoma Press, 1970.

Weltfish, Gene. *The Lost Universe: Pawnee Life and Culture*. Lincoln: University of Nebraska, 1965; New York: Basic Books, 1965; rev. ed. New York: Ballantine, 1971; repr. Lincoln: University of Nebraska Press, 1977.

Wissler, Clark. "General Discussion of Shamanistic and Dancing Societies." In American Museum of Natural History, *Anthropological Papers,* vol. 11, pt. 12, 853–76. New York: Trustees of the Museum, 1916.

Peoria

The tribal designation is a French corruption of the Algonquian word "Peouarea" or "Piwarea," "he comes carrying a pack on his back." Claude Allouez referred to them as "Peoualen," while Jacques Marquette called them "Peouarea."

LOCATION AND GOVERNMENT

The headquarters of the "Peoria Tribe of Indians of Oklahoma" is in Miami in Ottawa County, in far northeastern Oklahoma (about fifteen miles from Joplin, Missouri, and ninety miles from Tulsa). The tribe organized under the OIWA in June 1936, with a constitution adopted in October 1939 and a federal charter adopted in 1940. Their new constitution was ratified in 1981 and revised and approved in August 1997. The members of the business committee (made up of seven members including a chief) are elected to four-year staggered terms. The adult tribal membership in its annual March meeting serves as a General Council for tribal elections. The Peorias share a community center in Miami with the Ottawa Tribe. The tribal website is www.peoriatribe.com.

BUSINESSES

Peoria land was allotted individually from the time of their settlement in Oklahoma, and much remains in individual holdings. The tribe owned just 19 acres by the 1950s but now owns over 1,600 acres. The Inter-Tribal Council of Miami runs a gift shop in the council headquarters in Miami near the interstate highway. Using federal grant money, the tribe purchased 22 acres near Miami in late 1981. The large tribal casino, Buffalo Run, is located just off the Will Rogers Turnpike (Interstate 44, accessible from Miami), only two miles away from the Quapaw casino. A second casino, the Peoria Gaming Center, is in Miami on Highway 69A. Another major source of revenue is the Peoria Ridge Golf Course, located east of Miami.

NUMBER

The tribe has about 2,800 members.

The constituent tribes of the Illinois Confederacy all spoke Algonquian. The confederacy dominated the present states of Illinois, Wisconsin, Iowa, Missouri, and part of Arkansas. The confederacy's diverse makeup creates a challenging archeological background. Linguistics provides some insight into the Illinois tribes. Miami is one of the major languages, but the Illinois group also includes Peoria, Moingwea, Cahokia, Tamaroa (or Tamaroha), and many other languages. Peoria and Piankashaw are nearly identical. They differ dialectically from but are related to Wea and Kaskaskia. Proto-Algonquian, the mother language of all of them, existed about 3,000 years ago. Its home range is believed to be between Georgian Bay and Lake Ontario. As Ives Goddard pointed out, the language began to fragment at an early stage into at least ten increasingly distinct dialects. The name for the Illinois Confederacy came from Ilaniawaki or Illiniwek, "real or original ones" (shortened to "Illini," which the French altered to "Illinois"). The confederacy was loosely organized and was never as cohesive or formal as the Iroquois and Huron confederacies.

Illinois tribes like the Peorias erected a small earthen mound to mark the interment of respected leaders. The custom extended into the historic period. It harkened back to Woodland and Mississippian times, with sites such as Cahokia, named for an Illinois Indian tribe. Cahokia was the great North American urban mound center of the thirteenth century, located in what is now the state of Illinois across from St. Louis. Illinois peoples have been identified as descendants of Upper Mississippian peoples.

Illinois Confederacy members lived in pole and bark–covered residences called longhouses. Their permanent villages dotted the landscape through their territory. House structures sometimes were linked in an L-shape. Women tended their gardens and raised corn, beans, squash, and melons. They also gathered yellow pond lilies, pawpaws, nuts, and berries. Men hunted game and waterfowl as well as fished. Each year they left for the summer and fall communal bison hunts on the Plains and to seek deer.

Peorias looked to the Creator, the Master of Life, to offer bounty. The Creator formed this world after its earlier destruction in a great flood. Religious activity focused on an organized association of shamans. Peorias, like other Illinois Confederacy members, gathered for communal rites like the Fish Dance at spawning time, clan bundle feasts, adoptions, funerals, Calumet ceremonies, and other village-wide celebrations. The shaman associations publicly demonstrated their abilities. The Peorias probably divided their clans into Sky and Earth divisions, like other Illinois-speaking peoples.

As Jacques Marquette journeyed down the Mississippi River in 1673, he encountered the Peorias near the present site of the Illinois city of the same name. Illinois Confederacy people such as the Kaskaskias lived along the Illinois River, while others lived on the Mississippi River below the mouth of the Missouri. The Peoria village site (occupied after 1640) held 300 lodges, according to Marquette's account. The site is maintained today as Iliniwek Village State Historic Site (formerly the Haas/Hagerman archeological site of "Peouarea" that Marquette visited on June 25, 1673). Marquette and Louis Joliet spent three weeks among them. They identified them as the Peorias. The Indian chief gave Marquette a decorated peace Pipe as a sort of passport he could use on his travels. Marquette observed European trade goods like guns among the Peorias, who had visited the French post at Chemaquemegon (on Lake Michigan). Their descriptions of the lush lands to the south motivated him to launch his exploration into the new country. Peorias collected around the French fort and trading post established by Robert Cavelier, Sieur de La Salle, at Starved Rock on the upper Illinois River. Many Peorias had joined the Kaskaskias at their village. When the Kaskaskias left from Pimiteoui in 1700 and moved to the region of the Kaskaskia and Mississippi rivers, the settlement became known as Peoria. It still carries that name as a city in Illinois. Illinois tribes like the Cahokias and Michigameas moved into the American Bottom along the Mississippi River, which also realigned French settlements with their posts, forts, and missions.

At the site of present-day Peoria Jesuit Père Jacques Gravier looked after the mission and diligently worked on his Peoria dictionary, which survives. Marquette's April 1675 Immaculate Conception mission is now Starved Rock State Park on the Illinois River near its juncture with the Fox River. Below St. Louis the French built Fort Chartres after 1719. French missionaries made use of hymns to teach Indians about Christianity. Illinois Indians, on their part, were eager to obtain Europeans' power through religion as well as trade goods. Many Peorias remain Roman Catholic to this day.

As a result of their location, the Peorias traded extensively with riverborne traffic (especially the French) during the eighteenth century. Early French *voyageurs* found the Peorias living next to Kaskaskia on the southern shore of Lake Michigan. French officials believed that the future of

New France lay among the Illinois tribes, who could serve as intertribal links and could check English-Iroquois advances. But involvement with Europeans left the Peorias devastated. The half-century of warfare with the larger Iroquois Confederacy after 1650 left the population of the Illinois tribes reduced by 90 percent. Weakened, they moved westward but came into conflict with other more westerly tribes like the Sioux. The Peorias fled the Iroquois threat and moved west of the Mississippi River. The 1680 Iroquois invasion forced French traders like La Salle's lieutenant Henri de Tonti to flee the Illinois River Valley and find refuge among the Potawatomis at Green Bay.

The mixture of Native peoples became even more complicated. The movement of Indians in the wake of Iroquois attacks, refugee resettlement, shifting alliances, and migration to improve trade opportunities contributed to a bewildering mix of tribal peoples. About 1650 Eries (Westos) and Tionontatis sought shelter among the Illinois. The Kaskaskias took in remnants of the Michigameas, Cahokias, and Tamaroas, all Illinois Confederacy members. The more numerous Weas and Piankashaws were once bands in the Miami Nation but separated. The Weas and Piankashaws themselves incorporated the Pepikokias and others. The Moingweas, who had lived as Peoria neighbors in 1673 near the Des Moines River, merged with the Peorias. Cahokias also joined the Peorias.

The Illinois remained along the Illinois River through the eighteenth century but were drawn more deeply into imperial rivalries involving the European powers. The Peorias' loyalty to the French left them open to British-allied Indian attacks. Assaults from tribes in Wisconsin hit the Peorias located in the extreme north of Illinois country especially hard. The fury of the onslaughts forced the surviving Peorias southward.

Illinois warriors aided American general George Rogers Clark during the American Revolutionary War. In retaliation for the pro-American stance of the Illinois, British and Iroquois-allied Indian tribes launched a series of attacks against them. Internecine warfare continued throughout the region.

In 1814 Peorias and Piankashaws settled on the Black River near St. Genevieve in today's northwestern Missouri. There they joined kinfolk who had migrated to the location in the mid-1670s. Residents were anxious to be rid of the Indians and helped induce them to continue their journey. The Piankashaws had two villages at Paola with the Weas. Some Piankashaws moved to central Missouri along the St. Francis River. Peorias and Weas gradually drifted southwest to the White River.

The aftermath of the War of 1812 brought renewed U.S. efforts to evict Indians and obtain their land. Most moved. Chief Black Wolf led his Tamaroas, along with some Michigameas, upriver to the area between the Illinois and the Michigan rivers. Their descendants still live there. Kaskaskias and Peorias crossed the Mississippi River to present-day Kansas. The word "Mississippi" is derived from the Illinois name: Missisippuwe, "great river."

Americans pressed for land, even from allied tribes. The 1818 treaty at Edwardsville ceded 6.86 million acres of Illinois-Peoria land in return for $6,400 and 640 acres in Missouri. Under the Indian Removal Act of 1830, the United States brought even greater pressure on the Illinois Confederacy Indians to leave their homelands east of the Mississippi River and resettle west of it. The Weas came around 1827, followed by the Piankashaws and more Weas in 1832. In 1832 the Peorias and Kaskaskias made the trek to the Marais des Cygnes (Marsh of the Swans) River, then later to the Osage River in Kansas. The Peorias, Kaskaskias, Weas, and Piankashaws shared 365,000 acres there. Baptiste Peoria at Paola led a movement to revive Peoria Indian identity and at the same time accommodate to acculturation pressure.

Various members of the Illinois Confederacy came to reside in Kansas. The Peorias, Weas, Piankashaws, and Kaskaskias were the four major parts of the confederacy, but remnants of other groups also participated, such as Tamaroas, Cahokias, Michigameas, Moingweas, Pepikokias, Mascoutens, a few Kickapoos, and several Brotherton Indians. Squatters, swindlers, and railroad schemers connived with Kansas politicians over Indian lands. Growing pressure there through the 1840s led tribespeople to decide that they had to confederate to survive. In 1854 the Peorias, Weas, Piankashaws, and Kaskaskias came together. Under the terms of a treaty with commissioner of Indian affairs George Manypenny at the end of May that year, the United States recognized the "Confederated Peorias" and provided for allotment of 160 acres each (totaling 41,440 acres), citizenship, and opening the "surplus" land to white settlers. The federal government counted 259 Confederated Peorias. Another 163 Peorias migrated to Indian Territory. The Peorias obtained land for $24,000 in the northern half of the Seneca-Shawnee reserve and from a portion of the Quapaw reserve. It would be their third removal to a new "homeland." Through the Omnibus Treaty in February 1867 the United States provided for their removal to Indian Territory. Although 55 Citizen Peorias elected to stay in Kansas on allotments as citizens, most favored removal to Indian Territory, where they could begin anew.

The Miamis, a tribe closely related to the Illinois, settled to the west of them. In 1873 the Miamis united with the Peorias. The Omnibus Treaty mentioned the merger, but the union was not then formalized and quietly dissolved sometime during the 1920s.

Roman Catholic missionaries came early. Other missionaries worked among the Peoria tribes. Baptists labored after 1840 among the Weas. Children in Kansas attended the Shawnee mission school (Methodist) and a Presbyterian mission school for short periods. Under President Grant's peace policy, Quakers set up schools for Indian students in Indian Territory in the 1870s. The federal government assumed management of them during the following decade. The U.S. government opened Seneca Indian School to Peoria youths in 1897.

The Peorias were granted citizenship in 1890, and 153 individuals received allotments in 1893. Sales of Indian lands after 1902 eroded the tribal land base, so by 1915 no restricted tribal land remained and loss accelerated. The first lead ore that led to the mining bonanza in the Tri-State District, however, was discovered on the Peoria Reservation. John McNaughton, an intermarried Peoria, leased land after allotment to start mining operations. The Peorias opened the first Indian Territory lead and zinc mines. Some achieved great wealth that eased their lives. Others continued to prosper as farmers and laborers. Some Peorias served in the U.S. military in World War I and World War II.

In the immediate post–World War II period Congress authorized tribes to bring land claims suits in an effort to finalize and settle outstanding concerns. The Peorias began their claims case in 1946. An act of Congress (Public Law 364 in 1970) awarded the tribe $5.7 million to settle the claims. Much of it was distributed on a per capita basis to tribal members. A 1978 settlement of claims was awarded in 1984 and amounted to $6.5 million. Over two thousand descendants shared in the distributions.

As a result of the conservative political atmosphere in the 1950s, the federal government terminated supervision of the Peoria Tribe and its property under the terms of Public Law 84-921 in August 1956. After termination in August 1959, the only tribal land remaining was the four-acre Peoria cemetery. Congress reversed itself and restored federal recognition to the Peoria Tribe through Public Law 95-281 on May 15, 1978.

The Peorias today maintain old traditions, but in a modern context. They enjoy powwows with neighboring tribes, especially at the high bluff called the Devil's Promenade overlooking Spring River. Their own annual powwow celebration is held during June. In the 1990s the Peorias held their first South-Wind Dance in over a century. It was a stomp dance.

Peorias remain concerned about the possible impact of Tar Creek contamination in their region. They also are interested in the mascot issue swirling around the University of Illinois "Chief Iliniwek," because the Peorias historically resided in the region and are concerned about the portrayal of Indians in contemporary society.

The imprint of the Peorias remains on the geography as a lasting reminder of their legacy within their historic territory. Kaskaskia is the name of a township in Randolph and Fayette counties in Illinois as well as a river and state park. A city in Illinois and a small town in Indiana (in Miami County) are named Peoria, as well as similarly named towns in Iowa, Texas, Mississippi, North Carolina, and Oklahoma. There are towns named Paoli (a variant of "Peoria") in Kansas, Indiana, Pennsylvania, Wisconsin, Colorado, and Oklahoma. Wea Creek flows through Tippecanoe County, Indiana, before emptying into the Wabash River outside Lafayette.

Notable Peorias include Baptiste Peoria (Lan-e-pe-shaw), who moved to Miami County, Kansas, with the Peoria Tribe and became a storekeeper. Multilingual, he served as a chief and an interpreter. He led the Indians in a cultural revival and on their removal journey into Indian Territory. Fannie Kennerly (Wea) was an extra in Hollywood movies like *Cheyenne Autumn, Cimarron*, and *Daniel Boone*. In 1987 the National Congress of American Indians presented its Youth Leadership Award to Peoria tribal princess Charla Key Reevers for her outstanding record of achievement. Guy Willis Froman played baseball with the St. Louis Cardinals (1921–32) before becoming longtime tribal chief in 1947. David Froman was a stage and television actor. Moscelyne Larkin Jasinski was a splendid ballerina with the Ballet Russe.

SUGGESTED READING

Goddard, Ives. "Central Algonquian Languages." In vol. 15, *Northeast,* of the *Handbook of North American Indians,* 583–93. Washington, D.C.: Smithsonian Institution, 1978.

Kinietz, W. Vernon. *The Indians of the Western Great Lakes, 1615–1760.* Ann Arbor: University of Michigan Press, 1940.

Roberson, Glen. "The Homeless Peorias." In Robert E. Smith, ed., *Oklahoma's Forgotten Indians,* 39–52. Oklahoma City: Oklahoma Historical Society, 1981.

Valley, Dorris, and Mary M. Lembcke, eds. *The Peorias: A History of the Peoria Indian Tribe of Oklahoma*. Miami: Peoria Indian Tribe of Oklahoma, 1991.

Ponca

The Poncas refer to themselves as Ponka or Ppakkã, which was also the name of a clan or subclan among the Kansas, Osages, and Quapaws. Its meaning is unclear.

LOCATION AND GOVERNMENT

The headquarters for the "Ponca Tribe of Oklahoma" is at White Eagle in Kay County, about five miles south of Ponca City. The former school at White Eagle serves as the tribal affairs building. Tonkawa and Red Rock are nearby American Indian centers for neighboring tribes. The Ponca Tribe is organized under the provisions of the OIWA. It approved a constitution in 1950, which provides for four business committee members, a chair, a vice chair, and a secretary-treasurer, elected to staggered two-year terms. There is no tribal website yet.

BUSINESSES

The Oklahoma tribe gains most of its income from its Blue Star Gaming and Casino, located on Highway 177 near the tribal headquarters. The tribe owns 1,700 acres of trust land as well, and its members hold 13,000 acres of individual land allotments. The land provides farming, ranching, oil and gas, and leasing income.

NUMBER

The tribe has just over 3,300 members, most in communities and rural areas surrounding the tribal headquarters in Kay County. Others are out of state for employment, military service, and other reasons. There are approximately 2,600 members of the Ponca Tribe of Nebraska (terminated by Congress in the 1960s then reinstated in 1990), which has its headquarters in the community of Lake Andes in South Dakota just over the state line with Nebraska.

The Poncas are related to other Dhegiha Siouan–speakers like the Omahas, Osages, Kansas, and Quapaws. Dhegiha is a branch of the larger Siouan language family. According to academics and oral tribal tradition, these tribes were at one time a part of one mother group. Archeologists believe that they resided along the Ohio River or Wabash River south of Lake Erie and were a part of Oneota culture. They moved along the Ohio River as one people until they reached its mouth. There they began to separate. At the Mississippi River some went upriver (like the Omaha-Poncas), while others went downriver (like the Quapaws). The Omahas and Poncas lived in the area of modern St. Louis. At the mouth of the Osage River the Omahas and Poncas crossed the Missouri River and traveled to the red pipestone site in present-day Minnesota. Scholar Dale Henning concluded that the Dhegiha Siouans entered the Plains after A.D. 1300. Others suggest an earlier time frame. The Indians traveled southwest to the area near the Black Hills. Archeological records indicate that the large Oneota site called Blood Run was Omaha-Ponca for two centuries of its existence. The Indians resided on the Big Sioux River near present Sioux City, Iowa, until a terrible battle with the Dakotas, whereupon the Omaha-Poncas moved south. They met Arikaras in northeastern Nebraska, warred with them, then made peace. The Poncas learned how to build earth lodges from the Arikaras. Oral tradition states that the Omahas and the Poncas then separated. The Poncas were at the mouth of the Niobrara River. Omaha oral stories maintained that their famous sacred pole, housed for years in the Peabody Museum at Harvard University, was cut before the tribal split. The Poncas acquired their first horses from either the Lipan Apaches or the Comanches (called the Padoucas) and, in turn, passed some along to the Omahas, but after their separation.

The Omahas and Poncas may have been carriers of Mississippian traits onto the prairies after 1300 and later may have been at Mill Creek sites in South Dakota. Mill Creek peoples acquired Upper Republican and some Woodland traits, perhaps moving from Minnesota to Iowa to South Dakota, according to archeologist James B. Griffin. Poncas claimed long residence in the vicinity of the Niobrara River. Archeological investigation has not yet proven Ponca occupation of sites like Ponca Fort near the mouth of Ponca Creek (a tributary to the Missouri River) in Knox County, Nebraska. It was a village defended behind a palisade with bastions and a defensive ditch. The fort is believed to have been a late Ponca occupation and shows Arikara influence in later pottery remains. It may date to the 1790s and may show that some Poncas took Arikara wives who stubbornly clung to the use of old-fashioned clay pottery vessels when Ponca women used newer metal kettles for their cooking, since remains of both have been found at the site.

Linguists James Springer and Stanley Witkowski believed that the Dhegiha Siouans split from Proto-Chiwere-Winnebago Indians about A.D. 1000. Three centuries later the Dhegihans began separating from each other. Other linguists have placed the separations both earlier and later. Perhaps the Poncas still lived as one with the Omahas at the vast village called Blood Run in the late 1600s. James Howard suggested a separation date of 1715. After the 1790s Ponca settlements were identified on Ponca Creek, where they remained into the nineteenth century.

Chief Standing Buffalo's account in the nineteenth century told about the creation of the Poncas. Wakanda (or Wakkada), the Great Mystery or Powerful One, created the cosmos, the land, and the people. After placing the Poncas on the land, Wakanda instructed them to travel westward. For a long time the Poncas wandered, crossing a large body of water. One day they met another tribe, the Omahas. The two became friends and journeyed together toward the West. Wakanda gave the Poncas the bow and showed them how to hunt and also provided dogs to aid their hunting and to carry burdens for them. Wakanda provided the Poncas with a grain of corn and told them to plant it. The two nations eventually came to the Nishude (Missouri River), and the Omahas settled along it. The Poncas traveled upstream to the conjunction with the Niubthatha (Niobrara) and made their home there.

Omaha oral stories credited the Arikaras with introducing corn horticulture and the earth lodge to them and to the Poncas. Sometime around 1700 the Poncas adopted Arikara ceramics. The Poncas also were influenced by Teton and Yankton Dakotas. Ponca Fort (at the site called Nanza) archeological remains showed distinctive Coalescent characteristics, which are tied to the Arikaras. Pottery from the Redbird focus demonstrates possible relationships to the Lower Loup phase (ancestral Pawnee) of the central Plains and to the LaRoche focus (Arikara) of the Middle Missouri era. James Howard, who wrote extensively on the Poncas, accepted these links. Adaptations from the regional cultures where they set down their roots characterized all Dhegiha Siouan emigrants. It has not yet been possible to differentiate very many Ponca archeological sites with exactitude, because of the admixture of other cultural traditions in suspected sites.

The Poncas shared a similar social organization with the Iowas, Kansas, and Osages, all Dhegiha Siouans. They held to a dual division of their universe and their camps. They also adhered to common forms of religious ceremonies to placate the major forces in their lives, to award war honors, to name their children, and to mark births and deaths. Dhegihans shared an oral tradition of mythology about emergence from water and a subsequent creation of clans with Algonquian tradition, hinting at a connection in the dim past. Cultural similarities in their core beliefs and practices among the Dhegiha Siouans, the Chiwere Siouans, and Central Algonquian peoples imply a common prehistoric origin.

Poncas resided in permanent earth-lodge villages. Women raised corn, beans, and squash in their nearby fields. Men went out on an annual or semiannual buffalo hunt, sometimes with Omaha relations and sometimes with Tetons. The ultimate animosity of the Tetons, however, halted Ponca buffalo hunts after 1855. The Poncas were divided into Gray Blanket (Waixude) and Fish Smell (Hubdo) bands. The former camped near Ponca Creek, the latter in a location near the contemporary town of Verdel nearby. Each of the eight clans had a northern and a southern subdivision, with additional subgroupings.

The Poncas held a wide range of rituals. Supernatural power, *xube,* was everywhere and could be shared by those who underwent a vision quest or particular rituals or through medicine bundles and their owners. The major annual one was the Sun Dance, performed just prior to the buffalo hunt. Bundle rituals and renewals also took place during the summer, as well as ceremonies in the Medicine Lodge, which was similar to the Ojibwe Midewiwin. Very likely Poncas utilized priests on an individual basis for healing. They also put on their Pipe dance (Wa-wa) as their Calumet dance, which they may have received from the Pawnees.

The Poncas were patrilineal. Clans were further divided into subdivisions and subclans. The principal chief was the head of the leading clan (Wasabe, "black bear"), who cared for the tribal Pipe. He was advised on issues of peace and war by the first and second chiefs, who were also religious leaders.

The Omahas and Poncas are believed to have been platted on a 1718 map drawn by the French cartographer Guillaume de L'Isle. The Omahas (called the "Mahas") and the Poncas (termed "errant Omahas" or "wandering Omahas") are east of the Missouri River. Researcher James Howard did not discover them on any other early maps until one dated 1786, which placed the Poncas on the Missouri between Ponca Creek and the Niobrara River.

The Frenchman Jean-Baptiste Monier worked for the Spanish and traded with the Poncas in 1789 and thereafter received a monopoly to trade with them. French trader Jean Baptiste de Trudeau in 1794–95 set up Ponca House slightly north of the tribe on the Missouri River as a trade center. Other traders also worked the region. By 1795 the Poncas were stopping vessels on the Missouri River and confiscating their goods. They lived at their village above the mouth of Ponca Creek when visited by Lewis and Clark (1804), explorer H. M. Brackenridge (1811), and the Henry Atkinson/Benjamin O'Fallon party (1825). During this period Sioux attacks reduced the Ponca population. Many Ponca village sites have been identified along the Niobrara River at this time. The best-known of them was Backing Water Village situated on Bazile Creek (also called White Paint Creek).

Ponca leaders signed their first treaty (a treaty of friendship) with the United States in 1817 then another in 1825 for trade and commercial regulations under U.S. authority. White settlers squatted on rich river bottom land. Painter George Catlin visited the Poncas in 1841 and estimated that 500 people lived in a single village in buffalo hide "tents." The artist painted a portrait of the chief, Smoke. In 1858 the Poncas agreed to a reduced reservation along the Niobrara River in Nebraska. Delayed ratification and lack of annuity support led them to return to former lands, which by then had been occupied by white settlers.

A final treaty, at Fort Laramie (1868), assigned some 96,000 acres of Ponca territory to the Great Sioux Reservation. This was a flagrant violation of past pledges to the Poncas. In 1876 Congress claimed the remaining Ponca territory and authorized the tribe's removal to Indian Territory, all without telling the Poncas. The Indians reminded U.S. officials that tribal members had never taken up arms against the United States, but to no avail. Eight Ponca leaders were selected to accompany an official to locate a new area in Indian Territory. When the Poncas refused to choose new lands, the official abandoned them. The Indians walked more than five hundred miles back to their homes in forty days. Lieutenant John Bourke noted that as the Poncas journeyed they were "molesting nobody, and subsisted upon charity. Not a shot was fired at anyone; not so much as a dog was stolen."

After returning home, the Poncas continued to resist their eviction. They subsequently reported that the local Indian Office official withheld rations for two weeks then sent troops with fixed bayonets to kick in doors and force the Poncas onto waiting wagons. In the agent's defense, he claimed that he verbally persuaded recalcitrant tribe members of the futility of resistance and successfully prepared them for their journey. He always denied using any force. Of course, the agent himself did not use force; he ordered others to do so.

The Poncas refer to their trek as their "Trail of Tears." Conditions were miserable during the two months of travel, with heavy rains, floods, a tornado, constant illness, and deaths. Finally they arrived at their destination. The emigrants lived in tents at the Quapaw Agency just south of Baxter Springs, Kansas, in the far northeastern corner of what would become Oklahoma. While briefly at Quapaw, the Poncas made the acquaintance of southern Kansas cattleman George Miller, who would come to play a larger role, threading in and out of their lives. Dissatisfied with their surroundings and the lack of preparations for their arrival, the Poncas insisted on another location. They selected an area of 101,894 acres along the Salt Fork River above its junction with the Arkansas River in north-central Oklahoma. Poncas began filtering onto their new lands, with an official journey there in July 1878. Malnutrition, poor conditions, sickness, and death continued to stalk the Poncas. Within two years a third of the tribe had died. Thirty-six had remained in the North among their Omaha kinfolk.

During their sojourn leader Standing Bear attended to his family's needs. In Indian Territory his beloved eldest son died. Sixty-four others who were disheartened joined his reverse trek, to return his son's body for burial in the tribal heartland in Nebraska. U.S. troops arrested them, however, because they were absent from a reservation (and the authority of the agent, representing the U.S. government) without official authorization. Following a noteworthy trial in Omaha, Nebraska, the court in *U.S. ex rel. Standing Bear* v. *Crook* (1879) released the Ponca leader, stating that an American Indian was a person within the meaning of the law and thereby fell under the protection of the U.S. Constitution. American Indians, in other words, had individual rights when they voluntarily left their tribe. The decision foretold the thrust of the allotment policy that was soon to come. Standing Bear was freed to bury his son (the casket had been stored in an Omaha meat-packing locker during the trial).

Afterward a publicity tour of the East helped stir great public concern over the mistreatment of the Poncas and the cruelty of forced removals. Indian reform advocate Helen Hunt Jackson termed their forced removal a "high-handed outrage" and called for congressional action on their behalf. A Senate committee in 1880 announced that "a great wrong had been done the Ponca Indians," and a commission of inquiry concluded the following year that incredible government mismanagement had added to Ponca misery. That year Congress indemnified the Poncas $165,000. The money went toward infrastructure on their Indian Territory reservation. Standing Bear and about 170 Poncas remained in Nebraska (he died there in 1908). The Sioux negotiated for a return of some land for the Poncas, from which a reservation allotted individually to the Poncas was established in Nebraska. The 1879 difficulties split the Poncas into two divisions. Those who opted to stay in the North are known as the Osni-Ponka or Usni Ppakkã, "cold Poncas." Those who are in Oklahoma (who came under the guidance of Chief White Eagle) are called the Maste-Ponka or Maste-Ppakkaã, "warm Poncas" or "hot country Poncas."

The United States consolidated the Poncas with the Pawnees and the Otoe-Missourias into one agency in 1882. President Benjamin Harrison ordered allotment for the Poncas in 1890. In spite of fervent opposition, the reservation was allotted. The machinations of cattleman George Miller uniquely altered the face of Ponca landholding. His family leased much pasturage before allotment then after allotment "purchased" a considerable amount of the acreage for the famous 101 Ranch. Patriarch George Miller died in 1903, but his widow and sons carried on the ranching business. It is a coincidence that the cattle ranch's numerical designation matched the total amount of acreage of the Ponca Reservation. The Miller brothers' operation became a show place for Bill Pickett's steer wrestling, Wild West shows, and eventually early Western motion pictures featuring Tom Mix, Hoot Gibson, and others. Wrangler Tom Mix, a bartender in the Blue Belle Saloon in Guthrie to the south of the ranch, served drinks to the Miller brothers and was hired by them. Ernest Marland, an acquaintance of the Miller brothers, looked over the property, believed it had oil underneath it, obtained the Ponca leader's approval to drill, and brought in a gusher. Marland Oil Company was the forerunner of Conoco. The discovery of oil pushed the takeover of Indian land, and much of it passed into non-Indian hands. The exploitation of petroleum reserves on the reservation and on adjoining land gave great wealth to a few but polluted the groundwater and the streams and rivers of the former reservation.

Methodists established a mission at White Eagle, where the Ponca Boarding School (1880–1919) was also located. The town was the site of the agency. The railroad came in the mid-1880s, gradually increasing the population. Ponca City began with the Cherokee Strip land opening in 1893. A population explosion occurred in the aftermath of Marland's discovery of oil on the former reservation in June 1911.

In 1902 either a Cheyenne or a Tonkawa introduced the Peyote religion to the Poncas. Many adopted the Half Moon version of it. When followers incorporated in 1918, Frank Eagle (Ponca) was elected the first president of the main church and fellow tribesman Louis McDonald became treasurer. About the same time as the introduction of the Peyote ceremonies, the Pawnees brought the Ghost Dance as well as their hand game to the Poncas, who still play the game. The Heduska (or Heouska) was an important Ponca warrior society dance. It was a war dance in which the male dancer wore a headdress and a Crow belt (bustle) that denoted membership and rank in the society. The women's version was called the Nuda. After the Poncas were confined to the reservation about 1880 the dance took on a religious aura, likely derived from the Dream or Drum dance of the era, which swept through reservations. The performance now forms an integral part of evenings at powwow gatherings. Many powwows include Ponca songs for their drums and singers. Representatives from the Poncas of Oklahoma and Nebraska met in February 2007 on the campus of Haskell Indian University in Kansas to confer about preserving the Ponca language. It was their first meeting in 125 years.

In the early 1990s the Conoco refining company south of Ponca City responded to complaints of groundwater contamination by purchasing homes in the area, leveling them, and creating a stand of trees. The southern part became Standing Bear Park, named in honor of the nineteenth-century Indian leader. His statue, two stories tall, dominates the green space. There is another statue of Standing Bear in Niobrara, Nebraska. At the start of the twenty-first century tribal members joined with labor union representatives to protest alleged environmental violations as a result of emissions and pollution derived from the Continental Carbon Company plant (two miles south of Ponca City), which made carbon black used in tires. Eleven tribal households were in the area of a wastewater lagoon. There were allegations that the union exploited tribal fears as the result of a company lockout of union workers. The state's Department of Environmental Quality worked with the company to achieve a cleanup. The tribe subsequently received a $908,000 grant from the rural utilities services division of the U.S. Department of Agriculture for a wastewater treatment system in 2001. That was used to resolve a situation blocking the construction of a

Traditional dancer Abe Conklin (Ponca and Osage)

Photograph by Don Drefke. Courtesy Sandy Rhodes.

tribal wellness center for the community. It enabled the tribe to build infrastructure needed for long-term economic growth.

Ponca members today remain active on the powwow circuit. The tribal powwow is held annually in the last week of August at the tribal dance ground at White Eagle. Men engage each other in games of shinny, a lacrosse-like contest played on a grassy field through the month of April as a part of spring rites. Peyote ceremonies, dances, hand games, and other activities mark special calendar events like Easter, Christmas, New Year's, and other occasions. Veterans' and women's auxiliary groups support Poncas serving in military service in wartime. Ponca tribal members also participate in Baptist, Methodist, and Full Gospel church activities.

Notable Poncas include the late Abe Conklin (who was also Osage), an internationally recognized traditional dancer. Over the years he often served as a mentor to me. Casey Camp-Horinek acted in the Public Broadcasting System program *The Trial of Standing Bear* and played a leading role in the television series *Lakota Moon* on the Fox network. She also served as cultural advisor and hairdresser for actors in the ABC-TV miniseries *Son of Morningstar.* Clyde Warrior was an activist during the 1960s, calling on his fellow college-educated Indian youths to join the Indian militant cause. He co-founded the National Indian Youth Council in 1961. Thomas Roughface served devotedly for years as a pastor in

Activist Clyde Warrior (Ponca)
Courtesy Della Warrior

the Oklahoma Indian Missionary Conference of the United Methodist Church and was its superintendent at the time of his premature death. He was also active in powwow dances. His daughter, Barbara Warner, serves as executive director of the Oklahoma Indian Affairs Commission. Carter Camp was a rare "southern" Indian militant who was visibly active as an officer in the American Indian Movement (AIM) in the 1970s. He participated in the 1973 occupation of Wounded Knee in South Dakota. Ponca painters include Paladine Roy and Brent Greenwood (who is also Chickasaw). Yellow Thunder Woman is a lyricist and singer.

SUGGESTED READING

Bourke, John Gregory. *On the Border with Crook*. Lincoln: University of Nebraska Press, 1971 (quotation on 427).

Henning, Dale. "The Adaptive Patterning of the Dhegiha Sioux." *Plains Anthropologist* 38, no. 146 (November 1993): 253–64.

Howard, James H. *The Ponca Tribe*. Bulletin 195. Washington, D.C.: Bureau of American Ethnology, 1965; repr. Lincoln: University of Nebraska Press, 1995 (includes discussion of Griffin).

Jackson, Helen Hunt. *A Century of Dishonor* (originally published 1888). New York: Indian Head Books, 1993.

Logt, Mark van de. " 'The Land Is Always with Us': Removal, Allotment, and Industrial Development and Their Effects on Ponca Tribalism." *Chronicles of Oklahoma* 83 (Fall 2005): 326–41.

Mathes, Valerie Sherer, and Richard Lowitt. *The Standing Bear Controversy: Prelude to Indian Reform*. Urbana: University of Illinois Press, 2003.

Springer, James, and Stanley Witkowski. "Siouan Historical Linguistics and Oneota Archaeology." In Guy Gibbon, ed., *Oneota Studies*, 69–83. Minneapolis: University of Minnesota, 1982.

The Trial of Standing Bear. Lincoln: Nebraska Educational Television, 1988 (PBS program).

U.S. Senate. Select Committee. Testimony Relating to the Removal of the Ponca Indians, Sen. Report No. 670, 46th Cong., 2nd Sess., Serial Set No. 1898, 1880 (remarks of Chairman Henry L. Dawes, February 14, 1880, on 83).

Wishart, David J. *An Unspeakable Sadness: The Dispossession of the Nebraska Indians*. Lincoln: University of Nebraska Press, 1994; repr. 1997.

Citizen Potawatomi

NAME

The tribal name is derived from the Ojibwe word "Potawatomink" or "Potewatmi," "people of the place of the fire." The Potawatomis retained the council fire of the three related tribes or three brothers: Potawatomi, Ojibwe, and Ottawa. All shared the Algonquian language. There is, however, much debate over the meaning of the tribal name. The "Citizen" designation came from the Treaty of 1861 between the Potawatomis and the United States, which stated that those who consented to sell their Kansas land would become citizens and ultimately move to Indian Territory. The Citizen Potawatomis refer to themselves as Neshnabek or Nasnape, "true People."

LOCATION AND GOVERNMENT

The "Citizen Potawatomi Nation of Oklahoma" tribal headquarters is just south of the city of Shawnee (fifty miles east of Oklahoma City) in Pottawatomie County in central Oklahoma. The tribe organized under the OIWA. Its 1938 constitution was amended in 1985. The tribal government consists of a five-member business committee, including a chair. Members are elected to staggered four-year terms. Members voted in 1996 to delete the word "band" from their tribal name. In 2006 the tribe opened an impressive 30,000-square-foot Cultural Heritage Center in Shawnee, highlighting the tribe's history. The tribal website is www.potawatomi.org.

BUSINESSES

The Citizen Potawatomi Nation today owns a wide array of economic enterprises. They had modest economic beginnings: in 1971 the nation owned only 2.5 acres. The Citizen Potawatomis were the first tribe in the state to open a convenience store and smoke shop in the 1970s and now operate several smoke shops. FireLake Grand Casino opened in 2006 and is one of the largest in the state, with 125,000 square feet of gaming space. It is also Oklahoma's first large casino under a state-tribal compact giving the state a share of slot machine activity. It is thirty miles east of Oklahoma City at the Dale/Bethel Acres interchange on Interstate 40 (exit 178) for Highway 102 (see www.firelakecasino.com). The tribe funded the revamping of the exit and the widened entry roadway to the casino. There are plans to develop an adjoining 1,100 acres into two golf courses, a hotel, and a coliseum for events. The tribe also managed the FireLake Entertainment Center (casino) south of Shawnee, a restaurant and golf course near the tribal headquarters, an RV park, a concrete company, an apparel concern, tribal stores (FireLake Discount Foods in Shawnee, one of the largest grocery stores in the state, and FireLake Discount Grocery in Tecumseh), and a tribal gift shop. Both grocery stores incorporate tribal tobacco stores. Some tribal land has oil and gas leases. The tribe owns an AM radio station.

The Citizen Potawatomis bought 5.2 acres of land east of Rossville, Kansas, and built a community center and duplexes on the site. The center serves as a meeting place for the estimated 3,500 tribal members who reside within a fifty-mile radius of Topeka and recalls the tribe's residence in Kansas (1838–67). The Citizen Potawatomis also bought First National Bank and Trust Company in Shawnee. It is the largest Indian-owned bank in the United States and has branches in the region. The tribe brought $137 million to the county in 2005, making it the largest employer in the county. The tribe owned 1,200 acres of land (in sharp contrast to the 2 acres owned in the 1950s), and individuals held 6,360 acres of allotted land. The tribal contribution to charities in 2005 amounted to $209,000, while the tribe paid over $1.1 million in state and federal tobacco and fuel taxes or their equivalents.

NUMBER

The tribe has just over 26,000 members, with a descendancy roll. The approximately 5,000 Citizen Potawatomis in Oklahoma are concentrated in the towns of Shawnee, Maud, Tecumseh, and Wanette. It is the ninth largest tribe in the United States and the largest of the federally recognized Potawatomi groups.

Some twenty groups in the United States and Canada identified as descendants of nineteenth-century Potawatomis. The strategic Great Lakes location made the Potawatomis important players in history. Conflicts dispersed them into many remnant groups that stubbornly cling to their heritage and their homeland. There are approximately 4,900 members of the federally recognized Prairie Band Potawatomis in Kansas, about twenty miles north of the city of Mayetta (north of Topeka). They are descendants of horse nomads who roamed over the Plains. Fewer than 200 of the Prairie Band descendants left Kansas and returned to their homeland in the nineteenth century. They are called the Wisconsin Rapids Potawatomis. The Hannahville community in the Upper Peninsula of Michigan, near Wilson, is federally recognized and numbers about 300. About 600 Forest County Potawatomis reside in two settlements, Stone Lake and Wabeno, in that county near Crandon in northern Wisconsin. They are now federally recognized but had been in the region for some time and were considered landless, called "strolling" Potawatomis. Just before World War I they received a reservation in the county. In 1994 the 800-member Notawaseppii Huron Band of Potawatomis was granted federal recognition. They reside on a reserve in southwestern Michigan within Calhoun County near Athens and are Methodist farmers. The Gun Lake group near Dorr, Michigan, is also federally recognized (1999). Members of the small Pokagon Potawatomi group, who are Roman Catholic, reside in southern Michigan in Cass County at Silver Lake near Dowagiac and Rush River north of Watervliet.

Scholars James Clifton and David Edmunds have documented numerous other Potawatomi descendants. Illinois and Wisconsin Potawatomis migrated to western Missouri. They then moved to Iowa and merged with the Mesquakie or Fox Indians in Tama. About 2,000 Potawatomis fled into Canada (1837–40), settling among Ojibwes and Ottawas north of Lake Huron and on islands like Walpole and Manitoulin. A few Potawatomis who were in northern Wisconsin melded into the Menominees. They numbered about 300 and were followers of the Dream Dance religion. They reside at Zoar, Michigan. Perhaps 500 Potawatomis in 1833 joined the Kickapoo prophet Kennekuk and settled on the Kansas Kickapoo reservation. There are also descendants among the Mexican Kickapoos. In all, more than 45,000 people internationally claim Potawatomi heritage.

Linguistics offers insight into the prehistory of the Potawatomis. Ives Goddard and others noted that Proto-Algonquian was spoken perhaps 3,000 years ago in the region between Georgian Bay and Lake Ontario. It fragmented into at least ten increasingly distinct languages. Ojibwe, Potawatomi, and Fox were still connected at the start of the language separations. Lexical studies indicated that Potawatomi-speakers early on moved away from Ojibwes and settled near the Foxes along the present Lower Peninsula of Michigan. Ojibwe oral tradition located the split at the Straits of Mackinac. Some linguists placed the Potawatomi migration on the lower eastern shore of Lake Michigan about 1500 B.C. Others dated the separation earlier and pointed to "prairie" influences among the Potawatomis not seen in Ojibwe and Ottawa cultural traits. They argued for a much older independence.

Ancestral peoples of the Central Algonquians lived in the far North. They are called Shield Archaic peoples for the Canadian geographic region. Western Shield Archaic peoples were predecessors of Central Algonquian–speakers. They lived west of Hudson Bay and moved eastward south of that bay and southward. Some of them became the Potawatomis. Archeologically, as David Brose noted, the present Upper and Lower Peninsulas of Michigan shared what is called Peninsula Woodland culture. It was marked by sometimes fortified villages occupied seasonally. Oval bark-covered wigwams sheltered several families. There is evidence of trade, but the extent of cultural influences (such as Mississippian and Oneota) is not clearly known. After about A.D. 1000 the Upper Peninsula developed into Juntunen culture, which may have used pottery from Green Bay. Complexes to the south probably utilized corn.

The historic Potawatomis resided along shorelines in villages sometimes palisaded for protection. Women raised corn, beans, squash, and pumpkins. They also seasonally gathered nuts, roots, and berries and harvested wild rice in marshlands. Men hunted game and waterfowl and fished. Tapping maple trees for syrup became a major social occasion in the spring. After a long winter, marriage and naming ceremonies were held with feasting. The Potawatomi houses were domed wigwams covered in birch bark. Elders met occasionally in a council representing the villages that made up the Potawatomis. Their society was organized along lines similar to those of the Kickapoos and Sacs, their kin and neighbors. The Potawatomi clans were patrilineal. From a dozen villages at the start of their contact with Europeans, the Potawatomis expanded to a peak of over a hundred villages in 1800, containing a mix of Potawatomis, traders, and members of other tribes. Expansion of Potawatomi territory most often involved a clan establishing a new settlement in a new region while maintaining ties to the parent village and lineage.

Clan sacred bundles dominated Potawatomi religious life. An origin myth, selected rituals, and specific songs accompanied each bundle, believed to have been given to the Potawatomis by their culture hero, Wiske. Each individual in the village was part of the dual division of society reflected among most American Indian tribes, with a Central Algonquian twist. The alignment grew from the order of birth, so the first, third, and fifth children were on the "senior side," while the second, fourth, and sixth were born to the "junior side." The Potawatomis borrowed the Midewiwin (a private healing society) from their Ojibwe kinfolk in the early eighteenth century. In addition, a number of rituals, dances, and feasts were performed on a seasonal cycle. Potawatomis consulted individual medicine persons both publicly and privately.

According to the Potawatomi origin story, in the beginning there was no earth, only a watery world. A lone birch-bark canoe carried Our Grandfather, an old man. Chief Muskrat climbed aboard and spoke. They conversed about the absence of any land. Muskrat volunteered to dive for some mud. He surfaced with some mud in his mouth. Our Grandfather requested help for the muskrat, who called other water-dwellers to aid him. The beaver, turtle, and otter responded. Each of them dove deeply into the sea and brought up some dirt. Using the mud, Our Grandfather formed dry land. Next he planted the Great Tree. He created other growing things, rivers, and valleys across the earth. Our Grandfather was Master of All Life (Wiske to the Potawatomis). While walking northward, he encountered naked humans. They said they were Neshnabek, "true People." Wiske informed them that he would teach them all they needed: how to make wigwams, how to use bark canoes, how to make ceramics, what to hunt and how to gather, and what to plant (corn, beans, squash). Wiske also provided each clan and village its own sacred bundle, Pitchkosan, "watches over us." He instructed the People in proper rituals. Wiske's twin was Chipiyapos, a destroyer and the opposite of Wiske. He kept the netherworld and taught the People about bad behavior, troubles, disunity, and death.

Jean Nicolet was the first French trader known to have contacted the Potawatomis. He encountered them at Red Bank on today's Door Peninsula (the part of Wisconsin that juts into Lake Michigan). He came in 1634 from the St. Lawrence Valley. His Huron Indian guides noted that these new people made a fire, which the Frenchman wrote as *pouut-ouatami* (over the years, after many changes, it became "Potawatomi").

Jesuit Claude Allouez worked among the Ottawas and then in 1669 began work among the Potawatomis. He brought other missionaries like Claude Dablon (1670) and Louis André. Allouez founded St. Francis Xavier Church among the Potawatomis at Green Bay.

At the height of their dominance of fur trading in their lower Great Lakes region for over a century, the Potawatomis employed neighboring tribes to aid them. The Potawatomis ranged widely in dugout and birch-bark canoes, challenging the Ottawas for the role of intermediaries.

Beginning in 1640 the conflict called the Beaver Wars pushed the Potawatomis out of their homeland in what is today the Lower Peninsula of Michigan. Attacks by members of the Neutral Nation forced the Potawatomis to relocate, first to present-day Sault Ste. Marie then to Green Bay. The Winnebagos suffered an epidemic, which opened the Green Bay region to the Potawatomis. Ironically, during the next decade the Iroquoian tribes poured out of New York and over Neutral and Huron territory in Ontario. The Iroquois tribes spread their empire south of the Great Lakes, driving tribes like the Potawatomis, Foxes, and Kickapoos westward. The Potawatomis settled along Green Bay and were joined by more fleeing refugees. Several times the Iroquois unsuccessfully attacked this fortified refuge.

Archeologists believe that the Rock Island II site on Michigan's Upper Peninsula was the palisaded village where agents for René-Robert Cavelier, Sieur de La Salle, spent the winter of 1678–79 making allies and trade partners. Potawatomi leader Shimmering Light (Onanguisse) was among the strongest French advocates. The tribe developed long-lasting economic, political, and even marriage ties with the French. Mixed-blood offspring would assume leadership roles in the tribe in the years ahead. In a large council held in 1668 the Potawatomis agreed to work with Nicholas Perrot, siding with the French in the fur trade. Perrot left a written account of the several months he spent there.

As the Iroquois warfare died down, fur trade profits rose. In the 1680s the Potawatomis moved. Some migrated to the vicinity of what is now Milwaukee. A few, most of the Great Sea and Bear clans, returned to their homeland along the St. Joseph River in southern Michigan. The Potawatomis kept moving for over a century. Their territory eventually covered the region from Ohio west to the Mississippi River and south along the Illinois and Wabash river valleys.

The Potawatomis actively aided French imperial raiding and warfare. During the French and Indian War, Potawatomis accompanied French and allied tribes in the shattering defeat of British major general Edward Braddock in early June 1755 near Fort Duquesne (now Pittsburgh,

Pennsylvania). Located at the forks of the Ohio River, the fort dominated western Pennsylvania and served as a gatekeeper of the channel into the territory of the southern Great Lakes. The large number of British horses that the Potawatomis acquired transformed their transportation mode. They gave up their canoes for their horses. The British ultimately won the war in 1763, however, stopped giving presents to Indians, and drove the French traders out of the field. The Potawatomis joined a wide Native uprising against the British, called Pontiac's Rebellion, in 1763.

During the American Revolution, Potawatomi loyalties were divided. Some sided with the Americans, others with the British, and a few tried to remain neutral. Blackbird (Sigenak or L'Etourneau) led a Potawatomi contingent that successfully attacked British positions in 1781 through the St. Joseph River Valley. After the American victory and the eventual formation of the constitutional government, the Potawatomis joined the British as well as a confederacy of Northwest tribes opposed to land cessions to the United States. The Indians won early victories but were defeated in the decisive battle at Fallen Timbers in August 1794 in the vicinity of modern Toledo, Ohio. The following year the Indians ceded lands in present-day Ohio and Indiana in the Treaty of Greenville. In a desperate attempt to maintain their traditional lands, they rallied behind Tecumseh in an Indian uprising during the War of 1812. It was western Potawatomi leader Main Poc who visited the Shawnee Prophet in late 1807 and persuaded him to relocate from Greenville about 120 miles to Prophetstown. The new location was near what is now Lafayette, Indiana, strategically at the junction of riverine and overland trade routes. The Indians ultimately lost and suffered even more cessions of their territories to the United States.

The Potawatomis resided in territory that the new republic coveted. It had been well positioned to dominate European trade routes and was also prime midwestern farmland. Between 1789 and 1867 the United States negotiated almost sixty cession treaties with the Potawatomis, nearly twice as many as with any other tribe. At the same time conditions surrounding the Potawatomis radically changed. Trade evaporated; game vanished as a new white population pressed in; local residents seized Indian resources; the liquor trade demoralized tribespeople; and the influence of mixed-bloods increased. Beginning in the 1820s and continuing into the next decade, these forces fragmented the Potawatomis.

After the Indian Removal Act (1830), the Potawatomis were placed under great pressure to relinquish their lands. The St. Joseph Potawatomis were forced to leave their territory along the Wabash River in what is today northern Indiana in 1838 and to trek 620 miles to eastern Kansas over what they called the "Potawatomi Trail of Death." They were also called the Wabash, Mission, or Christian Band and were considered to be "progressives." They would later become the Citizen Potawatomi Nation of Oklahoma. Father Benjamin Petit accompanied them and left a touching written account of their sorrowful journey. In 1841 other Potawatomis traveled to Council Bluffs, Iowa. They were "traditionalists" who were called the Forest or Prairie Band. Potawatomis from Illinois and Wisconsin merged with them in 1847, and they all resettled on the Kansas River west of the present city of Topeka. They lived together until the post–Civil War era.

Fate placed the Potawatomis again on a major communication route. The Santa Fe Trail emerged out of Westport and passed along the Kansas River through the Potawatomi Reservation, and the Oregon Trail was close by. During the 1840s–50s some 250,000 people followed those routes through their valley, including a few Potawatomis who dispersed into the Far West. Railroad promoters also increased pressure on the Potawatomis, hoping to secure a central transcontinental route. Promoters arranged for a new treaty. Under the terms of a treaty (12 Stat. 1191) in 1861, members of the Mission Band accepted allotment in severalty and citizenship, but they quickly lost their lands as a result of unscrupulous speculators, taxes, and opportunists. They took the name "Citizen Band." The conservative Prairie Band nearby took a smaller eleven-square-mile reserve within their original reservation that they continued to own in common until it also was forcibly allotted and most of the land was lost. The bulk of the reservation "surplus" land went to the Atchison, Topeka, and Santa Fe Railroad.

The Citizen Band of Potawatomis, which was dominated by Roman Catholic mixed-bloods, responded favorably to the prodding of the BIA and signed a treaty on February 27, 1867, in Washington, D.C., that provided for removal to Indian Territory. They sold what little remained of their Kansas land and moved, as Joseph Murphy detailed in his history. Their new reservation encompassed 575,870 acres or 30 miles square next door to the Seminoles in central Indian Territory. From the enactment of 17 Stat. 159 on May 23, 1872, to 1891, the United States allotted a total of 215,679 acres to 1,498 Citizen Band Potawatomis. Although the Potawatomis gradually adjusted to Indian Territory, by the late 1920s the Indians at the Shawnee Agency, which included the Citizen Band, had per capita average incomes that were one-half the national average in the United States, according to the national Meriam Report.

Schools set up for the Potawatomis included Sacred Heart Mission, which began in 1876 under the guidance of Father Isidore Robot. Much later it served as the basis for St. Gregory's University (1913) in Shawnee. One of Sacred Heart's most notable graduates was Tony Hillerman, the novelist of the American Southwest. He and his brother lived on a nearby farm and were young enough to attend the girls' school at Sacred Heart. Another famous graduate was Jim Thorpe, the Sac and Fox Olympic athlete, whose mother was Citizen Potawatomi. Residents in the region established a series of day and mission schools through the early years. The girls' boarding school lasted until 1945.

Sacred Heart
School

*Hillerman
Collection,
Research
Division of
the Oklahoma
Historical
Society,
#21412.BH.85*

Potawatomi land claims against the U.S. government have proven to be exceedingly complex. Potawatomi contact with the American Republic goes far back in time, and Potawatomi territory extended across much of the western Great Lakes region. Claims are still pending. Conflict with the state tax commission through the 1980s also led to litigation. The state claimed lost tax revenue from tribal tobacco sales. The tribe pointed to its sovereignty. In *Citizen Band Potawatomi Indian Tribe* v. *the Oklahoma Tax Commission*, the U.S. Supreme Court issued a mixed opinion in 1991 that upheld both tribal sovereignty and the state's authority to tax sales to non-Indians. Several tribes thereafter entered into tobacco compacts with the state of Oklahoma. Nine years later the Supreme Court ruled that the tribe lost its sovereign immunity when it signed a roofing construction contract (with C&L Enterprises). The document required arbitration in a nontribal arena to settle disputes.

The Citizen Potawatomis in Oklahoma sponsor an annual Family Reunion Festival and Powwow. Large crowds participate in the June event. Citizen Potawatomis actively record elders and use the tribal language to teach their youth. The tribe pursues a language and cultural heritage effort using computer technology. A Potawatomi Language Advisory Committee was founded in 1994 as a multitribal body. The annual Gathering of the Potawatomi Nation, bringing representatives from all groups together, contributes to the study of the language. A 1996 international survey located only fifty-two Potawatomi-speakers. Elders bestow tribal names during local ceremonies.

Some Potawatomis remain ardently Roman Catholic. They visit the sites of now abandoned Sacred Heart Mission in Pottawatomie County and remember the mission in an annual powwow. Some also make a pilgrimage to St. Mary's in Kansas to pay homage not only to their faith but also to the sacrifices of their ancestors. The priests from Osage Mission fled to St. Mary's during the Civil War for safety. The church mission was also the location of the vision that founded the Potawatomi Dream Dance. St. Mary's Sugar Creek Mission is now called St. Philippine Duchesne Shrine. In addition, Potawatomi tribal members join in living history festivals in Indiana and participate in historic reenactments and period dances, music, and preparation of foods. State legislatures in Illinois, Indiana, Missouri, and Kansas passed resolutions in 1993–95 supporting the designation of the Potawatomi emigrants' route in 1838 as the Trail of Death Regional Historic Trail. Vehicle caravans have retraced the route as part of the commemoration. Members of the Bartlesville Indian Women's Club, including Potawatomi participants, sponsored a 1997 exhibit of appliqué clothing traditions in the museum at Prophetstown near Lafayette, Indiana. Some had ancestors who had resided there two centuries earlier.

Notable Potawatomis include the well-known painter Woody Crumbo, whose renditions of Spirit Horses adorn walls across the United States. Another painter in the tribe is Matthew Bearden. Jack Woolridge authored a series of children's fables during the 1990s. Country singer Kellie Coffey produced hit singles and CDs. Her voice sings "White Christmas" during the snowfall onto Main Street as tourists walk through Disneyland Theme Parks. Mike Rich writes screenplays for films such as *Miracle*, which told the story of the gold-medal-winning hockey Team USA in the 1980 Olympics. Jack Ackers was a Yankee relief pitcher, and John Henry Johnson pitched for Oakland. William Wano led the Arkansas Travelers team in winning the 1920 baseball Southern Association Pennant. Michigan-raised Simon Pokagon served as chief of the Potawatomis in that state and wrote a number of books on Indians. Albert Negahnquet, born in Kansas, was the first full-blood Indian Roman Catholic priest (1903) in the United States.

SUGGESTED READING

Brose, David. "Late Prehistory of the Upper Great Lakes Area." In vol. 15, *Northeast,* of the *Handbook of North American Indians,* 569–82. Washington, D.C.: Smithsonian Institution, 1978.

Chapman, Berlin B. "The Pottawatomie and Absentee Shawnee Reservation." *Chronicles of Oklahoma* 34 (Autumn 1946): 293–305.

Clifton, James A. *The Potawatomi.* New York: Chelsea House, 1987 (for young readers).

———. *The Prairie People: Change and Continuity in Potawatomi Indian Culture, 1665–1965.* Lawrence: Regents Press of Kansas, 1977; repr. Iowa City: University of Iowa Press, 1998.

Edmunds, R. David. *The Potawatomis: Keepers of the Fire.* Norman: University of Oklahoma Press, 1978.

Goddard, Ives. "Central Algonquian Languages." In vol. 15, *Northeast,* of the *Handbook of North American Indians,* 583–93. Washington, D.C.: Smithsonian Institution, 1978.

Horton, Loren N. "A Forest People on the Plains: The Potawatomi Indians." In Robert E. Smith, ed., *Oklahoma's Forgotten Indians,* 24–38. Oklahoma City: Oklahoma Historical Society, 1981.

Kraft, Lisa. "Thrice Purchased: Acquisition and Allotment of the Citizen Potawatomi Reservation." *Chronicles of Oklahoma* 86 (Spring 2008): 64–87.

Murphy, Joseph. *Potawatomi of the West: Origins of the Citizen Band.* Shawnee: Citizen Potawatomi Nation, 1988.

Unrau, William E., and H. Craig Miner. *The End of Indian Kansas: A Study of Cultural Revolution, 1854–71.* Lawrence: University Press of Kansas, 1978.

Quapaw

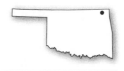

NAME

The tribe's name comes from "Okaxpa" (also spelled "Ug' Akhpa" and "Ugaqpa"), "downstream people," referring to the direction they took when separating from the rest of the Dhegiha Siouan–speakers and their movement down the Mississippi River. Earlier they were often called the Arkansas, but after about 1800 they became known as the Quapaws (named for one of the band villages).

LOCATION AND GOVERNMENT

The headquarters for the "Quapaw Tribe of Oklahoma" is located about three miles southeast of the city of Quapaw in Ottawa County (in the far northeastern corner of Oklahoma, just below Baxter Springs, Kansas) on the East 50 Road to Peoria. The tribal community center is south of Quapaw in the city of Miami, about twelve miles away. The tribe is not organized under the OIWA. It has no constitution. A business committee operates under the authority of a Governing Resolution adopted in August 1956. All eligible voters popularly elect the business committee of seven members, including a chair, for a two-year term. The tribe mandated staggered terms of office in 1994. The tribal website is www.quapawtribe.com.

BUSINESSES

Revenue comes from the tribe's large Downstream Casino with five restaurants (near Interstate 44), Quapaw Grand Casino (three and a half miles north of Miami), and Grand Lake Casino (located in Grove). The tribe also owns the 82-acre Spurto Industrial Park as well as a gas station and convenience store called O-Gah-Pah (located between Quapaw and Miami near the casino on the S 580 Road). The BIA purchased 528 acres south of the town of Picher in 1937 for the tribe, which converted the land into its industrial park in 1975 (now the site of one of the casinos). Some individual members receive royalty income from mineral leases and allotted lands.

NUMBER

The tribe has about 2,500 members.

Quapaw is a Dhegiha Siouan language, related to the languages of the Osages, Omahas, and Kansas. The distant past shrouds Quapaw origins in mystery. There is much controversy over whether the ancestors of the Quapaws had been in the Arkansas area since ancient times or whether they were relatively recent migrants. At the time when Southeastern Ceremonial Complex art was being produced throughout the Mississippian cultural world, peoples believed to be ancestral Quapaws in the central Mississippi Valley made distinctive polychrome-painted ceramics. They may have been part of a Late Mississippian trade network that stretched from the Red River through what is now Arkansas to the upper central Mississippi Valley. Archeologists point to possible ancient sites as being linked directly to the Mississippian cultural background. C. R. McGimsey argued that the Quapaws directly descended from the Mississippian peoples in present-day northeastern Arkansas encountered by Hernando de Soto in 1541. The temple-mound community that Soto found at Pacaha is located east of Crowley's Ridge near what is now Helena, Arkansas, and the St. Francis River. The Spanish commander sojourned at Pacaha (also called Cappa), Parkin, and other villages located in what would become the state of Arkansas.

Other archeologists believed that the Quapaws were remnants of a much-reduced Ohio Valley Mississippian population. That was the view of historian David Baird and of Arkansas archeologists Dan and C. A. Morse. Michael Hoffman more recently lent support when he suggested a link for the Quapaws with the Claborn-Welborn phase of the Ohio River Valley. Dhegiha Siouan oral tradition claimed a tribal migration from the region south of the Great Lakes down the Ohio River to its confluence with the Mississippi. The Quapaws shared the Dhegiha Siouan language with the Omaha-Poncas, Kansas, and Osages. Linguists believe that the Quapaw language was the first to separate from the larger group. In the oral story most of the migrating group turned to journey upstream and eventually became the other three tribes. The Quapaws, however, traveled downstream along the Mississippi River to their Arkansas homeland and became the sole Dhegiha Siouan–speakers in the Lower Mississippi Valley. Some Quapaw cultural traits are shared with southeastern Indian peoples, such as types of clans and stories of their rabbit trickster. Those traits are clearly not Plains. Other Dhegiha Siouan tribes possessed more marked Plains attributes in their oral tradition, such as featuring Coyote as trickster. They all had core social and religious institutions, which advocates for migration believed were derived from a common prehistoric Mississippian source in the Ohio Valley.

Linguist Robert Rankin found that the Quapaw language shared over 80 percent of its basic vocabulary with Osage. The close affinity not only implied a mutual Dhegihan root but pointed to recent separation of the two languages. It also suggested the recentness of the Quapaws' arrival at the mouth of the Arkansas River, where their first European visitors found them. As new arrivals, perhaps just after 1600, the Quapaws evicted the Michigamea, Tunica, and Koroa residents of the region. The late presence also meant that there had been little mixture with local Native peoples, either because they were pushed out of the way or because the Quapaws arrived quite recently. Linguists James Springer and Stanley Witkowski hypothesized that the Dhegiha Siouan language family began to split apart about A.D. 1300. Others like Michael Hoffman and Dale Henning argued for a more recent chronology, possibly as late as the start of the 1500s. Pointing to a recent arrival near the Mississippi River, they contended that the Dhegihan migration story is a generalized description of interrelationships and movements. Marvin Jeter maintained that the Quapaws arrived in the late 1500s and displaced the Tunicas and Koroas from present-day Arkansas and sent them southward only in the period just before 1700.

The origin story of the Quapaws is similar to that of their Siouan kinfolk. Water covered the earth for a long time. Shells sheltered the Quapaw people until they came onto dry land. Wah-kon-tah, the creative life force in the cosmos, guided them. Once on land, they formed clans and settled into their lives. Even today, when memorial feasts are held in the longhouse, a cup of water is placed at each setting as a reminder that from water comes life. Like their Siouan kinfolk, the Quapaws looked to Wah-kon-tah, who created everything in the universe, for guidance and help. In the celestial firmament the sun and the moon were special. On earth the serpent was of special spiritual significance. Wah-kon-tah also made lesser spirits to be helpers in this realm as well as individual guardian spirits (manitous).

Like Plains Indians, the Quapaws were patrilineal. They took their descent within the tribe from the father. The twenty-two clans (and subclans) had two divisions, the Sky People and Earth People, like their distant Osage kin. Leadership also had a dual division, one for peace and the other for war. Male subchiefs formed the council for major decisions, which were made inside a public council house. At the time of their final treaty with the United States, the Quapaws had four major bands, called the Quapaw, German, O-so-ta-wa, and Lost bands. They also had four chiefs: Hackaton, Sarassan, Tonnonjinka, and Kaheketteda. During the seventeenth century the Quapaws lived in four main permanent villages in clusters of bark-covered rectangular longhouses. Each sheltered several extended and related families. In the center of the arrangement of longhouses was a plaza for rituals and public events. Some Quapaw communities held sacred temples for priests to perform ceremonies. That was either an outgrowth of a Mississippian cultural heritage or an adaptation at the end of their journey. Quapaw women cultivated vast common fields for agricultural products. They depended on corn, beans, and squash as well as pumpkins, sunflowers, berries, and nuts. Men hunted for an abundance of game, including buffalo after journeys to the western prairie. Aquatic food sources also played a significant role in the Quapaw diet. A distinctive swirl design marked their pottery decoration. The Quapaws expanded their trade with Caddos on the Red River over a well-trodden route, participated in commerce with eastern tribes, and even tried to engage the Illinois in the North directly.

The Quapaws used a wide variety of ceremonies to appeal to supernatural forces. Their world was divided into an upper or sky world and a lower or earthly world, like that of many other American Indian peoples. Medicine men (*wapinan*) assisted people in their quest for help in this life. The priestly class also conferred names on newborns, bestowing good fortune with the proper name on the individual. The Quapaws held a number of major ceremonies, among them an annual Green Corn Ceremony for thanksgiving. One of the most noteworthy, described in French accounts, was their Calumet ceremony. It involved the ritual smoking of a two-foot-long Pipe decorated with designs and feathers and the elaborate welcoming of a visitor with rituals, speeches, dancing, and feasting. At its end the ceremony created a kinship bond of adoption between the visitor and the Quapaws. The relationship required mutual support and reciprocal service.

Hernando de Soto's expedition threaded its way through the southeastern forests in 1539–41. Toward the end of their journey in America they came to many chiefdoms or large villages on the western side of the Mississippi River, such as the mound-centers of Pacaha, Casqui, and Quizquiz, widely believed to have been in what is now Arkansas. Spanish chroniclers described "a very large, enclosed" town at Pacaha, whose palisade was "furnished with towers." Large towns were also nearby. The

Pacaha leader asked Soto to intervene in a long-standing enmity with residents of the rival province of Casqui. The Spaniards brought European weaponry, colonial trade items, and European-borne disease to Native peoples in the region for the first time. In the wake of Soto's passing, pigs that escaped the Spaniards turned wild and led to the razorbacks now famous in Arkansas as an athletic symbol.

The Quapaws occupied a prime communication route and were often visited. Jacques Marquette and Louis Joliet in July 1673 traveled down the Mississippi River for France and found the Quapaws. Marquette and Joliet spoke Algonquian Illinois. When asked who the hosts were, a captive replied that they were the "Akansea" in the Illinois language. The word was later anglicized into "Arkansas." The residents lived in four villages near the mouth of the Arkansas River. La Salle's expedition in March 1682 encountered the Quapaws first at the village of Kappa (or Kwapa) on the west bank of the Mississippi River just above the mouth of the Arkansas River. La Salle noted five large villages. The Quapaws greeted him with the Calumet ceremony, gifts, and feasting. La Salle's men took possession of the region for French ruler Louis XIV. Henri Joutel commented that two villages had later combined, based on the remarks of his informant. The impact of European diseases eventually reduced the Indians' population and led to further village consolidation. Henri de Tonti also passed through the Quapaw communities (1686) and left an account of them. He set up a small post in the village of Osotouy to anticipate the return of La Salle's party. The post was the forerunner of what would later become the famous trading center known as Arkansas Post.

The following year the remnant of the La Salle party returned to the area and was relieved to see a large wooden cross erected on the opposite bank of the Arkansas River. But Pierre Le Moyne d'Iberville after 1700 found the Quapaws collected on the Arkansas River and deeply affected by European disease. They also suffered attacks from Chickasaws and Michigameas (of the Illinois Confederacy). The Quapaws, however, remained staunch allies of the French. Historians point out that the French probably would have had no Louisiana Territory for the United States to purchase later if it had not been for Quapaw loyalty to the French cause and their blocking of English intrusion.

Other French explorers, trappers, and traders encountered the Quapaws in ensuing years. As the fur trade increased in the eighteenth century, European trade goods became more important for the Indians. The post that Tonti had set up grew. At its height of occupation it held some one thousand soldiers and other personnel. The establishment of Arkansas Post in the summer of 1721 as a permanent base for trade and alliance initially drew Quapaws for trade. It was a new experience for them. At that time the Quapaws resided on the west side of the river in their village of Osotouy. John House noted that Osotouy is believed to be the Wallace Bottom No. 2 site, a part of the White River National Wildlife Refuge today. It was there, according to House, that Tonti founded the post on the north side of the Arkansas River. It was the first European settlement in what later became the state of Arkansas. The post served as a magnet for commercial activity for years, even though its location shifted as a result of the changing course of the river. Bénard de La Harpe paused at the site in 1722 as he ascended the river to make contact with other tribes.

French authorities made presents available to the Quapaws to culti-vate their loyalty. The use of the Calumet ceremony, in turn made the French "kin" to the Indians. There were perhaps 15,000 Quapaws then. The French and the Quapaws had a symbiotic relationship in which the French gained a valued Indian ally strategically situated to block English incursions, while the Indians received French firearms and alliance. Both the French and the Quapaws opposed the English-supplied Chickasaws across the mighty river, as Morris Arnold noted. French trade made the Quapaws dependent on European-manufactured goods, to the detriment of the older modes of livelihood. When trade items like hides and buffalo fat became scarce, the Quapaws served as mercenaries for the French in their fighting throughout the valley.

Spain took over the Louisiana Territory in 1763 and renamed Ar-kansas Post as Fort Carlos. The Quapaws remained highly suspicious of Spanish motives and of their presence. In 1803 the United States took control of the Louisiana Purchase region and the Quapaws had to deal with a new rival. The Quapaws signed their first treaty with the United States negotiator, William Clark (governor of the Missouri Territory), in St. Louis in August 1818. The document gave up a large part of their terri-tory, some 16 million acres, to the United States in exchange for annuities and a reservation of 1.5 million acres below the Arkansas River from Ar-kansas Post to Little Rock. Botanist Thomas Nuttall toured the region in 1819 collecting plants and Indian stories. Nuttall viewed Chief Heckaton's parchment copy of the treaty, noted the sale price of a paltry $4,000, and lamented shady American negotiating tactics. Nuttall met and befriended mixed-blood Quapaws residing on isolated farmsteads.

Another treaty signed at Harrington in November 1824 ceded nearly all of the remainder of their Arkansas lands (for one-tenth of a cent per acre) and moved the fewer than five hundred Quapaws to a reservation at

Bayou Treache on the Red River near the log-jam called the Great Raft in the vicinity of what would become the city of Shreveport. The Quapaws reluctantly anticipated merging with the unwilling Caddos. Rumors of bribery accompanied the treaty signing. The Quapaws refer to the journey as their "Trail of Tears." Some mixed-blood French-Quapaws received Arkansas allotted land in fee. Chief Heckaton appealed to acting governor Robert Crittenden to be allowed to remain and not be pushed to the Red River. Heckaton pointed out that the Quapaws had never attacked settlers. On the contrary, the Indians had always befriended the newcomers. His appeal was rebuffed. In 1826 some 455 Quapaws left Arkansas. Under the terms of the treaty the Quapaws retained eighty acres below Pine Bluff, which included the remaining three tribal villages. Eleven mixed-blood Quapaw-French tribal members under the 1824 treaty retained about eighty acres each near Arkansas Post. Disastrous floods across their Red River parcel and attendant illnesses devastated the Quapaws and killed perhaps one-fourth of them by 1832. About one-quarter of the remaining Quapaws returned forlornly to their former homeland, now occupied by white settlers.

The Quapaws were now irrevocably divided. By 1831 many had gone back to Arkansas. A final treaty in May 1833 at Gascony provided for a reservation of 96,000 acres in the far northeastern corner of Indian Territory just below the Kansas boundary. The Reverend John Schermerhorn, later notorious for his dirty tricks during Cherokee removal talks, led the U.S. negotiations. Quapaws came from Arkansas and from the Red River region to Indian Territory. After arriving in the new territory, however, they discovered that they were residing on land that was not theirs (it was Seneca-Cayuga land). The Quapaws then separated into three bands and dispersed across the region, often on individual farms, beginning about 1838. A few Quapaws had intermarried with Europeans and Anglo-Americans and remained in Arkansas as ordinary citizens of that state. Some others left the Red River Caddo country to merge with Chief Bowles's Texas Cherokees but eventually ended up in a large village located near what is now Holdenville, Oklahoma, until the Civil War era. Still others moved to what is now Lexington, Oklahoma, while a few resided among the Choctaws.

Civil War strife and the violence between factions in Kansas overwhelmed the Quapaws. The turmoil of the Civil War era, which for Kansas also encompassed the late 1850s, brought other Quapaw, Seneca of Sandusky, Osage, and Shawnee refugees to the Quapaw reserve, seeking safety. Some Quapaws abandoned their reserve and sought refuge among the Ottawas near Ohio City in Kansas, while others tried to find shelter among their Osage kinfolk. The Reverend J. Owen Dorsey visited the Quapaws in 1882–83 as a part of his Bureau of American Ethnology research. He found the population reduced to fewer than two hundred on their own tract of land. The Ponca Indians temporarily settled on largely abandoned Quapaw land.

After the Civil War some Quapaws determined that they would improve their lot by moving to live near their distant relations the Osages in southeastern Kansas. Quapaw chief John Wilson (Pas-tee) negotiated with the Shawnee chief Theh-con-a-gah and purchased 14,863 acres of the Shawnee reserve held with the Senecas for a new Quapaw home in Indian Territory. It lay next to the land of the Peoria Confederacy. The Quapaws moved there in 1868–69. During their relocation John Wilson died while at the Osage Mission. A February 1867 treaty with the United States also ceded a half-mile-wide strip of land that lay inside Kansas near the borderline in exchange for a payment and educational support. Schools for Indians already existed in the region. Crawford School, named for the then commissioner of Indian affairs, had been opened in 1842 on Spring River (called the Pomme de Terre at the time) on the military road linking Fort Smith with Fort Leavenworth. Later the school was moved northward.

The Quapaws at first had been under the supervision of the Neosho Agency. Because of the distance between disparate groups, agent G. C. Snow recommended that a new agency be created. In February 1871 the Quapaw Agency came into being. Their reservation held about 202,000 acres east of the Neosho River. In the 1870s the number of Quapaws who remained on their Indian Territory reservation declined to such an extent that by 1878 only about thirty-five were left there. Nearby whites agitated for homesteading of the nearly deserted reservation. Quapaw residents took in members of other tribes (including many Miamis) as well as mixed-bloods of their own tribe, and some Quapaws returned to their reserve. Ironically, allotment brought even more back.

The Quapaws during that decade were the first tribe in Indian Territory to have their lands surveyed and platted. Abner W. Abrams, a Stockbridge Indian adopted as a Quapaw, served as tribal secretary. He proved instrumental because he drew up the Quapaw allotment plan. Tribal members opposed the federal government's efforts and found them too limiting. Uniquely, the Quapaws voted in support of their allotment agreement and in 1893 took over the oversight of their own allotment in severalty at Abrams's urging. Each of the 234 tribal members received 240 acres, with most of the assignments in connected parcels. No land remained as "surplus" to be opened to white settlers, because the entire reserve had been allotted to the Quapaws. They kept a substantial land base as a result. In 1895 Congress agreed. The official roll listed 215 Quapaws, with the Indian Office adding 22 adoptees. Townsite promoters began the town of Quapaw on the forty acres of Chief John Quapaw's allotment. Congress lifted restrictions against the sale of allotments in Public Law 306 in March 1909.

Profitable deposits of lead and zinc were discovered in 1905 on the seemingly worthless prairie land allotted to tribal members in the western portion of the reservation. Mining resulted in the founding of some leading families and brought great wealth to a few Quapaw allottees, especially after the federal government in 1913 tightened enforcement of regulations that reduced fraud and exploitation. The leases paid royalties to the Indian agency instead of directly to the Indian allotment owners, to their bankers, or to their storekeepers for alleged debts.

A boomtown atmosphere prevailed in the 1920s, with an estimated 22,000 people working to extract ore. For example, the mining community of Lincolnville sprang up and quickly had a population of 3,000. The region had 1,028 mining companies and 227 mills. The law at first required a separate mill for each leased tract. From 1900 to 1950 the Tri-State District (which included portions of Kansas, Missouri, and Oklahoma) was the leading producer of lead and zinc in the world. Bullets used in many wars came from the lead mined there. After 1920 the Interior Department gradually eased restrictions, which increased exploitation of Indian owners. Quapaws lobbied in Washington, D.C., to gain an extension of the measure mandating restrictions (which was due to expire at the start of 1921) as well as enactment of a measure extending restrictions to 1946 then to 1971 and later to 1996.

The Quapaw school had been established by Quakers under the Grant peace policy. The Quapaw and Seneca schools combined in 1898. The Quapaws had been exposed to the Roman Catholic faith upon the arrival of the first Frenchmen, including Father Marquette, Father Nicholas Foucault, and others. In the wake of the chaos and disruption of the reservation era, more Quapaws converted to Catholicism. The old Quapaw Mission School building was moved to Lincolnville to be used as a Catholic school. Priests periodically visited the Quapaws during their reservation experience. Katharine Drexel provided funds for the erection of a church, later called St. Mary's of the Quapaws. Father William Ketcham established it in 1894 as a church and school. In 1895–96 John Wilson (Moonhead), a Caddo-Delaware, made Quapaw converts to the Peyote ceremony, some of whom interlaced aspects of Catholicism into the ceremonies. The Big

Moon doctrine stressed right living and appealed to full-bloods in the mining region of their reserve. Following Wilson's death, Quapaw Victor Griffin was its priest. He was also elected tribal chief (1929–57).

The Quapaws rejected IRA- and OIWA-proposed reforms because they viewed their corporate structures as a direct threat to Native individualism. They continued their council and chief governance under Griffin. The Indian Office purchased 528 acres in 1937 for homes for landless Indians in the area. Smaller parcels were also purchased in subsequent years. Leaders filed a land claims case in 1946. A 1954 settlement (through Public Law 97 in 1959) brought nearly $1 million to tribal coffers, distributed to 1,144 members. The award breathed new life into tribal membership, as new members appeared. The BIA overthrew the traditional leadership and forced adoption of a business committee and new tribal government under chairman Robert Whitebird (1956), who oversaw the creation of a new tribal roll and distribution of the award. Quapaws prevented federal termination during the 1950s and also started economic development planning. The judgment payment revitalized the tribe because it focused attention on the tribal political entity and brought people back together.

Linguists consider the Quapaw language to be dormant, although other Dhegiha Siouan languages are still spoken. Because of their geographic location near the prairie, the Quapaws shared cultural traditions of both the Plains and the Woodlands. An annual powwow held on the Fourth of July next to the tribal headquarters on a campground is the oldest powwow in America and brings many people from afar to participate. It helps reunite tribal members and reasserts their cultural heritage, albeit much transformed. Their powwow celebration also includes stomp dancing. Flooding of their powwow ground led the tribe to move its dance ground to Devil's Promenade, the former Tall Chief allotment.

Reclamation efforts involving the Environmental Protection Agency's Superfund focused on a forty-square-mile region believed to be polluted by mining activity. It took its name from Tar Creek, a rust-colored stream flowing out of southeastern Kansas across northeastern Oklahoma, coursing through chat piles (mine waste) of lead and zinc. Mining residue, which included powdered lead, zinc, cadmium, and arsenic, leached through the soil, seeped into the groundwater, and blew in the air in the years following extraction. Children in the region had the highest levels of lead poisoning in the United States. High levels of lead contribute to severe developmental and learning disabilities. Picher (population 1,800) sat atop the ore remnant. The 300 miles of abandoned underground tunnels held 76 million acre feet of acid water. In 1978 an orange liquid oozed into Anglo rancher George Mayer's pasture and stained the legs of his prized horses. It would not wash off. Other residents joined the chorus of complaints. Later the area received Superfund designation (1983) for eventual cleanup. Schools, homes, and highways sat atop endless miles of tunnels, caverns, and potential sinkholes. For twenty-five years the Environmental Protection Agency squandered about $200 million on remediation of what is in effect a Love Canal situation. About half of the mining area is Quapaw tribal land. The issue was also tangled in multiple lawsuits (including BIA accounting for trust funds and royalty payments) as well as disputes over whether and how to relocate residents. Subsidence issues and agricultural runoff into area streams are also of concern.

In spite of vicissitudes through the centuries the Quapaws still occupy a portion of their aboriginal land. They are one of the few tribes indigenous to Oklahoma and are still there.

Notable Quapaws include Pontiac (1720–69), the leader of a famous rebellion. More contemporary members include composer Louis W. Ballard (who is also Cherokee) and poet and author Geary Hobson (who is also Cherokee and Chickasaw). Martha Moore Barker served as the first Miss Indian USA.

SUGGESTED READING

Arnold, Morris S. *The Rumble of a Distant Drum: The Quapaws and Old World Newcomers, 1673–1804.* Fayetteville: University of Arkansas, 2000.

Baird, W. David. *The Quapaw Indians: A History of the Downstream People.* Norman: University of Oklahoma Press, 1980.

———. *The Quapaws.* New York: Chelsea House, 1989 (for young readers).

Clayton, Lawrence A., Vernon J. Knight, Jr., and Edward C. Moore, eds. *The De Soto Chronicles.* 2 vols. Tuscaloosa: University of Alabama Press, 1993; repr. 1995 (quotations from Garcilaso de la Vega, "La Florida," vol. 2, 395).

The Creek Runs Red. Dallas: KFRA, 2006 (film on Tar Creek and Picher).

DuVal, Kathleen. *The Native Ground: Indians and Colonists in the Heart of the Continent.* Philadelphia: University of Pennsylvania Press, 2006.

Henning, Dale. "The Adaptive Patterning of the Dhegiha Sioux." *Plains Anthropologist* 38, no. 146 (November 1993): 253–64.

House, John H. "Wallace Bottom: A Colonial-Era Archaeological Site in the Menard Locality, Eastern Arkansas." *Southeastern Archaeology* 20 (Winter 2001): 257–68.

Joutel, Henri. *Joutel's Journal of La Salle's Last Voyage* (originally published 1714). New York: Corinth Books, 1962.

Sabo, George, III. *Paths of Our Children: Historic Indians of Arkansas.* Fayetteville: Arkansas Archaeological Survey, 1992.

Springer, James, and Stanley Witkowski. "Siouan Historical Linguistics and Oneota Archaeology." In Guy Gibbon, ed., *Oneota Studies*, 69–83. Minneapolis: University of Minnesota, 1982.

Stateline: The Other Side of the Creek. Oklahoma City: Oklahoma Educational Television Authority, 2004 (film on Tar Creek).

Tonti, Henri de. *Relation of Henri de Tonty [sic] concerning the Explorations of La Salle from 1678 to 1683.* Translated by Melville Anderson. Chicago: Caxton Club, 1898.

Young, Gloria, and Michael Hoffman. "Quapaw." In vol. 13, *Plains,* of the *Handbook of North American Indians,* 497–514. Washington, D.C.: Smithsonian Institution, 2001 (includes Hoffman, Jeter, McGimsey, Morse, and Rankin sources).

Sac and Fox

NAME

The Sacs and Foxes are independent peoples but closely related in language and culture. The name for the Sacs (or Sauks) derived from the Algonquian word "Osa'kiwug," "people of the yellow earth." They also referred to themselves as Asa-ki-waki, "people of the outlet" (for the region of the Saginaw River of Michigan from which the Iroquois drove them). The Fox name derived from Meshkwakihug, "red earth people." It was sometimes anglicized to Meskwakie or Mesquakie. That is the designation used by the Mesquakie Tribe at Tama, Iowa. The French took the Fox name of one clan, Wagosh, "red fox" group (*reynard rouge* in French), as the label for the entire tribe.

LOCATION AND GOVERNMENT

The headquarters for the "Sac and Fox Nation of Oklahoma" is located five miles south of Stroud in Lincoln County, in north-central Oklahoma. The reservation is approximately halfway (sixty miles) between Oklahoma City and Tulsa. It was also the halfway point for the old agency employees between Pawnee and Shawnee towns. The tribe is organized under the OIWA. The 1937 constitution was replaced with a new document in July 1987. The government consists of a five-member business committee (including a principal chief and other officers), elected to staggered four-year terms. The tribal website is www.sacandfoxnation-nsn.gov.

BUSINESSES

Major revenue comes from the Indian Country Bingo in Stroud and the casino on Westech Road in Shawnee (north of Interstate Highway 40 at exit 186). The tribe's Gallery (which opened in 1993) and the Tribal Mini-Mart sell to the public. The Tribal Museum offers exhibits on tribal history and arts and crafts and features athlete Jim Thorpe. The tribal RV park permits access to Veterans Lake for fishing and recreation. The tribe owns a 4,200-acre industrial park in Cushing and also owns about 1,000 acres in trust elsewhere. Individuals hold about 15,000 acres of allotted land. Leasing provides income from pasturage and oil and gas activity.

NUMBER

The tribe has about 3,000 members, primarily in and around towns near the tribal headquarters in Stroud as well as in Cushing and Shawnee. There are two clusters of Sacs and Foxes, a northern group around Cushing and a southern one near Shawnee. The tribal constitutional amendment enacted in 1995 dropped the blood quantum requirement to one-eighth. Like many other Indian nations, the Sacs and Foxes have kinfolk scattered across the continent. The Sacs and Foxes of the Mississippi River who settled along the Iowa River near Tama, Iowa, number about 600. They are more usually called the Mesquakies. The Sacs and Foxes of the Missouri, who have a reservation near Reserve in northern Kansas on the Missouri River, number about 300. Ethnographers view the Sacs and Foxes as two distinct tribes. Although closely related in language and culture, they were independent through much of their early history. After 1733, however, the two were forced together for survival. This discussion treats them as one nation, since that is how they are currently officially identified in Oklahoma.

Sac and Fox are Central Algonquian, closely related to Kickapoo. Linguists consider the three to be dialects of a single Algonquian language. All three perhaps formed one group with the Mascoutens, although that is conjectural, and were also closely connected with the Shawnees at one time. They culturally resembled the Potawatomis as well. The region of Wisconsin experienced pre-Mississippian cultural developments, whether these were local variations or resulted from outside intrusions. There were distinctive local cultural adoptions of palisaded villages with pyramid platform mounds. Local ceramic styles were carried over into Effigy Mound–Oneota cultural traits west of Lake Michigan. Archeologist Warren Wittry examined a late prehistoric village called the Bell site at Big Lake Butte des Mortes in southern Wisconsin on the Rock River within the Effigy Mound region. It is believed to be a Fox palisaded village dating to 1680–1730. By then French trade goods had replaced most Native items, although residents continued to use bone tools.

The Sac and Fox homeland was south of the Great Lakes. The Sac homeland was in what is today the Upper Peninsula of Michigan in the valley of the Saginaw River. The Foxes lived on the south shore of Lake Superior. Ojibwe expansion pushed the Foxes toward Green Bay. The Sacs and Foxes resided in villages on watercourses. The famously large main village of Saukenuk in the early nineteenth century rested on a point of land between the Rock and Mississippi rivers. Many families occupied one bark-covered longhouse. Women tended fields of corn, beans, squash, and melons. Nuts, berries, and plums abounded in the nearby countryside. Men hunted and fished. Able-bodied men and women left their village for the winter hunt. They returned with meat and furs, for spring planting duties. A council offered guidance in civil affairs. Civil chief positions were hereditary. Selected warriors carried the title of war chief. Clan membership was hereditary and patrilineal. The more numerous Sacs were more highly organized than the smaller Fox group.

For the Foxes, the ruler of the upper world or universe was the Great Manitou. Other spirits or manitous helped order the universe. The Foxes were the maternal aunts and uncles of their culture hero and creator, We Sahke Ha, who resided in the far north. The Foxes identified other manitous with the four directions, the most important being the sun in the East. A vision quest offered the individual spiritual guidance. Sacred packs were ritually honored through ceremonies, the main one during the summer, involving prayer, exhortation, singing, dancing, and feasting.

Father Claude Allouez in 1667 made the first European contact with the Sacs and Foxes. He found that, as a result of Iroquois and French pressure on the Sacs and Ojibwe pressure on the Foxes, both had been forced to the present Green Bay, Wisconsin. Allouez said that the tribes were located near his French mission at Chequamegon Bay. Two years later he estimated 600 residents in a wintertime village on the Oconto River that included Sacs and Foxes.

In 1670 Allouez visited Sac inhabitants of a community along the Fox River and a Fox village, Oestatinong, on the Wolf River. A year later he established the Mission of St. Mark among the Foxes. After the mission closed in 1678, the Foxes moved to a location on the west side of Lake Winnebago; in 1679 other Foxes resided near what would later become the cities of Green Bay, Chicago, and Milwaukee.

By about 1698 the Foxes dominated the river of their name and thereby controlled the river-borne French trade. When the Iroquois wars concluded in 1701, the French hosted a conference in Montreal for potential Indian allies. Afterward the French founded Fort Ponchartrain at what became Detroit, Michigan, dominating the west end of Lake Erie. The French tried to exterminate the Foxes as they did the Natchez. In their turn, the Foxes wanted to exclude the French from lucrative trade routes. In a 1712 battle French, Hurons, and Ottawas attacked and mauled Foxes and Mascoutens, who suffered an estimated 1,000 losses. This sparked the start of the so-called Fox Wars. Four years of internecine warfare took a toll on the Foxes. A French expedition in 1716 forced a Fox surrender and a pause in hostilities. The French sent Etienne de Venyard, Sieur de Bourgmont, in 1720 to secure an understanding that would end the Fox-Iowa-Otoe alliance and monopoly along their trade route. The French and the Foxes agreed to a final peace in 1726.

Wanting to dominate the fur trade in the West, the French established Fort Beauharnois in 1727 to cut off a feared Fox alliance with the Sioux. The following year the French led another expedition against the Foxes. In 1730 French and Indian allies again mauled the Foxes, who had moved near what is today the community of Leroy in Maclean County, Illinois. The Foxes moved again, to the lower Wisconsin River, where the Iroquois and Hurons sought out and killed many of them.

The Sacs offered shelter to Fox refugees and thus incurred more French wrath. Attacks in 1733 strengthened the Sac and Fox alliance. The two groups moved south to present-day Iowa under French assault. In a 1737 conference in Montreal, the French granted the two tribes a general pardon, finally ending the Fox Wars. The Fox survivors returned to Wisconsin, where most of the Sacs also relocated, although a portion moved to the Rock River.

About 1746 the Sacs moved to Sauk Prairie on the Wisconsin River in today's Sauk County, Wisconsin. The Foxes resided in a village on the north side of the same river below the mouth of the Kickapoo River. Their historic journey would take them from a woodland environment to the prairie. By the 1770s–80s some Sac and Fox mixed-bloods joined the merchant families of St. Louis through involvement in the lucrative fur trade.

The Sacs and Foxes migrated to the Mississippi River between Prairie du Chien and the Rock River then into Iowa and western Illinois. It was there that they built the Sac capital, Saukenuk. The Lewis and Clark expedition visited and estimated that it had a population of 2,000, including 1,200 Foxes. Saukenuk had about a hundred bark lodges, an impressively large community.

By this time there were two major bands of Sacs and Foxes, one near the Mississippi River and the other associated with the Missouri River. Some Sac and Fox chiefs of the Missouri band in 1804 visited St. Louis to accompany one of their members to a murder trial. While there, the Indians were induced to sign a treaty with U.S. representative William H. Harrison (governor of Indiana Territory and the District of Louisiana), in which the Indians ceded all their land east of the Mississippi River. The main bodies of each tribe claimed that the document was not official and was unauthorized, since they had not agreed to it. The federal government nonetheless enforced the treaty in ensuing years. Efforts to implement the terms of the treaty led to a split in the Sac and Fox alliance. In 1813 a young, untested mixed-blood Sac named Keokuk asked for and was granted permission to speak inside their council lodge to tribal leaders. His bold leadership during a time of crisis gave him a following. His eventual friendship with agent William Clark helped direct the Sacs and Foxes into siding with the Americans.

At the same time, perhaps a thousand tribespeople followed Black Hawk's "British Band" (so named for their support of the British during the War of 1812) toward their former homeland at Saukenuk in Illinois. The fraudulent 1804 treaty and its demands fed his followers' anger. They hoped Indian allies would sustain them but found little help. Their return to Iowa was blocked by the American army under General Henry Atkinson. Alarmed settlers had called for troops to protect them from the "renegades." Fighting began in mid-May of 1832, pushing the Indians into the southern Wisconsin area. In July a running fight between the Indians and pursuing U.S. troops took place as the Indians neared the Wisconsin River. The Indians, including many women and children, escaped, but at the start of August U.S. forces under Atkinson trapped Black Hawk's group as it tried to cross the Mississippi River south of the Bad Axe River near what is now Victory, Wisconsin. Over 150 Indians were killed and an equal number drowned. Survivors who reached the other shore were attacked by the Sioux, their long-time enemies. Black Hawk and his ally White Cloud surrendered to the United States at the end of August at Prairie du Chien. It was a tragic end to the final Indian war east of the Mississippi. Black Hawk, his sons, and the Winnebago Prophet were sent as prisoners of war under Lieutenant Jefferson Davis to incarceration at Jefferson Barracks (then Fort Monroe) on Chesapeake Bay. The Winnebago Prophet was buried in Washington, D.C. The prisoners were released back to their people after a short time. Many later Illinois politicians like Abraham Lincoln saw brief service in the war.

The Treaty of Fort Armstrong (located where the Rock River met the Mississippi) in 1832 ended Sac and Fox power on the frontier. The following year they moved to Iowa for thirteen years before moving to Kansas.

Historian William T. Hagan demonstrated a 50 percent drop in tribal population during the decade as a result of malnutrition, illness, conflict, and despair. A remnant group (called the Mesquakies) stayed in Iowa and was joined by more dissidents in 1859, with another trickle arriving in 1867. Poweshiek's Fox band twice returned to old villages on the Iowa River (1842–44) but was evicted by U.S. troops.

The United States appointed Keokuk chief, and in 1842 he ceded the remainder of lands in Iowa and agreed to move to 435,000 acres in Kansas. Although he had shown leadership through the preceding decade, the Sacs and Foxes were under intense pressure and suffered ongoing white encroachment onto their lands. Under the terms of a Washington, D.C., treaty of February 18, 1867, Keokuk's people exchanged their Kansas land for a larger reserve of 480,000 acres in Indian Territory. Congress failed to provide money for the removal, while squatters swarmed onto the Kansas reserve. The Indians finally completed their nineteen-day journey to Indian Territory in 1869. There they were joined in 1886 (under the terms of a March 1885 act, 23 Stat. 351, chap. 337) by about 200 members of Mokohoko's holdout Prairie band, which settled near Cushing. Some forlorn Sacs and Foxes returned to Kansas among kinfolk, but white attacks kept them homeless.

Quakers began a school in 1870 for Sac and Fox children. A three-story brick classroom building was erected in 1873 and the facilities at the site, on the agency grounds, served students until 1917. That year the agency and the mission school were moved to Shawnee (until 1919), and the old agency community became a ghost town. Baptists established a mission in 1874, also at the agency. Isaac McCoy was the first pastor. Late in his life Moses Keokuk, son of the chief, became a Baptist minister. In 1912 Sac and Fox members founded the Only Way Indian Baptist Church, and the following year a church was built nine miles north of Stroud. Missionaries worked diligently for converts. Presbyterian missionaries Samuel Irwin and William Hamilton worked on behalf of the Sacs and Foxes and served as intermediaries with whites. Scholar Joseph Herring revealed the ethnographic value of the missionaries' writings.

Their Indian agent persuaded the Sacs and Foxes to adopt the Osage constitution as theirs in 1885. The Osages also had a supreme court, but the frustrated agent disbanded the constitutional government in 1892. The Sacs and Foxes retained a smaller council. The BIA continued to manipulate tribal government. The Interior Department, frustrated that the council did not move fast enough on oil leases, abolished the council in mid-1909 and started a tribal business committee, with the BIA appointing its first members. The committee still failed to approve leases in 1915–16, so the BIA appointed three members to sign them. Oil and gas development after 1912 in the Cushing field provided wealth to a very few tribal families. Tribal government existed largely on paper through the 1920s. Allotment further split the tribes. The federal government allotted the reservation in 1891. The Mokohoko band ultimately took allotments across the northern part of the reserve in the Cushing area, while the remainder of the tribe members took theirs in the southern portion, near the later community of Meeker. The United States opened the "surplus" land in 1891 through a land run, the first in what would become the state of Oklahoma. Like other allotted American Indians, the Sacs and Foxes quickly lost the bulk of their lands.

A new governmental era began during the Indian New Deal of the 1930s. Non-resident Frank O. Jones, a quarter-blood, drafted his own version of by-laws in 1934, which was adopted by the Sacs and Foxes. (He was the brother of Smithsonian Institution anthropologist William K. Jones, who wrote extensively about Fox ethnography.) Under the guidance of the OIWA, the Sacs and Foxes adopted a constitutional government and elected half-blood Don Whistler as principal chief. That ousted Frank Jones from his council position. Jones and supporters formed the Ah-tha-kee-wah and Me-squa-kee Association as an opposing, and legitimate, traditional government. Whistler remained chief until his death in 1951.

The Sacs and Foxes formed a five-member Industrial Development Commission in 1983 to encourage economic development activity. The commission instituted a series of firsts. The tribe was one of the earliest to offer bingo to players. In 1984 it became the first tribe in the state to issue vehicle license plates to tribal members. A unanimous U.S. Supreme Court decision in 1993 upheld the legality of the tags for those tribal members who lived and parked their vehicles on tribal land. The tribe completed the first tribe–city governmental agreement, termed a compact, for business development (in 1985) and inaugurated the first complete tribal court system in the state.

The Sac and Fox Tribe officially changed its name in 1988 to the Sac and Fox Nation. That year the nation was one of the five tribes of the Shawnee Agency that decided to contract together to operate their own BIA programs. Early success led to Sac and Fox participation in the self-governance project that the Interior Department launched in the early 1990s.

At the start of 1992 tribal members were shocked by the tribe's application for a feasibility study for a nuclear waste storage facility. This sparked intense interest in the topic and added concern at the time of the conference that the tribe sponsored for the nationwide Indigenous Environmental Network.

In 1990 the Wisconsin legislature formally apologized for the excesses of the Black Hawk War. Members of the Sac and Fox Tribe attended the annual Black Hawk Powwow held in Rock Island, Illinois. Sometimes direct descendants of the chief participated.

For the first time in a century three Sac and Fox tribes came together in November 1994 in Reserve, Kansas. They discussed issues involved in the Native American Graves Protection and Repatriation Act and its effects on tribal remains.

A Sac and Fox suit against Tenneco Oil for pollution of water supply sources was successfully settled by the oil company's successor, El Paso Energy Corporation. The firm paid the tribe $1.16 million in 1997 in compensation for contamination and pledged to construct wells and a water supply delivery system and to restore some lands damaged by years of petroleum production. The construction and cleanup cost the company an additional $2.34 million. This was the culmination of a lengthy process, since the BIA initially began to study the issue in 1979.

There are still Sac-speakers in Oklahoma and Fox-speakers in Iowa. Linguists are honing computer language literacy programs. In 1995 the tribe formed a Sauk culture and language working group to foster retention efforts.

The annual Sac and Fox Powwow held outside of Stroud in July attracts many for dancing, crafts, and culture. The Oklahoma group hosts its Mesquakie kinfolk from Iowa. Unique to the Sacs and Foxes is the Swan or Crane Dance, which is still performed. The ancient Pipe dance is also demonstrated. Dancers wear ribbon work that continues the old floral designs, reflecting their Woodland heritage. The tribe is well known for its silk appliqué ribbon work. Elders confer tribal names on children, announcing which tribal division they joined. The tribe also sponsors an All-Indian Memorial Stampede Rodeo every summer. For a long time the tribal library has offered resources and community outreach on their heritage, research, and Native genealogy. I have used it through the years. There are some Native American Church practitioners who celebrate the sacrament of Peyote.

Sac and Fox names dot the landscape and maps of their former territories as reminders of their presence. Wapella, a Fox chief, gave his name to a county and a town in Iowa (Wapello) and a town in Illinois. Sac is the name of a town (Sac City) and a county in Iowa and a river in Missouri. The name of Saginaw, Michigan, is derived from a term meaning "place of the Sauks." The Fox chief Prairie du Chien lent his name to that settlement on the Mississippi River just above its confluence with the Wisconsin River north of present-day Dubuque, Iowa.

One of the most notable Sacs and Foxes is Black Hawk or Black Sparrow Hawk (Makataimeshekiakiah). His indomitable leadership of a band evading a pursuing military force as well as the deadly end of their odyssey lent an air of Greek tragedy to his legacy. Probably the most famous Sac and Fox is Jim Thorpe. He attended Shawnee Indian Boarding School, Sac and Fox and Sacred Heart Mission schools, then Carlisle Indian School. His athletic ability and determination led to two gold medals in the 1912 Olympics, for the pentathlon and decathlon. He was named the greatest athlete of the first half of the twentieth century in 1950 in an Associated Press poll. His daughter Grace Thorpe remained an environmental activist, most notable for opposing placing nuclear waste on Indian land. Gail Thorpe worked for the national Girl Scouts of America as well as other entities and then retired to Yale, Oklahoma, where she established the Jim Thorpe Museum in honor of her father. His granddaughter Dagmar Thorpe helped occupy Alcatraz Island in 1969 after a stint with Volunteers in Service to America (VISTA) and was later involved with various philanthropies.

Makataimeshekiakiah (Black Hawk), Sac (Sauk) chief

Print of colored lithograph by McKenney and Hall. Courtesy Creek Council House Museum.

Olympic athlete Jim Thorpe (Sac and Fox), painted by Charles Banks Wilson

Courtesy Oklahoma State Arts Council

Saginaw Grant (also Iowa) was well known from movie roles and poster portraits. He appeared in *Grey Owl* with Beau Bridges and in the television series *Harts of the West* and other serials. He also was an admired Southern Straight dancer in powwows and was involved in establishing the Narc Anon treatment program at the former Chilocco Indian School years ago. R. G. (Ronald George) Harris was a war dancer who performed and won championships widely throughout the United States and Canada. Antowine Warrior (who is also Shawnee) is a noted painter. The leading Indian historian in the United States, Donald L. Fixico, is enrolled Sac and Fox (as well as Shawnee, Seminole, and Creek).

SUGGESTED READING

Black Hawk, with the help of Antoine Le Claire and J. P. Patterson. *Life of Black Hawk: Ma-ka-Tai-Me-She-Kia-Kiak* (first published 1832 or 1833). Edited by Donald Jackson. Urbana: University of Illinois Press, 1955.

Crawford, Bill. *All American: The Rise and Fall of Jim Thorpe.* New York: Wiley, 2004.

Edmunds, R. David, and Joseph L. Peyser. *The Fox Wars: The Mesquakie Challenge to New France.* Norman: University of Oklahoma Press, 1993.

Hagan, William T. *The Sac and Fox Indians.* Norman: University of Oklahoma Press, 1958; repr. 1988.

Herring, Joseph. *The Enduring Indians of Kansas.* Lawrence: University Press of Kansas, 1995.

Jung, Patrick J. *The Black Hawk War of 1832.* Norman: University of Oklahoma Press, 2007.

Skinner, Alanson. *Observations on the Ethnology of the Sauk Indians.* Bulletin, vol. 5, nos. 1–3 (1923–25). Milwaukee: Public Museum of City of Milwaukee; repr. Westport, Conn.: Greenwood, 1970.

Thorpe, Dagmar. *People of the Seventh Fire: Returning Lifeways of Native America.* Ithaca, N.Y.: Akwekon/Cornell University Press, 1996.

Wittry, Warren. "The Bell Site, Wn9: An Early Historic Fox Village." *Wisconsin Archaeologist* 44, no. 1 (1963): 1–58.

Seminole

NAME

The name arose from the Mvskoke (Creek) word *simanoli* (also spelled *siminoli*), "runaway" or "wild," in the sense of "break-away." *Simanoli* referred to those who left or emigrated to settle anew elsewhere. Daniel Brinton said the term had originally been applied only to the Hitchiti Oconees. It also resembled the Spanish term for "wild," *cimarrón*. The word "Seminole" was first used in the 1760s.

LOCATION AND GOVERNMENT

The "Seminole Tribe of Oklahoma" headquarters is in Seminole County in central Oklahoma, with the National Council in the community of Seminole and the tribal administrative offices on the southern edge of the community of Wewoka. Tribal court sessions take place in the BIA building across the street from the administration building. The tribe was not organized under the OIWA but functions under a federally recognized 1969 constitution. Under Public Law 91-495 Congress permitted the Seminoles to elect their own officers. The tribe is controlled by a 28-member council with a principal chief and an assistant chief. Each of the traditional fourteen bands selects a representative to the council. Elections every four years select the officers. The tribal website is www.seminolenation.com.

The historic presence of the Seminoles in Florida is discussed only briefly here. Florida is home to some sixty tribal groups over time, making it a bewildering mix of Native ethnicities. The U.S. Congress created the Big Cypress Reservation (south of Clewiston) and the smaller Dania Reservation (now Hollywood Reservation, west of Hollywood) there in 1911. Residents of Big Cypress speak Mikasuke. Those on the Hollywood Reservation use both the Mikasuke and Mvskoke languages. In 1935 the federal government created a third reservation, Brighton, on the northwestern shore of Lake Okeechobee in Hendry County, whose residents also speak Mvskoke. Members of the three reserves make up the Seminole Tribe of Florida, established in August 1957. Their headquarters is in Hollywood. A fourth reservation, Miccosukee, was set up in 1962 with federal recognition, about forty miles west of Miami. Earlier this group had been referred to as Tamiami Indians because they resided along the highway (U.S. Highway 41) called the Tamiami Trail, connecting Tampa with Miami. There are also small clusters elsewhere in Florida. The Krome Avenue Miccosukees are located below Hollywood. The Alligator Alley Miccosukees are next to Big Cypress. The Immokalee Seminoles are northwest of Big Cypress. The Tampa Seminoles are north of that city. In 1996 the Cedar Key Seminoles near Altsena Otie Key on the Gulf Coast were federally recognized. Other Indians in Florida, many of them Seminoles, remain independent.

BUSINESSES

Major tribal revenue comes from four casino operations: Seminole Nation Bingo and Casino at the junction of Highways 99 and 59, the Seminole Casino at the junction of Interstate Highway 40 and State Highway 99 (exit 200), the Rivermist Casino near Konawa, and the Wewoka Gaming Center at Wewoka, all in Seminole County. The tribe owns five smoke shops. Travel plazas with convenience stores are located adjacent to major highways in the region. The tribe owns a motel near Seminole and a hotel in Ada. The tribe's various businesses make it the largest employer in Seminole County. The old Mekusukey Mission grounds are an industrial park south of Wewoka. There is also some leasing of land for oil and gas as well as pasturage for livestock. The tribe has about 35,000 acres of allotted land. Within the town of Seminole is a privately owned Seminole Nation Museum.

NUMBER

The tribe has about 15,000 members, two-thirds of whom live in Oklahoma, in the towns of Seminole and Wewoka and in rural areas of Seminole County. The second largest concentration is in Oklahoma City. There are 4,000 more Seminoles in Florida on reserves or remaining independent within that state.

Most Seminoles speak the Mvskoke (Creek) language (especially in Oklahoma), although there are Hitchiti-speakers in Oklahoma and Mikasuke-speakers in Florida. Hitchiti and Mikasuke are the same language, with dialectical differences. Prehistoric archeological sites are scattered across Florida. Some are ancient, others are Woodland, and still others are Mississippian cultures. The Seminoles were composed of remnants of many tribal nations and the Seminole-Creeks were latecomers to the peninsula, however, so the archeological sites do not have direct application to them. But a few of the remnant peoples who made up the Seminoles were connected to ancient residence in Florida. In addition, there are archeological burial sites of the historic residence of the Seminoles, of course, especially in their preremoval settlements and at gathering points for debarkation to Indian Territory.

Spanish explorers entered the Florida region in an increasing stream after Juan Ponce de León in 1513. Pánfilo de Narváez, Alvar Núñez Cabeza de Vaca, Hernando de Soto, and others trekked through the area and reinforced Spanish claims to the territory but also antagonized Native peoples. After the 1565 founding of St. Augustine, the first lasting European settlement in the Southeast, the Spanish also set up missions that dotted the southeastern landscape. They made converts among Timucuas, Calusas, and other tribes in Florida. But European diseases as well as attacks from rival neighboring tribes devastated the converted Indians. By the early 1700s the Timucuas and Calusas had almost vanished.

In the aftermath of their unsuccessful revolt against English settlers of 1715, Yamassee refugees fled into Florida. Other displaced Indians joined them, including a group of Muscogee Indians. After the English established the colony of Georgia, their runaway slaves also entered Florida. In 1763 Britain obtained control from Spain over Florida under the terms of its treaty negotiations at the end of the French and Indian War.

The Spanish interlude in Florida left behind remnants of the Apalachees, Calusas, Aises, Timucuas, and other Native peoples. They intermarried with the newcomers. The Spaniards had also welcomed Lower Creek residents into northern Florida, hoping that they would serve as a buffer against the English threat.

After turning Florida over to the British, the Spanish took with them most of the remaining Christianized and hispanicized Indians. Into the vacuum had come many remnant Native peoples, including Yamassees from the Carolinas, Oconees and Guales from Georgia, Chiahas and Apalachicolas from the Gulf region, Yuchis from Georgia and the Carolinas, Muscogees from the Alabama-Georgia area, and Hitchitis. Apalachicola, Yamassee, and Apalachee towns spoke Hitchiti. A Mikasuke town in northern Florida was formed by Apalachicolas and Chiahas, who also spoke Hitchiti, which was related to the language of the Upper Creeks. Oconees migrated from the river of the same name near present-day Milledgeville, Georgia, to Lower Creek territory in that colony after 1715 then into northern Florida. Oconees provided the early leaders of the Seminoles, such as Cowkeeper and Micanopy. Billy Bowlegs and John Jumper, later principal chiefs who extended their leadership into Indian Territory, were both nephews (sisters' sons) of Micanopy.

Lower Creek towns were shattered by European disease and military defeats, while economic shifts to the deerskin trade and away from chiefs' control led to chronic instability. The scattered people settled in the former Apalachee territory before 1780 near modern Tallahassee. Later migrants included Apalachicola, Sawaokli, Eufaula, and Hitchiti settlers of the Apalachee area as well as remnant Christian Apalachees and Yamassees. By the 1750s the Oconees of Cowkeeper (Wakapuchase in Mvskoke) gathered in Alachua territory in the area of present-day Gainesville. Perhaps the Oconees were heirs to the old Ocure chiefdom and moved to Florida to try to reassert it. Tamali-Ochisis, Yamassees, Yuchis, and Chiahas, nominally Lower Creeks, gathered as recent emigrants in the region of the forks of the Apalachicola River, where the present states of Georgia, Alabama, and Florida meet. By the 1820s they were frequently referred to as Seminoles.

Indians moved into and out of northern Florida both before and after 1700. By the 1760s Proto-Seminoles are considered to have become a subdivision of the Lower Creeks, with whom many had family and clan ties. In a real sense original Seminole towns had begun as colonies of Lower Creek towns, as ethnographer Richard Sattler has shown. Indian settlers, mestizos, maroons (escaped slaves), and others all contributed to the makeup of later Seminole towns. Trade, marriage, raiding, and migration in later years further added to the mixture of peoples.

Slaves escaped from the southern colonies, especially South Carolina, and settled along the Suwanee and Apalachicola rivers after 1700. There they engaged in commerce among Spanish, British, American, and Native traders. The Seminoles protected slaves within their villages under the guise of ownership. Their very presence fed southern slave-owners' demands to retrieve them, fostering undying conflict. Much of the subsequent warfare and history across the Florida peninsula officially focused on the Seminoles but was really about the presence of escaped black slaves. Free blacks and maroons lived among the Seminoles but were separate and were culturally distinct. They often aided Seminoles, worked with them, and sometimes served as a bridge between whites and Seminoles.

Shortly before the American Revolution, William Bartram traveled through Florida. He was a naturalist from Philadelphia who was interested in flora and Native uses of plants and left a valuable written account of what he saw. Bartram found that the Seminoles had comfortably settled into the region. He observed that they were gradually adapting European cloth for their dress. Women quickly made use of metal utensils. The Seminoles grew new crops like oranges and watermelons and raised domesticated animals like pigs, cows, and horses, which Europeans introduced to them. Seminole town life mirrored that of the Muscogees. After 1700 Seminole towns subsisted on both agriculture and game. Abundant wildlife such as deer, bears, and turkeys joined aquatic food sources such as fish, turtles, and more to sustain the Indians. Dry land amid the swampy areas (called hummocks) and sandy pine barrens offered good agricultural opportunities. Seminoles raised food in garden plots adjacent to their homes and tended larger "town fields" some distance from their villages. In 1774 Bartram watched Seminole families cultivating corn, beans, cowpeas, squash, sweet potatoes, melons, and pumpkins. They also tended stock animals. The grassy savannahs of summer were covered with several feet of water during the winter.

The newly developing United States, after the 1783 reversion of Florida to Spain, took increasing interest in the peninsula. Settlers violated Indian lands, southern slave-catchers accused Seminoles of harboring slaves, and pressure for the Seminoles to move continued to rise. Some mixed-blood Creek Indian Red Sticks massacred residents in Fort Mims in southern Alabama, sparking the Creek War of 1813–14. The fighting, the punitive peace terms, and continuing white encroachments into Native territory led more Indians to enter Florida. The new refugees tripled the Seminole population and greatly increased the Muscogee presence among them. The earlier Seminoles like the Tamali-Ochisis were mostly Lower Creeks, who spoke Hitchiti. After the dissident Red Stick defeat, a large influx of Upper Creeks flooded into Florida. That changed the makeup of the Seminoles. Upper Creek immigrants spoke Mvskoke and further doubled the existing population. That does not count the number of black slaves who also escaped into the region.

Ongoing skirmishes and escaped slaves provided the United States with an excuse to grab Florida from Spain. In the First Seminole War (1818–21), Andrew Jackson of Tennessee became well known, drove the Seminoles south away from the border, and forced Spain to sell the region to the United States in 1819. It really had been Jackson's punitive filibuster. Blacks played a pivotal role in saving the population of the town of Billy

Bowlegs during the conflict. Two years later the Florida territorial governor agreed with Indian leaders near St. Augustine on a reservation of 5 million acres for them in central Florida. They relinquished 30 million acres. Historian Annie H. Abel called this one of the worst Indian treaties ever made by the United States, because it inflamed conflicts instead of solving them. As a result of the poor execution of the agreement's terms and U.S. refusal to pay annuities, some Seminoles starved during their removal. The treaty had been signed in September 1823 at Camp Moultrie on the creek of that name below St. Augustine. Northern Florida quickly filled with white settlers, who continually harassed the Seminoles.

Under the Indian Removal Act (1830), the federal government tried to pry the Seminoles away from their latest lands. Fifteen Seminole headmen signed the treaty with the United States in May 1832 at Payne's Landing on the Oklawaha River. It became the Seminole removal document. Seven Seminoles ventured to Indian Territory to examine proposed lands and were tricked into agreeing to a removal treaty in March 1833 at Fort Gibson. The notorious John Schermerhorn served as U.S. negotiator. He would go on to infamy over his actions leading to the Cherokees' removal treaty. At Fort Gibson he received help from Montfort Stokes and Henry Ellsworth. The seven Seminoles had no authority to act for the tribe, but U.S. officials used the document as the excuse to undertake the tribe's removal.

Seminole warriors struck before the deadline, and the Second Seminole War (1835–42) erupted. Nine months after Seminole agent Wiley Thompson attempted to enforce removal in his official capacity, Osceola led an Indian attack that killed Thompson. Other Seminoles killed members of the Dade command. The Seminole War flared anew. It would prove to be the single costliest war in U.S. history and was also one of the most brutal. It cost the United States over $40 million and 1,500 soldiers' lives. At its height, one-fifth of all American military forces were engaged in the warfare. New tactics like amphibious landings were used, along with older tactics such as employing bloodhounds (which the Spanish had used much earlier). General Thomas Jessup's aggressive approach after December 1836 dampened down the Indian warfare only to see it rekindle after the treachery of Osceola's capture and death in captivity. Jessup's offer to free black slaves took them out of the conflict in 1838.

Attrition finally led some Seminoles to surrender and remove to Indian Territory. Some of them were taken in chains aboard cattle steamers. Conflict and illness killed others. Overall, the war era reduced the Seminole population by about 40 percent. Osceola's heir Wild Cat (Cooacoochee) finally surrendered in the spring of 1841. Up to five hundred holdouts melted into the Everglades swamp. The war dwindled away without a treaty ending it. A formal tripartite agreement was finally signed by the Seminoles, the state, and the United States in 1962. Between 1835 and 1842 approximately 4,400 Seminoles emigrated to Indian Territory. There they began once more. George Catlin painted a group of Seminoles at Fort Moultrie, including Osceola. The emigrants tended to be northern Florida residents who spoke Mvskoke, including Red Sticks, according to linguist Jack Martin. In the 1830s a portion of Apalachicola Seminoles, made up of Iolee, Tamali, and Ochisi bands under John Blount, migrated to the Trinity River in Texas and joined earlier Alabama and Koasati settlements. A series of skirmishes in the 1850s involving Billy Bowlegs, called the Third Seminole War, eventually led his group of 162 to relocate into Indian Territory too. A few Seminoles left for Mexico, settled at Nacimiento de los Negros near Muzquiz, Coahuila (across the international border from Eagle Pass), then in the 1870s served with distinction in the U.S. Army's Seminole-Negro Indian Scouts out of Brackettville, Texas. (Black Seminoles are referred to as Afro-Seminoles, Black Indians, maroons, and freedmen.) Black Seminoles today maintain descent groups.

Once in Indian Territory the Seminoles had difficulty adjusting to their new homeland. Kiowas and Comanches plundered their livestock. Their own Seminole identity was subordinated to the far larger Creek Nation. Half the Seminoles lingered around Fort Gibson for three years before traveling west to the Little River to set up their shelters. The Seminoles and blacks among them chafed under restrictive Creek laws regarding slaves and free blacks. Finally, the Indian Office authorities used the separation of the Choctaws and Chickasaws the year before as the model for an August 1856 official separation of the Seminoles from the Creeks. The Seminoles received 2.17 million acres in a strip between the Canadian River and the North Fork of the Canadian River in exchange for $1 million paid to the Creeks. The enlightened help of the commissioner of Indian affairs, T. Hartley Crawford, in reality saved Seminole identity and prevented them from being wholly absorbed into the Creek Nation.

In 1849 more than a hundred Seminoles under Wild Cat and blacks under John Horse (also called Gopher John) moved to Mexico, where Wild Cat and others served with distinction in the Mexican army. Some of the Indians and blacks returned to Indian Territory before the American Civil War. Ultimately there were about twenty Seminole towns in Indian Territory. Among these Indian towns also were black towns, which were made up of most of the five hundred blacks who had emigrated from Florida. They provided the model for later all-black communities in the early Oklahoma statehood period. Wewoka, the contemporary county seat, began in 1849 as a settlement by Gopher John.

The Seminoles underwent changes in organization during the eighteenth century. Before 1784 they were considered an extension of the Lower Creeks. Seminole bands were arranged according to red or white divisions, similar to Creek towns. Red division members were concerned with war. White division members provided civic leadership and dealt with matters of peace. There may have been local confederacies for Apalachees under Tonaby of Talahassi and for Alachuas under Cowkeeper of Cuskowilla at the start of the century. The band constituted the main political unit. Each band had its own "medicine" (*hiliswa* in Mvskoke). If the band had its own sacred fire and square ground, it was self-governing. It then operated under its own sacred charter. An informal council evolved in the 1820s to deal with increasing American demands and various removal schemes. The council became more formal during the next decade. It followed a Muscogee model; because it was developed in Alachua territory, the office of the principal chief evolved into a hereditary office held by the Alachua paramount chiefs of old. Seminole political identity only unified during their removal, which also forged their polity.

Osceola, Seminole chief
Print of colored lithograph by McKenney and Hall. Courtesy Creek Council House Museum.

In Florida and in Oklahoma the Seminoles resided in towns called *talofa* or *etalwv* or *tulwa* (in Mvskoke), further divided into separate Mvskoke-speaking and Mikasuke-speaking towns. The residents of the towns, made up of log cabins, cultivated the rich bottomland. They identified with the town of their birth. Matrilineal clans regulated family life in the towns. Each town had a band headman or chief (called a *meko* or *mico* in Mvskoke) as well as an assistant or second chief (*heniha*) and a war leader (*tustvnvke* or *tustanugy*). They, in turn, had representatives on the Seminole general council, which supervised national affairs. The Seminole polity reflected a strong Muscogee sociopolitical structure. The council selected a principal chief. The effective Micanopy was chief until his death in 1848 or 1849. Wild Cat served as his counselor. After Micanopy, Jim Jumper served as principal chief until his death and was succeeded by John Jumper.

Missionaries slowly established schools for the Seminoles. The Reverend and Mrs. John Lilley opened Oak Ridge Presbyterian Mission in 1849 about three miles southeast of present Holdenville in Hughes County. It had limited success and closed on the eve of the Civil War. A family member opened Pond Creek Mission near Oak Ridge. The educational endeavor of John Bemo at Prospect Hill after 1844 was also short-lived. He joined the efforts of Joseph Samuel Murrow, a Baptist, after 1859. Following the Civil War the Lilleys began Seminole Presbyterian Mission north of Wewoka. There were ultimately four Presbyterian mission schools for the Seminoles. Seminole chief John Jumper became a Baptist convert. He led members of his Oconee-Alachua band and mixed-bloods to his faith. The building for Spring Indian Baptist Church was moved to his property near Sasakwa ("goose" in Mvskoke). The congregation celebrated its 150th anniversary in 2000. The original church (restored) is still used. After statehood the Seminoles combined Mekusukey boarding school with Emahaka (1911).

The sixty Seminole Indian Christian churches, of which fourteen are Baptist, replicated their old *etalwv* (town) structure. The hierarchy saw the pastor in a position that equaled the earlier *mico*; the assistants or speakers (similar to earlier *heniha*) became deacons. The church building faced east, the direction of the rising sun, which played such a prominent role in traditional ceremonies, and the direction from which Indian Christians anticipate the Savior will return. Use of Native languages in hymns and sermons helped perpetuate a sense of being Indian. Author Jack Schultz argued that these aspects contributed to a unique traditional Seminole identity within an Anglo world: a distinctive arrangement using the Seminole language, hymns, and worldview.

The passions of the Civil War divided the Seminoles as it did most of the United States. John Jumper became an officer of the First Regiment of Seminole Mounted Volunteers. Like Lower Creeks under Daniel and Chilly McIntosh, the Confederate Indian forces saw action in the war. Other Seminoles such as Billy Bowlegs remained loyal to the Union and joined Creeks under Opothleyahola, who led followers toward the Kansas haven. Bowlegs later commanded Union troops in Company F of the First Indian Home Guards. Refugees from both sides suffered terribly from malnutrition, climate, and destitution. Their homeland experienced the depredations of guerrillas, outlaws, and profiteers. In their March 1866 Reconstruction treaty, the Seminoles ceded their entire domain for fifteen cents an acre and paid fifty cents an acre for 200,000 acres in the western part of Creek territory. After the convulsions of their removal and the Civil War eras, the following forty years were the longest period of respite for the Seminoles since 1818. Even that era of quiet would not last.

Stubborn resistance to allotment in severalty among the Five Tribes under the Dawes Commission led Congress to enact the harsh Curtis Act (1898). It abolished most of the Seminole Nation's court structure, school system, and tribal government. Under allotment, completed in 1902, 3,119 Seminoles received an average of 120 acres each (with 355 children added in March 1905 to the list of those receiving land). Afterward the BIA appointed principal chiefs when a signature was needed to deed tribal land to a private owner. A monument to the exploitation of Indians and freedmen during the petroleum boom around World War I is the former W. D. Grisso mansion north of the town of Seminole. During the late 1920s Seminole was the greatest oil field in the world.

The distinctive multicolored designs on women's skirts and men's jackets, called patchwork, mark Seminole clothing. Oklahoma Seminoles adopted patchwork in the 1960s from their Florida kinfolk. The designs are symbols of objects and events out of their heritage and provide a notable motif for their clothing. About a quarter of the Seminoles in Oklahoma speak the Mvskoke language. Hitchiti is lapsed among them, and Mikasuke is about to be.

The presence of freedmen has always been a unique feature of the Seminoles. In the 1960s the federal government included freedmen in the reestablished Seminole Tribe, although the U.S. government excluded freedmen from the judgment funds settlement. (Statehood further separated Seminoles and freedmen because of imposed statewide segregation.) A tribal vote in 2000, disputed in court, amended the tribal constitution and excluded freedmen from membership and abolished the council seats of the two freedmen bands (Dosar Barkus and Caesar Brunner). The Indian Claims Commission in 1976 awarded $16 million to the Seminoles as compensation for Florida lands lost. For the first time in over a century, representatives of Oklahoma and Florida Seminoles met under federal auspices to negotiate the terms. Disagreement over how to distribute the judgment fund delayed the payment until a 1990 settlement allocated 75 percent of the $48 million fund (which had grown from accumulated interest) to the more populous Seminole group in Oklahoma and 25 percent to the smaller Florida Seminole group.

The federally recognized Seminole tribes cooperated in 1998 to develop guidelines for repatriating ancestral remains under the terms of the 1990 Native American Graves Protection and Repatriation Act. It was the first time the tribes had officially collaborated in 150 years.

Among the most notable Seminoles is the mixed-blood Osceola. His mother took him from the Horseshoe Bend battle in 1814 into Florida, where he became the leader of Seminole resistance against removal. Billy Bowlegs, known as Hulbutta Mico or Alligator King, was the last Seminole chief to be removed to Indian Territory. Enoch Kelly Haney is widely recognized as a painter and artist as well as a politician, including serving as tribal chief. His sculpture *The Guardian* atop the State Capitol dome honors the memory of his son. He served for many years as a representative and a senator in the state. Michael Stephen Haney (who was also part Lakota) was an activist member of AIM who spoke against many injustices, including the use of Indian mascots for sports teams. Mary Jo Watson is a leading American Indian art history professor at the University of Oklahoma. Johnny,

Sculptor Enoch Kelly Haney (Seminole) in front of *The Guardian,* 2002
Courtesy of the artist

Dana, and Jerome Tiger are painters of note. June Lee is a master of patchwork. Jack Larkin created remarkable folk art sculpture in stone at Chiaha (Ceyvha) outside Wewoka. Mary Youngblood (Aleut-Seminole) was one of the first American Indian women to record Native flute music. Among her CDs was one titled *Beneath the Raven Moon.* Comedian Redd Foxx as well as Willie Stargell and Johnny Ray (who were both baseball players for the Pittsburgh Pirates) claimed Seminole heritage. National Public Radio commentator Sarah Vowell (also Cherokee) is of tribal heritage. Episcopal bishop William Wantland served as attorney general for the tribe and as a justice on the tribal court. Sterlin Harjo (who is also Creek) is a filmmaker.

SUGGESTED READING

Abel, Annie H. "History of Events Resulting in Indian Consolidation West of the Mississippi." In *Annual Report of the American Historical Association for 1906,* vol. 1, 233–450. Washington, D.C.: Smithsonian Institution Press, 1908 (quotation on 330).

Black Indians: An American Story. Dallas: Rich Heape Films, 2000 (film).

Black Warriors of the Seminole. N.p.: Florida Humanities Council, 1991 (film).

Brinton, Daniel G. *The American Race: A Linguistic Classification and Ethnographic Description of the Native Tribes of North and South America.* New York: Hodges, 1891.

Burke, Jerry. "Oklahoma Seminole Indians: Origin, History, and Pan-Indianism." *Chronicles of Oklahoma* 51 (Summer 1973): 211–23.

Elder, John L. *Everlasting Fire: Cowokoci's Legacy in the Seminole Struggle against Western Expansion.* Edmond, Okla.: Medicine Wheel, 2004.

Howard, James H., and Willie Lena. *Oklahoma Seminoles: Medicine, Magic, and Religion.* Norman: University of Oklahoma Press, 1984.

Hudson, Charles. *The Southeastern Indians.* Knoxville: University of Tennessee Press, 1976.

Johnson, Dolores. *Seminole Diary: Remembrances of a Slave.* New York: Macmillan, 1994 (for young readers).

Lancaster, Jane F. *Removal Aftershock: The Seminoles' Struggles to Survive in the West, 1836–1866.* Knoxville: University of Tennessee Press, 1994.

Littlefield, Daniel F., Jr. *Africans and Seminoles: From Removal to Emancipation.* Westport, Conn.: Greenwood, 1977; repr. University: University Press of Mississippi, 2002.

Mahon, John K. *History of the Second Seminole War, 1835–1842.* Gainesville: University of Florida Press, 1967; repr. 1985; rev. ed. 1991.

Martin, Jack. "Languages." In vol. 14, *Southeast*, of the *Handbook of North American Indians*, 68–86. Washington, D.C.: Smithsonian Institution, 2004.

Medearis, Angela Shelf. *Dancing with the Indians.* New York: Holiday House, 1991 (for young readers).

Miller, Susan A. *Coacoochee's Bones: A Seminole Saga.* Lawrence: University Press of Kansas, 2003.

Missall, John, and Mary Lou Missall. *The Seminole Wars: America's Longest Indian Conflict.* Gainesville: University Press of Florida, 2004.

Mulroy, Kevin. *Freedom on the Border: The Seminole Maroons in Florida, the Indian Territory, Coahuila, and Texas.* Lubbock: Texas Tech University Press, 1993; repr. 1998.

———. *The Seminole Freedmen: A History.* Norman: University of Oklahoma Press, 2007.

Porter, Kenneth W. *The Black Seminoles.* Edited by Alcione M. Amos and Thomas P. Senter. Gainesville: University Press of Florida, 1996.

Sattler, Richard. "*Siminoli Italwa*: Socio-political Change among the Oklahoma Seminoles between Removal and Allotment, 1836–1905." Ph.D. dissertation, University of Oklahoma, 1987.

Schultz, Jack M. *The Seminole Baptist Churches of Oklahoma: Maintaining a Traditional Community.* Norman: University of Oklahoma Press, 1999.

Trimble, Vance H. *Alice and J. F. B.: The 100-Year Saga of Two Seminole Chiefs.* N.p.: Market Tech Books, 2006.

Waselkov, Gregory A., and Kathryn E. Holland Braund, eds. *William Bartram on the Southeastern Indians.* Lincoln: University of Nebraska Press, 1995.

Welsh, Louise. "Seminole Colonization in Oklahoma." *Chronicles of Oklahoma* 54 (Spring 1976): 77–103.

Seneca-Cayuga

"Seneca" derives from the Iroquoian word "Onodowohgah," "people of the hill top." Some refer to Nun-da-wa-o-no, "the great hill people." It was anglicized from Dutch to "Seneca." "Cayuga" is derived from the Iroquoian name "Kwenio Gwe," "the place where the locusts were taken out." The Oklahoma Cayugas designate themselves as either Hodinqh Syq:ni', "Iroquois," or Kayohkhonq, "Cayuga" (see the "Cayuga" entry).

LOCATION AND GOVERNMENT

The "Seneca-Cayuga Tribe of Oklahoma" has its headquarters in Miami in Ottawa County, in far northeastern Oklahoma (about twenty miles southwest of Joplin, Missouri). The Seneca-Cayugas were the first in Oklahoma to organize after the enactment of the OIWA, with their constitution approved by the interior secretary in April 1937 and by tribal vote the following May 15. They revised their constitution in 1973. The seven-member business council, with a chief, serves as the governing body. Members have staggered two-year terms. An annual tribal meeting elects officers. The Senecas have had an elected council form of government since at least the 1870s. The tribal website is www.sctribe.com.

BUSINESSES

Revenue arises from the tribes' Grand Lake Casino north of the community of Grove; two smoke shops; and Tobacco Company. All are located in the area of Grove, on the east side of the Grand Lake O' the Cherokees. Skydancer-brand cigarettes are manufactured locally and are distributed globally. In addition, the tribes co-own about 4,000 acres, of which under 3,000 acres are held as individually allotted land.

The tribes have about 4,200 members. Many reside in northeast-ern Oklahoma, but many also live throughout the United States and across the globe due to military service, intermarriage, and job opportunities.

Because of their long contact with Europeans and their north-eastern location in history, Senecas today live in many areas. Ca-yugas today also reside in New York, while a large group can be found on the Six Nations Reserve in Canada.

Senecas and Cayugas belong to the Five Nations (later called the Six Na-tions) of the Iroquois League. Their languages are Iroquoian. The Senecas are the westernmost members of the League of the Iroquois. The Cayugas are Younger Brothers in the league and lived between the Senecas to their west and the Onondagas to the east. The league abolished the practice of the blood feud and determined to work as a unit, especially out of their home base in central New York. The French used the label "Iroquois" to designate a variety of Native languages spoken on either side of the St. Lawrence in the Northeast. Seneca is one of ten Northern Iroquoian lan-guages. Linguists maintain that Seneca split from the main core relatively late (perhaps a thousand years ago), just before Mohawk-Oneida, the last to divide. Cayuga, in contrast, according to linguists Wallace Chafe and Michael Foster, separated much earlier but interacted with Proto-Seneca more than once and was influenced by those episodes.

Theories abound for the origin of Iroquoian peoples. Current think-ing favors local in-place development, although migration stories are prevalent. Archeologists use the term "Owasco" for the stages through the centuries before the emergence of the historic Iroquois tribes. Evi-dence indicates that the early Senecas gradually moved northward out of what is now termed the Boughton Hill site (earlier called Gannagaro). There are other sites between Seneca Lake and the Genesee River of New York. Cayuga village locations have been found on both sides of Cayuga Lake in that state. After about A.D. 1000 the population drifted away from riverine and lake villages to stockaded settlements on defensible hilltops. There was increasing warfare after 1300, as Iroquois legend at-tests. By mid-point in the following century Seneca and Cayuga tribes perhaps had emerged from consolidated villages. Longhouse residence, ceramics, and other features characteristic of the Iroquois had appeared by then. Paleo-Indian and Archaic Native ancestors lived in small camps.

They moved across their landscape in small bands as they hunted and gathered their food. Pottery appeared during the Late Archaic, followed about 700 B.C. by manufactured tubular tobacco pipes. Domesticated plant use marked the Woodland period, which eventually included corn, beans, and squash.

Woodland Iroquois towns were only lightly influenced by Hopewell, Adena, and then Mississippian cultural traits. Iroquois towns in the 1400s were heavily fortified on top of hills, commanding the surrounding valley fields. Matrilineal clans dominated civil affairs, which were conducted inside longhouses. Both the Senecas and the Cayugas had elected leaders, likely hereditary among the Cayugas. Because of their constant movements, details of their form of leadership are not well known. To add to the confusion, both tribes were often called the Mingos. They carried their council form of government with them into Indian Territory.

According to the Seneca origin story, an angry husband hurled his wife from the upper world into a void. She had come to sit and view the hole created when the husband knocked over the sacred tree, with its white roots extending through to the earth below. Birds aided the wife's descent and landing on the back of a turtle. When the muskrat brought up mud from the depth of the ocean and smeared it over the turtle's back, the earth grew. The woman dropped seeds that she had grabbed before she fell and used dirt that she held to offer a bed for the seeds. The woman gave birth to a daughter, who grew very rapidly. The daughter gave birth to two boys, one good and one bad. The bad son killed his mother. From her grave sprang beans, squash, corn, and tobacco plants as gifts to the People.

In the historical record, the Senecas and Cayugas resided in what is now the state of New York. The Senecas, the largest of the Five Nations, occupied a region between the Genesee River and Canadaigua Lake in what are now Livingston and Ontario counties in New York. A pronounced east and west division of the Senecas extended from late prehistory into the historic period. The smaller Cayuga group resided in New York between Cayuga and Oswego lakes in what is now Cayuga County.

The arrival of Europeans, especially the Dutch and the French after 1609, thrust outside influences into long-standing intertribal warfare between the Iroquois and the Algonquians of the northeastern region. During the century of English-French wars that ended in 1673 the Iroquois generally sided with the English. The Iroquois gradually gained the ascendancy until the 1770s. They attempted neutrality when the American Revolution began, but the effects of warfare devastated their New York homeland. Postwar treaties with the new United States ceded Iroquois territory and confined the Six Nations (the Tuscaroras joined as the sixth in 1712–15) to reservations. The Treaty of Big Tree (1797) alienated most of the Seneca lands in western New York.

After about 1660 and well through the following century a varied group of tribal peoples entered present-day Ohio. The Ohio Valley was a natural extension out of western Pennsylvania, which was drained by that river. The name "Ohio" is derived from the Seneca designation (meaning "Fine River") for that watercourse. Native peoples, mostly Iroquois (especially the Senecas), followed the natural riverine channel into what would later become Ohio, first as hunters then as settlers. The eventual mix of tribal peoples included Delawares, Wyandottes, Shawnees, and others, and they were identified with the Iroquois, who made up their largest number.

The western Iroquois were commonly known in the eighteenth century as the Mingos. They resided in western Pennsylvania and in the eastern region of the Ohio Valley. The Mingos were a group of allied bands of Iroquois, made up of Cayuga, Mohawk, Oneida, Tuscarora, Onondaga, Erie, and Conestoga Indians. One of the most famous Mingos was the leader named Logan. Logan is believed to have guided British agent George Croghan in 1765 into the Illinois country to open that region to English trade. It was the massacre of Logan's family in April 1774 that started Lord Dunmore's War in the Pennsylvania border region. The Ohio Iroquois tended to support the Americans during the War of 1812. Under the terms of an 1817 treaty the Mingos obtained a 40,000-acre reserve on the Sandusky River in Ohio. They thereby became known as the Senecas of Sandusky. Treaties in 1817–18 ceded northwestern Ohio lands to the United States but also created two small reserves there: for the Senecas of Sandusky near Fremont and for the Mixed Band of Senecas and Shawnees near Lewistown. After the American Revolution, Cayugas in New York sold their lands and also moved to Ohio, where they too took up residence on the Sandusky River after 1800. On the Sandusky they were joined by Shawnees as well as some other members of the Iroquois League.

The Senecas and Cayugas who lived in Ohio relied upon agriculture. Their farming communities remained in village homes during warm weather to tend crops. During cold weather, however, the population dispersed for hunting and fur trapping. They prospered on their fertile farms. That success brought demands for their removal so the lands would fall to white settlers. In February 1831 the tribes sold their land in Ohio and agreed to relocate to a reservation within the Cherokee Nation in Indian Territory. Finally, 231 Senecas boarded a canal boat then a steamboat and traveled to St. Louis through late 1831 and into 1832, followed by

110 Senecas and 58 Delawares on horseback. Their journey took eight months, and the miserable travelers were beset by blizzards, illness, and deaths. Perhaps a third died.

When the Senecas and Cayugas arrived in Indian Territory, they realized that their new lands of 67,000 acres overlapped with those of the Cherokee Nation. The newcomers first settled on Cowskin or Elk River. Another band of 220 Mixed Senecas and Shawnees traded their land in Ohio in July 1832 for a new 60,000-acre reserve in Indian Territory. They also discovered that their land lay inside the Cherokee Nation. They were without a country.

President Andrew Jackson authorized United States commissioners Montfort Stokes, Henry Ellsworth, Samuel Stambaugh, and the Reverend John Schermerhorn to adjust Seneca boundaries. A December 1832 treaty on Buffalo Creek, a branch of the Cowskin near the Seneca Agency, provided new boundaries and recognized the "United Nations of Seneca and Shawnee." This treaty was the first that the United States made with emigrant Indians inside what would become Oklahoma. The Indians gained an official reservation east of the Neosho (or Grand) River outside Cherokee Nation borders. It was called the Neosho Reservation. The Mixed Band got the northern half; the Seneca-Cayugas (the Senecas of Sandusky) the southern portion. The Seneca-Cayugas were the eastern Indian pioneers in that area. An 1837 census identified 200 Senecas of Sandusky, 211 Mixed Band members, and 50 Mohawks on the reservation.

A small number of Iroquois ventured from New York to Kansas between 1846 and 1852. Many returned to New York, while some moved to Indian Territory before returning to Kansas. A few, mostly Cayugas, remained in Indian Territory. In the 1870s emigrants from the Six Nations Reserve arrived from Canada, married, and added to the mix of reserve peoples.

Under the guidance of Confederate representative Albert Pike, the Senecas and Seneca-Shawnees signed a treaty with the Confederacy in Tahlequah (Park Hill) in October 1861. Repeated wartime incursions by Kansas Union forces and threats from Confederates led most of the Seneca-Cayugas to flee to Kansas. They resided on the Ottawa Reservation through the remainder of the war. Some Senecas and Shawnees performed military service during the early warfare. Fighting ended the Roman Catholic mission at Seneca (established for the Seneca-Cayugas and for some Shawnees and Cherokees), which had begun in 1853.

Federal negotiators in February 1867 achieved an Omnibus Treaty that sold a part of the Seneca-Cayuga lands for future use by other Kansas tribes, such as Ottawas, Peorias, and Wyandottes. Federal authorities separated the Shawnees, who became the Eastern Shawnees. In the future the Senecas of Sandusky and the Senecas of the Mixed Band were to be known simply as the Seneca Tribe. The 1867 document took effect in 1869.

Missionaries after the Civil War entered the reservation seeking converts. The Society of Friends established a Seneca School in 1870. It was located in Ottawa County near the town of Wyandotte. Tribal member Joe Kagey served with distinction as superintendent from 1928 to 1956. The following year the BIA placed the Seneca-Cayugas under the jurisdiction of the Quapaw Subagency. Methodists operated a school among the Wyandottes, which was open to Seneca-Cayuga pupils. Roman Catholic priests visited the region too. Some of the Wyandotte and Cayuga residents were at least nominally Catholic. One of them, Mathias Splitlog, supported the establishment of St. Mary's of the Quapaws as well as the Cayuga Mission Church, which was willed to the Catholic Church upon his death. The Cayuga Church was lovingly restored in the 1950s and is now a Baptist church.

In 1881 over a hundred Cayugas journeyed from Canada, joining some Cayugas from New York to settle among the Senecas in Indian Territory. Indian Office officials opposed any additional members on the reservation and blocked the Canadians' absorption. A few of them returned to Canada, but most remained. Some of those who returned to the North walked home amid incredible hardships. There were repeated removals in both directions. Some Senecas took allotments into 1891 after the enactment of the 1887 Dawes Act. Another 372 members were allotted lands in 1902–1903. "Surplus" lands were opened to white settlers. Ultimately, many Indian allotments were lost to whites.

It took nearly two years of discussions before the Seneca-Cayugas agreed to come together under the OIWA for their tribal constitution and by-laws in the 1930s. During the Indian New Deal they joined Civilian Conservation Corps (CCC) and Works Progress Administration (WPA) programs as well as arts and crafts programs. Among their CCC products is the stone events building on their tribal grounds, which is still used annually. Some of their members also worked for the Grand River Dam project. Seneca-Cayugas served in the European theater during World War II.

A swath of Seneca-Cayuga land, including about half their ceremonial area, was inundated by the waters of Grand Lake following the completion of the dam in 1940. Half of their Bassett Grove ceremonial grounds (also termed Turkey Ford) was lost to the waters. More recently Seneca-Cayuga tribal members have been concerned with the potential hazards to their territory from downstream contamination from Tar Creek runoff. The Tar Creek Superfund Site of the Environmental Protection Agency has been a focus of concern for many years as a result of tailing waste from mining activity. Lead, zinc, and other heavy metal waste invaded the groundwater. Residents in the region are concerned about the pollution of the air, water, and soil, of native plants, and of their lives. Linked caverns from mining threaten cave-ins across a 40-square mile swath of territory. Poultry runoff into local streams is another issue.

The tribes built a new longhouse in 1968. The former rural Charloe School was remodeled as a tribal meeting hall. Tribal members eagerly anticipated the 1973 settlement of a long-standing claims award arising out of their treatment in 1789. The tribes also contributed to an enlargement of Indian jurisdiction and economic development in a noteworthy court opinion. A 1985 federal court decision (*May v. Seneca-Cayuga Tribe*) limited state jurisdiction over Seneca-Cayuga bingo that operated on Quapaw land in northeastern Oklahoma.

The tribal claims to their historic lands in order to undertake lucrative gaming enterprises are a source of ongoing controversy with residents of New York. The parcel that the Seneca-Cayuga Tribe sought is near Cayuga Lake in the known homeland of the Cayugas. In late 2004 the governor of New York agreed with the Cayugas of Oklahoma in a settlement of the tribal claim. The Indians dropped their share of the $248 million awarded in a 2002 federal judgment and their claim to 64,000 acres of land that the tribe asserted was wrongly taken in a 1795 treaty. The governor agreed to a 100-acre plot in Sullivan County, including the community of Monticello, for a casino in the Catskill Mountains until an adverse court opinion in another case (*City of Sherrill* in 2005) upset the deal.

Today the Seneca-Cayugas continue their rituals as well as ceremonial dances such as the Green Corn Ceremony. Members of the north and south clans sit on opposite sides of the longhouse. Four rites sustain the Green Corn Ceremony: the personal chant, turtle shell dance, thanksgiving dance, and peach seed game, which is played on the second day. Many return to Oklahoma to maintain connections to kin and to reinforce their Indian identity. During their major annual ceremony Seneca-Cayuga members play a ritual football game, mirroring the practice of their Shawnee, Delaware, and Quapaw neighbors. At the Bassett Grove/Turkey Ford ceremonial ground the Pot Hangers (the six clan mothers, who are also referred to as Faithkeepers and Workers of God) who guide it, as well as six men, recall the rituals and the names of clan affiliations from Iroquois heritage. The Pot Hangers manage the ceremonies and set dates for them to be performed. They offer songs for the thunders, the sun, the moon, and the earth. A Rain Dance or Sun Dance is held twice a year, at the beginning of the ceremonial season and at the end of the ritual cycle. There is also a Strawberry Ceremony to honor the first fruits in the springtime. Their Blackberry Ceremony in July offers thanks to grandmother Moon. Dancing precedes the baby-naming ceremony. Some members belong to the Iroquois False Face Society as well as medicine societies. Some also continue to participate in Peyote meetings. Wakes and funeral gatherings include feasts. Among the Seneca-Cayugas there are also Quaker, Baptist, Catholic, and Methodist church members. Oklahoma tribal members continue to interact with their New York and Canadian kinfolk as well as with neighboring Northeast Eight Oklahoma tribes for ceremonies, athletic contests, and powwows. Kinfolk maintain connections to Six Nations Reserve residents and exchange visits to participate in rituals. Additionally, New York Senecas teach Native language courses at the Miami, Oklahoma, satellite campus of Northeastern State University.

Notable Seneca-Cayugas include Michael Justus, an award-winning artist known for his paintings. Te Nona Kay Kuhn was honored in 1997 as Outstanding Young Woman of America by the United States Jaycees for her numerous contributions to her community.

SUGGESTED READING

Bass, Althea. *The Thankful People.* Caldwell, Idaho: Caxton, 1953 (for young readers).

Chafe, Wallace, and Michael Foster. "Prehistoric Divergences and Recontacts between Cayuga, Seneca, and the Other Northern Iroquoian Languages." *International Journal of American Linguistics* 47, no. 2 (1981): 121–42.

Foreman, Grant. *The Last Trek of the Indians.* Chicago: University of Chicago Press, 1946; repr. New York: Russell and Russell, 1972.

Nieberding, Velma. "Seneca-Cayuga Green Corn Ceremonial Feast." *Chronicles of Oklahoma* 34 (Summer 1956): 231–34.

Absentee Shawnee

The tribal name is derived from Shawnunogi, "southerners," in the Central Algonquian languages. The phrase "Absentee Shawnees" arose when a group of Shawnees separated in the mid-1840s from the main portion of the Shawnees in Kansas. They journeyed to Texas and continued to be "absent" when allotments in Kansas were assigned under an 1854 treaty. Under the terms of that treaty, a portion of the Kansas land was set aside for those who were absent. The Absentee Shawnees refer to themselves as Shaawanwa (which cannot be translated). (See also the "Eastern Shawnee" and "Shawnee Tribe [Loyal Shawnee]" entries.)

LOCATION AND GOVERNMENT

The headquarters for the "Absentee Shawnee Tribe of Oklahoma" is located on the southern edge of the city of Shawnee in Pottawatomie County, in central Oklahoma (approximately thirty-five miles east of Oklahoma City). The government of the Absentee Shawnee Tribe exists under the OIWA, with a December 1938 constitution, amended in August 1988. The government consists of five officers and executive council members, who are elected by the tribal General Council (made up of all eligible enrolled members over the age of eighteen). Members of the council are elected to staggered two-year terms. A governor presides. The current government has two branches, the judicial and the legislative/executive. The tribe was one of the first seven tribes in the United States to become a self-governing nation during the 1990s. The tribal website is www.astribe.com.

BUSINESSES

The focus of revenue is Thunderbird Wild West Entertainment Center (at www.okthunderbirdcasino.com) on State Highway 9 east of Norman on the east side of Lake Thunderbird. It is halfway (seventeen miles) between Norman and the tribal headquarters.

The tribe also owns a medical supply and garment manufacturing firm as well as a shopping mall called Tecumseh Square, two smoke shops (and one more leased), and a convenience store (in the city of Tecumseh) and offers recreational facilities at the lake. It contracts with a printing company in Shawnee. The Absentee Shawnees gain revenue from a tribal tax on goods and services within their boundaries. The tribe's business entities are under the control of the federally chartered Absentee Shawnee Economic Development Authority. Individual allotted land totals about 11,000 acres, while the tribe owns about 400 acres, and some oil and gas income is derived from leases.

NUMBER

The tribe has about 3,000 members, with 800 of them concentrated in the area extending from Norman to Little Axe to Tecumseh to Shawnee. There is a one-fourth blood quantum requirement for membership. Because of the tribe's many moves, Shawnee descendants are widely scattered throughout the United States and Canada.

Linguistics provides insight into Shawnee origins. The Shawnees speak a dialect of Algonquian. Because Shawnee is related linguistically to the languages of other Central Algonquian-speakers like the Sacs and Foxes, Kickapoos, and Ojibwes, scholars believe that the Shawnees ultimately share a common background. Proto-Algonquian was spoken perhaps 3,000 years ago in the region of Georgian Bay on Lake Ontario. At an early stage the language fragmented into at least ten distinct languages as peoples migrated. Some of those Proto-Algonquian peoples formed what is termed Central Algonquian culture and moved through the boreal forest south of Hudson Bay into the region south of the Great Lakes.

By the time of the Middle Ages in Europe, Fort Ancient peoples lived over the remains of earlier Adena and Hopewell cultures in an arc from present-day Ohio into West Virginia. The origin of Fort Ancient culture is unknown, but its people used plaza architecture and corn as a staple, like the Mississippians of mound-building fame. Some of the Fort Ancient villages had stockade fortifications. Early Shawnee bands occupied some of the Fort Ancient sites. Whether Fort Ancient societies were late prehistoric Shawnees is conjectural. But some Shawnee cultural traits like their town structure and rituals seen as southeastern probably derived from a Mississippian background. Iroquois oral history claims that they drove the Shawnees out of the central Ohio Valley. If that occurred far enough back in time, the Iroquois presence may have helped split Algonquian-speakers and contributed to the creation of languages and tribal entities. Historic Shawnee territory was just south of Lake Erie, especially in the central Ohio area. English colonists even found Shawnees in Georgia and South Carolina in 1692. The ever-fragmented Shawnees rarely resided there but were found far and wide (from present-day Ohio into Maryland, Pennsylvania, Alabama, and South Carolina) through the seventeenth century. Consequently the Shawnees cannot be identified with only one "homeland," with the exception of Ohio.

The Prophet relayed their origin story to C. C. Trowbridge in 1824. The Great Spirit made the earth and a Shawnee man and woman to inhabit it. The Great Spirit opened up the door of the skies, and the twelve Indians peered down on the Island below. He told them that they must journey to the Island and that it would take them twelve days. He provided corn, beans, and squash as well as melons and game for the Indians to live on. The Great Spirit gave a portion of his heart so that all might share at least a part of something good.

In another version the Supreme Being made a female presence with formative power. The Creator for the Shawnees is Our Grandmother (Kokomthena) or Cloud Woman. She created the earth as well as the turtle supporting it. After her grandson Rounded Side (or Cloud Boy) sent a flood that destroyed earth, Our Grandmother re-created it. She also created the Shawnees and instructed them on how to live and how to perform proper ceremonies. She gave the Shawnees their twelve laws. Our Grandmother also provided sacred bundles to the five divisions of the Shawnees (termed "septs") and gave instructions on their proper use.

The Shawnees' strategic location along the Ohio Valley meant that the English and French fought over control of the area. The contest for the area shattered the Shawnees. Iroquois expansion between 1662 and 1673 drove them from the valley. The Shawnees were repeatedly scattered and moved during the ensuing years. Their diaspora divided them permanently.

Some Shawnees who were dispersed starting in the late seventeenth century settled amid Delawares in the area of eastern Pennsylvania. They intermarried and together moved back to present-day Ohio but later crossed the Mississippi River. Following the Iroquois cessation of out-right hostility, the Shawnees in western Pennsylvania became associated with the Mingos, a segment of the Iroquois (mostly Senecas and Cayugas) who later became better known as the Senecas of Sandusky. The Shawnees had kinship connections with the Creeks, Cherokees, and Yuchis in the Southeast. Each Shawnee group within those tribes traced its membership back to a different major Shawnee division.

Shawnee warriors joined Pontiac's Rebellion (1763). Pennsylvania Indian agent George Croghan, sent to persuade tribal members to rejoin the American colonies peacefully, remarked that the Scioto and other river valleys in Ohio were Shawnee country and that their towns in the vicinity of present-day Chillicothe were "where Pontiac's conspiracy was largely fomented." Shawnee warriors also engaged in combat during Lord Dunmore's War (1774, over Kentucky) and were in the forefront of the Indian coalition fighting American expansion after the Revolutionary War. Interpreter Frederick Post toured the region in the prerevolutionary era and remarked on how distressing it was to observe the landscape "deserted and laid waste." In the wake of the end of the Revolution, U.S. claims to the region below the Great Lakes led Indians to meet in 1783 on the Sandusky River. The Indians formed an alliance to resist the invasions. Some spectacular successes in 1789–91 were followed by a shattering defeat in 1794. With other allies, the Shawnees participated in the punitive Treaty of Greenville the following year. The Indian signatories, including the Shawnee chief Blue Jacket, ceded to the United States the Old Northwest Territory, including the Ohio Valley. Their experience against the expanding American frontier would lead naturalist Thomas Nuttall, who later visited some of their camps in Arkansas, to state that the Shawnees among all the tribes were the ones who migrated most often and farthest.

Tenskwatawah (The Prophet), Shawnee
Print of colored lithograph by McKenney and Hall. Courtesy Creek Council House Museum.

The two most famous Shawnees were Tecumseh and his brother, The Prophet (Tenskwatawah). Tecumseh continues to be one of the most important Indian leaders of all time because of his attempt to forge an Indian coalition against American expansion. Encroachments continually threatened the Shawnees. Between 1774 and 1782 Tecumseh's family had to flee invading armies. His father and two brothers died in battles. Tecumseh devoted his energy to uniting widely separated tribes into a confederacy, while The Prophet preached a nativistic philosophy emphasizing a return to traditions. When British aid failed to come, the Native resistance collapsed. Tecumseh died leading his troops in the Battle of Moraviantown on the Thames River near present-day Chatham, Ontario, in October 1813. The profile of Tecumseh adorns the Absentee Shawnee tribal flag today.

Some of the Shawnee survivors held out in their Ohio homeland. The Indian Removal Act of 1830 finally forced the remaining Shawnees to leave Ohio and travel to Kansas, just west of the current Missouri boundary line. The Shawnees who advocated peace during the American Revolution emigrated from Ohio to present-day Cape Girardeau in southeastern Missouri, which then lay within Spanish territory. Some Shawnees among the Creeks joined the Missouri Shawnees, as did some Shawnees from Ohio. Other Shawnees in Ohio were forced to relocate under a removal agreement signed in August 1831.

Shawnees and Delawares settled amid a French-Canadian, mixed-blood, and slave population. Spanish officials persuaded the French-Canadian Louis Lorimer to attract the residents of two Shawnee towns and one Delaware village to a 625-square-mile grant in Missouri. He was named commandant of the District of Cape Girardeau. Shawnee chief Black Bob of the Chalakaatha division and his followers eventually ceded Cape Girardeau lands in 1825 to the United States and also ended up in Kansas, just west of Kansas City and south of the Kansa River.

In 1839 some Shawnees from the Cherokee area of Texas under Cherokee chief Bowles settled in what are now the Shawnee, Tecumseh, and Little Axe regions. Some settled along the Canadian River and in Shawneetown in what is now McCurtain County as well as elsewhere. Kansas Shawnees in the 1840s added to the number of Shawnees on the Canadian River. Shawnee residents of the Brazos Reserve in Texas augmented their numbers when they were forced across the Red River in 1859 to the Washita River. An 1854 George Mannypenny treaty with Shawnees in Kansas allotted their 1.6 million acres and ultimately led to more movement. The treaty left a reservation of 200,000 acres (what would later become Johnson County, with some leftover land extending to the town of Eudora). Pressure from squatters, tax collectors, and thieves as well as Civil War activities devastated the area of Black Bob's band, forcing it into new villages at Olathe and Eudora and then to flee to Indian Territory. In 1854 the U.S. government officially designated the Shawnee groups in central Indian Territory and in Texas as the "Absentee Shawnees" because they were not present in Kansas for the allotment of that reserve under the terms of the treaty. The Absentee Shawnees consisted of the Thawikila, Pekowi, and Kispokotha divisions of the tribe. Kansas Shawnees were mostly from the Chalakaatha and Mekoche divisions, according to anthropologist James Howard and historian Stephen Warren.

Confederate threats drove most of the Absentee Shawnees to sanctuary among their Ohio kin near Bellemont, Kansas. Some of the Shawnees saw military service in Union Indian companies. Survivors returned to their Indian Territory homes after the war. Congress seized lands of the Black Bob band, forcing its relocation. About 80 percent of the band members joined the Absentee Shawnees in what would become Oklahoma. An unratified treaty in 1867 permitted the Absentee Shawnees to select land west of the Seminole Nation. The federal government recognized their separate sovereign status in 1872 (act of May 8, 1872, 17 Stat. 160). The tribe received title to land through the congressional act of May 23, 1872, while the Citizen Band Potawatomis occupied another part of the reserve. A later survey discovered that the Shawnee land lay within the Potawatomi reserve. The confusion, affirmed in an appellate court decision (*Potawatomi* v. *Collier* in 1998), in effect left the Shawnees as a people without a land base. They continue to occupy their Oklahoma lands but cannot place any new land into trust status without the permission of both the Potawatomi and U.S. governments.

Allotment during the 1870s split the Absentee Shawnees (under the act of May 23, 1872, 18 Stat. 160). Allotment began in 1875 and increased under an agreement with the Cherokee Commission on June 26, 1890. Ultimately 70,791 acres were allotted to 563 Absentee Shawnees. Members recalled the devastation in the wake of allotments during the 1850s in Kansas. The followers of Big Jim and Sam Warrior refused to countenance allotment and moved to live among the Kickapoos outside of Harrah, Oklahoma. They resided there for a decade. The Indian agent in 1886 brought U.S. troops and forced the Absentee Shawnees who lived along the Deep Fork River among the Kickapoos to relocate south of the Canadian River along Hog Creek (now under Lake Thunderbird) and the Little River in Cleveland County. They were called the Big Jim band and later were known as the Little Axe. Big Jim was a grandson of Tecumseh. Around 1900 white land schemers tried to persuade the Absentee Shawnees to move to Mexico and vacate their Oklahoma land. The ploy ended when smallpox among the Mexican Kickapoos who were being visited by the Shawnees tragically killed nearly all of the Shawnee party. A larger group of Absentee Shawnees known as the White Turkey band, Thawikila division, remained near the town of Shawnee in Pottawatomie County.

The Society of Friends had made initial contacts with the Shawnees in 1740 in Pennsylvania, during the time of William Penn. That association continued through the ensuing years. Under president Ulysses S. Grant, church denominations assumed direction of Indian agencies. The Friends came back to the Shawnees. After 1869 missions and schools served the Indians on and around the Sac and Fox Agency, which included the Shawnees. Joseph Newsom came in the very early 1870s as the first missionary teacher. The Friends' presence offered not only religious instruction and education but also food, agricultural advice, and a community focus. One of the original seven Shawnee students, Thomas Alford, returned in the 1920s as the Sunday school teacher for the mission. Alford was a great-grandson of Tecumseh and served as the superintendent of the Shawnee boarding school. Methodists, Baptists, and Quakers continue to have Shawnee participants in their religious services.

The Absentee Shawnees support several ceremonial grounds in and around the Little Axe community. The return of spring begins the ceremonial cycle: a Spring Bread Dance is held, paying homage and respect to all things that are associated with this time of year. The Kispokotha clan takes charge during the summer months and holds a War Dance, acknowledging past and present warriors. Traditional chiefs then take charge during the autumn and perform a Fall Bread Dance to give thanks for all that has been provided for the people, closing the ceremonies for the year. Stomp dances are interspersed through the ceremonial season.

Shawnee ceremonialism today, seen in symbols of gardening/food (female) and hunting/meat (male) as well as ritual centered on the drum and singing

Courtesy the Absentee Shawnee Tribe

Visitors attend the ceremonies to participate in the dancing, feasting, and camaraderie. Although outdoors, the ceremonial ground reproduces the basic structure of the old Shawnee council house. Within its bounds, Shawnee men and women take part in age-old ceremonies and leaders offer prayers for prosperity and well-being. The songs and dances that are performed today continue traditions that were described by early colonial visitors to the Shawnees.

Painter Benjamin Harjo (Shawnee and Seminole)

Courtesy Benjamin Harjo, Jr.

Famous Shawnees include Tecumseh and his brother, The Prophet. Foster Hood acted in the *Bonanza* television series. Anita Chisolm for years headed the American Indian Institute at the University of Oklahoma. She guided and aided countless Indian students and staff who passed through the institution. The painter Earnest Spybuck (1883–1948), a member of the Thawikila division, attended Shawnee Indian Boarding School and Sacred Heart Mission. He became one of the early famous Indian artists in the nation. His art vividly portrayed Indian culture and ceremonies in central Oklahoma. Benjamin Harjo (also Seminole) is an award-winning painter.

SUGGESTED READING

Alford, Thomas Wildcat, as told to Florence Drake. *Civilization.* Norman: University of Oklahoma Press, 1936; repr. 1979.

Chapman, Berlin B. "The Pottawatomie and Absentee Shawnee Reservation." *Chronicles of Oklahoma* 24 (Autumn 1946): 293–305.

Croghan, George. "A Selection of George Croghan's Letters and Journals Relating to Tours in the Western Country." In Reuben Gold Thwaites, ed., *Early Western Travels,* vol. 1, 45–173. New York: AMS, 1966.

Edmunds, R. David. *The Shawnee Prophet*. Lincoln: University of Nebraska Press, 1983.

———. *Tecumseh and the Quest for Indian Leadership*. Boston: Little, Brown, 1984.

Foreman, Grant. *The Last Trek of the Indians*. Chicago: University of Chicago Press, 1946; repr. New York: Russell and Russell, 1972.

Howard, James H. *Shawnee!: The Ceremonialism of a Native Indian Tribe and Its Cultural Background*. Athens: Ohio University Press, 1981.

Noe, Randolph. *The Shawnee Indians: An Annotated Bibliography*. Lanham, Md.: Scarecrow, 2001.

Post, Christian Frederick. "Two Journals of Western Tours." In Reuben Gold Thwaites, ed., *Early Western Travels*, vol. 1, 177–291. New York: AMS, 1966.

Trowbridge, Charles C. *Shawnese Traditions*. Edited by Vernon Kinietz and Ermine W. Voegelin. Occasional Contributions from the Museum of Anthropology, No. 9. Ann Arbor: University of Michigan Press, 1939.

Warren, Stephen. *The Shawnees and Their Neighbors, 1795–1870*. Urbana: University of Illinois Press, 2005.

Eastern Shawnee

The tribal name is derived from the Central Algonquian word *shawun,* "south," and from Shawnunogi, "southerners." They refer to themselves as Sahwahwankee ("People of the south").

LOCATION AND GOVERNMENT

The Eastern Shawnee lands are in far northeastern Oklahoma near the Missouri border. The headquarters for the "Eastern Shawnee Tribe" is located in West Seneca, Oklahoma, about fifteen miles southwest of Joplin, Missouri. (The former headquarters was in Quapaw in Ottawa County, Oklahoma.) Entry into the tribal complex is from Seneca, Missouri. The state boundary runs through the eastern edge of the tribal complex, so the Eastern Shawnee headquarters is located in both Missouri and Oklahoma. From the highway, the tribal complex and casino to the north are hidden by the Milnot Plant in the foreground (which is itself divided into Missouri and Oklahoma segments for the sale of its dairy products in each state). The tribe is governed through a business committee made up of six members, including a chief. Elections are held annually by a General Council of all enrolled members eighteen years of age or older. The tribe organized under the OIWA and approved a constitution in April 1994, revising the document of November 1939. The tribal website is www.easternshawnee.org.

BUSINESSES

A large tribal casino in West Seneca, Oklahoma, near Interstate 44 called Bordertown Bingo and Casino (at www.bordertown-bingo.com) provides major revenue. A smaller Casino and Travel Center is located on Highway 10 near the state line. The tribe also owns two Vision Clinics (one in Seneca, Missouri, and one in Claremore, Oklahoma), offering eye care to the paying public. The Eastern Shawnees own a financial lending institution, the

People's Bank, in Seneca. The tribe also owns a public park near its tribal headquarters. The land was purchased under provisions of the OIWA. The tribe owns and operates a Best Western Motel in Fort Scott, Kansas. The Eastern Shawnee Tribe also has a travel center, smoke shop, and convenience store just east of the town of Miami. It owns about 800 acres, 200 of which are contiguous acreage in Ottawa County. The tribe maintains partial interest in some oil wells in the region.

NUMBER

The tribe has just under 2,000 members, mostly concentrated in the counties of Ottawa, Craig, and Rogers in northeastern Oklahoma and in Newton County, Missouri, just across the state boundary. Membership is based only on lineal descent from predecessors. There are Shawnee descendants scattered widely throughout North America (see also the "Absentee Shawnee" and "Shawnee Tribe [Loyal Shawnee]" entries).

The early history of the Shawnees is covered in the "Absentee Shawnee" entry. Shawnee life focused on their town. Women tended garden plots and fields, while men hunted. Their main game was elk. Active men and women left their town and participated in long hunting forays through the fall and winter, bringing home not only game for food but also pelts for the fur trade. Residents of the town lived in bark-covered longhouses similar to those of the Sacs, Foxes, Kickapoos, and Iroquois. The central structure was the large council house in which leaders performed rituals and presided over public gatherings. Clan membership was patrilineal. Like the Delawares, the Shawnees did not have moieties or clusters or divisions of clans. The Shawnees did have peace and war divisions of their towns. The peace chief represented his town in the national tribal council when important issues faced the nation. Women chiefs oversaw crop planting and the fate of prisoners.

The Shawnees led resistance to Anglo-American expansion along a thousand-mile-long Ohio River frontier line following the American Revolution, which ended only with Tecumseh's death during the War of 1812, as ethnographer Colin Calloway noted. In the aftermath of the War of 1812 over a thousand Shawnees remained under Black Hoof at the large village of Wapakoneta in the Ohio area in an attempt to reach some sort of accommodation with the growing number of American settlers in the region. The Treaty of Fort Meigs ceded 4.2 million acres of northwestern Ohio to the United States. In that 1817 land grant the Lewistown band, under the leadership of Quah-tah-wah-peeyah or Colonel Lewis, responded to increasing American pressure and settled in western Ohio on a reserve of forty-eight square miles. The Wapakoneta reserve was ten square miles, while the adjoining tract for Hog Creek was twenty-five square miles (both along the Ottawa River). There they shared the region with an independent band of mixed Seneca and Cayuga Indians who had allied with the Shawnees. Authorities divided the Lewistown reserve for the Seneca-Shawnees into a northern half for the Senecas and a southern half for the Shawnees. By 1830 the Lewistown band was known also as the Mixed Band of Senecas and Shawnees. Two years later the Mixed Band migrated from Ohio directly to northeastern Indian Territory. On July 20, 1831, their leaders signed a treaty with the United States, ceding their lands in Ohio at Wapakoneta and Hog Creek. The death of Black Hoof that year fed the melancholy determination to give up and move. The Shawnees endured hardships due to inadequate government provisions and illnesses as they moved first to Kansas then to Ottawa County in what is now Oklahoma. Missionary Henry Harvey wrote: "I saw more real suffering during that time among the Shawnee, for food, than I had ever expected to witness in my whole life." Holdouts joined them the following year. During their sojourn in Kansas, missionary activity, Indian agent manipulation, and new mixed-blood leaders forged a merged Shawnee national government under an 1852 constitution.

In the American Civil War the Eastern Shawnees maintained ties to the Union and also shared the label "Loyal Shawnees" with their kinfolk. Others signed an 1861 treaty with Albert Pike of the Confederacy. Most fled to Kansas, where they sought shelter among the Ottawas. An 1868 treaty recognized the Seneca-Shawnees in Kansas and bought Cherokee land in Oklahoma. In June of the following year the Cherokees granted 722 Shawnees membership in their tribe. They settled in what is now Craig County, Oklahoma. The town of Bluejacket recalls the prominent Shawnee leader and his descendants. In 1867 the Shawnees took the name "Eastern Shawnees" to differentiate themselves from others within Indian Territory. That year the Mixed Band split, separating into Seneca and Shawnee groups, each with their own assigned lands (see the "Seneca-Cayuga" entry).

Some Eastern Shawnees participated in a famous court case in Kansas. In 1860 Kansas Territory declared all Indians citizens and their lands subject to taxation so that those lands could be seized. In the celebrated case of *Charles Bluejacket* v. *County Commissioners of Johnson County*, which the United States Supreme Court eventually decided in 1866, the federal judiciary held that Shawnee lands were not taxable. That only increased the Kansans' frenzy to obtain the Indian lands, leading to the Eastern Shawnees' departure for Indian Territory in 1869.

The Eastern Shawnees adopted a constitution under the OIWA in November 1939 and organized formally in a December 1940 referendum, with a business committee form of government. They separated from the Senecas. For depredations during the Civil War the Eastern Shawnees shared a $110,000 claims payment from the federal government (1965). With foresight tribal members dedicated a 157-acre industrial park at the end of 1977. It lay behind the Milnot Plant on the state boundary line. Travelers must still cross to the other side of the tracks to enter the tribal complex. The tribe has attempted to secure trust land for gaming in Kansas City and Branson, Missouri, as well as in Ohio, but so far without success.

Eastern Shawnees participate in the powwow and stomp dance culture of northeastern Oklahoma and in family rituals. They begin their ceremonial season like their Shawnee relations in other tribes with an Indian football game in the spring. There are a few adherents of the Peyote way among them. Other traditions are still practiced. For some of the tribal members the traditional burial is still the norm. They build a fire at the head of the grave, keeping watch for three consecutive nights, and ritually burn cedar.

Notable Eastern Shawnees include Blue Jacket. The tribal community center is named for him. He participated in the American Revolutionary War and led various tribal groups south of the Great Lakes involved in a loose confederation from the 1770s through 1808, including his own Shawnees as well as Delawares, Miamis, and Wyandottes. Blue Jacket led the battlefield defeats of Arthur St. Clair and Josiah Harmer in the Ohio country. He himself led a siege of Fort Miami in 1793 and was one of the signers of the August 1795 Treaty of Greenville. Blue Jacket is considered one of the greatest American Indian diplomats who ever lived.

SUGGESTED READING

Calloway, Colin G. *The Shawnees and the War for America.* New York: Viking/Penguin, 2007 (Harvey quotation on 164–65).

Sugden, John. *Blue Jacket: Warrior of the Shawnee.* Lincoln: University of Nebraska Press, 2000.

Shawnee Tribe
(Loyal Shawnee)

NAME

The tribal name is derived from a variation of the Central Algonquian word "Shaawanwa," "southerner." It designated a warm climatic location, akin to the southern branch of the family. The dictionary of linguist C. F. Voegelin designated the Loyal Shawnees as Khkipakaakamii-thaki, "blue water persons" (for the Cumberland River that flowed through Kentucky and Tennessee, where some Shawnees lived about 1756), but also as Kaatheewithiipiiki-Shaawanuwaki, "Shawnees at the Kaw River," a reference to their Kansas residence. The term "Loyal" originated during the travails of the American Civil War, when those Shawnees who remained steadfastly tied to the Union were deemed to be loyal. They were also called the Cherokee Shawnees because they lived within the historic boundaries of the Cherokee Nation (see the "Absentee Shawnee" and "Eastern Shawnee" entries).

LOCATION AND GOVERNMENT

The headquarters for the "Shawnee Tribe" is located in Miami in Ottawa County, in far northeastern Oklahoma. A new Loyal Shawnee tribal headquarters building sits next to the Ottawa tribal administrative building. (The Loyal Shawnee offices were previously inside the Inter-tribal Council Community Building nearer Steve Owens Boulevard in Miami. Before that the headquarters was in Jay, Oklahoma.) The Loyal Shawnee Tribe was recognized by the state of Oklahoma in 1998 and federally recognized in 2000. The Loyal Shawnees operate under a business committee with eight members elected for two-year terms, headed by a chair. The tribal website is www.shawnee-tribe.org.

BUSINESSES

The Loyal Shawnees have no businesses. They are in an unusual situation in that the Shawnee Tribe has no separate jurisdiction and no land base. The tribe in 2007–2008 attempted to secure

359

trust status for a casino site in Oklahoma City (located south of the Frontier City amusement park at Wilshire Boulevard along Interstate 35) but met fierce opposition.

NUMBER

The tribe has just over 1,600 members, sprinkled across northern Oklahoma in Craig, Rogers, and other counties. The membership, based only on descent, is largely focused ceremonially on White Oak in Craig County outside Vinita. When the tribe began its bid for separation from the Cherokee Nation, it had about 7,000 members, most of whom remained members of the Cherokee Nation. There are Shawnee descendants scattered far and wide, as mentioned in the "Absentee Shawnee" entry.

The linguistic and historic background for the Shawnees is presented in the "Absentee Shawnee" entry. Some Shawnees remained in Ohio but moved during the 1830s to Kansas after the passage of the Indian Removal Act at the start of that decade. When they were joined by the Black Bob band, of the Chalakaatha tribal division, there was great contention. In 1869 the Ohio Shawnees formally joined the Cherokee Nation in northeastern Indian Territory.

Some Shawnees, especially members of the Chalakaatha and Mekoche divisions, advocated ongoing hostilities against the Americans. They continued to live in the Ohio area near Wapakoneta and Hog Creek. A treaty with the United States in 1831 ceded their territory and led to their relocation to present-day Kansas the following year. Inadequate rations, sickness, and swindlers plagued the migrants en route. Holdouts joined them a year later.

Following the conclusion of the conflict, the United States signed a treaty with the Shawnees in October 1868 and consented to pay them for livestock and other property that soldiers had seized during the war. Payment was finally made in the early 1930s. Intimidation against the Shawnees in Kansas is referred to as the "reign of terror." The Loyal Shawnees and Delawares left Kansas and moved to northeastern Oklahoma after the Civil War. The Shawnees settled near White Oak and Vinita. Both tribes signed a June 7, 1869, treaty placing themselves under the jurisdiction of the Cherokee Nation, within whose boundaries they resided. The Cherokees pledged to include the Shawnees in allotments. The Shawnees paid $50,000 to the Cherokees for their reserve. The federal government hoped that the incorporation would reward the Shawnees for fidelity while punishing the Cherokees for Confederate sympathies. In spite of legal incorporation in the Cherokee Nation, the Loyal Shawnees maintained their own cultural traditions and political identity.

The 145 Loyal Shawnees received a federal payment in the early 1930s for their tribal losses during the Civil War (under the terms of Public Law 2 in December 1927 and Public Law 1017 in December 1929, both arising from article 12 of their October 14, 1868, treaty). The Loyal Shawnees filed an Indian Claims Commission suit for lands seized in contravention of treaties in 1825, 1831, and 1854. They finally won a judgment in 1959. After that effort they formed the Loyal Shawnee tribal business committee as their official tribal entity in a December 1960 meeting at White Oak (also spelled as one word). With Cherokee Nation aid, the Loyal Shawnees arranged for the purchase of thirty acres in White Oak to serve as a multipurpose center, which opened in 1991. The center became the community focus of the Loyal Shawnees and helped motivate and unify the membership. A 1994 visit of members to their homeland in Ohio led to renewal of old ties. Shawnee State University in Portsmouth, Ohio, consented to provide scholarships for qualified tribal youths to attend college.

The Loyal Shawnees continue their traditional ceremonies on an annual cycle, centered at White Oak. In the spring women and men participate in ritual preparations at their camps as a part of the Bread Dance. Women select the date for the encampment and make the bread. It is a high honor. The women clean and prepare the dance ground area and choose men to dance as a part of the ceremony. A football game (using a small, hand-sewn ball stuffed with deer hair) is played prior to feasting. A stomp dance concludes the activities. There is also a fall Bread Dance to close out the ceremonial season. In between, various gatherings and dances are held, often involving members of other ceremonial grounds who lend their supportive assistance. Loyal Shawnees retain one of the five sacred bundles of the Shawnees. The Loyal Shawnee bundle is for the Chalakaatha division. They celebrate the Green Corn Dance during their ceremonial season. (Shawnee captive Oliver Spencer observed one in 1792 and wrote a description of his experiences.) Their Green Corn Dance is immediately followed by a Buffalo Dance. It is not performed at the other Shawnee grounds. There are some Peyote adherents among the Loyal Shawnees.

Beginning with an official resolution to the Cherokee Nation in 1996, Loyal Shawnees sought separation from the larger tribe. The state of

Oklahoma recognized the Shawnee Tribe in 1998 and Public Law 106-568 (Title VII) at the end of 2000 granted federal acknowledgment. After 132 years within the Cherokee Nation, the Loyal Shawnees were once again a mostly independent tribe. Part of their separation involved a pledge not to seek trust land within the host Cherokee Nation.

All three of the Shawnee tribal groups participate on a joint repatriation council housed in Tahlequah to address issues of human remains.

Notable Loyal Shawnees include Ruthe Blalock Jones, long-time Indian art instructor at Bacone College in Muskogee. The Loyal Shawnees also claim Tecumseh and The Prophet as forbears.

SUGGESTED READING

Callender, Charles. "Shawnee." In vol. 15, *Northeast*, of the *Handbook of North American Indians,* 622–35. Washington, D.C.: Smithsonian Institution, 1978 (C. F. Voegelin dictionary designation on 634).

Howard, James H. *Shawnee!: The Ceremonialism of a Native Indian Tribe and Its Cultural Background.* Athens: Ohio University Press, 1981 (Spencer account on 225).

Nieberding, Velma. "Shawnee Indian Festival." *Chronicles of Oklahoma* 42 (Autumn 1964): 253–55.

Parker, Linda. "Indian Colonization in Northeastern and Central Indian Territory." In Arrell M. Gibson, ed., *America's Exiles,* 104–29. Oklahoma City: Oklahoma Historical Society, 1976.

Thlopthlocco

"Thlopthlocco" in the Mvskoke language means "lily pad." It may have become the designation for the town because residents resided near a pond and utilized the pads seasonally for food.

LOCATION AND GOVERNMENT

The headquarters for the Thlopthlocco tribal town is outside Clearview in Okfuskee County, in east-central Oklahoma (eighteen miles west of Henryetta). It can be reached at the Clearview exit (227) on Interstate 40, six miles east of Okemah.

Thlopthlocco is a tribal town in the Creek Nation. Members of the community adopted their own constitution under the OIWA and were separately recognized by the federal government as a tribal entity (in this case, a chartered tribal town). The Thlopthlocco Business Committee consists of a king (*meko* in the Mvskoke language) and four town warriors as the elected officers. The designations for members of the committee reflect ancient tradition. Officials serve four-year terms. There is an annual town meeting for all enrolled members.

BUSINESSES

The tribal town operates a gaming facility (the Golden Pony) and a smoke and gift shop, located at its headquarters on Interstate 40. The smoke shop opened in 1984.

NUMBER

The tribe had about 650 members in 1991 and has about 1,500 now, some 600 of whom live in the town.

According to ethnologist John Swanton, Thlopthlocco is a branch of Thleware. Both were red towns among the Upper Creeks in the Southeast. European and American incursions into their region both altered their lifeways and led to migration away from the enlarging frontier settlement. The Thlopthlocco Indians removed into Indian Territory with other Creeks. They farmed and attempted to regain their lives in their new land. During the conflict over Creek Nation leadership in late 1882 involving Isparhecher of Nuyaka, Thlopthlocco members were caught in the clash between followers of Tukachtchee Harjo and those of Samuel Checote with Wewoka lighthorse (tribal police) on Battle Creek outside of Okemah. Most of the casualties of the clash were from Thlopthlocco. Tempers eventually cooled, and the Indians returned to their farms.

Along with Alabama-Quassartes and Kialegees, members of the Thlopthlocco community took advantage of the provision within the 1936 OIWA to organize under that act. They adopted an OIWA constitution in mid-November 1938 and also obtained a federal charter. Town members met at the Thlopthlocco Methodist Episcopal Church building, which served as their headquarters. Starting in 1939, a separate building was erected for the town out of native sandstone from the North Canadian River using WPA labor. The building is three miles northeast of the church. Roley Canard was selected to be the first tribal town king (*meko*) after the federal charter.

During this period the town owned a granary and made use of a gas-fired hot bed to raise onion and sweet potato sprouts for sale. It used New Deal funding to purchase land and to lease 40-acre mini-farms for families who had lost their allotments. The town owned 2,400 acres of riverine land. Federal monies also subsidized the purchase of farm equipment and livestock. Farm tenants kept some of their produce but contributed a portion to the town granary. A 1942 flood and wartime employment opportunities led to the end of the attempt to sustain a utopian farming community.

Town government continued with periodic meetings to discuss leasing of land, but the town was largely inactive until the 1960s. Individual Indian Money (IIM) account funds (that is, money held in trust by the BIA) were tapped, and the business committee became more active during that decade. In 1977 the town bought 120 acres of land near Interstate Highway 40, which was placed into trust. The town eventually established a casino on the land.

A BIA ruling in late 1989 determined that the tribal town could directly contract with the federal government for program funding under Public Law 638. That undermined the overall authority of the Muscogee Nation. The BIA reasoned that the tribal town had separate federal recognition.

Thlopthlocco town members participate in activities at nearby ceremonial grounds. Members also belong to Indian churches in the vicinity.

Johnnie Diacon, a tribal town member, is a well-known artist.

SUGGESTED READING

Swanton, John. *The Indians of the Southeastern United States.* Bureau of American Ethnology Bulletin 137. Washington, D.C.: Government Printing Office, 1946; repr. Washington, D.C.: Smithsonian Institution Press, 1979.

. . . *to Keep the Drum . . . to Tend the Fire: History and Legends of Thlopthlocco.* Oklahoma City: Oklahoma Indian Affairs Commission, 1978; repr. Oklahoma City: Mvskoke Language Institute [1991?].

United Keetoowah Band of Cherokee Indians

NAME

"Keetoowah" (or "Kitua" or "Kituwa") means "principal People" in the Cherokee language. It is also the name of the mother town and seat of authority, located in the Great Smoky Mountains of western North Carolina, which they claim as their homeland.

LOCATION AND GOVERNMENT

The headquarters of the "United Keetoowah Band of Cherokee Indians" is in Tahlequah (on Highway 62 leading into town from the south, two miles from the larger headquarters of the Cherokee Nation of Oklahoma). Members are spread throughout the surrounding fourteen counties and elsewhere. The tribal website is www.ukb-nsn.gov.

BUSINESSES

The United Keetowah Band operates a casino at the tribal headquarters.

NUMBER

The band has about 12,000 members.

Tracing its name to the ancient seat of Cherokee authority in North Carolina, the United Keetoowah Band of Cherokee Indians (popularly shortened simply to "Keetoowah" or abbreviated as "UKB") arose from a confluence of events. Baptist missionary Evan Jones switched political allegiance as the American Civil War loomed in Indian Territory. He led abolitionist followers into the Union camp. The more militant identified themselves with crossed pins on their jacket lapels: hence the name "Pins." Their enemies viewed them as a secret organization of violent thugs. Keetoowahs authored their first written constitution in 1859 under the guidance of Bud Gritts. They were full-blood Union Cherokees who fought against mixed-blood Confederate Cherokees during the American Civil War.

Following the warfare, the Keetoowah Society exercised control over Cherokee Nation politics, influencing or determining the election of chiefs, from Lewis Downing, who was a head captain of the Keetoowah Society in 1859, through the 1893 election of Dennis Bushyhead as principal chief. During the allotment era the Keetoowah Society opposed any allotment agreement as flagrantly illegal and in violation of treaties. It demanded that the federal government uphold solemn treaty pledges. As a result of the disputes, a series of splits took place within the society. At the turn of the twentieth century so-called Nighthawks broke off from the Keetoowah Society. The father of famed religious leader Redbird Smith, who rekindled Cherokee ceremonialism, was a Keetoowah member in Arkansas. The Nighthawks continued opposition to allotment until Redbird was jailed, but they maintained revived ceremonies. The Nighthawks themselves split in the late 1930s into a group centered around their town or square (located north of Vian and named for their founder, Redbird) and another ground outside the community of Stillwell (named for its founder, Stokes Smith, the youngest son of Redbird). Both grounds are separate entities from the UKB, although it maintains ties with and some support for the Redbird group as well as the Echota ceremonial ground and the Long Valley Kituwah Association. All encourage Cherokee nationalism, language, and pride.

In 1905 the Keetoowah Society incorporated in district court in Tahlequah. Additional divisions further fractured the society through the 1920s. The Keetoowah Society, Inc., itself divided in 1939. One group later became the United Keetoowah Band of Cherokee Indians in Oklahoma, which Public Law 715 officially recognized in August 1946. Members had worked diligently with the congressional delegation from the state, avoiding the opposition within the local Indian agency and regional BIA offices. The UKB incorporated under section three of the OIWA, which granted Indians in the state the right to organize for the common welfare. The two groups reunited in 1950 after the Interior Department approved documents submitted by the Keetoowahs. A vote by members ratified them. The UKB is federally recognized and is separate from the Cherokee Nation of Oklahoma (also headquartered in Tahlequah), which has attempted to absorb the Keetoowahs.

Keetoowah members, two-thirds of whom are full-bloods and speak the Cherokee language fluently, do not stomp dance as a group. UKB members do participate in ceremonial dancing as individuals, however, and during their annual festival. The Keetoowahs hold an annual tribal celebration at their headquarters in late September. They also join in their Indian church activities in their Native language. In 1950 the UKB began the first of its annual singing events at its celebration grounds.

Notable United Keetoowah Band members include the late law professor Allogan Slagle and linguist and educator Durbin Feeling.

SUGGESTED READING

Cherokee History as You've Never Heard It: A History of the United Keetoowah Band of Cherokee Indians in Oklahoma. Tahlequah: UKB, 2006 (booklet).

Leeds, Georgia Rae. *The United Keetoowah Band of Cherokee Indians in Oklahoma.* New York: Peter Lang, 1996.

Wichita

The origin of the tribal name is unknown. Frenchmen who encountered the Wichitas referred to them as "Ouatchitas." After 1800 the Choctaws used the term *wia chitoh*, "big arbor," for their grass houses. Americans in the 1835 treaty referred to the Wichitas as the "Witchetaus," from which the anglicized current spelling is derived. Tribal leader Burgess Hunt maintained that the name came from *wits eta*, "men of the north." They refer to themselves as Kitikiti'sh, "raccoon-eye," from the heavy decorative tattooing around men's eyes. That designation is used on Wichita tribal license plates.

LOCATION AND GOVERNMENT

The headquarters for the "Wichita and Affiliated Tribes" (Wichitas, Tawakonis, Wacos, and Kichais, who formally organized under this designation in 1960) is located about three miles north of Anadarko (across the Washita River) in Caddo County, in southwestern Oklahoma. The mailing address is Anadarko. Their headquarters is located on ten acres of the grounds of the old Riverside Indian School. The Tawakonis and Wacos are Wichita-speaking groups but historically were separate tribes. The Kichais do not speak the same language but are culturally related: hence the "affiliated" designation. The Wichita Tribe is not organized under the OIWA but did adopt a tribal governing resolution in August 1961. The tribe has no written constitution or by-laws but continues to operate under tribal resolution. The chair and a council have four-year terms of office. There is a museum within the tribal headquarters. The tribal website is www.wichita.nsn.com.

BUSINESSES

In 2008 the Wichita Tribe opened its Sugar Creek Casino in Hinton, about fifty miles from Oklahoma City. The tribe jointly owns the Fortune Bingo facility with the Caddo and the Western Delaware tribes (a 25,000-square-foot building located along U.S. Highway 61). In 1974 the tribe erected a 30,000-square-foot building that it then leased to the Bureau of Indian Affairs. The tribe owns the lucrative CrossTimbers restaurant, situated on a restricted allotment, on the west edge of Anadarko. The Wichitas joined the Caddos and Western Delawares to form WCD Enterprises for light industry and erected buildings in an industrial park. The three tribes also share ownership of 2,602 acres of trust land in Caddo County, most of which are leased for income from farming. Ten acres of Riverside Indian School land went to the Wichitas in the 1950s. The tribe built a community building, a dance pavilion, and camping facilities on the site. Some tribal income is derived from the commonly held lands on which oil and gas wells operate.

NUMBER

The affiliated tribes have about 2,000 members.

The Wichitas share the Caddoan linguistic family with the Caddos, Pawnees, and Arikaras. Wichita belongs to the Northern Caddoan branch. According to linguist Douglas Parks, Wichita separated from Proto–Northern Caddoan some 3,000 years ago. Caddo belongs to the Southern Caddoan branch. Wichita, Tawakoni, and Waco arose from Northern Caddoan, as did Pawnee (although long ago). Wichita oral tradition dates their split from the Pawnees around A.D. 1100–1450. Wichita and Pawnee oral tradition both also maintain that they were together as one people that migrated from the Southwest to the Arkansas, Missouri, or Platte River (depending on which version) before separating.

Ancestors of the Wichitas belonged to a confederacy that shared a common culture and heritage. By 1100 they are believed to have occupied a region extending from the Smoky Hill River in what is now central Kansas southward through Oklahoma into north-central Texas, with an east-west range from Arkansas to New Mexico. After seventy-seven days of travel through the oppressively hot summer of 1541, Francisco Vásquez de Coronado visited their settlement, which he called Quivira. His chronicler noted that they had "the same sort of appearance as the Teyas" (or Caddos), meaning that they were heavily tattooed. He found the Teyas or Quivirans residing next to or in the grass houses of the elder daughter's family (called matrilocality). Female-related kinfolk resided nearby in a "thickly settled province." They were agriculturalists who raised corn, squash, pumpkins, and melons and lived in tall, straw-thatched conical houses in semisedentary villages. The structure of their houses reflected Wichita cosmology. Four upright cedar poles representing the cardinal directions supported the framework. The entrance faced eastward. These villagers are believed to have been Proto-Wichitas, who were also encountered by Juan de Oñate 1601. They resided in the area of south-central Kansas near present-day Arkansas City during what is termed the Lower Walnut phase.

Evidence from excavations reveals that these villagers actively traded and interacted with their distant kinfolk in northeastern Texas, implying some merging of peoples. Later changes that accompanied the Europeans led the widely dispersed Wichita villages to consolidate as well, a process that had been going on for some time. As the groups merged, they lost much of their earlier independence and separate character. The Wichitas supplemented their diet with buffalo hunting. For a part of the year they resided in semipermanent villages and tended their plants. After their harvest, they left their settlements and became tepee-dwelling bison hunters on the Plains.

Wichitas engaged in extensive trade involving flint, agricultural products, salt, bison fat, and animal hides. For trade, the Wichitas produced parched corn, plaited dried pumpkin strands, cured tobacco, and processed hides and robes. Travelers strode the Wichita Trace that skirted the Cross Timbers, the wooded thicket that stretches across portions of Oklahoma into Texas. The Wichita Trace route would be used much later by freighter Jesse Chisholm and still later by cattle drivers along the Chisholm Trail. The ancient Wichitas also used the riverine system of communication and trade.

The Wichita origin story was reported by George Dorsey. Kinnikasus ("man never known on earth") created a man, Kiarsidia (also spelled Kata-us-t'skis, "having power to carry light," or Morning Star), and a woman, Watsikatsia (also spelled Na-ahsee-ya-sikits, "bright shining woman," or the Moon). The man traveled to the east and learned how to build grass houses and to use the bow and arrow. The woman received different types of corn, the four Corn Mothers, through her dreams. They propagated the human race and founded Wichita culture. The spirits of the wind looked after the first humans. After teaching their descendants, the man and the woman ascended into the sky.

The Wichitas had a complex cosmology. They believed that four pivotal epochs make up the cyclical existence of the world. The last, in which we currently reside, will lead to destruction of this world and the start of a new cycle. The Wichitas held a number of dance and ritual ceremonies honoring the creative force. The Deer Dance of medicine men acknowledged the first harvest and sought prosperity. Various rituals involved medicine bundles, the sacred bear medicine bundle being among the most noteworthy. Women performed the Turkey Dance to celebrate their heritage and pivotal events. The Pipe or Calumet ceremony established alliances and made "kin" of individuals and outsiders. Some have credited the Wichitas with beginning the Calumet ceremony and spreading it northward. The Pawnee Chawi band's Hako Ceremony, involving feather-decorated pipe stems and elaborate rituals of adoption, derived from the Wichita word for "pipe." Scholars John Swanton and Ian Brown, however, argued for a much more recent diffusion of the ceremony, pointing to French assistance in its spread through the Illinois country.

Population estimates vary widely for the Wichita Confederacy, from 30,000 to 100,000. Their loose confederacy consisted of up to thirteen distinct tribes, such as the Panis Piqués (a French designation for "tattooed Pawnees," that is, the Wichitas), Teyas, Mentous, Panioussas, Taovayas, Guichitas, Akwits, Tokanes, Escanjaques, Yscanis, Tawakonis, Wacos, and Kichais. The numerous constituent tribal entities through history made for a great amount of confusion among outsider observers. The extensive tattooing of Wichitas and other Indians led to further mislabeling. Many early observers in the 1690s simply lumped them all together under the rubric "Jumanos," which only added to the confusion.

The ancient ancestry of the Wichita peoples is dizzyingly complex, compounded by movements of groups and mergers and remergers over time. Archeologists have given different labels (usually derived from geographic features) to the varied phases. The peoples of the earliest Woodland period (called the Cooper phase in northeastern Oklahoma and the Cuesta, Walnut, and Keith phases in Kansas) are predecessors of the Wichitas. There were also other groups in the region. Around A.D. 1250 the Turkey Creek people (who became Garza complex people) started making more use of bison products to supplement their farming. Three hundred years later they moved north into the Arkansas River Valley but continued to hunt bison along the Canadian River, which was also part of their territory. Through time the tribal peoples who would later make up the Wichitas moved across their homeland. Some remained in their ancestral home area (present-day Kansas or the Texas Panhandle or elsewhere). Others migrated onto the Plains to pursue bison, while some traveled south toward the Red River basin.

Proto-Wichitas can be traced back in time to the Great Bend aspect and Norteño phase and to the Antelope Creek, Turkey Creek, and Paoli phases, according to Waldo Wedel and other archeologists. Wedel provided the broad outline of Wichita development. In the Upper Republican phase the earliest Pawnees and some Wichita peoples shared with others the Central Plains Tradition. In their Great Bend aspect in today's central Kansas, they also shared cord-roughened pottery with the ancestral Pawnees of Lower Loup and Upper Republican sites. Ancestral Wichita peoples were part of the prehistoric southern Plains tradition (the Antelope Creek, Neosho, Turkey Creek, and Washita River phases, among others). Using ethnological accounts of Spanish explorers like Oñate's 1601 encounter with Quivirans, ethnologist Mildred Wedel hypothesized that the Wichitas reached their northernmost penetration of the Plains in present-day Kansas at about that time on the Smoky Hill River and began their swing southward.

The Wichitas left their name across the landscape of their traditional territory. The city of Waco on the Brazos River in Texas and Tawakoni Creek in the same area carry the names of major Wichita bands. The city of Wichita Falls on the Red River, the Wichita Mountains of Oklahoma, and the city of Wichita on the Arkansas River in Kansas also mark their presence. In 1994 tribal descendants dedicated a highway bridge near Illinois Bend, Texas, named for the Taovayas.

Members of the Coronado expedition of 1540–42 traveling from Mexico and the American Southwest crossed the Arkansas River about where the community of Fort Dodge is now and met pedestrian Native bison hunters, who are believed to have been from the Larned site. Coronado's men visited the "Tancoas," who were horticulturists and bison hunters of the Little River phase of Kansas (part of the Great Bend aspect), near either present-day Hutchinson or Lindsborg, Kansas (Waldo Wedel favored the latter). They can be traced back to about the fourth century A.D. and became the Tawakonis. Eventually they migrated into the Three Forks region of northern Oklahoma. (Some scholars believe that the Tancoas were Tonkawas.)

Tawakoni stone "council circles" have been found at five Little River sites on the south side of the Little Arkansas River in Rice and McPherson counties in Kansas. Waldo Wedel's research clearly demonstrated their astronomical and semicardinal directional alignments, indicating solar observation (such as at the winter and summer solstices) by prehistoric peoples. Clark Mallan's investigations also found a possible astronomical link for the so-called serpent dug-out land form (referred to as an intaglio) found in the same region. Trade items from the American Southwest showed long-range connections. Locals also likely traded finely made elbow pipes and chert diamond-beveled knives to Red River Caddos and Fort Coffee–phase peoples. Archeologists believe that the Lower Walnut–phase peoples of the Great Bend aspect who resided near Marion, Kansas, could have been the "Tabas" of Coronado and perhaps the "Uayam" of Oñate. Some Lower Walnut people resided at the Deer Creek and Bryson-Paddock sites after 1760. Perhaps the extensive Wichita network of interaction reaching into the eastern frontier Pueblos helped direct Spanish settlement in that direction.

Coronado was gravely disappointed that his hoped-for city of Cíbola was only a series of ancestral Wichita villages near the Great Bend of the Arkansas River in a province the Spaniards called Quivira. Pedro Castañeda, one of Coronado's captains and author of one of the accounts of the Spaniards' trek, described the ancestral Wichitas, who "all paint themselves" with tattoos and reside in a "thickly settled" region inside their distinctive beehive thatched houses. A small Mexican force under Francisco Layva de Bonilla and Antonio Gutiérrez de Umana crossed Quivira and was largely annihilated by Indians in 1593. New Mexico's Governor Oñate headed a Spanish expedition in 1601 that heard accounts of the Tancoas but visited the Lower Walnut people of the Great Bend aspect, whom he called the "Etzanoas," in south-central Kansas near today's Arkansas City: a large population estimated at 20,000 lived in villages with grass houses similar to historic Wichita residences. Their fields surrounded the villages. The Bryson-Paddock archeological site in Kay County near Newkirk is believed to be a Wichita village from around 1700.

French trader Bénard de La Harpe visited the Red River Caddoans in 1719 then contacted several Indian villages deep inside today's Oklahoma. He estimated that one Tawakoni village contained six thousand people, who were soon joined by another thousand for trade. The Wichitas asked La Harpe to provide them with merchandise, including "arms in order to defend themselves against" Osages, Apaches, and other enemies. La Harpe's aide Henri Joutel reported that they lived in grass-thatch houses that looked like a "Bee-Hive" in appearance. The village was close to the contemporary community of Leonard south of Tulsa on the south bank of the Arkansas River. George Odell has described it. (These Tawakonis may have been the same ones that Juan Jaramillo of the Coronado expedition described.) At about the same time, Claude Du Tisné, who headed westward from Kaskaskia and the mouth of the Missouri River, reached a composite village with a Taovaya leader. It is believed to be near present

Neodesha in southeastern Kansas. French traders later worked at Ferdinandina (Deer Creek), a moat-protected village in Wichita territory near what is now Ponca City in far northern Oklahoma.

Wichita tribes felt the effects of ongoing Apache and Osage conflict and desired easier access to European trade goods. For about 150 years, into the mid-eighteenth century, Wichita tribes like the Taovayas steadily moved southward out of Kansas and all the way into Texas, while their kinfolk remained behind on ancestral lands. Those who moved entered into an uneasy relationship with Spaniards in Texas, who had contacts with French traders. When the Spanish reversed themselves and made peace with the Apaches and established San Sabá Mission for the Lipan Apaches (1757), the Wichitas determined to act. The next year the Wichitas and their Indian allies destroyed the mission and then repulsed Colonel Diego Ortiz Parilla's punitive expedition in a major battle a year later when it struck a heavily fortified Taovaya village on the Red River, at the Longest site. Historian Todd Smith vividly demonstrated that by entering into trade with Spanish and French colonial interests the Wichitas became both generators of wealth for the European imperial powers and buffers along the frontier against hostile tribes. The Wichitas suffered as a result of both roles. European diseases devastated them, while exposing them to constant attacks from their Indian enemies.

Dragoons under the command of Colonel Henry Dodge contacted a Wichita village in 1834 near present Lugert, Oklahoma. Painter George Catlin accompanied the expedition and depicted the tattooed males and females who were described to him. The next year the Wichitas signed their treaty of peace and friendship at Camp Holmes (near the modern city of Purcell) with the Americans. Negotiators Montfort Stokes, Matthew Arbuckle, and F. W. Armstrong used the collective name "Wichita" for all the associated tribes.

Texans struck at Wacos and Kichais, forcing them to abandon their villages along the West Fork of the Trinity River (near the present city of Arlington) in 1841. Waco and Tawakoni raiding helped keep the Texas frontier in turmoil.

In 1846 and 1850 the Indians signed treaties with the United States, which had annexed the Texas Republic in 1846. Helen Tanner's research demonstrated that American representative M. S. Lewis took the expedient course during the negotiations in 1846 at Council Springs when Indians proved reluctant to come to terms. He simply gathered separate sheets of marks as the signatures of Indian leaders and then wrote the finished treaty after he returned to Washington, D.C., and appended the signatures.

In any case, Texas repudiated the treaty terms permitting Indians to keep their land. The Texas legislature reluctantly agreed to a reservation for small tribes on the upper Brazos River (1853–54), but ongoing turmoil, anti-Indian feeling, and lawless outbursts led authorities to escort Wichita tribal groups like the Tawakonis, Wacos, and others (about a thousand in all) across the Red River in 1859 into Indian Territory for a new reserve in the Leased District of the Choctaws and the Chickasaws under the terms of an 1855 treaty with the latter. Wichitas also had sought refuge near Fort Arbuckle under Indian superintendent Elias Rector. He selected 69,120 acres of former Seminole territory in a rectangular tract on the north side of the Canadian River for the Wichitas and affiliated tribal groups. All of the land had at one time been the Wichitas' ancestral homeland. In a council with the Indian leaders, Rector and Robert S. Neighbors assured them that the reservation would be theirs forever. U.S. troops under the command of Captain Earl Van Dorn in pursuit of Comanche raiders the year before had mistakenly attacked a Wichita village on Rush Creek in what is now Grady County. The survivors fled to Fort Arbuckle. After the 1859 removal of Wichita bands into the Indian Territory, the United States set up Fort Cobb nearby for protection and aid to the Indians.

After hesitating, Wichitas signed a treaty with Confederate commissioner Albert Pike in 1861. Most Wichitas fled to Kansas during the American Civil War, giving their name to a city there. During this period trader Jesse Chisholm set up a trading post at the mouth of Chisholm Creek near today's Wichita, Kansas. The Indians suffered terribly during their exile, which was made worse by an exploitative agent who pocketed their subsistence funds. The Wichitas finally returned to Indian Territory in 1867 but missed the big treaty council held at Medicine Lodge. Throughout the second half of the nineteenth century the federal government lumped the Wichitas and smaller related tribes together as the Wichita and Affiliated Tribes (including bands directly related to the Wichitas, like the Tawakonis and Wacos, as well as others such as Kichais, Caddos, and Delawares).

In 1872 some 743,610 acres were set aside for the Wichitas, who agreed to this during their leaders' visit with officials in Washington, D.C. But Congress never ratified the agreement. Because their reservation existence was not officially approved by Congress yet continued, historian Berlin Chapman pointed out that it achieved a position of "peculiar importance in the history of the lands of Oklahoma Territory." The tribes officially held their lands under right of occupancy only. The United States relocated Kiowas, Comanches, and Plains Apaches as well as Cheyennes and Arapahos into the same leased region (1868–69). Wacos, Tawakonis, Kichais, and Wichitas settled into separate communities. The federal government combined the Kiowas, Comanches, and Plains Apaches with the Wichita Agency in Anadarko in September 1878. Seven years earlier federal authorities had opened a school near the agency. In 1871 Quaker Jonathan Richards from Philadelphia became the subagent (for fellow Quaker Indian agent Lawrie Tatum at the KCA Agency) at the Wichita Agency. Medical missionaries Fordyce Grinnell and his wife, also Quakers, assisted in the religious life at the agency. Creek John F. McIntosh brought the Baptist faith in 1878. Other missionaries set up their presence nearby. Physician-traders John and William Shirley removed with the Brazos Reserve Indians and set up their mercantile operation anew at the Wichita Agency.

The Wichitas embraced the Ghost Dance (1890–91) and long continued its songs as a part of healing rituals. Wichitas also embraced the sacrament of Peyote sometime around 1902. Tribal members opposed negotiations of the Jerome Commission until headmen and some others signed an agreement in June 1891. It was the first Indian agreement for the commission that year. Litigation over terms delayed allotment until 1901. Terms for the assignment of 160-acre plots to the Wichitas and affiliated tribes were roughly the same as in the Cheyenne and Arapaho agreement. Assignment of 965 individual allotments broke up the local band communities on the Wichita reserve. The whole allotment process was confused and poorly managed. The government opened the "surplus" land for white settlement. Today about 53,000 allotted acres remain in individual Indian ownership.

The United States Court of Claims at the end of the 1930s paid $675,000 to the Wichitas and affiliated tribes for the surplus lands on their reservation. In 1985 the Wichita Tribe settled its land claims suit filed in the 1970s against the federal government for land taken in Kansas, Oklahoma, and Texas. The tribe received $14 million. The Wichitas are the sole Indian nation of the southern Plains who remain in their place of origin. The tribe has used various grants to record the Wichita language and heritage. One fluent speaker of the language remains. In 2004 there were five persons reasonably familiar with it. Wichitas hold various powwow events at their dance pavilion and participate in the activities of others who make use of it. The tribe's annual powwow is held each August. The Wichitas continue their ancient visitation cycle with the Pawnees during the summertime, including use of tobacco, singing, hand games, giveaways, visiting, and feasting.

SUGGESTED READING

Brown, Ian. "The Calumet Ceremony in the Southeast and Its Archaeological Manifestations." *American Antiquity* 54 (April 1989): 311–31.

Castañeda, Pedro. *The Journey of Coronado.* Ann Arbor, Mich.: University Microfilms, 1966.

Chapman, Berlin B. "Establishment of the Wichita Reservation." *Chronicles of Oklahoma* 11 (December 1933): 1044–55.

Dorsey, George A. *The Mythology of the Wichita.* Norman: University of Oklahoma Press, 1995.

La Vere, David. "The Wichitas." In *The Texas Indians,* 128–33. College Station: Texas A&M University Press, 2004.

Mallan, Clark. "The Serpent: A Prehistoric Life-Metaphor in South Central Kansas." *Kansas Anthropological Association Journal* 5, no. 2 (1984): 40–83.

Newcomb, William W., Jr. *The People Called Wichita.* Phoenix: Indian Tribal Series, 1976 (for young readers).

Odell, George H. *La Harpe's Post: A Tale of French-Wichita Contact on the Eastern Plains.* Tuscaloosa: University of Alabama Press, 2002.

Parks, Douglas. "Northern Caddo Languages." *Nebraska History* 60 (1979): 197–213.

Smith, F. Todd. *The Caddos, the Wichitas, and the United States, 1846–1901.* College Station: Texas A&M University Press, 1996.

———. *The Wichita Indians: Traders of Texas and the Southern Plains, 1540–1845.* College Station: Texas A&M University Press, 2000.

Swanton, John. *The Indian Tribes of North America.* Bureau of American Ethnology Bulletin 145. Washington, D.C.: Government Printing Office, 1952; repr. Washington, D.C.: Smithsonian Institution Press, 1995.

Tanner, Helen H. "The Territory of the Caddo Tribe of Oklahoma." In David A. Horr, comp., *Caddoan Indians IV,* 9–144. New York: Garland, 1974 (1846 negotiations on 102).

Wedel, Mildred Mott. "The Wichita Indians in the Arkansas River Basin." In Douglas H. Ubelaker and Herman J. Viola, eds., *Plains Indian Studies: A Collection of Essays in Honor of John C. Ewers and Waldo R. Wedel*, 13–37. Washington, D.C.: Smithsonian Institution Press, 1982.

Wedel, Waldo R. "The Council Circles of Central Kansas." *American Antiquity* 32 (January 1967): 54–63.

———. *Prehistoric Man on the Great Plains*. Norman: University of Oklahoma Press, 1970.

Winship, George P. "The Coronado Expedition." In *Fourteenth Annual Report of the Bureau of American Ethnology for 1892–93*, part 1, 329–593. Washington, D.C.: Government Printing Office, 1896; repr. Chicago: Rio Grande, 1964.

Wyandotte

The tribal name is derived from the Iroquois word "Wendat," "islanders" or "dwellers on a peninsula." It became anglicized to "Wyandotte," which has been spelled a variety of ways (including "Wyandot"). The Wyandottes speak an Iroquois language, like the tribes of the Six Nations. The Mohawks referred to them as Skawenat, "[those of] one language." They were called different names by various peoples. The designations changed over time. In the seventeenth century the French and the English referred to the Wyandottes as the Tionontatis, Petuns, the Tobacco Nation, or a variant. The Petuns resided in perhaps ten major villages in Ontario and are considered allies of the Wyandottes. The Pennsylvania traders used "Wyandot" for those who moved to Ohio. Others referred to them as the Hurons. When meeting twice with Wyandottes outside Sandusky, Ohio, in September 1748, Pennsylvania envoy and interpreter Frederick Post called them Wyandots, Tobacco Hurons, and Petuns alternatively, acknowledging their constituent groups.

LOCATION AND GOVERNMENT

The headquarters for the "Wyandotte Nation" is in Wyandotte (about twenty miles from Miami) in Ottawa County, about a hundred miles northeast of Tulsa. The tribe organized under the OIWA and operates according to a 1995 constitution and by-laws. It is governed by a business committee composed of a chief, a second chief, a secretary-treasurer, and two council members, elected every two years. They meet monthly. The tribal website is www.wyandotte-nation.com.

BUSINESSES

The dual ravages of allotment in the 1890s and federal termination in the 1950s left the tribe virtually landless. Today the Wyandotte Tribe owns 213 acres. It has a convenience store and fuel stop (called Turtle Stop) on the outskirts of the community of Wyandotte and the Lucky Turtle Casino located in it. Major revenue comes from the Wyandotte Palace Casino in downtown Kansas City, Kansas, which opened in September 2007. Members raise pumpkins on five acres of tribal land for local consumption and for sale and also harvest timber from tribal land. The tribal campground on Highway 60 near the tribe's headquarters serves visitors to the popular Grand Lake recreational area. The tribe owns an operation that refines and markets petroleum products. Its NetTel firm supplies fiber optic information services to U.S. government entities. The tribe also owns Collegiate Systems, which operates Metropolitan Colleges, offering technical training in five cities across the United States.

NUMBER

The tribe has about 3,600 members in Oklahoma and nation-wide. Wyandotte descendants are scattered throughout Canada and the United States because of the long history of interaction between Wyandottes and Europeans and Americans. Some are in Ontario in Essex County, others at Indian Lorette in Quebec, Canada. More kin are found among the Senecas, while a few remained in Detroit, Michigan, during tribal moves in the past. In 1999 over 10,000 Wyandotte descendants were scattered mainly across the Great Lakes region of Canada and the United States and elsewhere.

French explorer Jacques Cartier sailed up the St. Lawrence River in 1536–43 and found Wyandottes in what is now the Canadian province of Ontario. The Wyandottes and their allies spoke different languages but basically shared Northern Iroquoian cultural traits. The Wyandottes maintained Iroquois rites and rituals in their longhouses. They observed an annual Green Corn Ceremony. They maintained a Blackberry Feast honoring the moon and kept annual feasts for their dead. Medicine persons interceded for individuals in the realm of the supernatural.

In the Wyandotte origin story, spirit beings lived in the sky. A brilliant shining tree lit their world. After being married for many years, the wife of the chief became pregnant. Her husband was suspicious. His anger grew until eventually his frustration exploded, and he threw the tree then his wife into the void below. She fell downward but was rescued by a passing flock of ducks. When the birds yelled out for help, a huge turtle arose from the depths of the ocean. On the back of the turtle was an old lady, Grandmother. She looked after the wife, who gave birth to twins, the bad one called Flint and the good one called Sapling. The twins grew rapidly and created things in this world.

Wyandottes lived in their northeastern villages at the edge of lakes and watercourses. There they raised corn, beans, squash, sunflowers, pumpkins, and melons. Their birch-bark canoes glided over waterways carrying foodstuffs as well as other items for trade. They had twelve clans as well as four matrons who guided decision-making for each clan.

Around 1650 the French referred to the Wyandottes as Hurons or Petuns. That name came from the French word *hure*, "head of the wild boar" (meaning rough or spiky bristles). It stood for the roached hair on the heads of warriors that resembled the bristles of a boar's head. The Wyandotte Tribe refused to accept the name "Hurons." By the 1670s the English called them the Wendats.

The Wyandottes generally resided south and east of Georgian Bay. A long-standing hostility with the Iroquois Confederacy erupted into years of outright warfare. A massive Iroquois strike in 1649 obliterated the homeland of the Wyandottes (then called the Hurons) and sent survivors scattering over a wide area, seeking refuge. They would move many times. Many fled to Mackinac Island (also called Michilimackinac) in present-day Michigan, where they established a long-lasting friendship with the Ottawas. The Wyandottes reestablished their trade with the French, but renewed Iroquois attacks kept them continually on the move. They shifted to the Mississippi River then returned to the lake country, settling at Chequamegon on Lake Superior during the 1660s. During the following decade they went back to Michilimackinac and opened trade with both the French and the English. The Wyandottes were later swept into a complex and dangerous game of balancing French-English-Iroquois trade and imperial interests. In 1701 delegates established a peace in Montreal, enabling Laumet de la Mothe Cadillac to found Detroit as a key point of access to the upper Great Lakes. The Wyandottes gradually shifted from Michilimackinac to the Detroit area, near neighboring Ottawas and Potawatomis. Wyandotte settlements occupied the banks up and down the Detroit River, which controlled traffic between Lake Erie and Lake Huron. A breakaway Wyandotte village was set up at present-day Sandusky, Ohio, on the shore of Lake Erie. Traders from Pennsylvania opened commerce with the Wyandottes and other Indians at Sandusky in 1745. There was considerable intermarriage of Wyandottes, Shawnees, Delawares, Senecas, Cayugas, and others in the vicinity. The Wyandottes played a pivotal role through history due to their location in the Ohio region. Because Ohio was "prodigious rich" and "one of the finest countries in the world," in the words of Indian agent George Croghan at the time of Pontiac's Rebellion, American colonists coveted the entire region.

The Wenros resided through the northern Niagara frontier region, in the direct path of Iroquois expansion. Wenro refugees in 1638 merged with the Eries, who merged with the Hurons. Similarly, the Neutral Indians lived in what is now Ontario. In the aftermath of 1652 attacks, some of the Neutral survivors also joined the Hurons.

The Wyandottes participated on the French side in the defeat of General Edward Braddock's force near Fort Duquesne (1755) but then shared in the overall French loss in the French and Indian War (1754–63). Wyandottes joined Pontiac's siege of Detroit and attacks elsewhere, especially at the battle of Bloody Bridge in present-day Michigan. The Wyandottes finally signed a peace agreement with the British at Presque Isle, Pennsylvania. The Indians also sided with the British during the American Revolution and suffered U.S.-led assaults on their settlements. Before the Revolutionary War the Wyandotte war leader Katepakome dominated the Ohio country.

In the latter half of the eighteenth century a remnant of the Hurons settled along the Detroit and Sandusky rivers. There they merged with the Petun and Neutral tribes to form the Wyandottes. They carried on trade and resisted encroachments from the Americans. The Wyandottes and other Indian allies suffered a crushing defeat by the forces of General Anthony Wayne at the battle of Fallen Timbers in 1794. The following year the Treaty of Greenville ceded most of Wyandotte territory (about two-thirds of present-day Ohio) to the United States. The Pipe smoked at the Greenville negotiations and the wampum belt were kept by the Wyandottes, who were the first to sign the document. Treaty documents in 1805 and 1807 nibbled away additional lands. Sentiment about the expansion of the United States divided the Wyandottes during the War of 1812. Wyandottes near Detroit supported Tecumseh and the British, while Wyandottes at Sandusky sided with the Americans. An American agreement in 1815 acknowledged Wyandotte assistance and provided a small reserve territory. But it was short-lived. Four years later the United States negotiated a treaty under which the Wyandottes relinquished their claim to most of that region and were confined to a small reservation near Detroit.

In the Treaty of Fort Meigs (also termed the Treaty of the Rapids of the

Maumee) in September 1817 the Wyandottes lost the remainder of their Ohio territory, some 3.36 million acres. They ultimately kept three reserves, two on the upper Sandusky called the Grand Reserve and Big Spring and one on the west side of the Sandusky River. Another treaty relinquished Michigan lands except for a reservation along the Huron River.

Under the terms of the 1830 Indian Removal Act, the Wyandottes signed an 1832 treaty ceding their final Ohio and Michigan lands. The following year 750 of them entered eastern Kansas. In mid-1843 the Wyandottes under chief Floyd Hicks boarded the river boats *Nodaway* and *Republic*, which transported them down the Ohio River to the Mississippi. They were the last tribe removed from Ohio. Their former Grand Reserve expanded into Wyandot County. The Wyandottes planned to buy land from the Shawnees, but that did not materialize. In December the Delawares sold thirty-six sections of their 2 million acres to the Wyandottes for $46,080. The land was at the junction of the Missouri and Kansas rivers. The Delawares gratefully recalled past friendship with the Wyandottes. The Wyandotte tract, including additional church and school land, totaled 24,960 acres. The U.S. Senate approved the deal in 1848. (A monument on the Kansas City Community College campus dedicated in 1997 commemorates the sale.) Uniquely, the 1842 treaty pledged a section of land (640 acres) to each of the thirty-five Wyandottes who took unoccupied land farther to the west in Kansas. These were called "floating" grants or the "Wyandotte floats." Ironically, the Wyandottes prospered in Kansas.

California gold fever, transcontinental railroad plans, and the Kansas-Nebraska Act of 1854 led commissioner of Indian affairs George Manypenny to negotiate a treaty with the Wyandottes to cede their Kansas reservation lands. The violence of Bleeding Kansas swept over the Indians. Pro-slavery forces murdered their agent William Gay in 1856. The 1855 Manypenny document gave state citizenship to allotted Wyandottes who received forty acres, ended the tribal organization, and led many to remove. Their Kansas reserve became the modern city of Kansas City, Kansas, and Wyandott County. Many of the Wyandottes who remained in Kansas quickly lost their land, and a few became homeless. Some Wyandottes returned to Ohio, while others traveled to Canada. About two hundred Wyandottes under Matthew Mudeater removed to the Seneca Reserve in northeastern Indian Territory in 1857. Many years before, the Wyandottes had befriended the Senecas and provided them 40,000 acres on the Sandusky River of Ohio in an 1817 treaty. The Senecas pledged to return the favor if needed in the future. In 1857–58 Seneca chief Little Tom Spicer arranged to grant a strip of land four miles wide across the northern portion of their reserve to the Wyandottes. Congress affirmed the arrangement under the Omnibus Treaty of 1867. The treaty set up a commission to determine the amount of taxes that Kansas had illegally collected from the Wyandottes and at the end of May 1872 awarded $11,704 to the tribe, with an additional $5,000 for resettlement expenses. The Wyandottes paid $20,000 to the Senecas for 20,000 acres.

During the Civil War era the Wyandottes fled to safety in Kansas. After the war the U.S. government tried to clarify the situation of the Wyandottes remaining in Kansas. Through 1872 tribal members emigrated to Indian Territory and were reintegrated into the tribe. The tribal organization had been reestablished in Indian Territory a year earlier.

The Wyandottes shared the Quapaw Subagency as their BIA headquarters with other Indians. They turned to farming and to farm labor. Some rented or leased their land to whites. Members of the Society of Friends arrived in 1869. In 1872 Quaker Jeremiah Hubbard established the Seneca Indian School on 160 acres of Wyandotte tribal land; it eventually was opened to youths of nearby tribes. In later years the school also served as an orphanage for the neighboring tribes. Allotment in the late 1890s individualized the reservation lands. Intermarriage with neighboring whites altered the makeup of the tribal membership. The Quaker mission to the Wyandottes is still active. The Council House Friends Church is twelve miles east of Wyandotte, Oklahoma.

During the early 1920s the Wyandottes' agency moved to Miami then in 1947 to the Five Tribes' Agency in Muskogee. In the post–World War II period congressional delegates pushed to terminate federal supervision over selected American Indian tribes. At the start of August 1956 the Wyandottes were terminated under Public Law 887. The legislation contained a provision permitting the Wyandottes to sell the two-acre Huron Cemetery in downtown Kansas City. The controversy over the proposed sale split the tribe. Congress underwent a change of attitude in subsequent years. In 1978 (through Public Law 95-281) the tribe was reinstated with federal recognition. But its land base was gone. In 1970 the tribe turned to a Kansas City urban renewal grant to restore the Huron Cemetery grounds. Under the long-term leadership of Leaford Bearskin, the Wyandottes won a settlement from the United States for long-standing land claims in Ohio then spearheaded investing the $560,000 settlement payment.

The Wyandotte Tribe of Oklahoma has claimed territorial rights in a number of locations. In 1996 the federal government recognized the tribe's ownership of an old Masonic Lodge building on a half-acre across from the City Hall in Kansas City, Kansas. It is called the Shriner Tract. The tribe opened a casino in trailers on the property, but state officials raided it and seized cash and equipment. In 2004 the National Indian Gaming Commission ruled that the operation was illegal because the tribe had no historic claim to the area. The tribe countered with a land claim to Kansas City property under the terms of the 1855 treaty. Circuit court opinions in April and July 2006 reopened the possibility for gaming on the tract. The tribe's Palace Casino occupies the site. The tribe also tried to obtain a casino location at the popular Kansas Speedway location.

After they fled their homeland in 1649, the Wyandottes settled in a variety of locales. At each major turn Jesuits reestablished missions for them, the first being St. Esprit at Chequamegon then St. Ignace at Michili-mackinac. Some Wyandottes make a pilgrimage to St. Mary's Church in Pottawatomie County, Kansas, to pay homage to their heritage. In the early nineteenth century Protestantism made some inroads among the Wyandottes. They host an annual powwow in June. In addition Wyandotte tribal members share in the ceremonies of their neighboring tribes. They dance in the Seneca Green Corn Ceremony annually and in the Eastern Shawnee Bread Dance.

In late August 1999 representatives from the Wyandottes of Oklahoma, the Wyandots of Kansas, the Huron-Wendats of Quebec, and the Wendats from Michigan met for the first time in 350 years at Midland, Ontario. They came together for a commemoration of the survivors of the 1649 destruction of the Huron-Wendat society at the hands of their Iroquois attackers. Huron territory was then near Georgian Bay and its environs.

Contemporary Wyandotte concerns include the impact of long-standing pollution from mining waste and from agricultural and poultry farm runoff in the region. Aside from the threat to members' health, the pollution posed the problem of long-term impact on recreational lake use. The tribe opposed a poultry plant in the area. There were also fears that contamination from the Tar Creek Superfund region would end up in Grand Lake. Tar Creek empties into the Neosho River, which in turn feeds Grand Lake.

Notable Wyandottes include Leaford Bearskin, who returned home to retire after a successful career in the U.S. military. He came out of retirement to run for tribal chair and succeeded in pointing the tribe in the direction of long-term economic development. In 2005 Miami University of Ohio awarded him an honorary degree in recognition of his long service to his people and their heritage. Bertrand O. Walker was a poet and writer. Tribal member Joe Kagey was a long-time educator.

SUGGESTED READING

Croghan, George. "A Selection of George Croghan's Letters and Journals Relating to Tours in the Western Country." In Reuben Gold Thwaites, ed., *Early Western Travels*, vol. 1, 45–173. New York: AMS, 1966.

Foreman, Grant. *Last Trek of the Indians.* Chicago: University of Chicago Press, 1946; repr. New York: Russell and Russell, 1972.

Gaff, Alan D. *Bayonets in the Wilderness: Anthony Wayne's Legion in the Old Northwest.* Norman: University of Oklahoma Press, 2004.

Smith, Robert E. *Keepers of the Council Fire: A Brief History of the Wyandot Indians.* Joplin: Missouri Southern State College Press, 1974.

Trigger, Bruce G. *The Children of Aataentsic: A History of the Huron People to 1660.* 2 vols. Montreal: McGill-Queen's University Press, 1976.

———. *The Huron: Farmers of the North.* New York: Holt, Rinehart and Winston, 1969.

Willig, Timothy D. *Restoring the Chain of Friendship: British Policy and the Indians of the Great Lakes, 1783–1815.* Lincoln: University of Nebraska Press, 2008.

Yuchi/Euchee

NAME

The tribal name is translated "situated yonder at a distance" by ethnologist Frank Speck. Perhaps it was the response to the question "Who are you?" or "Where do you come from?" He also gives the derivation of Yuchi as yu', "at a distance," plus *tci*, "sitting down." There is considerable difference in the views of ethnologists, linguists, and the Yuchis about the derivation of their tribal designation. The Yuchis refer to themselves as Tsoyaha or Tsoyah, "children of the sun." Some Yuchis refer to themselves as Yu Ge Ha. All of them use the name "Yuchi," which is also spelled "Uchee" and "Euchee" (the latter from the name of their boarding school, which closed in 1928).

LOCATION AND GOVERNMENT

The headquarters of the "Yuchi/Euchee Tribe" is in Sapulpa in Creek County, in east-central Oklahoma. There are several communities of Yuchis outside the southern reaches of the city of Tulsa. They reside in both rural and urban areas in the region but congregate regularly at their three ceremonial grounds at Duck Creek (southest of Bixby), Polecat/Kellyville (outside of Kellyville), and Iron Post/Sand Creek (south of Bristow). The ceremonial grounds operate as religious congregations but represent town governments, encompassing secular life as well. Yuchis also gather at their churches.

The Yuchis are not (yet) federally recognized. They rely on their ceremonial ground leadership for political and governmental guidance. The Yuchi Council is made up of the three ceremonial ground chiefs, two other members of the grounds, and three representatives selected at large. The Muscogee Nation chartered the Yuchi communities separately in 2001. They have their own community centers for their members. The tribal website is www.euchee.org.

BUSINESSES

Yuchi businesses are under the umbrella of the Muscogee Nation and so are not owned by the Yuchis. Their Duck Creek Casino is well south of Tulsa on State Highway 75, but it is also under the control of the Muscogee Nation.

NUMBER

There are about 1,000 Yuchis, with maybe two to three times that number of people of Yuchi descent. They reside in Tulsa, Creek, and Okmulgee counties. Bigpond town consolidated with Sand Creek at the turn of the twentieth century. The Polecat ceremonial ground includes members of the Long Tiger group.

Linguistics offers only controversy regarding the Yuchi language. It was once thought to be connected to Siouan then to Iroquoian but is now viewed as a language isolate by both the Yuchis and linguists. That fact combined with the lack of any migration legend among the Yuchis led to the claim that the Yuchis were among the oldest residents of the Southeast.

According to the Yuchi origin story, Gohantone, the Master of Breath or Creator, oversees the universe. To create the earth, crawfish dove into the primordial ocean and brought up mud. From that mud dry land expanded into the earth. Gohantone created the sun and the moon. The moon was in her monthly period. A drop of blood fell to the earth. From it sprang a person. The sun claimed the human as his son. He became the predecessor of the Yuchis, called the Children of the Sun or Tsoyaha. The sun instructed the Yuchis in proper ceremonies and rituals in the celestial square ground, which in the Yuchi language equates with the Rainbow and the Big House. There continues to be an emphasis on reciprocity (between genders, between ancestral spirits and the living community, and among residents of Yuchi towns as well as allies in other tribes).

The Yuchis are unique among southeastern Indians in a number of cultural aspects. They claim a solar origin and descent from the sun. Descent for their leaders was patrilineal, unlike most southeastern Indians. Their male society was dually divided into chiefs and warriors. The patrilineal kinship system resembled that of their neighbors like the Shawnees and the Sacs. Yuchi individuals joined the ceremonial ground of their mother, however, at one time. Now that clan system is obsolete. Yuchi oral history asserts that they gave the Green Corn Ceremony to other southeastern Indians.

Early ethnologist John Swanton claimed that Hernando de Soto's expedition did not directly contact the Yuchis but that the commander sent men to venture into "Chisca" province, which is thought to be eastern Tennessee. The chronicler mentioned Cofitachiqui as the queen of the province. Although the Yuchis resided in the Southeast for a long time, they responded to disruptions in the precolonial and colonial periods by moving long distances, so their residential locations vary greatly over time. European colonial strife led the Yuchis to disperse. Some lived on a tributary of the Savannah River in Georgia. British settler Timothy Barnard married a Yuchi woman and settled in today's Macon County, Georgia, on the Flint River. Various writers have reported that Yuchis resided at one time in present-day South Carolina, Alabama, Tennessee, Georgia, and Florida. In historic times the Yuchis occupied sites on the Tennessee River near Muscle Shoals, at what may now be Manchester, and along the Hiwasee River. Rogue traders from South Carolina and their Cherokee allies in 1714 attacked and largely wiped out Yuchis in a town in southeastern Tennessee. It was the last Yuchi settlement in the Tennessee River Valley.

By 1729 some Yuchis resided among Creek towns on the Flint and Chattahoochee rivers. After 1770 U.S. Indian agent Benjamin Hawkins assisted the consolidation of the Creek Confederacy, which included the Yuchis. Botanist William Bartram traveled through the Southeast in 1791. He stopped at a Yuchi town on the Chattahoochee, which he spelled "Chata Uche." The largest Yuchi town on the eve of removal was on the present site of Fort Benning in Georgia. Bartram and agent Hawkins noted that the Yuchi town was an outgrowth of the marriage alliance with Chief Ellick of the Creek town of Cusseta. Bartram observed that most Yuchis, although members of the Creek Confederacy, were fiercely independent at the same time and stubbornly maintained their own identity.

The Yuchis lived in villages arranged in a layout similar to that of other southeastern Indians. Men hunted, fished, and looked after defense. They were associated with collective ritual and with animal foods. Women were associated with plant foods. They tended gardens and their fields of corn, beans, and squash. Yuchi oral tradition paints a picture of a small, mobile tribe in the Southeast. That mobility increased in subsequent years after the Europeans arrived and stirred up rivalries.

Ethnologist Jason Jackson pointed out that in the colonial period the Yuchis sided with the British until after the American Revolution, when the Yuchis followed the lead of the Creek Confederacy. Yuchis allied with the Red Sticks during the 1812–14 Creek civil war. Yuchi Lower Town chief Timpoochee Barnard, however, was a colonel under Andrew

Jackson, commanding one of his army divisions. Other Yuchis moved to Florida, where they sided with the Seminoles in those wars.

Yuchis fought against removal but were captured by Georgia and Creek troops and forcibly evicted from the Southeast during the 1820s–30s. Some Yuchis came to Indian Territory as late as the 1850s. Once in Indian Territory, the Yuchis were politically incorporated into the Creek Nation. The bands settled along watercourses in the vicinity of the modern communities of Sapulpa and Bristow and lent their names to ceremonial grounds: Polecat, Little Deep Fork, and Bigpond. The Yuchis lived in a more dispersed settlement pattern than they had in their compact towns in the Southeast. Farmsteads were the arrangement in the West, but the community focus remained on the ceremonial square ground and its religious and political activities.

Yuchis returned from Kansas exile after the Civil War. Some settled in the vicinity of Wealaka. Their Snake Creek community formed the basis for the contemporary Duck Creek community. After Tullahassee Mission burned (1880), a new edifice was erected for a school in Wealaka. The Wealaka Mission was near present Leonard in Tulsa County near a bend of the Arkansas River. Wealaka Mission was home for the Reverend Robert Loughridge while he was superintendent from 1881 to 1884.

Yuchi chief Samuel W. Brown, Sr., who traded near Wealaka, was instrumental in helping to found Euchee Boarding School, which opened in 1894. It was located on the east side of Sapulpa. Members alive today fondly remember the boarding school. The Creek Nation operated it from 1918 to 1925 for Yuchi girls then from 1925 to the 1940s for boys. It is the site for the present Sapulpa High School.

By 1891 the number of Yuchis was about five hundred. The Dawes Commission lumped the Yuchis in with the Creek Nation for the purposes of allotment in severalty.

Yuchis after World War II sought an aboriginal land claim in July 1951, separate from the Muscogee Nation. But they were unsuccessful in their Indian Claims Commission suit for compensation for 11.2 million acres in the Southeast taken under terms of an 1814 treaty. Although they were turned down in the mid-1950s, the roll prepared in 1957 now serves as the basis for Yuchi identity.

Under Indian education acts in the 1970s, a Yuchi parent advisory committee brought in federal educational grant money for programs. The Yuchi Community Organization evolved from the educational endeavor. They were especially concerned about repatriation issues and their tribal distinctiveness. The Yuchis took concrete steps to lay the foundation for independent recognition (called federal acknowledgment) as a tribe separate from the Muscogee Nation. They sent lobbyists to Washington, D.C., in 1986, but without success. Three years later the Yuchis began meeting in the home of Ann Rolland Holder and eventually formed the Yuchi Tribal Organization, which received federal funding for an office in Sapulpa. In that same year the tribal members founded EUCHEE (Euchees United Cultural, Historical, and Educational Efforts) to foster tribal identity. Their 1991 petition for recognition was denied by the BIA in 2000 because of a lack of tribal enrollment. The Yuchis responded with a more concerted attempt to obtain acknowledgment. They set up the more permanent Euchee (Yuchi) Tribe of Indians (1992), incorporated under state law, and undertook many projects (such as constitution writing, an enrollment endeavor, teaching their language, culture, and history, and seeking grant support for their many activities).

The Yuchis celebrate a series of rituals through the year. Ceremonial activities focus on the square grounds, called *yu-ah* (Rainbow), the Big House. Their ritual season starts with Indian football games in the springtime, followed by a series of stomp dances. In the summer Yuchis hold first their Arbor Dance then their Green Corn Ceremony, offering thanks for the bounty of the harvest. It marks the climax of the ceremonial season and the transition from female-dominated spring to male-dominated fall rituals. The three Yuchi ceremonial grounds hold their new year, new fire, and new green corn celebration at that time. Their Soup Dance marks the end of their summer ritual cycle and the start of the fall hunting season. Family camps encircle the central square, preserving the social order of Yuchi towns in the ancient Southeast. Yuchis continue to maintain close contacts and visits with Absentee Shawnees, Creeks, and northeast Oklahoma tribal communities for ceremonies. Euchee Heritage Days, first held in 1997, attracts many people for athletic contests, fashion shows, crafts, and participation in the Yuchi cultural heritage.

During the 1920s or 1930s the use of Peyote was introduced to the Yuchis. Their close ties to the Sacs and Foxes continued through their Peyote association. Yuchis also continued their links with Delawares, Shawnees, and other northeast Oklahoma groups. The Yuchis practice the Little Moon version of the Peyote religion. Under the guidance of Walter Thompson, they, in turn, took Peyote to the Navajos in the Southwest. Along with Peyote rituals, Yuchis are also involved in United Methodist Church activities at Pickett Chapel, constructed in 1915 near Sapulpa, and at Mutteloke Church in Bristow.

Only about four fluent speakers of the Yuchi language remain. Grants support linguistic training among tribal members, including an effort to develop a standardized, accepted alphabet for the language. Scholar Jason Jackson pointed out that the Yuchis are the most culturally divergent minority group within the Muscogee Nation. In the nineteenth and twentieth centuries the Yuchis represented about 15 percent of the total Muscogee Nation population. The Yuchis share cultural patterns with northeastern Indians like the Shawnees. They still maintain close ties to the Absentee and Loyal Shawnees as well as to neighboring Sacs, Muscogees, and other tribes.

Notable Yuchis include several chiefs who were named Samuel Brown. They were descendants of the granddaughter of Cosenna Barnard (also called Barnett) and direct descendants of the early British settler Timothy Barnard. Greg Bigler is an attorney and tribal judge; Daniel Wildcat is co-director of Haskell Indian University's Environmental Research Studies Center and co-author of a book on Indian education, *Power and Place* (2001), with Vine Deloria, Jr. Richard Ray Whitman is a well-known artist in the media of drawing, photography, and video, who also had a part in the movie *War Party*. His brother, Joe Dale Tate Nevaquaya (part Comanche), is also an accomplished artist. Steve Deo and Wanda A. Green (also Creek) are painters. Actress Harmony Revis (also Choctaw) appeared in the film *The Princess Diaries*. Merwyn Garbarino is an anthropologist. The wealthy and eccentric Creek oil baron Jackson Barnett (also Barnard), who attained such notoriety during the 1920s, was part Yuchi.

SUGGESTED READINGS

Euchees: Past & Present. Sapulpa, Okla.: EUCHEE, 1997 (booklet).

Foreman, Carolyn Thomas. "The Yuchi: Children of the Sun." *Chronicles of Oklahoma* 37 (Winter 1959–60): 480–96.

Jackson, Jason Baird. "Architecture and Hospitality: Ceremonial Ground Camps and Foodways of the Yuchi Indians." *Chronicles of Oklahoma* 76 (Summer 1998): 172–89.

———. *Yuchi Ceremonial Life: Performance, Meaning, and Tradition in a Contemporary American Indian Community*. Lincoln: University of Nebraska Press, 2003; repr. 2005.

Pearson, Julie. "Invisible Too Long." *Oklahoma Today* 42 (May/June 1992): 23–26.

Speck, Frank G. *Ethnology of the Yuchi Indians.* Anthropological Publications, vol. 1, no. 1. Philadelphia: University of Pennsylvania Museum, 1909; repr. Lincoln: University of Nebraska Press, 2004.

Swanton, John. *The Indians of the Southeastern United States.* Bureau of American Ethnology Bulletin 137. Washington, D.C.: Government Printing Office, 1946; repr. Washington, D.C.: Smithsonian Institution Press, 1979.

Waselkov, Gregory A., and Kathryn E. Holland Braund, eds. *William Bartram on the Southeastern Indians.* Lincoln: University of Nebraska Press, 1995.

Index